Algeria

WORLD BIBLIOGRAPHICAL SERIES

General Editors:
Robert G. Neville (Executive Editor)
John J. Horton

Robert A. Myers   Hans H. Wellisch
Ian Wallace   Ralph Lee Woodward, Jr.

John J. Horton is Deputy Librarian of the University of Bradford and currently Chairman of its Academic Board of Studies in Social Sciences. He has maintained a longstanding interest in the discipline of area studies and its associated bibliographical problems, with special reference to European Studies. In particular he has published in the field of Icelandic and of Yugoslav studies, including the two relevant volumes in the World Bibliographical Series.

Robert A. Myers is Associate Professor of Anthropology in the Division of Social Sciences and Director of Study Abroad Programs at Alfred University, Alfred, New York. He has studied post-colonial island nations of the Caribbean and has spent two years in Nigeria on a Fulbright Lectureship. His interests include international public health, historical anthropology and developing societies. In addition to *Amerindians of the Lesser Antilles: a bibliography* (1981), *A Resource Guide to Dominica, 1493-1986* (1987) and numerous articles, he has compiled the World Bibliographical Series volumes on *Dominica* (1987), *Nigeria* (1989) and *Ghana* (1991).

Ian Wallace is Professor of German at the University of Bath. A graduate of Oxford in French and German, he also studied in Tübingen, Heidelberg and Lausanne before taking teaching posts at universities in the USA, Scotland and England. He specializes in contemporary German affairs, especially literature and culture, on which he has published numerous articles and books. In 1979 he founded the journal *GDR Monitor*, which he continues to edit under its new title *German Monitor*.

Hans H. Wellisch is Professor emeritus at the College of Library and Information Services, University of Maryland. He was President of the American Society of Indexers and was a member of the International Federation for Documentation. He is the author of numerous articles and several books on indexing and abstracting, and has published *The Conversion of Scripts and Indexing and Abstracting: an International Bibliography*, and *Indexing from A to Z*. He also contributes frequently to *Journal of the American Society for Information Science*, *The Indexer* and other professional journals.

Ralph Lee Woodward, Jr. is Professor of History at Tulane University, New Orleans. He is the author of *Central America, a Nation Divided*, 2nd ed. (1985), as well as several monographs and more than seventy scholarly articles on modern Latin America. He has also compiled volumes in the World Bibliographical Series on *Belize* (1980), *El Salvador* (1988), *Guatemala* (Rev. Ed.) (1992) and *Nicaragua* (Rev. Ed.) (1994). Dr. Woodward edited the Central American section of the *Research Guide to Central America and the Caribbean* (1985) and is currently associate editor of Scribner's *Encyclopedia of Latin American History*.

VOLUME 19

Algeria
Revised Edition

Richard I. Lawless

Compiler

CLIO PRESS
OXFORD, ENGLAND · SANTA BARBARA, CALIFORNIA
DENVER, COLORADO

British Library Cataloguing in Publication Data

Algeria – 2nd Rev. ed. (World Bibliographical Series;
Vol. 19)
I. Lawless, Richard I. II. Series
016.965

ISBN 1–85109–130–0

ABC-CLIO Ltd.,
Old Clarendon Ironworks,
35A Great Clarendon Street,
Oxford OX2 6AT, England.

ABC-CLIO Inc.,
130 Cremona Drive,
Santa Barbara,
CA 93116, USA.

Designed by Bernard Crossland.
Typeset by Columns Design and Production Services Ltd., Reading, England.
Printed and bound in Great Britain by Bookcraft (Bath) Ltd., Midsomer Norton.

THE WORLD BIBLIOGRAPHICAL SERIES

This series, which is principally designed for the English speaker, will eventually cover every country (and many of the world's principal regions), each in a separate volume comprising annotated entries on works dealing with its history, geography, economy and politics; and with its people, their culture, customs, religion and social organization. Attention will also be paid to current living conditions – housing, education, newspapers, clothing, etc. – that are all too often ignored in standard bibliographies; and to those particular aspects relevant to individual countries. Each volume seeks to achieve, by use of careful selectivity and critical assessment of the literature, an expression of the country and an appreciation of its nature and national aspirations, to guide the reader towards an understanding of its importance. The keynote of the series is to provide, in a uniform format, an interpretation of each country that will express its culture, its place in the world, and the qualities and background that make it unique. The views expressed in individual volumes, however, are not necessarily those of the publisher.

VOLUMES IN THE SERIES

Contents

Contents

Contents

Preface

Like the first edition of this bibliography, which appeared in 1980, this new revised edition has been prepared primarily for an English-speaking audience, as indeed are all the bibliographies in ABC-CLIO's *World Bibliographical Series*. Until recently Algeria was little known outside France and the francophone countries. Traditionally Anglo-American authors have shown little inclination to work on North African topics, and Algeria, together with the rest of the 'Maghreb', was regarded as very much a French preserve. Algeria first attracted the attention of Anglo-American writers in the late 18th and early 19th centuries, through the activities of the 'notorious Barbary pirates', and after the French conquest beginning in 1830 it became a winter playground for a few wealthy English and American travellers. An English colony became established at Mustapha in Algiers in the 1850s formed by rich convalescents wintering in the Algerian capital and survived until the late 1920s as a self-contained community with little contact with either the French or the Arabs. Paradoxically, however, the only detailed bibiography covering this period in Algeria's history is that of Sir R. Lambert Playfair, an Englishman, who was for many years British consul in Algiers; while the only comprehensive study of the English in Algeria is Joelle Redouane's doctoral thesis presented at the University of Rennes, entitled *Les Anglais et l'Algérie 1830-1930*. It was the Allied landings in North Africa during the Second World War and the growth of nationalism culminating in the outbreak of the War of Independence in 1954 which resulted in a marked revival of interest in Algeria among English and American writers. Through the reports of journalists and of other news media, the herioc struggle of the Algerian people won the sympathy of a large section of Anglo-American public opinion, a development which proved extremely valuable to the Algerian nationalists in their battle to gain international support for an independent Algerian state. Indeed, of all periods in Algerian history it is the revolutionary era (1954-62) which has stimulated the greatest interest of Anglo-Saxon authors. Perhaps inevitably many Anglo-American contributions on Algerian history have been strongly influenced by French studies and opinions, but a growing volume of original research has been undertaken. Even though dependent on French documentary sources, American and British scholars have been able to offer new insights into the country's recent history.

Since Algeria won its independence from France this interest has been sustained and strengthened, encouraged by the new economic and cultural links forged between Algeria – anxious to reduce its dependence on France – and the Anglo-Saxon world. In addition to a number of important analyses and interpretations of political trends in the new republic, American and British scholars have critically assessed Algeria's experience in worker self-management, and have turned their attention to the ambitious development programme embarked upon during the Boumediène era and its economic, social and spatial impact. Many of these studies are based on original research and fieldwork in Algeria and cover a wide range of subjects including migration and emigration, urbanization, industrialization, the oil and gas industry, land reform and rural settlement.

In the fifteen years since the first edition of the bibliography appeared, the number of books and articles on Algeria has increased dramatically, though English-language publications remain a mere fraction of the literature available in French. This period has brought profound changes to Algeria: the introduction of economic reforms leading to a free market economy; the end of single-party rule; political pluralism; the dramatic resurgence of political Islam in the form of the Front islamique du salut; and the country's tragic descent into virtual civil war following the military *coup d'état* in January 1992. Anglo-American researchers have made a valuable contribution to the analysis of recent political developments in Algeria, especially the rise of Islamism, to a range of social issues, for example patriarchy, class and gender, to demographic trends, rural settlement policy and regional inequalities. But historical research has not been neglected and American scholars in particular have played their part, together with Algerian and French researchers, in shifting the focus of research on the period of French rule from the 'colonizer' to the 'colonized'. In addition, some of the works of leading Algerian writers such as Mohammed Dib and Assia Djebar are now available in English translation, and through its journal and monographs the Centre d'Etudes sur la Littérature Francophone de l'Afrique du Nord at Temple University in Philadelphia has become an important source of information in English on Algerian literature and Algerian writers.

The number of young Algerians undertaking postgraduate research in America and Britain has continued to grow. The wide range of topics studied by these students relating to Algeria is illustrated by the list of selected theses and dissertations in English on Algeria provided at the beginning of this bibliography. The results of their research are often published in English and there is now a small but influential group of Algerian scholars who write in Arabic and English rather than in French. Those Algerians with postgraduate experience in America or Britain who have achieved political importance include former prime minister Abdelhamid Brahimi, who had been a senior representative of SONATRACH, the state oil company, in the USA, where he graduated from university, and Abassi Madani, the imprisoned leader of the banned Front islamique du salut, who obtained his doctorate at the University of London's Institute of Education and is married to an Englishwoman.

Over two-thirds of the entries in this revised edition of the bibliography are new and only those items which remain useful references have been retained from the first edition. A wide range of bibliographical sources has been used in the preparation of this work, including electronic databases that were not available during the preparation of the first edition. Wherever possible, priority has been given to books and articles in English, although given the dominance of French-language publications on Algeria, in many sections of the bibliography major works in French have also been included. French-language publications have also been included on subjects where works in English are limited in number or unsatisfactory and, for example, as in the case of the sections on the colonial period and the War of Independence, to provide information about the results of new research. The aim is to provide a range of basic references on all key aspects of the country and its people. Every effort has been made to ensure that the bibliography is as comprehensive as possible and that it incorporates the most recent books and articles, and those which are readily available in the United Kingdom and the USA. Algerian government publications such as statistical yearbooks, census materials and development plans are unfortunately not widely diffused and are almost exclusively in French or Arabic; for this reason they have been excluded from this bibliography. The reader is introduced to the country's geography, history, politics, foreign relations, and economy; to the people, their social organization, language, religion, customs and culture. Every item included in the bibliography is annotated to provide the reader with a short summary of the scope and content of the book or article. Inevitably in any classification system the demarcation of topics cannot be wholly satisfactory, but a comprehensive numerical cross-referencing system has been incorporated together with author, title and subject indexes.

I am especially grateful to Avril Shields of the Middle East Documentation Unit, University of Durham, England for her skilful assistance in identifying many of the references for this new edition.

Finally, no bibliography is ever complete and I apologize for any errors, or references which have inadvertently been omitted.

Introduction

Algeria takes its name from the Arabic words *Al-Jazair* meaning 'the islands', in this case the little rocky islands off the coast from Algiers, the capital. With an area of 2,381,741 sq. km., Algeria is the biggest political unit in Africa and the Middle East after Sudan, and yet with some 26 million inhabitants it has only half the population of Egypt and less than one-third that of Nigeria. The country's geography helps to explain this apparent anomaly. Almost nine-tenths of its total area (some 2 million sq. km.) is desert, part of the vast and arid Saharan domain characterized by vast gravel plains, huge sand seas (*ergs*) and dominated in the south-east by the great Ahaggar (Hoggar) massif rising to almost 3,000m., where the erosion of volcanic and crystalline rocks has produced a lunar landscape of extreme ruggedness. Very high temperatures, often associated with violent duststorms, and low rainfall with several years of absolute drought result in the extreme sparseness of vegetation and very low population densities; less than one-tenth of the country's population live in the Saharan territories.

In contrast, the northern coastlands are more humid and are dominated by the Atlas mountains which form two parallel chains running from west to east: the rugged Tell Atlas in the north, a complex series of plateaux and massifs separated by deep valleys and gorges; and the more open Saharan Atlas to the south. These ranges are separated by monotonous interior plains studded with salt flats (*shotts*) at a height of over 1,000m. The western coastlands are lower than the east and the arid interior steppelands are more extensive. The eastern coastlands, on the other hand, are dominated by high mountains, Greater Kabylia rising to 2,300m. and the Aurès Massif to 2,000m. The climate of northern Algeria is of the Mediterranean type with warm, wet winters and hot, dry summers, giving way on the southern margins to semi-arid steppe conditions where summer drought lasts for five to six months and winters are colder and drier. The higher and wetter parts of the Tell Atlas once supported extensive forests of Aleppopine, cork oak and evergreen oak, but deforestation, overcultivation and overgrazing have had a destructive effect and only a few scattered remnants survive. South of the Tell there is very little woodland except on the higher and wetter parts of the Saharan Atlas, and the surface of the interior high plains is bare or covered with scattered bushes and expanses of esparto and other coarse grasses.

The northern coastlands of Algeria are part of the Mediterranean world and over the centuries they have been influenced by a variety of different civilizations. Their history stretches back to preclassical times. The Berbers are the earliest inhabitants identified historically in Algeria, but they have rarely been united or free; constant domination by and resistance to diverse invaders – Phoenicians, Romans, Vandals, Arabs, Spanish, Turks and the French – is one of the most important themes in the country's history.

From the 12th century BC the Phoenicians used ports on the Algerian coast as staging posts on the route from Carthage to their distant trading establishments in Morocco and Spain. After the overthrow of Carthage in 146 BC the Romans formed the province of Africa, roughly corresponding to present-day Tunisia, and by the middle of the 1st century AD they had annexed two Berber kingdoms, Numidia and Mauretania, thereby extending their control over the northern coastlands of Algeria. The Romanization of these lands and their inhabitants remained superficial, and Berber resistance to Roman penetration manifested itself in numerous revolts and tribal incursions. After the adoption of Christianity as the official religion of the Roman Empire in the early part of the 4th century AD, this resistance expressed itself forcibly in the Donatist religious schism, provoking violent civil war and religious strife throughout the period. Roman power slowly disintegrated during the 5th century and was effectively terminated towards the end of the century by the Vandal invasion. The Vandals, like the Romans before them, failed to exert any real control over the Berbers, who established a number of independent Christian kingdoms. The Byzantine reconquest in the 6th century only extended as far as eastern Algeria and left the rest of the country under Berber control.

A more serious threat to Berber independence appeared in the middle of the 7th century when Arab armies, fresh from their victorious conquests in Syria and Egypt, invaded North Africa. The Arabs faced fierce Berber resistance, particularly in Algeria, and after more than a century the region had not been subdued. Yet the religion of the newcomers, Islam, was firmly planted and the vast majority of Berbers eagerly embraced the new faith, and, enrolling in its armies, the Berbers went along with them to the conquest of the western Maghreb and Spain. So complete was the process of Islamization that Christianity disappeared completely and few traces of Judaism survived. However, the Berbers were slow to adopt the Arabic language. The first Arabs to settle in the region were few in number, and as soldiers, administrators and traders they were mainly urban dwellers. The invasion from Egypt in the 11th century by tribes of Arab nomads, the Beni Hillal and Beni Solaym, quickened the pace of Arabization in rural areas, but the process was by no means complete. Even today almost one-fifth of Algeria's population, concentrated in the eastern mountains in Greater Kabylia and the Aurès, remain Berber-speaking. The majority of Algerians are therefore Arabized Berbers and the distinction between Arabs and Berbers is linguistic rather than ethnic.

The unity which the Arab invasion brought to the North African territories did not long endure. The Berbers adopted Muslim heresies as eagerly as they had previously embraced Christian ones: Kharijism, a radical Muslim sect, in the 8th century and Shia doctrines in the 10th century. A period of anarchy ensued but some order was restored in the 11th century by the Berber dynasty of the Almoravids who gained control of the western Maghreb including much of what is now western Algeria. But their power was short-lived and in the following century they were succeeded by the Almohads who unified the whole of the Maghreb with Muslim Spain. This was followed by a brief period of economic prosperity and cultural achievement but the precarious unity of the empire collapsed in the 13th century. Out of the political vacuum created by the decline of Almohad power, three states emerged: Ifriqiya (present day Tunisia and eastern Algeria) under the Hafsids, the far Maghreb (present day Morocco) under the Merinids, and the central Maghreb (central and western Algeria) under the Abd al-Wadids.

Each of these new political units was governed by a Berber tribe or family, each struggling to revive the power, prestige and traditions of the Almohads. The Abd al-Wadid Sultanate possessed much poorer physical resources than either of its neighbours and a much weaker political structure. In the central Maghreb the northern extension of the arid steppelands of the interior high plains reduced the Mediterranean zone to a narrow coastal strip. The state lacked a firm peasant base and a diversified economy, while the important nomadic and semi-nomadic element in the population caused numerous disputes over pasture, and general instability. Consequently, for long periods the Abd al-Wadid Sultanate was reduced to a vassal state of the Merinids, and there was interference in the internal affairs of the state from both its neighbours.

Introduction

By the early 16th century, the authority of the Abd al-Wadid rulers did not extend much beyond the limits of their capital, Tlemcen, and their survival for another half century mainly resulted from the conflicts between Spaniards, Turks and Moroccans which prevented any one group from permanently annexing the Sultanate.

At the beginning of the 15th century, Spain, having completed the reconquest of the Iberian peninsula from the Muslims, carried its crusade across the Mediterranean, occupying a number of ports in the central Maghreb. Mers el Kebir fell to the Spaniards in 1505, Oran in 1509, and Bougie in 1510, while Tenès, Dellys, Cherchel, Mostaganem and finally Algiers agreed to pay tribute to Spain. The major check on the Spanish advance came not from the local rulers but from a new force, the Ottoman Turks. The architects of Ottoman expansion in the region were the Barbarossa brothers, Aruj and Khair al-Din, Muslim corsairs originally from the Greek island of Mytilene.

They took possession of Algiers in 1516, drove out the Spaniards from their coastal strongholds and expanded their control over the interior of the central Maghreb. In 1518 Khair al-Din, in order to consolidate his position, placed all the territory which he controlled under the protection of the Ottoman Sultan. His action is memorable because it marked the first emergence of Algeria as a political concept.

A regular Ottoman administration was introduced, headed by a succession of *beylerbeys, pashas, aghas* and *deys*, but from the mid-16th century real power in Algiers passed into the hands of two main bodies: the janissary corps or Turkish garrison, the nominal representative of Ottoman power; and the guild of corsair captains who for over three centuries were the main financial support of the province. Ottoman rule became a convenient fiction. The Regency of Algiers reached the peak of its prosperity in the course of the 17th century. During this period the rulers entered into diplomatic relations with the leading maritime states of western Europe – England, Holland and France – and these countries maintained consuls or agents in Algiers. The profitable trade of piracy flourished throughout the century, bringing great wealth to Algiers in the form of captured ships, cargoes and men, and earning it notoriety as the centre of the 'Barbary' slave trade; there were an estimated 35,000 Christian slaves in the prisons of Algiers at this time. Throughout the 17th and 18th centuries Algiers looked outwards to the sea and maintained little interest in or effective control over the interior of the province.

As the 18th century progressed, however, the growth of European seapower brought about a decline in corsair activity and in the prosperity of Algiers. In 1816 when a British fleet under Lord Exmouth bombarded the city there were no more than 1,200 captives left in its prisons. The increasing weakness of Algiers encouraged European intervention and in July 1830 the capital fell to a French expeditionary force and the ruler, the *dey*, and most of the Turkish officials were sent into exile. The occupation of Algiers had been designed to enhance the declining prestige of the French monarchy, but before plans for the consolidation and extension of French rule could be put into effect, the Bourbon dynasty and its government were overthrown by revolution. Four years of indecision and confusion elapsed before the new government of Louis Philippe decided that the occupation must continue, and the need to secure territory already won generated fresh expansion. The history of Algeria for the next quarter of a century is mainly concerned with the gradual reduction of the country by France against bitter and continuing opposition.

Early resistance to the French conquest was organized by the leader of one of the largest religious orders, Emir Abdel Kader, a reforming Muslim, a brilliant guerrilla commander and a skilful diplomat. For a time he succeeded in gaining the allegiance of the tribes in western Algeria and in constructing the foundations of a modern state, but was finally defeated in 1847 by the persistence and ruthlessness of the French commander General Bugeaud, the real architect of French rule in Algeria. Later, during the 1850s, the tribes on the northern edge of the Sahara were pacified and although further revolts erupted throughout the 19th century, the conquest was virtually completed by the brutal suppression of the fiercely independent Berber republics of Kabylia in 1857.

Military conquest was closely followed by officially sponsored settler colonization. Algeria was declared an integral part of French territory and French citizens in Algeria were able to elect deputies to the Assembly in Paris. The coastal region was divided into three departments, like those of France, and these, from 1858, elected departmental councils; elected municipal government was also set up in the principal towns. By a policy of confiscation and expropriation of tribal lands, vast tracts of the best agricultural land in the coastal lowlands were made available to the growing influx of European colonists who came mainly from France, Spain and Italy. They eventually acquired over a quarter of the country's cultivated lands which were developed to produce cash crops (soft wheat, vines, olives, citrus fruits, tobacco and early vegetables) for export to markets in metropolitan France. After phylloxera ravaged vineyards in southern France in 1878 vast areas in central and western Algeria were planted with vines, and wine became the country's most important single export. Later Algeria's extensive mineral resources, notably phosphates, iron ore and – at the very end of the colonial period – Saharan oil and gas, were exploited by the French, but there was little industrialization and only those activities which did not compete with French industry were permitted.

The European population reached its peak in 1954 when the settlers, known locally as *pieds noirs*, numbered just over one million or one-tenth of the country's total population. By that time about four-fifths of the European residents lived in towns, many of which were French creations, where they were mostly administrators, bankers, technicians, traders, professional men and skilled workers, though some had lesser jobs, and their influence was far in excess of their numbers. Their concentration was greatest in the big cities with Algiers, the capital and major port, containing over one-third of all Europeans. The dualistic shaping of the economy and the creation of a modern sector in which agriculture, mining, industry and trade were organized to serve the interests of the metropolitan power was also accompanied by the polarization of political, social and economic power. The ·settlers exercised power and enjoyed privileges and high incomes, while the Algerian majority suffered loss of status, subservience and poverty. Few Algerians received any education or technical training, and few Algerian workers participated in industry or other non-agricultural activities. As a result of the conquest, the majority of Algerians (8.4 million in 1954) had been forced out of the fertile plains into the more inhospitable mountains and steppes where they eked out a meagre existence on the land on small, fragmented holdings occupying the less productive land. After 1930 and particularly after the Second World War the high rate of population increase among the Algerians further aggravated the pressure of population on resources, resulting in an acceleration of rural-to-urban migration and a quickening in the rate of urbanization. The migrants crowded into existing Muslim quarters and then into squalid squatter settlements or *bidonvilles* (cities made out of tin cans) which mushroomed in and around the major cities. Few jobs were available in the urban economy for these new migrants, many of whom merely exchanged underemployment in the countryside for unemployment in the towns.

So profound had been the destruction of the Muslims' economic, social and political organization during the conquest and so apparently invincible was the privileged position and ascendancy of the European settler community that the first stirrings of nationalism among Algerian Muslims only emerged after the First World War. The early Algerian nationalist movement was composed of a number of very different strands. One, the Etoile Nord Africaine led by Messali Hadj, emerged among the Algerian workers in France and initially had close links with the French Communist Party. From the outset it pursued a nationalist and radical programme which as early as 1927 included the independence of

Algeria, the withdrawal of French troops, the creation of a national army and the nationalization of large estates. More moderate doctrines were put forward in the postwar years by a group of French-educated Muslims drawn from the small, educated Muslim élite. Under the leadership of Ferhat Abbas the aims of the Fédération des Elus Musulmans, formed in 1930, were firmly assimilationist. They demanded representation in the French parliament, the suppression of legislation descriminating adversely against Muslims, and that Muslims should be given the same rights as the French in Algeria without renouncing their Muslim status. A third strand in the diverse fabric of Algerian nationalism was the Ulama's Association created in the early 1930s by the Muslim theologian Ben Badis. Initially this movement was directed towards religious reform and attacked the popular religious practices of the religious brotherhoods and their close association with the colonialists. Later Ben Badis became increasingly concerned with political questions and directly contradicted Ferhat Abbas by firmly opposing assimilation. His concern with the problems of Islam provided an immunity from French civilization, which was so central to the ideas of many of his contemporaries, and his contribution to the development of nationalist opposition increased the importance of Islam as part of Algerian identity. His guiding principle 'Islam is my religion, Arabic is my language, Algeria is my country' was later to be echoed by other nationalists.

The victory of the Popular Front in the French elections of 1936 gave hope that at least some of the more moderate nationalist demands might be achieved peaceably. The French Prime Minister Blum, with the advice of Violette, a former Governor-General of Algeria, put forward a plan which would have granted full right of citizenship to some 25,000 Algerians without renunciation of Muslim status. Even this modest reform was denounced by the European settlers and their reaction had sufficient support in Paris for the proposal to be dropped without even being discussed in the French parliament. One result of the failure was that Ferhat Abbas, now the major spokesman of a steadily growing nationalist opinion, began to abandon his assimilationist views. His appeal in 1943, called the 'Manifesto of the Algerian People', represented a turning point in the growth of Algerian nationalism and became a charter for a new political movement. It demanded liberty and equality for Muslims in their own country, in language, education and religion; the abolition of colonization together with agrarian reform; full and immediate participation of Muslims in the government of their country; and recognition of the political autonomy of Algeria as a sovereign state.

The defeat of France in the Second World War, the Anglo-American invasion of North Africa in 1943, and some American interest in

Introduction

Algerian nationalism all contributed to a strengthening of nationalist aspirations and a rejection by Muslims of their inferior status. The end of the war brought a dramatic outburst of nationalist feeling in Algeria. At Sétif in May 1945 a Muslim demonstration to celebrate the Allied victory turned into a riot and was viciously suppressed by French military forces, resulting in the deaths of several thousand Muslims. The incident deeply shocked the Muslim community and many who later joined the Algerian Revolution became committed to the nationalist movement at this time.

After the liberation of France successive French governments were committed to reform in Algeria and certain legislative measures were passed. In 1944 an *ordonnance* gave equal rights to both Muslims and French, removing discriminatory legislation and opening civilian and military careers, while Muslim representation on municipal councils was increased. Three years later a new statute decreed that Algerian Muslims were to become French citizens with the title of Muslim French, while keeping their personal Muslim status. The reformers hoped that a middle group of Algerian moderates and French liberals would develop and hold together a political system, with the result that violent nationalism would be defused. They failed completely because of the obstinate resistance of the European community in Algeria. The settlers prevented successive Governor-Generals from implementing French policy and in some cases enlisted their help in order to ensure that elections were manipulated to serve European interests. Growing frustration because political expression was blocked by electoral trickery turned some nationalist leaders towards armed struggle as the only means of gaining their objective.

As early as 1947 several young men of the Mouvement pour le Triomphe des Libertés Démocratiques (MTLD), the party created by Messali Hadj at the end of the war, formed the Organisation Secrète (OS) which collected arms and money from supporters and built up a network of cells throughout Algeria in preparation for armed insurrection and the establishment of a revolutionary government. The OS was quickly broken up by police action but regrouped in 1954 as the Comité Révolutionnaire d'Unité et d'Action (CRUA) to prepare for an immediate revolt against French rule. The leaders were Krim Belkacem, Rabah Bitat, Ben Boulaid, Larbi Ben M'Hidi, Mohamed Boudiaf, Mourad Didouche, Ben Bella, Aït Ahmed and Muhammad Khider, who became known as the nine 'chefs historiques' of the revolution. From the start their aim was the independence of Algeria but first they had to win over the Muslim population to their cause and establish their movement as the sole representative of the Algerian people. On 1 November 1954 the revolt was launched in the Aurès mountains and by 1956 guerrilla activities had spread throughout the settled areas of Algeria.

Indiscriminate punitive raids by French forces on Algerian villages merely drove more of the Muslim population into the nationalist camp.

Once the revolt was underway the CRUA changed its name to the Front de la Libération Nationale (FLN) and in 1956 was joined by Ferhat Abbas and the religious leaders of the Ulema. This made the FLN representative of nearly all shades of Algerian nationalism; ideological differences were temporarily shelved in the interests of the independence struggle. Only Messali Hadj's party, renamed the Mouvement National Algérien (MNA), remained an intransigent though unsuccessful rival of the FLN. In August 1956 the FLN held its first conference in the valley of the Soumman. It was a major achievement. The deep rivalries among the leaders were kept in check, and the movement was given a formal organization, a command structure, and a political programme.

At the outset the French government was convinced that only support from Egypt sustained the FLN offensive, and Cairo was perceived as the centre of a virulent and contagious Arab nationalism orchestrated by President Nasser and threatening to undermine Western interests. Their exaggeration of Egypt's role in the Algerian problem led to French collusion with Britain and Israel in the abortive invasion of Egypt at the end of October 1956. Not only did the Suez operation fail to topple President Nasser and stop the Algerian struggle, it actively strengthened the FLN's position by increasing support from newly independent and non-aligned states.

In the face of the weak government in Paris, the French military in Algeria began to assert their independence of the politicians whom they regarded as divided and irresolute. The notorious 'Battle of Algiers' destroyed the FLN position in Algiers and the construction of electrified barriers along the Tunisian and Moroccan frontiers cut their supply lines. By employing psychological warfare, intelligence operations and extensive use of torture, the French forces, which numbered half a million men, became increasingly successful in their operations against the guerrillas. In May 1958 when the European community took to the streets of Algiers in mass demonstrations calling for strong government, the army commander General Salan took over military and civilian power in Algeria. This coup brought down the Fourth Republic and paved the way for a return by General de Gaulle who became first President of the Fifth Republic of France in January 1959.

Once in power de. Gaulle quickly initiated a major programme of economic development for Algeria, known as the Constantine Plan, and appointed many more Muslims to administrative posts. But in the highly charged situation his first pronouncements on the political future of Algeria were cautious and highly ambiguous. It was not until September 1959 that he spoke of self-determination for Algeria, an announcement which inevitably provoked the opposition of those who had contributed to de Gaulle's return to power in the belief that he would follow a single policy of integrating Algeria with France. Europeans in Algeria and segments of the French army formed the Organization de l'Armée Secrète (OAS) to resist a negotiated settlement and the transfer of power from European hands, and in April 1961 a group of senior army officers, including Generals Challe, Zeller, Jouhaud and Salan, planned a new army *putsch* to halt the progress towards negotiation and an 'Algerian republic', a phrase which de Gaulle had used for the first time on 4 November 1960. De Gaulle's authority and determination were sufficient to crush the challenge, but it became clear that a wide gulf now separated the French in Algeria, including the ultras of the army, and those in France.

On the military side the war continued to go against the nationalists, but on the diplomatic front the FLN won some notable successes, especially after 1958 when they established a provisional government of the Algerian republic (GPRA). The GPRA secured diplomatic recognition from the Arab states and also, as a result of an energetic campaign at the United Nations, from a growing number of African and Asian members. At the same time the repressive policies adopted by the French army in Algeria, above all the extensive use of torture, provoked widespread criticism within the international community, especially in western Europe and America, but also in France itself.

It was against this background that negotiations began between France and the FLN in 1960, and, in spite of a wave of terrorism launched by the OAS to prevent an agreement, the peace talks culminated in the Evian accords concluded on 18 March 1962. The objectives of the revolution were achieved at Evian, and the FLN was acknowledged as the sole representative of the Algerian people. Algeria became independent with full control over its own affairs including foreign policy and defence; France agreed to provide continued economic and technical assistance and substantial foreign aid; the new state's territorial integrity was confirmed and French insistence that they retain control of the Saharan territories with their vast oil and gas reserves was dropped; all French troops were to be withdrawn; and although the rights of the European minority were safeguarded, they were not accorded special protection as a community within the Algerian state. The signing of these agreements was the signal for a final desperate outburst of terrorist activity by the OAS which provoked violent reprisals from the FLN. In the ensuing chaos an increasing number of Europeans and Jews left Algeria for France so that when de Gaulle proclaimed Algeria an independent republic on 3 July 1962 over half the Europeans had departed.

The declaration of independence was followed by an intense struggle for power among different factions within the FLN from which Ben Bella and his group, supported by Boumediène, the commander of the Armée de Libération Nationale (ALN), eventually emerged victorious. Ben Bella, who was personally popular in the country, gradually concentrated more and more power in his own hands, becoming Prime Minister, Secretary-General of the FLN (now declared the sole political party), and in September 1963 the first president of the Algerian republic. But he remained heavily dependent on the support of Boumediène who was named Minister of Defence and Commander-in-Chief of the armed forces.

Ben Bella's government meanwhile faced enormous economic and social problems. The war had claimed the lives of several hundred thousand Algerians and forced half a million to seek refuge in Morocco and Tunisia. Over 2 million people in rural areas had been uprooted from their homes by the French army as part of its pacification programme and resettled in 'protected' villages, often under harsh conditions. Many more people had left the insecurity of the countryside and flooded into the towns and cities. It has been estimated that half the Algerian rural population were displaced during the war in circumstances that were among the most brutal ever recorded. In the major cities, principally Algiers and Oran, urban guerrilla warfare, murders and assassinations had intensified during the last two years of colonial rule, accompanied by the destruction of much public and private property. Many Algerians who had fought for the French (the *harkis*) were murdered in a series of bitter reprisals and others in fear of their lives fled to France. The majority of the European community representing almost all the administrators, technicians, teachers, doctors and skilled workers had left the country in a massive exodus; factories and shops were closed down and farms were abandoned. Their departure paralysed the economy and merely intensified the already chronic problems of underemployment and unemployment. An estimated 70 per cent of the population of the new republic were unemployed and over four-fifths were illiterate, while rapid population growth resulted in an extremely youthful population, almost half of whom were under 15 years of age.

During the first three years of independence the problem of power lay at the centre of political conflict in the new republic. Ben Bella's régime was challenged by opposing factions within the FLN, and there were revolts against the central government in the mountains of Kabylia and in the south. To these difficulties were added border disputes with Algeria's neighbours, Morocco and Tunisia. The most serious clashes occurred between Algeria and Morocco, where long-standing disputes over areas along their common frontier in the Sahara flared into open conflict in October 1963. The actual hostilities were not on a large scale and were soon brought to an end by the efforts of other African states, but they left a legacy of bitterness between the two countries.

On the economic front the Constantine Plan (1959-64) had achieved little. It represented the first attempt by the French at economic planning and it was intended to reawaken the traditional countryside and industrialize Algeria, but the industrialization drive had never really begun and by 1961 a tide of disinvestment was beginning to rise. Nevertheless the new republic inherited an important technical, industrial and agricultural infrastructure, and her economic potential was considerable. But although the national government inherited the material foundations laid during the colonial period, there was no one to man them and no one to serve. Furthermore, the modern sector of the Algerian economy had been created to serve the needs of the metropolitan power, not the Algerians themselves. The new republic remained heavily dependent on the former colonial power for its economic survival as indeed the Evian accords intended that it should. At independence agriculture made the largest single contribution to GDP, and agricultural produce comprised 80 per cent of all exports, wine alone representing 53 per cent. Almost all exports went to France, which in turn supplied the bulk of Algeria's imports. The Tripoli programme agreed at a FLN congress in May 1962 set as major objectives radical agrarian reform, the establishment of state and cooperative farms, nationalization of large establishments in all sectors, and the adoption of socialism as ideology and system. In practice, however, in its approach to economic matters the Ben Bella government was influenced by one primary factor: its own political survival. Furthermore, events marched faster than legislation or institutional arrangements. In the summer and autumn of 1962 many thousands of workers took over the management of farms and factories abandoned by the Europeans in order to keep these units in production and to protect their own jobs. When Ben Bella issued the famous March Decrees in 1963 legalizing the position of these workers' committees it was essentially to gain their political support. Factories run by self-management committees were relatively unimportant, but by the end of 1963 the *secteur autogéré agricole* controlled about a third of the total cultivated area, from which the bulk of the country's agricultural exports were produced. Algerian worker self-management rapidly attracted international attention. It was not, however, a system of land reform nor the answer to the Algerian peasant's land-hunger and social stagnation. In agriculture the self-management sector employed less than 200,000 workers, and together with their families they probably amounted to about one million people out of a rural population of 8 million. Yet *autogestion* monopolized the government's attention and financial means at the expense of traditional agriculture. In practice the majority of workers on *autogestion* estates did not fully understand the nationalization decrees, and effective power within the self-management committees was exercised by the directors appointed by the Ministry of Agriculture. The workers simply regarded themselves as state employees. The committees were also dependent on state organizations for credit and for marketing their produce, and this almost totally removed any possibility of independent action. Algeria's declared socialist approach to development was in fact a myth. Under Ben Bella no real attempt was made to make the self-management sector an organized political and economic force. Indeed, the only committed support for this system of economic organization came from a relatively small group of revolutionary intellectuals and from the trade unions. Another minority group within the Algerian political élite favoured private capitalism, but this faction was relatively small because of the weakness of the Algerian bourgeoisie. In fact the majority of the political élite, mainly of *petit bourgeois* origins, remained hostile to both worker self-management and private capitalism. Instead they favoured the establishment of an economic system dominated by state capitalism.

This trend towards state capitalism was substantially reinforced after Ben Bella was deposed by a swift and bloodless military *coup d'état* led by Boumediène on 19 June 1965, an event celebrated in Algeria as the 'revolutionary resurgence'. Boumediène, at the head of a twenty-six man Revolutionary Council and surrounded by young technocrats, set out to transform Algeria into a centrally planned economy, No further additions were made to the self-management sector and the new régime's approach to economic development was one of capital-intensive modernization under the direction of economic managers such as Belaïd Abdessalam, the powerful Minister of Economy, Smaïl Mahroug, the Minister of Finance, and Ahmed Ghozali, the head of SONATRACH, the state oil company. A series of nationalization measures, culminating in the take over of the major French oil companies operating in the country in 1971, secured state control over all key sectors of the Algerian economy. At the same time the government embarked on a programme of rapid industrialization which gave priority to huge capital-intensive projects including steelworks, petrochemical complexes, oil refineries and gas liquefaction plants. A high rate of investment, one of the highest in the Third World, was needed to implement these ambitious economic policies and to finance the rapid expansion of the educational system to produce skilled workers and managers for the new factories. Revenues from oil and gas, now the country's major source of foreign exchange, were inadequate, and the government was forced to borrow heavily from European and American banks by mortgaging future oil and gas exports. As Algeria's oil reserves are much smaller than those of other major

Middle Eastern producers, priority was given to exploiting the country's huge reserves of natural gas in order to finance future economic development. The Algerian people themselves were called upon to make new sacrifices in order to maximize productive investment, and living standards, already low, were held down by a deliberate policy of austerity. The agricultural sector, however, where over half the population gained their livelihood, was neglected, and in spite of a belated land reform programme launched in 1971, production remained stagnant. By the mid-1970s Algeria was spending one-third of its oil revenues on food imports. Migration from the poverty-stricken and neglected countryside to the towns continued unchecked and merely aggravated the already acute housing crisis in the overcrowded cities. No radical redistribution of wealth was put into effect and a state bureaucracy enjoying privilege and wealth quickly established itself. In theory this 'class' was open to talent and the government was committed to educating skilled managers; in practice, however, the way to the top was very much easier for those who started with an educational advantage which in turn depended on social class. The régime's commitment to modernization did not mean a rejection of religion and tradition. Islam continued to provide a unifying ideology and practice, relating 'revolutionary Algeria' to its past, incorporating the modern sector into a national whole, and maintaining some measure of outward cohesion in a divided society.

During the Boumediène era Algeria's activities in international affairs were as ambitious as its development strategy. In any conventional analysis Algeria ranks as a small power, yet the record of Algerian diplomacy is impressive. Boumediène's ministers often expressed a grand concept of Algeria's role in the world and Abdelaziz Bouteflika, the influential Foreign Minister, described Algeria as the central country in the Maghreb: on the borders of the Mediterranean, with a double attachment to Africa and the Arab world, and thus ideally placed to be the crossroads of three continents, Europe, Africa and Asia.

The country's major successes in world affairs have been in oil politics and among the non-aligned states. Algeria joined OPEC in 1969 and, as a minor producer, quickly became one of the organization's leading 'hawks', consistently campaigning for the maintenance of high prices for oil. Among the non-aligned states Algeria argued persuasively in favour of nationalization and producer cartels and used the example of its own experience to demonstrate that the struggle for development should be seen as an extension of the struggle for liberation. These policies were promoted energetically at the fourth conference of non-aligned states held in Algiers in September 1973 and again in April 1974 when Boumediène addressed a special session of the UN General Assembly.

His call for a 'new international economic order' to redress the economic disparities between the Western industrialized countries and the Third World heralded Algeria's efforts to set up an international forum to tackle these problems through dialogue rather than confrontation. Algeria's success in mobilizing the non-aligned world, the 'seventy seven' developing countries, the United Nations and OPEC in support of these initiatives, even though the practical outcome was negligible, won it new prestige and almost universal recognition as a diplomatic leader of the Third World.

In spite of the militancy of Algerian rhetoric in international affairs and its vociferous support for liberation movements, in practice its foreign relations have been tempered by a good deal of pragmatism. Anxieties in the West that Algeria might become a Soviet satellite proved unfounded and cooperation with the Soviet Union has been limited essentially to the supply of military equipment for Algeria's armed forces, while the technology for its development drive has been purchased mainly in western Europe and the United States. Thus, although Algeria denounced American actions in Latin America, the Middle East and Vietnam, by 1976 the USA had replaced France as its major trading partner. However, increasing contact with the Anglo-Saxon world inevitably produced new strains in Algeria's intense but uneasy relations with its former colonial power, France; these relations had already been aggravated by the nationalization of French oil interests and by the inability or unwillingness of the French police to protect Algerian workers living in France. In 1973, following a series of racist incidents in the south of France directed against Algerians, the Algerian government suspended all new emigration to France, and some observers were convinced that Algeria would break off diplomatic relations with France if these incidents were not brought rapidly under control. A new cause of friction arose in 1975 when the Spanish Sahara was annexed and divided between Morocco and Mauritania following their Tripartite Agreement with Spain. Algeria denounced the annexation and gave active support to the Saharan resistance movement, Polisario, which proclaimed the Saharan Arab Democratic Republic in 1976. France, on the other hand, supported the Moroccan position and in May 1978 French jet fighters based in Dakar, Senegal, intervened to assist Mauritanian ground forces against Polisario guerrillas. After 1975 Algeria's dispute with Morocco over the future of the western Sahara dominated the country's foreign policy and there were real fears that a new war would break out between the two countries over the Saharan issue.

At home Boumediène's régime enjoyed a remarkable degree of stability after the debilitating rivalries and uncertainties of the first few years of independence. The majority of the population greeted the new régime with indifference, but active opposition – from certain left-wing elements in the government, army and trade unions opposed to the imposition of a technocratic and centralist form of socialism – was crushed after an abortive coup in 1967. Opposition groups were driven into exile, and within the country discontent continued to be expressed openly only by some school and university students. After 1967 no real attempt was made to democratize the structure of political control. Algeria continued to be governed by a few men and a few institutions, with the army and the administration having central importance as executors. The FLN, once a successful mass political movement, ceased to play an effective role, and although a number of attempts were made to revive it, the heavy hand of the state and the army denied it any independent political activity. In the late 1960s a process of political education was introduced with the creation of elected local and provincial assemblies, but their role was essentially advisory and they operated within a framework determined by the central government. This policy was extended in 1975 when Boumediène announced that national elections for an Assembly and a President were to be held and that a National Charter would be drawn up to provide the state with a new constitution. Public discussion of the National Charter was vigorous and often critical of local and central government, but it received almost unanimous approval in a referendum held in June 1976. The essence of the Charter was the irreversible commitment of Algeria to socialism, though a socialism specifically adapted to Third World conditions. The dominant role of the FLN was reasserted, but as a concession to more conservative sentiment Islam was recognized as the state religion. The following November a new constitution embodying the principles of the Charter was also approved by referendum and in December Boumediène was elected President unopposed. Finally, to complete the new formal structure of power, a National Assembly was elected in February 1977 from candidates selected by a committee of the FLN. Steps were taken yet again to strengthen and enlarge the FLN in order to make it the guiding political force envisaged in the National Charter. But before a national FLN congress could be held, Boumediène suddenly became ill, and on 27 December 1978 he died of a rare blood cancer.

Boumediène died without naming a successor. The choice of Colonel Chadli Bendjedid, a senior army officer and commander of the Oran military district, as the new president rather than Bouteflika, the minister of foreign affairs or Yahiaoui, the head of the FLN, who were regarded as more obvious potential successors, came as a surprise both inside and outside Algeria but unquestionably reaffirmed the political primacy of the armed forces. Chadli was inaugurated as president on 9 February 1979, after his candidature had been approved by a reassuring 94 per cent of the electorate. Nevertheless, at first the Chadli government was in a weak position because the president's own supporters were in a minority. However, the existence of a number of factions within the régime gave the new president some room to manoeuvre and enabled him gradually to exert his control over the state apparatus. Influential personalities from the Boumediène era, such as Bouteflika, Yahiaoui and Abdessalam, were removed from the Politburo and then from the Central Committee of the FLN, paving the way for the removal of potential opponents at lower levels of the system. With his reappointment as secretary-general at the FLN's fifth party congress in December 1983, Chadli automatically became the party's candidate in the presidential election held in January 1984 when he was re-elected for a second five-year term as head of state, gaining 95 per cent of the vote. After his re-election Chadli quickly strengthened his position by carrrying out a major reshuffling of both party and government posts.

On coming to power Chadli had declared that he would uphold the policies of Boumediène, the 'irreversible option' of socialism and 'national independence' in both political and economic spheres. But it soon became clear that despite the official rhetoric about 'continuity' Boumediène's policies were to be revised, reversed or abandoned. Until the late 1980s the Chadli régime directed most of its attention to the economy, introducing a range of economic reforms. Even before the death of Boumediène an evaluation of the 1967-77 decade of social and economic development was in progress. Yet instead of providing a much needed constructive criticism of this phase of the development experience, the evaluation was used rather to discredit the strategy adopted by the Boumediène régime. The large state conglomerates established during this period as the backbone of the industrial sector were singled out for intense criticism and their poor performance highlighted. The new five-year plan (1980-84), whose slogan was 'for a better life', denounced the priority given to industrialization up to 1979. Major industrial projects devised by the former régime were to be frozen and the functioning and management of existing industries 'rationalized'. A package of reforms was quickly introduced to restructure the state conglomerates and make them profitable by dividing them up into smaller 'entreprises nationales'. Priority in investment shifted to agriculture, light manufacturing and consumer goods. The new régime sought to encourage the national private sector to invest in downstream light industries while portions of state-owned farmlands and their commercial networks were privatized.

Some analysts have interpreted these reforms as a pragmatic attempt to deal with the country's economic problems; others have accused the Chadli régime of implementing a policy of de-Boumediènization, of consolidating the gains of the new industrial bourgeoisie and encouraging the gradual 'compradorization' of the Algerian economy and society. There is no doubt that the impact of the liberalization programme was uneven and had unintended consequences. The rate of capacity utilization remained low in the restructured state enterprises which continued to make financial losses. Restructuring did not provide a reformed organization at the state level capable of dealing with, and following up, the complexities of the restructured industrial sector. To some extent the economic reforms merely amplified economic distortions instead of invigorating the performance of the public sector. Far from transforming the pattern of trade, the country became almost completely dependent on oil and gas for its export revenues. The liberalization of the deeply troubled agricultural sector failed to stimulate food production, though it paved the way for the enrichment of certain private farmers specializing in speculative products such as the so-called 'milliardaires de légumes' who control the supply of fresh vegetables. By the early 1990s Algeria had the most precarious food security situation in the region with up to 80 per cent of its food supply imported. The private sector, formal and informal, legal and illegal, expanded dramatically. Those entrepreneurs who benefited the most from economic liberalization were those close to the state who could cut their way through the stifling bureaucratic red tape because of their association with often highly placed state officials. At the top end of the informal economy, this produced serious and high level corruption – what Algerians refer to as 'the mafia'. While the IMF and the World Bank estimate the informal or parallel economy at some 10 per cent of the official economy, some researchers believe that the figure may be as much as 50 per cent.

The dramatic collapse in the price of oil in 1986 together with the devaluation of the US dollar had a devastating effect on Algeria. The world price of oil fell from almost $40 a barrel in 1979 to under $10 in 1986, impacting immediately on Algeria's balance of payments. Receipts from crude oil sales dropped in real terms by 80 per cent and as the government had insisted on linking prices for its natural gas exports to that of crude petroleum, overall hydrocarbon export receipts fell from $12,970m in 1985 to $7,633m the following year and remained depressed for the rest of the decade. Algeria was particularly vulnerable because it had incurred heavy foreign debt, estimated at some $22-23,000m in 1986, to finance its ambitious development programme on the assumption that rising oil revenues and growing revenues from industrial exports would easily allow it to service the debt. But following the fall in oil prices, servicing the debt swallowed up a growing proportion of the country's export revenues. Debt service ratios rose at an alarming rate from 26 per cent in 1980 to 76 per cent in 1988.

The government responded to the crisis by taking measures to reduce both imports and public spending and planned investment projects were modified, postponed or cancelled. Imports of capital goods, semi-finished products and spare parts, on which the country's industrial sector was heavily dependent, were either curtailed or suppressed. In place of the slogan 'for a better life', the single party urged 'work and rigour to guarantee the future'. A second phase of reforms was introduced to speed up economic liberalization, including legislation granting considerable managerial autonomy to the restructured state enterprises that were now required to operate by the laws of supply and demand rather than by the dictates of central planning. Laws were also passed to accelerate the privatization and exploitation of state-owned lands. Subsidies on basic consumer staples were reduced and price controls lifted from state industrial and agricultural sectors in order to allow market forces to regulate resource distribution. The social costs of these reforms were high, particularly for the vulnerable strata of society. Inequalities in income widened and while a privileged minority was enriched, the vast majority of Algerians were hard-hit by rising prices and cuts in both social benefits and public-sector jobs. Unemployment rose and the purchasing power of the majority of families declined drastically.

The tensions that had been building up in Algerian society erupted in widespread rioting in late 1988. In September 1988 the country was hit by a wave of paralysing strikes, particularly around the Rouiba vehicle assembly plant on the outskirts of Algiers, orchestrated in part by the Union Générale des Travailleurs Algériens (UGTA), the national trade union. In early October rioting broke out in Algiers and other cities, but unlike previous violent incidents involving Berberists and Islamists in the early 1980s or riots in the Algiers casbah in 1985 and in Constantine in 1986, these disturbances proved difficult to control. When the police were unable to cope, the army was called in and incurred intense popular anger at the brutal way it subdued the rioters. Between the 6 and 11 October hundreds were killed and thousands injured. There were rumours at the time that left-wing elements within the FLN and from the clandestine communist party, the Parti de l'Avant-garde Socialiste, which was influential in the UGTA, had been responsible for provoking these disturbances in an attempt to force the government to slow down the pace of its economic liberalization programme. Whether these rumours are true or not, the riots rapidly became an opportunity for the release of long pent-up feelings of intense frustration and alienation by Algerian youth against a régime that was perceived to have marginalized and abandoned them.

The riots also saw the open re-emergence of the Islamist movement into the mainstream of Algerian political life. Islamist militants did not start the riots but represented the only organized movement to voice the frustrations of the rioters. Islamists became prominent targets for the security forces in the subsequent repression. Algerian Islamism may be regarded as heir to the Islamic reform movement of Ben Badis and to the FLN. The Islam of the Reformers was crucial to the formation of Algerian national consciousness but although the Association of Reformist Ulema had rallied to the support of the FLN in 1956 it was deprived of its autonomy. The avowed purpose of the FLN was 'the restoration of the sovereign, democratic and social Algerian state within the framework of Islamic principles', yet the state which the FLN established is certainly not an Islamic state. The new nation-state maintained strict control over the religious sphere, transforming the ulema into its salaried officials. The development of a radical Islamist movement may therefore be interpreted as a belated reaction to the continuing subordination of Islam to the FLN state.

The movement did not become a major feature of Algerian political life until after the death of Boumediène. On coming to power Boumediène had vigorously reasserted the state's monopoly over the religious sphere, suppressing the al-Qiyam (the Values) association which had demanded official support for Islamic rites and duties and had campaigned against the manifestation of Western cultural values in Algerian society, while incorporating some of their demands into his own programme. But the left-turn in government policy beginning in the early 1970s and Boumediène's attempt to implement a wide ranging programme of radical social reforms, described as 'la Révolution socialiste', resulted in a revival of Islamist agitation. Despite the banning of al-Qiyam, its leaders had remained the focus of the various currents of Islamist opposition which found collective expression in the semi-clandestine movement Ahl el Da'wa (the People of the Call). Moreover, the movement was reinforced by Islamist ideas and literature imported from the Arab East, often brought by Egyptian teachers recruited as part of the country's Arabization programme, many of whom had been influenced by the Muslim Brotherhood. The Islamist movement also gained a growing number of adherents in the universities where 'Islamic associations' were formed, following the example of the informal group organized within the Central Faculty of the University of Algiers under the intellectual patronage of Malek Bennabi, one of the major figures in al-Qiyam.

The Islamist movement was greatly strengthened after the death of Boumediène. There is evidence that at first the Chadli régime quietly encouraged the Islamists as a means of intimidating the left and the Berberists. The government's controversial 'Family Code', promulgated in June 1984, represented a major concession to Islamist sentiment and a defeat for the small but vociferous Collective des femmes. Unlike its rivals in opposition, the Islamists did not hesitate to employ violence to promote their cause. In their effort to re-conquer the religious sphere, many state-controlled mosques were taken over by force, in some cases after violent clashes with the authorities, and hundreds of unofficial mosques outside state control were established. In their zeal to uphold public morality, stocks of alcohol were destroyed and brothels attacked in several towns. The universities in particular became the scene of violent confrontation between militant Islamists and their principal rivals, notably the left and the Berberists. The first armed resistance was launched by a former FLN war veteran, Mustafa Bouyali, who from 1981 to 1987 embarked on an armed struggle against 'the impious state' in the name of *jihad* (holy war). In August 1985 Bouyali's group robbed a factory of its payroll and a few days later attacked a police barracks making off with arms and ammunition. By revising the old *maquis* traditions in the mountains the rebels defied the security forces for over a year before Bouyali was finally killed. The partisans of political violence were never disarmed and after the army-backed coup, which denied the Islamists victory in the national elections in January 1992, the armed struggle was renewed.

Chadli's response to the October 1988 riots was to implement a new phase of reforms more far-reaching than any that had gone before. Economic reforms were speeded up, especially after the appointment of Mouloud Hamrouche as prime minister in September 1989, and Algeria was placed on the road to a free market economy. Major laws voted included the official abolition of the 'Agrarian Revolution', the re-distribution of nationalized land to the former owners, and permission for foreign capital to participate in a wide variety of enterprises. But these economic reforms were for the first time accompanied by sweeping political reforms. Constitutional reforms were approved by referendum in November 1988 and the organization, power and position of the FLN in state and society was fundamentally revised. The FLN was officially separated from the state and its monopoly of power was eliminated. The president was to stand above day-to-day politics and the government was made responsible to the legislature, the National Assembly. The military withdrew from any formal participation in political life. After Chadli's re-election as president in December 1988, further constitutional amendments were approved by plebiscite in February 1989. They signaled a clear ideological break with the past. The 'irreversible commitment to socialism' was abandoned completely, freedoms of expression, association and organization were guaranteed, as were the right to unionize and strike, but most important of all 'associations of a political nature' were allowed to compete with the FLN so long as their platforms were neither religious nor regionalist. A law on political associations passed in July 1989 opened the way to a controlled multiparty system.

Within a few months some thirty political parties representing a wide range of ideological tendencies had been officially registered. Apart from the previously banned Front des Forces Socialistes (FFS) of Hoceine Aït Ahmed, one of the 'chefs historiques' of the Algerian revolution, and the newly created Rassemblement pour la culture et la démocratie led by Said Sadi, both of which drew their support mainly from the Berbers in Kabylia, together with Ahmed Ben Bella's Mouvement pour la Démocratie en Algérie, most parties were small and insignificant with the exception of the Islamist Front Islamique du Salut (FIS) which quickly emerged as the only serious nationwide competitor to the FLN. Although there were three other Islamist parties, the FIS gathered together the major if diverse elements of the Islamist movement into a political coalition which had a well-organized and well-financed party network, strongly rooted at the local level in the many neighbourhood mosques. The party attracted support from those members of the technical and intellectual élite who saw the FLN-controlled state as the principal obstacle to their professional mobility and political participation, as well as from the vast mass of the urban poor, especially young Algerians from the cities' slums, the main victims of the régime's economic reforms. The FIS became a vehicle for very heterogeneous social and political demands and its internal contradictions and divergences were reflected in its senior leadership: Abassi Madani, the middle-aged, middle-class university professor with his university-educated retinue; and Ali Benhadj, the fiery young imam from the popular quarter of Bab el-Oued in Algiers who appealed to deprived and frustrated urban youth – the new 'wretched of the earth'.

The new multiparty system was put to the test in June 1990 when municipal and provincial elections were held. Despite a high rate of abstention, the FIS won a sweeping victory obtaining 55 per cent of votes cast and gaining control of 856 of the 1,541 communes – including every commune in the three major cities, Algiers, Oran and Constantine – and 31 of the 48 provincial assemblies. Only in Berber-speaking Kabylia and in the south did the FIS fail to win convincingly. In contrast, its chief rival, the FLN, which had entered the elections deeply and irreparably divided, was completely humiliated, obtaining only 32 per cent of the vote and taking control of only 487 communes and 14 provincial assemblies. Just before the elections, a former prime minister, Abdelhamid Brahimi, had dropped a bombshell by alleging that party and government officials had pocketed $26,000m over the years in bribes and commissions – a sum equivalent to the entire foreign debt. The FIS victory was widely interpreted as a crushing rejection of rule by the FLN establishment, rather than as an endorsement for the project and worldview of radical Islamism.

Yet for all the FIS's populist rhetoric against 'the thieves of the FLN', some analysts have argued that in its impatience to exert influence the party allowed itself to be manipulated by Chadli and the reformers who attempted to use the Islamists in their own battle for supremacy against the 'old guard' of the FLN. They point out that whereas Chadli and his associates had been the target for the Islamists' wrath in October 1988 by the middle of 1989 the FIS focused its attack on the FLN in general and more particularly on Chadli's enemies within it. They accuse the FIS of opportunism and hypocrisy, pointing in particular to the FIS's tacit support for the policy of economic liberalization even though these reforms had imposed a crushing burden on the urban poor, from which the party drew much of its support. If indeed the FIS was manipulated by Chadli and his allies, the president's strategy backfired when the FIS won such an overwhelming victory in the local elections.

Iraq's invasion of Kuwait in August 1990 and the ensuing Gulf crisis obliged the authorities to postpone the long-awaited elections for the National Assembly. It was not until the beginning of April 1991 that the government announced that national elections would be held in two rounds in June and July. A range of measures were introduced, including some major revisions to the electoral law, designed to weaken the FIS's electoral performance. These actions were interpreted by some as an excess of self-confidence by the presidential entourage and especially the prime minister Hamrouche, who, it was argued, believed that the FIS had been weakened by their militant and essentially opportunisitic support for Iraq and the devastating defeat suffered by Iraqi forces in the war. Despite its close links with Saudi Arabia and the other Gulf monarchies, the FIS, anxious to maintain its popular base, had been the most vociferous and militant supporter of Iraq during the crisis. In the event Hamrouche's self-confidence proved to be misplaced.

The FIS decided to confront the authorities and at the end of May its leaders called a general strike. There was only a limited response but it raised the political temperature and soon FIS supporters, especially unemployed youths, took to the streets of Algiers as part of a campaign of peaceful mass protest. However, at the beginning of June when riot police were ordered to clear the streets fierce fighting broke out as armed FIS supporters set up barracades in two of the city's main squares, transforming them into battlefields. On 4 June, in a dramatic midnight announcement, President Chadli declared a state of siege, cancelled the elections planned for the end of the month and dismissed prime minister Hamrouche and his government. By the early hours of the morning, the army had occupied key positions in Algiers. Armed with extensive powers, the military then re-established relative peace on the streets of the capital.

A few days later, Abassi Madani and Ali Benhadj called off the strike and the protest campaign, announcing that the president had agreed to hold both parliamentary and presidential elections before the end of the year and to change the disputed electoral laws to ensure that elections would be 'clean and fair'. But what appeared to be a victory for the FIS clearly antagonized elements within the army bitterly hostile to the Islamists. Army leaders demanded a crackdown on the militant fringe of the Islamist movement which quickly resulted in renewed tension between the FIS and the government. When army units moved into FIS-controlled communes at the end of June and ordered the removal of Islamic slogans from municipal offices, further violent clashes erupted as FIS militants confronted the security forces. The army arrested at least 2,500 Islamist militants in a major crackdown on FIS activities, culminating in the arrest of Abassi Madani and Ali Benhadj on 1 July; they were accused of having led an armed conspiracy against the security of the state in an attempt to take power. Despite rumours that an army-backed régime was to be installed, the army did not take power at this time but waited a further six months before intervening decisively. One explanation put forward is that leading members of the military hierarchy were persuaded that the FIS would not be able to repeat their success in the forthcoming legislative elections; an alternative view is that the army leadership was poised to take over but, with an eye to international opinion, waited until it could claim that the incompetent Chadli régime had let the political situation get out of hand and that it had to intervene to protect the integrity of the state against the threat of an Islamist takeover.

The state of siege was lifted at the end of September 1991 and in mid-October President Chadli announced that the postponed legislative elections would be held in two rounds on 26 December 1991 and 16 January 1992. The army remained vigilant. Two leading members of the military hierarchy had entered the government: General Khaled Nezzar as minister of defence and later, General Larbi Belkhair as interior minister with responsibility for the general elections. The FIS remained deeply suspicious of the government's intentions, especially as its two leaders were awaiting trial by military court, and it was not until the last minute that the party agreed to participate in the elections. In the first round of the elections the FIS won outright in 188 of the 430 constituencies. The FFS came second with 25 seats and the former ruling party, the FLN, was relegated to a humiliating third place with only 15 seats. The FIS seemed set to win a majority of the remaining seats on the second round of voting planned for 16 January 1992 and thus control the Assembly. The other Islamist parties, Nahdah, Hamas and Umma, instructed their supporters to vote for the FIS against the FLN in the second round, but the secular parties failed to declare their support for the FLN.

In the wake of the first round of the elections protest was widespread, led by professional and women's organizations and by secular parties such as the FFS, which organized a huge march through the centre of Algiers on 2 January in support of democracy. But President Chadli, who had resigned from the FLN the previous year, reaffirmed that he would respect the election results and indicated his willingness to 'cohabit' with a FIS government. Confident that they could probably win two-thirds of the seats in the National Asembly, the FIS rejected the possibility of sharing power, demanded the appointment of Abassi Madani as prime minister and called for immediate presidential elections. They would only accept Chadli's continuation in office if he dismissed the two members of the army high command, Generals Nezzar and Belkhair, from the government. Such an arrangement was clearly unacceptable to the military who intervened in what one analyst described as not so much a *coup d'état* as a *coup de grâce*.

Despite some attempt to observe constitutional niceties, the heavy hand of the army was all too clear. On 4 January the president was forced to dissolve the National Assembly and on 11 January, five days before the second round of the elections was due to take place, Chadli resigned 'to safeguard the interests of the country' as a result of intense pressure from senior military officers. As tanks and heavily-armed troops were deployed around key buildings in the capital, the High Security Council, dominated by three senior generals, defence minister Nezzar, interior minister Belkhair and Abdelmalek Guenenaizia, the army chief-of-staff, and also including the prime minister, and the ministers of justice and foreign affairs, took power with the declared aim of preserving public order and national security. The second round of the general elections was immediately cancelled. On 14 January the Council appointed a five-member High State Council to act as a collegiate presidency until December 1993, when Chadli's presidency would have expired. The High State Council was headed by Muhammad Boudiaf, one of the historic leaders of the War of Independence who was recalled from self-imposed exile in Morocco where he had lived since 1964, but also included defence minister Nezzar, the new régime's strongman.

Some analysts have argued that the military takeover put an end to Algeria's inevitable transformation from a one-party authoritarian state to a liberal multiparty democratic polity and that the 1992 *coup d'état* marked a retreat of the Algerian state back to its authoritarian past.

However, the general elections themselves were deeply flawed and there are serious doubts that a FIS-dominated government would have preserved democracy once it came to power. Although the FIS gained a majority of seats in the first round of the elections, its victory was based on just 3.3m votes from an electorate of 13.3m. There were almost a million spoiled ballot papers and accusations of intimidation and malpractice in FIS-controlled municipalities that may have prevented a further one million from voting. But more important, the political rhetoric of the FIS was highly intolerant and the statements of its leaders left no doubt that the party's aim was an Islamic state and an end to multiparty democracy.

On taking power, the military junta moved quickly against municipalities, newpapers and mosques controlled by the FIS. Security forces took control of the FIS offices and arrested leading FIS officials who were accused of inciting soldiers to desert. Violent clashes between the army and demonstrators broke out across the country and on 9 February the authorities declared a twelve-month state of emergency giving the security services sweeping powers of arrest and detention. Thousands of FIS supporters were arrested, and by the end of March some 9,000 were held in special detention camps in remote parts of the Sahara. Already over a hundred people had died in clashes between Islamist militants and the security forces. At the beginning of March, following a court judgement, the FIS was outlawed. The repressive policies of the military increasingly forced the movement underground and provoked the growth of several armed and clandestine Islamist groups. By May some 400 people had been killed. In June FIS leaders Abassi Madani and Ali Benhadj were tried before a military court and later sentenced to twelve years in prison.

On 29 June 1992 Muhammad Boudiaf, the chairman of the HSC, who had been installed as a figurehead to give a measure of legitimacy to the new régime, was assassinated during an official visit to the eastern city of Annaba. Widely respected as a man of integrity, Boudiaf had begun to show that he had ideas of his own. In particular his efforts to root out corruption had threatened many at the highest levels of the ruling establishment; he had ensured that at least one senior army officer, Mustafa Beloucif, was charged before a military tribunal for embezzling millions of dinars. The assassination took place in full view of the television cameras, and the assassin, a sublieutenant in the special anti-terrorist unit responsible for the president's security that day, was arrested almost immediately. A commission was set up to investigate but its report, which was heavily censored, while concluding that the assassin had not acted alone, declined to state who had ordered the killing. Few people, including Boudiaf's family, believed that the FIS were responsible and popular suspicion fell on the mafia and its allies in the administration and army, often referred to as the *hizb fransa* – the party of France. Ali Kafi, the head of the Algerian War Veteran's Organization, succeeded Boudiaf as chairman of the HSC.

Ali Kafi appointed Belaid Abdessalam to form a new government. Abdessalam, a former minister of energy and heavy industry, had been the architect of the ambitious economic development programme initiated during the Boumediène era. He had opposed the liberalization policies of the Chadli régime and belonged to the group within the FLN that the former president and his allies had sought to outmanoeuvre by encouraging the FIS. Untainted by the corruption that permeated the ruling establishment, the new prime minister was given increased powers. The economic and political challenges that confronted his government were daunting. Earlier in the year an official report had revealed that the economic crisis was even more serious than many observers had believed. Much of the country's industry was operating at only half its capacity because of shortages of spare parts and other essential inputs. 1.3m people were unemployed, over a fifth of the working population, living standards were falling and servicing the massive foreign debt was absorbing over three quarters of the country's foreign exchange earnings. Abdessalam immediately made it clear that economic liberalization policies would be halted and some reversed. He stated that the government's priority was to deal with inflation and tackle social issues, rather than to pursue reform policies which resulted in the loss of jobs and triggered price increases. The economy had to be put on a war footing and imports cut to a bare minimum. He rejected debt rescheduling, devaluation and further trade liberalization. In contrast to previous policies of opening up the economy, which had been encouraged by the International Monetary Fund (IMF), his economic programme, published in September 1992, envisaged a ban on imports that competed with locally produced goods. On the other hand, the policy of encouraging foreign investment, especially in key sectors such as hydrocarbons, was continued though within clearly defined limits to protect Algeria's economic sovereignty.

The security situation continued to deteriorate. At the end of August 1992 a series of bombings, including an attack on Algiers international airport which killed nine people and injured 100, marked a dangerous escalation in the cycle of violence. The prime minister called for 'total war' against supporters of the banned FIS. Tough new security laws were introduced, special state security courts were set up to try Islamist suspects speedily and with authority to impose harsh sentences, including the death penalty, and media reporting on security matters was strictly controlled. In January 1993 the first two Islamists were executed and more executions followed, including that of Hocine Abderramane, a close associate of Abassi Madani. The curfew which had been imposed in Algiers and several neighbouring provinces was extended and the state of emergency renewed indefinitely. Amnesty International reported a dramatic increase in the use of torture by the security forces. These tough policies found support among some elements within Algerian society, but for the vast majority of the population, especially the urban poor, the crude techniques of mass repression provoked popular resentment and drove some into the arms of the Islamists.

After the FIS was banned and its political organization dismantled in early 1992, the initiative had passed from the political wing to a number of armed clandestine opposition groups, some of which derived from an earlier phase of armed Islamist resistance to the state in the 1980s led by Mustafa Bouyali. The Mouvement Islamique Armé (MIA) under the leadership of Abdelkader Chebouti, a former associate of Bouyali, and Said Mekhloufi, an officer who had deserted from the army, though formally linked to the FIS, appeared to operate with a degree of autonomy. It was active throughout the country but was particularly strong in the west, in the Oran region. Its rival, the Groupe Islamique Armé (GIA), linked together several more or less autonomous cells including many so-called 'Afghanists' – Algerian Islamists who had fought with the *mujahidin* in Afghanistan during the struggle against the Soviet occupation – and which had opposed the electoral strategy of the political wing of the FIS. The GIA had its power base in the eastern suburbs of the capital, Algiers, and in nearby towns such as Blida while other groups were active around Sidi Bel Abbes in the west and the Jijel district in the north-east. Whereas the MIA has never seriously aimed at a revolutionary seizure of power and has mainly targeted the security forces and low level government officials in order to force the régime to the negotiating table, the GIA rejected negotiation and called for the violent overthrow of the state, liquidating prominent public figures, intellectuals, journalists, teachers and foreign nationals. The group warned all foreigners to leave the country by the end of November 1993 or die, provoking an exodus of foreign nationals. However, there is evidence that some of the more spectacular assassinations may have been the work of military security which is believed by some to have infiltrated the GIA and used it to eliminate those critical of the military junta. The appalling acts of violence perpetrated by the GIA certainly proved a major embarrassment to the FIS and at the same time strengthened the hand of the faction within the military-backed régime opposed to a negotiated settlement.

In August 1993, after only a year in office, Abdessalam was replaced as premier by foreign minister Redha Malek, a former career diplomat.

There had been speculation about the departure of Abdessalam since July, and both the French and US Governments, it was reported, had favoured the appointment of Malek. The new prime minister expressed his commitment to maintaining a hard line against the Islamist militants and his support for a free market economy. He appointed Mourad Benachenhou, formerly Algerian representative at the World Bank and an advocate of debt rescheduling, as minister of economy. Talks with the IMF recommenced in December but it was not until April 1994 that a package of reforms was agreed. The economic situation was precarious, exacerbated by the depressed petroleum prices, with the result that at the beginning of 1994 Algeria was forced to cease repayment of most of its medium- and long-term debt. The IMF agreement provided some $1000m in loans over the next twelve months and commited Algeria to a package of reforms including a 40 per cent devaluation of the dinar and the restructuring of state companies. The IMF standby agreement paved the way for the rescheduling of more than half of the country's $26,000m foreign debt, reducing debt repayments dramatically. Without rescheduling, debt repayments for 1994 had been forecast to exceed hydrocarbon revenues.

The mandate of the HSC was scheduled to expire on 31 December 1993, and in October the formation of an eight-member National Dialogue Commission was announced, which was to organize a gradual transition to an elected government. But the commission made little progress in its negotiations with legal opposition parties about the creation of a transitional régime. The only significant parties, the FLN and the FFS, had strongly opposed the *coup d'état* in 1992 and the interruption of the electoral process and had refused to cooperate with the military-backed governments installed since then. Indeed the power structure itself had become deeply divided since 1992, with two tendencies confronting one another, those who rejected any compromise with the FIS and the Islamist militants and insisted on the brutal suppression of the Islamist movement – *les éradicateurs* – and those who recognized that the political crisis could only be solved by compromise and dialogue with the Islamist opposition – *les conciliateurs*. The main 'eradicators' were those senior army officers who had served in the French army and who had occupied key positions in the army high command since 1988. Support outside the army for this hard-line tendency was limited to the leadership of the trade union movement, a few minor political parties such as the Berberist Rassemblement pour la Culture et la Démocratie and the former communist Ettahadi party, feminist groups and most of the Francophone press. The 'conciliators' could count on less formal support among the senior officer class but included all the main political parties, human rights activists and the courageous intellectuals and journalists grouped around the journal *Naqd* and the weekly *La Nation*.

In mid-December 1993 the HSC issued a statement indicating that it would not disband itself until a new presidential body had been inaugurated and proposed to hold a national dialogue conference at the end of January 1994 to choose a new collective leadership. The conference proved to be a fiasco as it was boycotted by almost all the main political parties. The HSC then appear to have abandoned the idea of a three-man presidency to rule during the transitional period from 1994-96 in favour of a single strong hand to restore confidence and coherence to government policy. Hard-liners in the régime, such as generals Nezzar, Belkheir, Gheziel and Mediene, favoured Abdelaziz Bouteflika, Boumediène's foreign minister, but the High Security Council eventually named defence minister General Lamine Zéroual as president and he was sworn in on 31 January. Zéroual, regarded as one of the most respected members of the senior officer corps, was believed to share the views of the conciliators. He never served in the French army but joined the Armée de Libération Nationale at the age of sixteen and fought in the guerrilla struggle inside Algeria during the War of Independence, giving him a measure of personal legitimacy. In his first public statement the new president called for 'serious dialogue' to find a way out of the country's crisis and made cautious overtures to those members of the banned FIS who renounced violence. In April he removed Redha Malek, one of the eradicators, from the premiership together with the hard-line interior minister Selim Saadi and appointed a new government team made up mainly of technocrats or senior civil servants led by Mokdad Sifi. The following month he reorganized the army high command, placing his own supporters in key posts; notably there were changes to five out of the six *wilayat* or regional commanders. But the president remained tough on security, leaving security operations under the control of hard-liners such as Generals Lameri, Mediene and Touati.

Efforts to promote dialogue proved cautious. In May Zéroual inaugurated the Conseil National de Transition, an interim legislature of 200 appointed members which was supposed to provide a forum for debate until new parliamentary elections were held. Of the main political parties, only the 'moderate' Islamist party, Hamas, agreed to participate in the new body which became the target of ridicule in the media. Indeed, the régime consistently failed to involve a majority of the leading legalized political parties in its efforts to promote dialogue. It was not until August that the president managed to get five leading legalized parties to join dialogue talks aimed at drawing up an acceptable peace formula, and then there was disagreement among the parties over whether or not to include the banned FIS. In March two high-ranking FIS members – Ali Djeddi and Abdelkader Boukhamkham – had been released from prison in order to explore the possibilities for dialogue with the Islamist opposition, but little progress was made. It was not until late August that a breakthrough appeared to have been made. In a letter to Zéroual, imprisoned FIS leader Abassi Madani agreed to respect the 1989 Constitution and the principle of the alternation of power, and while not explicitly renouncing violence, spoke of a possible 'truce'. In early September Zéroual ordered the release of both Abassi Madani and Ali Benhadj from prison and their transfer to house arrest.

Several factors are thought to have brought about a change in the FIS's intransigent stance towards the military-backed régime, but the most important is believed to have been its fear of marginalization by the extremist GIA. It has been argued that the appalling acts of violence perpetrated by the GIA guerrillas alarmed at least some of the FIS leaders who felt that it was not in their interest for the extremists to gain the upper hand. But this may be only part of the explanation. From the middle of 1994 there were persistent reports of splits, mergers and conflicts within the Islamist opposition – reminiscent of the wartime FLN – and in particular uncertainty about the relationship between the political and military wings of the FIS and between the FIS and its more radical rival, the GIA, whose forces dominated the military struggle against the régime. For example, it has been claimed that the MIA, renamed the Armée Islamique du Salut in the summer of 1994, may not be under the control of the civilian wing of the FIS, that it frequently cooperates with the GIA in the field and has committed its share of nihilistic attacks and assassinations. After the transfer to house arrest of the two FIS leaders, the GIA reiterated its rejection of any ceasefire, reconciliation or dialogue and threatened to kill Islamist leaders who participated in talks with the 'renegade' régime. However, two months earlier Anouar Haddam, the FIS spokesman in the USA, had issued a statement claiming that an agreement had been reached in May to merge the armed forces of the FIS with those of the GIA. A communiqué from Rabah Kebir in Germany, the most senior FIS spokeman in exile, immediately denied that any such merger had taken place. Haddam later denied joining the GIA and stated that he was still a member of the FIS. There was further confusion in August when the GIA announced that it was creating a government in exile entitled the caliphate and named Haddam as foreign minister. In September it was reported that Mohammed Said, a former university professor and senior FIS official who had defected to the GIA, had been appointed GIA leader. There was some speculation that Said's appointment might guide the GIA in a more moderate direction and perhaps signaled a move by the GIA to seek greater credibility as a political movement. However, other reports stated that Said would remain with the the FIS and named Abu-Khalil Mahfouz as the new GIA leader. Accurate information about the leadership structures of the Islamist militant groups and the frequent power struggles between shifting rival factions in the Islamist opposition is difficult to obtain. Numerous defections of FIS activists to the GIA do appear to have taken place.

The release of Abassi Madani and Ali Benhadj failed to break the deadlock between the régime and the FIS and entice the FIS to the negotiating table. At the end of October 1994 Zéroual announced that neither Abassi Madani nor Ali Benhadj were willing to renounce violence or participate in talks. Before his release, Abassi Madani had stated that he was willing to consider calling a halt to the military campaign if certain conditions were met. Zéroual was unable to concede on a number of these points, namely rescinding the ruling outlawing the FIS in order to restore the party to legality, releasing all imprisoned FIS members, and allowing its armed wing into the dialogue talks. Zéroual's ability to compromise was limited because of the objections of leading eradicators in the military, while the political leadership of the FIS was under pressure from radical militant groups opposed to any dialogue with *l'état impie*. In a speech on 31 October marking the fortieth anniversary of the start of the War of Independence, Zéroual spoke of the failure of dialogue with the FIS and his decision to hold presidential elections before the end of his mandate in 1996. In the same speech the president accused the FIS leadership of consolidating extremism instead of acting to halt the violence. He also used the occasion to announce the promotion of chief-of-staff Muhammad Lameri, the leader of the eradicators, to the newly created rank of General of the Army Corps, the highest ever in the Algerian military, a move interpreted by some as marking the resurgence of the eradicators.

For all the talk of dialogue during 1994, the suicidal slide into civil war continued and some of the barbarous acts reported recalled the worst days of the struggle for independence. Indiscriminate terror tactics by both Islamist guerillas and the security forces have turned the conflict into a dirty war. The régime admitted in September 1994 that 10,000 had died in the conflict since early 1992. Amnesty International put the death toll at 20,000, half of them ordinary citizens who bear the brunt of the violence. These figures almost certainly underestimate the scale of the death toll as daily killings go unreported in a heavily censored media; as many as 30,000 lives have probably been lost since Feburary 1992 with around a thousand killed every week by the end of 1994. An Amnesty International report released in October 1994 painted a grim picture of a country where civilians were living in a state of fear, threatened and killed by Islamist militants for not obeying their orders and by the security forces in retaliation for Islamist raids. In addition to their campaign of assassinations, Islamist guerrillas have burnt down schools and colleges and instituted a reign of terror in areas under their control; anyone violating Islamist *diktats* risk mutilation or murder. In their campaign against Islamist guerillas the security forces have resorted to air attacks using napalm, punitive raids, torture and psychological warfare. Army repression has been harsh especially in popular quarters of Algiers and other large cities where many young men suspected of Islamist sympathies have been picked up in raids by the security forces, tortured and summarily executed. Latin American-style death squads have appeared carrying out revenge killings against victims selected at random. In Kabylia, a region traditionally alienated from the régime but strongly opposed to the Islamist militants, Berber villages began organizing armed patrols. Early in 1994 the USA, Britain, Spain, Japan and France advised their nationals to leave; some countries have closed their embassies in Algiers, making it difficult for Algerians to travel abroad. About 6,000 French citizens have left Algeria and in March 1994 the French Ministry of Foreign Affairs announced that it was closing all French schools and cultural centres, except for the Lycée Decartes at Staoueli outside Algiers. Claude Pierre, the head of the French community in Algeria, stated that the closures marked the end of the French presence there. On the whole the hydrocarbon sector has not been targeted by Islamist guerrillas, and the Saharan region as a whole has been less affected by the violence which has engulfed the northern regions of the country. Nevertheless, in mid-April 1995 security measures were reinforced in the four 'exclusion zones' at Ouargla, Laghouat, El Oued and Illizi which protect the Saharan oil and gas fields providing 95 per cent of Algeria's export revenues. The government announced that access to these areas would be restricted to staff working on the oil and gas installations and local inhabitants, all of whom would be required to carry special identity cards. Yet despite these new measures on 5 May five *coopérants*, two French, one British, one Canadian and one Tunisian, were killed at the industrial zone of Bounoura close to Ghardaia by 'a group of armed terrorists' according to official sources. The five men were employed by Anabib, the Algerian subsidiary of the American company Bechtel which is responsible for the construction of the Algerian section of the Maghreb–Europe gas pipeline. The murders at Ghardaia, which received wide coverage in the international press, brought the number of foreigners killed since September 1993 to eighty-two, twenty-nine of them French. Damage to the country's infrastructure as a result of the conflict is estimated at $3000m, and destruction of forests by the security forces will have severe environmental consequences. The rising tide of violence also calls into question the government's ability to implement the economic reforms demanded by the IMF.

Following the failure of dialogue with the Islamist opposition, the army embarked on the most extensive military operations of the conflict and confident of eventual victory appeared to have abandoned any restraint in its efforts to root out suspected Islamist sympathizers and guerrilla units. At the end of December 1994, president Zéroual told local officials that the state was determined to put an end to violence by all means. Some analysts believed that the main reason for the régime's new hard line was that it could count on the all-out support of France, fearful of the consequences of an Islamist victory in its former colony. Charles Pasqua, the powerful French Interior Minister, enjoys close links with the Algerian generals, and France is believed to have been the main supplier of sophisticated military equipment to the régime for use in anti-guerrilla warfare. In response to the régime's strategy of maximum force, the Islamist guerrillas stepped up their campaign of violence. The GIA, with over 10,000 men under arms, organized into forty groups, reaffirmed its commitment to a prolonged war in order to destroy the régime, calculating that state repression would continue to swell their own ranks particularly from the unemployed youths of the city slums. On 24 December Algeria hit the international headlines when four GIA guerrillas hijacked an Air France airbus at Algiers airport and murdered three passengers before forcing the plane to fly to Marseilles where the plane was stormed by French counter-terrorist police and the hijackers killed. It was claimed that the guerrillas planned to blow up the plane over Paris. In retaliation four Catholic priests, three French and one Belgian, were murdered by the GIA in Kabylia. At the beginning of January 1995 the GIA called for war on France because of 'its military presence in Algeria' and its support for the 'oppressive régime'. On 30 January 1995 a massive car bomb exploded in the centre of Algiers killing 42 people and injuring more than 250. Both the AIS and the GIA claimed responsibility for the attack, the biggest terrorist operation since the conflict began.

The plan to hold presidential elections, announced by Zéroual in October 1994, was rejected by several leading legalized opposition parties and condemned by the exiled FIS leadership. In a surprise move the opposition parties seized the initiative and after talks in Rome under the aegis of the Sant'Egidio Roman Catholic community in early January 1995, eight opposition parties agreed a 'platform for a national contract', setting out the basis for a negotiated end to the conflict and a return to democracy. The document was signed by representatives of the three 'fronts' – the FIS, FLN and the FFS, which between them won more than

80 per cent of the votes in the first round of the general elections of December 1991 – together with former president Ben Bella's Mouvement pour la démocratie en Algérie, the Trotskyist Partie des travailleurs, the Mouvement de la naissance islamique, Jazair musulman contemporaine and the Ligue algérienne de défense des droits de l'homme. Anouar Haddam and Rabah Kebir, who represented the FIS at the talks, made strange bedfellows with Trotskyist *pasionaria* Louiza Hanoune, the leader of the Partie des travailleurs.

The Sant'Egidio pact made a urgent appeal to both parties in the conflict to end their hostilities and allow the restoration of civil peace. It recommended the establishment of a transitional government in which both the military-backed régime and the political parties would be represented which would prepare the way for free multiparty elections as quickly as possible. All parties must guarantee to respect the results of the elections. Before any negotiations, the participants called for the release of the FIS leadership and of all political detainees, the restoration of the FIS to legality, and an immediate end to the use of torture and of attacks on civilians, foreigners and public property. The participants also agreed certain general principles, the renunciation of violence to achieve or retain power, respect for human rights, for popular legitimacy, multipartism and the alternation of power, and the guarantee of fundamental liberties. They recognized that the main elements of '*la personnalité algérienne*' were '*Islam, arabité et l'amazighité* (Berber culture)' and that both the Arab and Berber languages must be recognized as national languages. Finally they called for the withdrawal of the army from politics and its return to its constitutional role of protecting the unity and integrity of the national territory. Ali Benhadj and Abassi Madani both endorsed the Rome peace platform, whereas the GIA condemned it and reaffirmed their commitment to the establishment of a 'caliphate' by armed struggle.

The military-backed régime condemned the Sant'Egidio meeting even before it had begun claiming 'foreign interference in its national affairs'. Some days after the Rome platform was announced a government spokesman rejected its proposals '*en bloc et en détail*', a reaction which the US State Department greeted unfavourably. The French foreign minister, Alain Juppé, also voiced his disappointment, prompting some observers to detect a shift in the French government's position from strong backing for the generals in Algiers to support for the process of dialogue. The Italian, Spanish and US Governments had supported the Rome talks and had urged the junta to join the peace process. Whereas some analysts have argued that the Rome document confirms that the FIS is distancing itself more and more clearly from the Islamist radicals, anti-Islamist organizations in Algeria saw the Sant'Egidio pact as no more than a ploy by the Islamists to take power; with the army neutralized they would abandon all pretence to democracy and impose their intolerant rule. There was also criticism of the FLN and the FFS for their participation in the Rome meeting. The FLN was accused of attempting to throw off its discredited image after thirty years of corrupt, single-party rule by forming an alliance with the Islamists against the military-backed régime in a mistaken bid to return to power. In the intense debate about the Rome platform some argued that it was the only way to resolve the current crisis, while others believed that it merely paved the way for the Islamists to take power. In early April 1995 president Zéroual attempted to regain the initiative by resuming talks with the legalized opposition parties, but this time individually, about preparations for the presidential elections planned for the end of 1995. Separate meeings were held between the president and the leaders of the FLN and the FFS and former president Ben Bella of the Mouvement pour la Démocratie en Algérie also responded positively to the president's invitation, prompting speculation that the unity achieved at Rome might prove to be short-lived. The FFS had previously refused to take part in any dialogue with the military-backed régime. But talks with the FLN and FFS quickly broke down when Zéroual once again refused to include the FIS in any dialogue. The FLN and FFS agreed to take part in the presidential elections only if the FIS was allowed to participate. The government reiterated its demand that the FIS must renounce violence and accept the constitution before it could take part in the elections. On 17 April it was announced on state radio that the president would limit dialogue to those opposition parties which had agreed to participate in presidential elections on the government's terms; nine parties had accepted these terms. It was also reported that the army would call up reservists to ensure security during the elections. Foreign minister Dembri stated that international observers, including observers from the UN, would guarantee the fairness of the elections. At the end of May the government issued an electoral law decree prepared by the Conseil National de Transition stipulating that any candidate for the presidential elections must obtain 75,000 signatures before standing for election. Candidates must sign a declaration stating that they respect the constitution, reject violence and agree not to use Islam for partisan aims. No date was given for the elections but the government stated that they would be held in December 1995 at the latest. It was announced that in preparation for the elections President Zéroual would continue bilateral meetings with six opposition parties, the FLN, FFS, Hamas, Ennahda, the Mouvement pour la Démocratie en Algérie, and the National Party for Solidarity and Development, suggesting that he had not given up hope of securing the participation of two out of the three biggest parties. At this stage the régime did not name its candidate for the presidency. Zéroual himself has indicated privately that he does not wish to be a candidate. Other names mentioned include Mohamed Salah Yahiaoui, who headed the FLN under Boumediène, former prime minister Hamrouche, Ahmed Taleb Ibrahimi, and UGTA leader Abdelhaq Benhamouda.

There was speculation that unofficial talks were continuing between the government and the FIS leadership. After being returned to prison in February, Abbasi Madani and Ali Benhadj were reported to have been placed under house arrest at the end of March. The two men were reported to be held in separate residences west of Algiers but refused permission to meet with FIS supporters. However, in early June interior minister Cherif stated that the two men had been returned once again to prison. Nevertheless, it was rumoured that contacts with the FIS leaders had been renewed and that discussions centred on the possibility of FIS support for the presidential elections and restoring the party to legality. At the end of June in an interview with a French weekly, interior minister Cherif expressed optimism that the violence would soon be over and that if the majority of Algerian people 'were for the FIS' in the forthcoming presidential elections the government would 'respect their decision'. Sources close to FIS, however, denied that any agreement was about to be reached with the military-backed régime.

In mid-July the presidency announced that talks with the leaders of the banned FIS had broken down once again. The official communiqué denounced the 'intransigence' of the leaders of the Islamist movement. There were fears among the Algerian people that the breakdown in talks might lead to a new escalation of the violence. The Algerian press, for the most part hostile to the FIS, criticized the authorities for embarking on a new round of talks with the Islamist opposition. *Le Matin* accused the régime of not learning from the experience of earlier talks with the FIS leadership and insisted that the Islamists only participated in dialogue to gain time not to seek peace. *Liberté* warned the régime that its efforts to seek dialogue with the FIS were interpreted as a sign of weakness. Only *El Moudjahid* commented that some progress had been made during the recent discussions because for the first time the president had succeeded in involving Abassi Madani. Some observers argued that, despite the hostility of hardliners on both sides to an accord, the authorities and the FIS leaders were convinced that a political solution had to be found because there could be no military solution.

By the summer of 1995 there was evidence that the Algerian conflict had spread to France. In July 1995 two gunmen assassinated Sheikh Sahraoui, a leading spokesman in France for the Algerian Islamist opposition, outside the mosque in the rue Myrha in Paris. Claims that the Algerian régime was responsible for the murder were strongly rejected by

Introduction

Algeria's ambassador to Paris, Hocine Djoudi. Sheikh Sahraoui's murder was followed by threats from the GIA against FIS officials and supporters in Europe, and Moussa Kraouche, president of Fraternité algérienne en France, was placed under police guard for his own protection. When bombs exploded at the Saint-Michel metro station in Paris in July and near the Arc de Triomphe in August, suspicion inevitably fell on the GIA.

There are those analysts who are convinced that the future of Algeria is Islamist and that most people accept this. It has been argued that the FIS leadership, unable to exert control over the armed extremists, may be content to let the army eradicate the GIA by force. According to this scenario, such a military victory would only be achieved at enormous human cost and that popular rage against state terrorism would force the army to negotiate a deal with the FIS. A FIS-led government would be inevitable and the army would be forced to return to its barracks. This view questions whether the FIS would then seek to impose its model on all of Algerian society or would be willing to cede some space to those who do not share its vision. The existence of the FFS, with strong support among the Berbers of Kabylia determined to win recognition for their cultural and linguistic rights, is seen as the best hope that the interests of democrats will not be ignored by the FIS or the army.

The inevitablility of Islamist rule is contested by others who are convinced that the Algerian people, horrified by the outrages commited by the Islamist guerillas, now reject the FIS and believe that Islamism can be eradicated by military force. The anti-Islamist tendency, which includes professional associations, trade unions and feminists, stress that Algeria in early 1995 is very different from the Algeria of December 1991 when the FIS won almost half of the votes cast in the first round of the general elections. Certainly there are signs of a reduction in the level of support for the Islamist guerrilla groups in both social and geographical terms. Islamist militants are getting younger and are now almost all recruited from among the unemployed urban youth. Though it is too early to be certain, some observers believe that the army has forced the Islamist guerrillas to fall back to the major cities where they can wage their campaign only by assassinations. Nevertheless, they still have access to an almost inexhaustible supply of recruits. For its part, the army, with some 165,000 men under arms, can only mobilize around 60,000 of these for anti-terrorist operations, which may explain why, despite their successes, the security forces have been unable to consolidate their control over areas won from the guerrillas. The war between the armed groups of the state and the Islamists, both deeply divided, could be prolonged. Ordinary civilians are involved in this struggle only as victims. Yet Algerian society has shown immense resilience in the face of appalling violence. Witness the fact that every morning teachers throughout the country bravely open their schools even though some 600 school buildings have been burnt down by the GIA and 200 teachers killed since the crisis began. Will democracy eventually be allowed to take root or are Algerians condemned to endure either the authoritarianism of the junta or the intolerance of Islamist rule?

Selected Theses and Dissertations in English on Algeria

A. Abba. 'Traditional architecture in Algeria: from the past to the future', MPhil thesis, York University, England, 1986.

M. Abbad. 'Educational wastage and its effects on socio-economic and manpower provision in Algeria', PhD thesis, University of Wales, Cardiff, 1983.

Manssour Ahmad Abou-Khamseen. 'The first French-Algerian war (1830-1848): a reappraisal of the French colonial venture and the Algerian resistance', PhD thesis, University of California, Berkeley, 1983.

M. Achouri. 'The structure and performance of Algerian industry 1920-1980', MA thesis, Keele University, England, 1986.

M. C. Adad. 'Technology transfer for Algeria, with particular reference to the use of the CLASP system', MPhil thesis, Sheffield University, England, 1987.

A. Adamou. 'Community action for the rehabilitation of the housing stock: the Casbah of Algiers', MPhil thesis, York University, England, 1988.

K. E. Adamson. 'Labour and industrialization in the Maghreb', PhD thesis, Leeds University, England, 1984.

M. Aiche. 'The improvement of school building design in rural areas in Algeria with particular reference to the region of Mila', MPhil thesis, Sheffield University, England, 1987.

A. Aimar. 'Foreign co-operation and development: the Algerian case', PhD thesis, Manchester University, England, 1990.

Louisa Ait-Hamou. 'The divided self and separate audiences: an evaluation of Camus's and Fugard's political thought through a comparative and contrastive study', PhD thesis, University of York, England, 1990.

F. Ait Si Selmi. 'Phonological issues in Berber: evidence from French borrowings into Kabyle, Algeria', MPhil thesis, York University, England, 1985.

K. E. A. Ait Si Selmi. 'A socio-linguisitic study of the performance at the phonological level of a group of Algerian pupils learning English as a foreign language', MPhil thesis, York University, England, 1985.

M. Alem. 'Migration and its effects on a local community in Algeria', PhD thesis, Hull University, England, 1981.

Mohammed Abdallah Aljerrah. 'Trade balance instability and the optimal exchange rate régime: the case of OPEC countries (Algeria, Kuwait, Libya, Saudi Arabia, United Emirates)', PhD thesis, The University of Nebraska-Lincoln, 1993.

Boussetta Allouche. 'Small states and international mediation: the case of Algeria', PhD thesis, University of Maryland College Park, 1987.

Mohamed Alwan. 'Algeria before the United Nations', MA thesis, The American University, 1959.

M. Amirech. 'Land tenure, class structure and political discourse in Algeria: 1830-1982', PhD thesis, University of Wales, Bangor, 1987.

Y. Amirouchen. 'Building on the perimeter: a study of its relevance to traditions of built-form in Algeria', MPhil thesis, Nottingham University, England, 1989.

C. Anderson. 'Peasant or proletarian? Wage labour and peasant economy during industrialization', PhD thesis, University of Lund, Sweden, 1986.

A. G. Angal. 'The conflict between the built environment created by the recent housing schemes in Algiers and the expectations of those for whom they are designed', PhD thesis, Newcastle University, England, 1990.

A. Aouabed. 'A methodological investigation into the decay of an Algerian historical city: Constantine', DPhil thesis, York University, England, 1989.

Elmentfakh Aouad. 'Variation in the pronunciation of French loan-words in Western Algerian Arabic', MPhil thesis, University College, London, 1980.

A. Aoued. 'The problematicial nature of mixed jurisdictions: the Algerian approach', LL M thesis, Glasgow University, Scotland, 1980.

L. Assassi. 'Non-alignment as an ideological framework for the analysis of Algeria's foreign policy behaviour', MPhil thesis, City University, 1985.

Omar Assous. 'Arabization and cultural conflicts in Algeria', PhD thesis, Northeastern University, 1985.

A. A. Attal. 'Monetary policy in Algeria 1962-1977', MA thesis, Keele University, England, 1980.

A. A. Attal. 'Financing economic development in Algeria 1967-1977', PhD thesis, Keele University, England, 1983.

Rose-Marie Avin. 'Money windfalls and oil-exporting developing countries: a comparative study of Algeria, Ecuador, Trinidad and Tobago, and Indonesia', PhD thesis, University of Maryland, 1986.

S. Ayadi. 'Foreign trade and the economic development of Algeria', MA thesis, Keele University, England, 1986.

M. F. Azzi. 'The Algerian state and development', MSc Econ thesis, University of Wales, Aberystwyth, 1982.

Bertrand Babinet. 'Algeria: Boumedienne's régime: structures, values and achievements', MA thesis, The American University, 1971.

Elena Ruocco Bachrach. 'Oil and development: the case of agriculture in Nigeria and Algeria', PhD thesis, Northwestern University, 1988.

Yousef Farhan Bader. 'Kabyle Berber phonology and morphology: outstanding issues', PhD thesis, University of Illinois at Urbana-Champaign, 1984.

Fawzia Muhammad Bariun. 'Malik Bennabi's life and theory of civilization', PhD thesis, University of Michigan, 1988.

M. Barkaoui. 'The *New York Times* and the Algerian revolution 1956-1962: an analysis of a major newspaper's reporting of events', PhD thesis, Keele University, England, 1988.

Adnan Khalil Basha. 'Malek Bennabi and his modern Islamic thought', PhD thesis, University of Salford, England, 1992.

Abderrezak Belaid. 'Farmers risk attitides in the Eastern High Plateau region of Algeria: an application of the experimental approach', PhD thesis, Oregon State University, 1985.

H. C. Belhoul. 'The performance of public industrial enterprises in Algeria: an empirical study', PhD thesis, Keele University, England, 1984.

B. Belkacemi. 'French railways in Algeria 1850-1900: a contribution to the study of colonial history', PhD thesis, University of East Anglia, England, 1984.

C. Belkacemi. 'A linguistic survey of the Arabic dialect of Ras-El-Ma', MA thesis, Manchester University, England, 1982.

C. Belkacemi. ' Aspects of noun-modification in Algerian Arabic, with reference to the relative clause', PhD thesis, Manchester University, England, 1985.

Noureddine Belkhamza. 'Development and improvement of the telephone network in Algeria as a communication and environmental problem: analysis and modeling', PhD thesis, Rensselaer Polytechnic Institute, 1982.

A. Belkhiri. 'Phytochemical investigation of some Algerian cruciferae', PhD thesis, Manchester University, England, 1990.

A. Beloucif. 'A survey of geography teaching in Algerian secondary schools', MLitt thesis, Glasgow University, Scotland, 1991.

Laroussi Beloulou. 'Hydrogeological study and evaluation of water resources of the Collo Basin, Skikda, Algeria', MS thesis, The University of Arizona, 1987.

Linda Caroline Benabdi. 'Arabization in Algeria: processes and problems', PhD thesis, Indiana University, 1980.

A. Bendania. 'Development and evaluation of a model for teaching comprehension in Algerian secondary schools', PhD thesis, London University, Institute of Education, 1988.

R. Bendib. 'Hydrocarbons, rent and the Algerian growth strategy: a critical appraisal of the process of building an "independent and national economy"', PhD thesis, Glasgow University, Scotland, 1988.

R. Bendib. 'University libraries in the Arab countries with special reference to Algeria', MA thesis, Strathclyde University, Scotland, 1986.

M. A. Bendifallah. 'Workers' self-management in Algerian agriculture', MA thesis, Keele University, England, 1981.

S. Ben Mohamed. 'Export marketing: an investigation of the Algerian manufacturing sector: a case study', MCom thesis, Strathclyde University, Scotland, 1989.

Abdelmedjid Bennamia. 'Palestine in Algerian foreign policy, 1962-1978', PhD thesis, University of Exeter, England, 1988.

Mahfoud Bennoune. 'Impact of colonialism and migration on an Algerian peasant community: a study of socio-economic change', PhD thesis, University of Michigan, 1976.

D. Benouared. 'A study of alternative methods to industrialize the traditional house in Algeria', MSc thesis, Bath University, England, 1984.

M. Benrabah. 'The intelligibility of Algerian speakers of English: a phonetic/phonological study', PhD thesis, University College, London, 1987.

Abed Benkhadouma Benzina. 'Culture-specific guidelines for the design of medium and high density settlements in northern Algeria', DArch thesis, Catholic University of America, 1991.

N. Benrabah. 'Algerian intonational proficiency in English: an empirical study', University College, London, England, 1990.

Aziz Beziou. 'On ethnic political mobilization: the case of the Berber movement in Algeria', PhD thesis, University of Denver, 1993.

M. Bouabdallah. 'Aspects of anthropomorphic figurative usage of English and Algerian Arabic', MA thesis, Manchester University, England, 1981.

Sherazade Boualia. 'Gender and ethnicity: language attitudes and use in an Algerian context', EdD thesis, Columbia University Teachers College, 1993.

Ali Bouamrane. 'Aspects of the sociolinguistic situation in Algeria', PhD thesis, Aberdeen University, Scotland, 1986.

A. Bouceid. 'Agrarian reform and agricultural development in Algeria 1962-1984', MA thesis, Keele University, England, 1986.

Y. Bouchagour. 'Teaching English for specific purposes: the organization of a communicative approach for higher education in Algeria', PhD thesis, University of Wales, Cardiff, 1984.

S. M. Bouchenak-Khelladi. 'Planning energy use in Algeria: a study for the choice of energy in the domestic sector', PhD thesis, University of Wales, Swansea, 1983.

R. Boudebaba. 'Socio-economic development and migratory labour: the case of Algeria and France', MPhil thesis, Hull University, England, 1982.

R. Boudebaba. 'Urban growth and housing policy in Algeria: a case study of a migrant community in the city of Constantine', PhD thesis, Hull University, England, 1990.

Belgacem Bouguerra. 'The question of the Asiatic mode of production and pre-colonial Algeria', PhD thesis, The American University, Washington, DC, 1986.

F. A. N. Bouhadiba. 'Aspects of Algerian Arabic verb phonology and morphology', PhD thesis, Reading University, England, 1988.

F. Bouhass. 'Communication in the additional oral classes: towards improving students' oral fluency in English at Oran University', MPhil thesis, Warwick University, England, 1988.

H. Boukara. 'Ideology and pragmatism in Algerian foreign policy', PhD thesis, Lancaster University, England, 1986.

Y. Gacimi Boukhedimi. 'Testing EFL in Algerian secondary schools', MPhil thesis, Manchester University, England, 1988.

A. Boukhemis. 'Recent urban growth patterns and migration: a case study of Constantine', PhD thesis, Glasgow University, Scotland, 1983.

K. Boukhemis. 'Algerian development and urbanization: a case study of Skikda', PhD thesis, Glasgow University, Scotland, 1983.

Liess Boukra. 'Controversial problems in the theory of precapitalist societies and the concrete study of precolonial Algeria', MA thesis, The American University, 1979.

S. Boulmessaoud. 'An examination of centrally state planned agrarian reform: the Algerian case', MSc thesis, Stirling University, Scotland, 1982.

B. Boumarafi. 'Library and information education in Algeria: a framework for curriculum development', PhD thesis, Loughborough University, England, 1989.

Cherif Boumaza. 'Guests' perceptions of quality service in major Algerian hotels', MS thesis, Eastern Michigan University, 1993.

M. Boumaza. 'Ammonia plant availability: a study of the causes of ammonia plant failures and their outages in developing countries and an examination of ways of improving their performance with particular reference to Algeria', PhD thesis, Bradford University, England, 1988.

Karima Radja Roudesli Bourenane. 'English learning in Algeria: an analysis of errors and attitides (ESL)', PhD thesis, The University of Texas at Austin, 1984.

Chaoura Bourouh. 'Industrialization and class structure in Algeria', PhD thesis, The American University, 1985.

D. Boussaa. 'Housing design: towards a responsive approach: Dellys as the setting of research', MPhil thesis, York University, England, 1988.

S. Boutemine. 'A study of the Algerian correctional system for juvenile delinquents', MPhil thesis, Lancaster University, England, 1988.

K. Bouzebra. 'Culture and political mobilization in Algeria', PhD thesis, University of East Anglia, England, 1982.

A. Bouzida. 'The socio-economic structures of post-independence Algeria', MPhil thesis, Sheffield University, England, 1981.

A. Brahim-Bounab. 'The Algerian development strategy, income distribution and poverty', PhD thesis, Glasgow University, Scotland, 1989.

P. A. Brebner. 'Physical planning as an agent of ideology: an analysis of Qacentina, Algeria', PhD thesis, Glasgow University, Scotland, 1982.

Charles Scott Brunger. 'The development of the internal market in Algeria, Nigeria, and the Ivory Coast', PhD thesis, New School for Social Research, 1983.

Stuart James Bullion. 'Priorities of mass communication development: the Algerian case', PhD thesis, University of Minnesota, 1981.

Riec Eileen Iwirtzt Canjar. 'A structural comparison of spatial organization in conventional and unconventional military systems: the case of the 1954 Algerian revolution', PhD thesis, University of Michigan, 1983.

Caroline Elizabeth Card. 'Tuareg music and social identity (Algeria, Niger)', PhD thesis, Indiana University, 1982.

Hal Victor Cartwright. 'Revolutionary Algeria and the United Nations: a study in agenda politics', PhD thesis, University of Maryland, College Park, Maryland, 1974.

N. Chabbi. 'Towards a socio-cultural approach for the design on the house/settlement system – a case study in Ghardaia, Algeria', PhD thesis, Newcastle University, England, 1988.

Z. Chebchoub. 'A sociolinguistic study of the use of Arabic and French in Algiers', PhD thesis, Edinburgh University, Scotland, 1986.

M. N. Chenef. 'Changes in values and the meaning of the built environment in Algeria: a case study of Bou-Saada', PhD thesis, Nottingham University, England, 1988.

A. Chenini. 'The demand for money in a controlled economy: the case of Algeria', MPhil thesis, Loughborough University, England, 1988.

S. Cherchalli. 'Learners' reactions to their textbook (with special reference to the relation between differential perceptions and differential achievement): a case study of Algerian secondary school learners', PhD thesis, Lancaster University, England, 1988.

Boumediene Chergui. 'On optimization methods for gas liquefaction production in Algeria and for a firewater safety system for the holy area of Mina in Saudi Arabia', PhD thesis, University of Texas at Austin, 1986.

Boutheina Cheriet. 'Specific socialism and illiteracy amongst women: a comparative study of Algeria and Tanzania', PhD thesis, University of London, Institute of Education, 1987.

Suzanne Mary Chester. 'Dominance, marginality and subversion in French postcolonial discourse', PhD thesis, Louisiana State University and Agricultural and Mechanical College, 1991.

N. Chouakria. 'Capital accumulation and food crisis in Algeria: the contradictions of a capitalist development', PhD thesis, Glasgow University, Scotland, 1988.

M. T. Chouchane. 'Education and socio-economic development in Algeria, 1962-1982/84', PhD thesis, Manchester University, England, 1986.

Allan Christelow, Jr. 'Baraka and bureaucracy: Algerian Muslim judges and the colonial state (1854-1892)', PhD thesis, University of Michigan, 1977.

Julia Ann Clancy-Smith. 'The Saharan Rahmaniya: popular protest and desert society in south-eastern Algeria and the Tunisian jarid c. 1750-1881', PhD thesis, University of California, Los Angeles, 1988.

S. Collingwood-Whittick. 'The colonial situation in Algeria and its literary reflection', PhD thesis, Birkbeck College, London, 1980.

S. Debache. 'Problems of mass housing production, with particular reference to Algeria', MPhil thesis, Leeds University, England, 1987.

H. Dekkiche. 'The appropriate physical expression of habitat in the Algerian context', PhD thesis, Glasgow University, Scotland, 1989.

Ammar Deliou. 'Technocracy and Third World foreign policy development: the case of Algeria', PhD thesis, State University of New York at Albany, 1992.

Monica Dell'Osso. 'The Ministry of Algeria and the Colonies (24 June 1854-24 November 1860): an experiment in civil government', PhD thesis, University of Virginia, 1989.

A. Derbal. 'The problem of non-performance of contractual obligations and the provided means of release under English, Scottish, French and Algerian laws', LL M, Glasgow University, Scotland, 1989.

A. Derradji. 'The Algerian guerrilla campaign strategy and tactics', PhD thesis, Reading University, England, 1989.

A. Diafat. 'Improvement and maintenance of the old housing stock of Sétif, Algeria', MPhil thesis, York University, England, 1988.

M. Dieddour. 'Modern housing in Algeria: a study of spatial practices', PhD thesis, Manchester University, England, 1988.

P. D. Dine. 'French literary images of the Algerian war: an ideological analysis', PhD thesis, Stirling University, Scotland, 1990.

Aissa Djabelkhir. 'Africa and the Third United Nations Conference on the law of the sea: case study of Algeria', PhD thesis, University of Miami, 1984.

A. Djeghdjegh. 'A critique of dependency models of development in North Africa: a case study of Algeria', MSc thesis, Strathclyde University, Scotland, 1984.

Anne Donadey. 'Polyphonic and palimpsestic discourse in the works of Assia Djebar and Leila Sebbar', PhD thesis, Northwestern University, 1993.

A. Dridi. 'Aspects of Algeria's relations with France since independence', MSc Econ thesis, University of Wales, Cardiff, 1983.

D. Eddaikra. 'A socio-phonetic study of Algerian Arabic: its implication for the teaching of English pronunciation', PhD thesis, UWIST, Wales, 1988.

Lesley Anne Emerson. 'Internal migration in Algeria, 1966-1977: an empirical analysis', PhD thesis, University of Maryland College Park, 1992.

L. Q. Escobar. 'The process of workers' participation in the management of Algerian manufacturing enterprise during 1971-1982 period', PhD thesis, Hull University, England, 1989.

Daho Faghrour. 'Revolutionary causality in theory and practice, case study: Algeria 1830-1954', PhD thesis, University of Denver, 1984.

Salah Fellahi. 'An assessment of Algerian development (planning, decentralization, bureaucracy)', PhD thesis, Syracuse University, 1985.

A. Ferhaoui. 'Legal powers, duties and liabilities of management (with particular reference to Algerian company law)', LL M, Glasgow University, Scotland, 1990.

C. Ferhat. 'Indigenous housing forms in relation to housing problems in Algeria', PhD thesis, Leeds University, England, 1989.

F. Ferhat. 'American policy towards Algeria between 1940 and 1962', PhD thesis, Keele University, England, 1986.

Hocine Fetni. 'Law and development in the Third World: a case study of Algeria', PhD thesis, Universiy of Pennsylvania, 1992.

A. Fodil. 'Reported armed conflict: The Times coverage of the outbreak of the Algerian revolution', MEd thesis, University of Wales, Cardiff, 1986.

Judith E. France. 'AFL-CIO foreign policy: an Algerian example, 1954-1962', PhD thesis, Ball State University, 1981.

S. Gadi. 'Textile marketing in Algeria', MSc thesis, Strathclyde University, Scotland, 1983.

S. Z. Gaid. 'Urban renewal programmes appropriate for inner areas of Algerian cities', MPhil thesis, Oxford Polytechnic, England, 1989.

Patricia Geesey. 'Writing the decolonized self: autobiographical narrative from the Maghreb', PhD thesis, Ohio State University, 1991.

Peter Maxwell Geismar. 'De Gaulle, the army, and Algeria: the civil-military conflict over decolonization, 1958-1962', PhD thesis, Columbia University, New York, 1967.

E. H. Ghedjghoudj. 'Alternative energy strategies with particular reference to the oil industry of Algeria', MPhil thesis, Polytechnic of Central London, 1987.

B. Ghodbane. 'The Times' coverage of the Algerian Revolution 1954-1962', MA thesis, Keele University, England, 1985.

Mabrouk Ghodbane. 'The Algerian policy of foreign borrowing and its development strategy: a dependency theory perspective', PhD thesis, State University of New York at Albany, 1985.

Diane Gill-Duremberg. 'Algerian chronicles', MA thesis, Antioch University, 1991.

N. Guella. 'A linguistic investigation of the Arabic dialect of Nédroma (Algeria)', PhD thesis, Manchester University, England, 1983.

C. Guermat. 'Economic and time series analysis of electricity consumption in Algeria', PhD thesis, Exeter University, England, 1991.

H. Guenoune. 'Cooperative villages in Algeria: a case study in Bouira Wilaya', MPhil thesis, Nottingham University, England, 1989.

Z. Guernina. 'A study of behaviour and adjustment at home and in school in a sample of Algerian children between the ages of 11 and 16', PhD thesis, University of Wales, Cardiff, 1984.

O. Hachemi. 'The teaching of English language specialists in Algerian universities: the role of African literature', MA thesis, Warwick University, England, 1987.

Ibrahim Naji Al-Hadban. 'Aborted transition: the case of the failure of the democratization process in Algeria, 1989-1992', PhD thesis, Ohio State University, 1993.

Fatiha Haddar. 'Seismic vulnerability of urban housing in Algeria and related risk mitigation strategies', MPhil thesis, Oxford Polytechnic, England, 1991.

K. Hadjri. 'Techniques for an appropriate housing delivery system and a more responsive housing environment in Algeria', MPhil thesis, Oxford Polytechnic, England, 1989.

Abdel-Kader Haireche. 'Conflict, conflict management and cooperation in North Africa', PhD thesis, New York University, 1993.

M. Hamaizia. 'Evaluation of new towns in the context of a national human settlements strategy', MPhil thesis, South Bank Polytechnic, England, 1990.

C. Hamzaoui. 'The structure and control of public enterprises in Algeria: problems and reforms', PhD thesis, Glasgow University, Scotland, 1988.

Alexander Harrison. 'An oral history approach to the study of the counter-revolution in Algeria, 1954-1962', PhD thesis, New York University, 1980.

R. Harrouche. 'The impact of socio-economic development on worker-management relations, with particular reference to absence from work: a case study in an Algerian tractor factory', PhD thesis, Keele University, England, 1982.

Lindsay James Haslett. 'Ends and means in the moral and political thought of Albert Camus', DPhil thesis, University of Ulster, Northern Ireland, 1986.

Z. Hassane-Bensafi. 'The Spanish and French influence in western Algeria: a case of borrowing', PhD thesis, University of Bath, 1984.

Jamshid Heidarian. 'The effect of petroleum exports on the Algerian economy: a quantitative analysis', PhD thesis, Howard University, 1987.

Abd al-Majeed N. Mahmod al-Heeti. 'State capitalism and the agricultural sector: aspects of political and economic development of Algeria 1962-1982', PhD thesis, University of Durham, 1987.

A. Hemal. 'Industrialization through the import of technology and local technological development in LDC's: the case of Algeria', PhD thesis, Bath University, England, 1986.

A. Henouda. 'Agrarian policy and social transformation in Algeria since pre-colonial times', MA thesis, Keele University, England, 1988.

Donald C. Holsinger. 'Migration, commerce and community: the Mizabis in nineteeth-century Algeria', PhD thesis, Northwestern University, 1979.

Ahmed Houiti. 'Industrialization and economic development: the experience of post-independence Algeria, 1962-1984', PhD thesis, The American University, 1986.

A. Ikhef. 'Impact of technology and industrializaton on housing in Algeria', MPhil thesis, York University, England, 1985.

B. Iratni. 'Foreign policy and nation-building in Algeria 1962-1985', PhD thesis, Warwick University, England, 1986.

N. Jones. 'The fertility attitudes and behaviour of women in contemporary France: a study of French and Maghrebine women in Marseilles', PhD thesis, University of Kent, England, 1984.

R. Kabache. 'The land to those who work it: agricultural workers' management in Algeria', MSc Econ, University of Wales, Aberystwyth, 1982.

Y. Kadri. 'Educational aims and policies in three Arab countries with socialist political options: a problem solving approach', PhD thesis, Durham University, England, 1986.

Z. Kadri. 'Hospital design for Algeria in the light of developments in Great Britain', MPhil thesis, Sheffield University, England, 1987.

Mustapha Kara. 'Problems of development financing in Algeria', PhD thesis, University of Pittsburg, 1978.

S. Keddad. 'An analysis of French-Arabic code-switching in Algiers', PhD thesis, Birkbeck College, London, 1986.

N. Khababa. 'The management of the public sector in Algeria – a study of the Algerian planning experience 1960-1985, with particular reference to the education sector', PhD thesis, University of Wales, Cardiff, 1986.

Mowaffaq Ali Al-Khalil. 'Oil and economic development in OPEC countries, with case-studies about Iraq and Algeria', PhD thesis, The Florida State University, 1984.

Hamid Kherbachi. 'Structural change and employment in Algeria', PhD thesis, Rensselaer Polytechnic Institute, 1984.

A. Khettabi. 'Workplace industrial relations in Algeria – a case study of oil and chemical industries', PhD thesis, Keele University, England, 1990.

Abdou-Elkadir El-Amir Khiati. 'Investigation of the need for professional guidance and psychological counseling program in Algerian high schools', PhD thesis, Rensselaer Polytechnic Institute, 1988.

Hocine Kouache. 'Peasants, dependency and underdeveloped areas of Algeria: the case of Beni-Chebana', PhD thesis, Michigan State University, 1985.

T. Kouider. 'A study of thermal indoor environment in selected new housing in the hot, dry climatic regions of Algeria', MPhil thesis, Oxford Polytechnic, England, 1992.

L. Kouloughli. 'The Algerian fundamental polytechnic school: a "problem approach" to the Algerian trial to reconcile the social and economic demands on the educational system', PhD thesis, Institute of Education, University of London, 1985.

B. Laabas. 'A macroeconometric model for Algeria: a medium term macroeconometric model for Algeria 1963-1984, a policy simulation approach to Algerian development problems', PhD thesis, Bradford University, England, 1989.

B. Lahouel. 'The origins of nationalism in Algeria, the Gold Coast and South Africa, with special reference to the period 1919-1937', PhD thesis, Aberdeen University, Scotland, 1984.

Merouane Lakehal-Ayat. 'The leading sector approach to economic development: the case of Algeria', PhD thesis, University of Denver, 1990.

A. Lama. 'Agrarian transformation and the agricultural sector in Algeria: a long-run perspective on the process of change under the colonial and post-colonial régimes', PhD thesis, Salford University, England, 1990.

Djamel-eddine Laouisset. 'The growth of the Algerian iron and steel industry', PhD thesis, University of Miami, 1983.

A. Laraba. 'A linguistic description of the Algerian Arabic dialect of Constantine', PhD thesis, Manchester University, England, 1981.

Mounir Laraba. 'A comparative study of nationalist expressions of the Algerian community under French domination (1919-1954) and the black community in the United States of America during the 1960s (1969-1970)', PhD thesis, University of Keele, England, 1988.

Azzedine Layachi. 'Images of foreign policy: the United States and North Africa', PhD thesis, New York University, 1988.

Benaouda Lebdai. 'Rachid Boudjedra and Ngugi Wa Thiong'o: a comparative study of two post-independence African writers', PhD thesis, University of Essex, England, 1988.

T. Ledraa. 'The adjustment process of urban migrants in Constantine, Algeria', PhD thesis, Nottingham University, England, 1989.

Robert Deemer Lee. 'Regional politics in a unitary system: colonial Algeria, 1920-1954', PhD thesis, Columbia University, New York, 1972.

Larbi Lezzam. 'Balanced or unbalanced "industrializing industries" and the theory of the leading sectors: Algeria, 1967-1984', PhD thesis, The American University, 1990.

Elliott Burton Litsky. 'The Murphy-Weygand Agreement: the United States and French North Africa (1940-1942)', PhD thesis, Fordham University, 1986.

Paricia M. E. Lorcin. 'France and the Kabyles: stereotyping, prejudice and race in nineteenth-century Algeria', PhD thesis, Columbia University, 1992.

Lisa M. Lowe. 'French literary Orientalism: representations of 'others' in the texts of Montesquieu, Flaubert and Kristeva', PhD thesis, University of California, Santa Cruz, 1986.

A. Maghni. 'Teaching English to social science students in Oran University, Algeria – implications for E. S. P. syllabus design', PhD thesis, University of Wales, Cardiff, 1986.

A. Mahdi. 'The impact of colonial and post-colonial change on marriage, kinship and the family in Algeria', MA thesis, Keele University, England, 1990.

Abassi Madani. 'Wastage in the Algerian system of education: a comparative study of policy solutions in France and in the UK', PhD thesis, Institute of Education, University of London, 1974. *(Noteworthy only because Abassi Madani, an FLN veteran and professor at the University of Algiers, became one of the main leaders of the Front Islamique du Salut. He was arrested in June 1991 accused of having 'formented, organized, unleashed and led an armed conspiracy against the security of the state in an attempt to take power'. He was released from prison in September 1994 to be held under house arrest.)

D. Madani. 'Some aspects of the provision and operation of bus services in Algiers', MSc thesis, Salford University, England, 1984.

James Michael Malarkey. 'The colonial encounter in French Algeria: a study of the development of power asymmetry and symbolic violence in the city of Constantine', PhD thesis, University of Texas at Austin, 1980.

A. Mana. 'Juvenile delinquency and social change in modern Algeria: a study in comparative criminology', PhD thesis, Hull University, England, 1983.

Rosemary Averell Manes. 'The "pieds-noirs": a case study in the persistence of subcultural distinctiveness', PhD thesis, Syracuse University, 1991.

A. Mansouri. 'Rural housing in Algeria with reference to Zeribet El-Oued', MPhil thesis, York University, England, 1988.

Abdelhamid Mansouri. 'Algeria between tradition and modernity: the question of language', PhD thesis, State University of New York at Albany, 1991.

Rita Rudges Maran. 'Torture during the French-Algerian war: the role of the "mission civilisatrice"', PhD thesis, University of California, Santa Cruz, 1987.

K. Matallah. 'The development of the Algerian oil and gas industry, 1962-1982', MA thesis, Keele University, England, 1985.

K. Matallah. 'An input-output study of the integration of the hydrocarbon sector in the Algerian economy', PhD thesis, Keele University, England, 1988.

John Joseph McGrath. 'Comparative analysis of the national liberation movements in Northern Ireland, South Africa and Algeria with specific reference to the development and interrelationship of political ideology and military strategy', PhD thesis, Fordham University, 1990.

A. Meddour. 'Parasites of freshwater fishes from Lake Oubeira, Algeria', MSc thesis, Liverpool University, England, 1988.

M. Medjbeur. 'An approach to urban area conservation: the case of Tlemcen in Algeria', MPhil thesis, York University, England, 1989.

A. Medjedel. 'Science, technology and development in less-developed countries: the Algerian case, 1962-1986', MPhil thesis, Leeds University, England, 1987.

Abderrahmane Megateli. 'Petroleum policies and national oil companies: a comparative study of investment policies with emphasis on exploration of SONATRACH (Algeria), NIOC (Iran) and PEMEX (Mexico), 1970-1975', PhD thesis, The University of Texas at Austin, 1978.

N. E. Megharbi. 'The question of Algerian-American attitudes and policies, 1954-1962', MPhil thesis, Manchester University, England, 1985.

F. B. Meghezzi. 'The architecture and thermal performance of modern and traditional housing in the desert town of El Oued, Algeria', MPhil thesis, Sheffield University, England, 1987.

N. Mellouk. 'Productivity and workers participation: the example of Algeria', MLitt thesis, Aberdeen University, Scotland, 1982.

Rafika Merini. 'The subversion of the culture of voyeurism in the works of Leila Sebbar and Assia Djebar: a socio-literary study', PhD thesis, State University of New York at Binghamton, 1992.

Gil Merom. 'Blood and conscience: recasting the boundaries of national identity (France, Algeria, Israel, Lebanon)', PhD thesis, Cornell University, 1994.

T. Messaoud-Nacer. 'The colonial heritage of Algiers, past and future', MPhil thesis, York University, England, 1988.

Mohammed Meziane. 'Toward computing in Algerian higher education: assessment, perceptions and alternatives', EdD thesis, United States International University, 1987.

F. Midane. 'Factory and society in contemporary Algeria: an enquiry into industrial accidents at the Sonacome State Enterprise at Rouiba', MSc thesis, Bristol University, England, 1983.

M. B. Miliani. 'Objectives, curriculum design and methods for the teaching of ESP in Algeria, with special reference to the teaching of English in the Institute of Economic Sciences in Oran', PhD thesis, UWIST, Wales, 1985.

Nora Fatima Mitiche. 'An investigation of selected lexical items in Kabyl Berber', PhD thesis, The University of Texas at Austin, 1985.

L. Mokhtari. 'The agrarian revolution in Algeria: a sociological study', PhD thesis, Brunel University, England, 1983.

Joan Phyllis Monego. 'Algerian man in search of himself: a study of the recent novels of Mohamed Dib', PhD thesis, Case Western Reserve University, Cleveland, Ohio, 1975.

Mildred Palmer Mortimer. 'The Algerian novel in French: 1945-1965', PhD thesis, Columbia University, New York, 1969.

Robert Amsden Mortimer. 'Foreign policy and its role in nation-building in Algeria', PhD thesis, Columbia University, New York, 1968.

M. Moulai-Hadj. 'Living in two cultures: the Algerian factory worker between traditionalism and modernity', MPhil thesis, Leicester University, England, 1987.

M. T. Naimi. 'Toward a theory of postrevolutionary social change: a six nation comparative study (Algeria, Bolivia, Cuba, Ecuador, Haiti, Sudan)', PhD thesis, Washington State University, 1985.

A. Nait-Ladjemil. 'The responses of private peasants to changes in state policy in Algerian agriculture', PhD thesis, Reading University, England, 1991.

Phillip Chiviges Naylor. 'Conflict and cooperation: French-Algerian relations, 1962-78', PhD thesis, Marquette University, 1980.

M. S. Nedjai. 'The socio-educational experience of Algerian immigrants' children in France and Algeria', PhD thesis, Bath University, England, 1989.

I. Nezha. 'Comparative study between local authority and private small and medium scale industries in Algeria: case study of Setif wilaya', MPhil thesis, Nottingham University, England, 1987.

Rahima Kenza Osmane. 'Land expropriation and assimilation: a comparative study of French policy in Algeria and Federal Indian policy in the United States during the nineteenth century', PhD thesis, University of Keele, England, 1988.

David Blackburne Ottaway. 'The socialist revolution in Africa: party (Guinea) and state (Algeria) revolutionary systems', PhD thesis, Columbia University, New York, 1972.

A. Oucief. 'The Algerian model of development (1965-1980): a critical assessment', MPhil thesis, Sheffield University, England, 1988.

Mostafa Abdelhamid Ouki. 'Adjustments to a boom in hydrocarbon export revenue: a CGE analysis of the Algerian economy', PhD thesis, University of Pittsburgh, 1990.

M. Ould Hamou. 'Beneficiation of Algerian phosphate tailings by electrostatic methods', PhD thesis, Leeds University, England, 1990.

A. Oussadou. 'Residential satisfaction in the new urban housing projects in Algeria: a case study of Ain-Allah, Algiers', PhD thesis, Nottingham University, England, 1988.

Karen Pfeifer. 'Agrarian reform and the development of capitalist agriculture in Algeria', PhD thesis, The American University, Washington, DC, 1981.

David Lewis Porter. 'The role of workers' self-management in Algerian political development', PhD thesis, Columbia University, New York, 1968.

Nourredine Rabah. 'Colonial domination and the origins of state capitalism: the case of Algeria. An economic and socio-political analysis of colonialism and its impact on the emergence of a bureaucratic-military oligarchy in independent Algeria, 1962-1965', PhD thesis, The American University, 1991.

Mohammed Rabhi. 'External debt: a comparative analysis for Algeria and Venezuela – a linear quadratic control theory illustration', PhD thesis, The University of Texas at Austin, 1979.

Robert Bernard Revere. 'Consensus in independent Algeria, 1962-1965', PhD thesis, New York University, 1970.

Aicha Rezig. 'Gender, resources and attitudes toward marital role equality: a comparison of Algerian and American students', PhD thesis, University of Massachusetts, 1985.

Malcolm Lynn Richardson. 'French Algeria between the wars: nationalism and colonial reform, 1919-1939', PhD thesis, Duke University, Durham, North Carolina, 1975.

Jack Blaine Ridley. 'Marshal Bugeaud, the July Monarchy and the question of Algeria, 1841-1847: a study in civil-military relations', PhD thesis, University of Oklahoma, Norman, Oklahoma, 1970.

Richard A. Roughton. 'French colonialism and the resistance in central and western Algeria 1830-1839', PhD thesis, University of Maryland, College Park, Maryland, 1973.

Lynette Rummel. 'Privatization in Algeria: implications for development theory', PhD thesis, University of California, Los Angeles, 1989.

Zohra Saad. 'Language planning and policy attitudes: a case study of Arabization in Algeria', EdD thesis, Columbia University Teachers College, 1992.

Belkacem Saadallah. 'The rise of Algerian nationalism: 1900-1930', PhD thesis, University of Minnesota, Minneapolis, Minnesota, 1965.

M. Sadeg. 'A study of the relationships between organizations and environments and their implications for organizational performance in Algerian state-owned enterprises', PhD thesis, Leeds University, England, 1990.

M. Saidi. 'The planning of new towns: a study of some European examples and their relationship to the growth of Algiers', MSc thesis, Bath University, England, 1984.

Carol Richman Saivetz. 'Socialism and Egypt and Algeria, 1960-1973: the Soviet assessment', PhD thesis, Columbia University, 1979.

A. Salem. 'The economic relations between the Maghreb states and the European Economic Community', MA thesis, Keele University, England, 1984.

Mohamed Salem. 'Training in maintenance of industrial equipment: its contribution to technology transfer to industrializing countries (Algeria)', EdD thesis, Harvard University, 1989.

K. Salhi. 'Nedjma and Algeria in the works of Kateb Yacine: towards a national identity', PhD thesis, Exeter Univesity, England, 1991.

Egya N. Sangmuah. 'The United States and the French Empire in North Africa, 1946-56: Decolonization in the age of containment', PhD thesis, University of Toronto, 1989.

A. Z. Saouli. 'The revival of traditional housing: the case of Biskra', MPhil thesis, York University, England, 1989.

Adam Schesch. 'Popular mobilization during revolutionary and resistance wars: Vietnam, China, Yugoslavia, Ireland, and Algeria', PhD thesis, University of Wisconsin, Madison, 1994.

A. Sedoud. 'A comparison of urban fabric as found in Algiers and Edinburgh', MSc thesis, Bath University, England, 1985.

M. Seffari. 'Workers' participation in management: the case of Algeria's industry', PhD thesis, Keele University, England, 1984.

N. E. Sellamma. 'Social organization and attitudes to work in Algerian collective farming', PhD thesis, Reading University, England, 1988.

M. Y. Selmane. 'Modern Algerian theatre: translations and critical analysis of three plays by Kateb Yacine, Abdelkader Alloula and Slimane Benaissa', PhD thesis, Leeds University, England, 1989.

A. Seray. 'The Casbah of Algiers: a study in conservation', MPhil thesis, York University, England, 1987.

F. Serour. 'A comparison of the land problem in Algeria and Kenya in its historical, social, political and economic contexts to the mid-1970s, with special reference to the effects of settler dominance', PhD thesis, Aberdeen University, Scotland, 1984.

A. Slimani. 'The teaching/learning relationship: learning opportunities and learning outcomes, an Algerian case study', PhD thesis, Lancaster University, England, 1988.

Z. Smail. 'Themes in the Francophone Algerian novel', PhD thesis, Exeter University, England, 1991.

William Henry Smith. 'International exploration decision-making for independent oil companies: case-studies in areas of Pakistan, China, and Algeria', PhD thesis, Colorado School of Mines, 1989.

Khalifa Ali Solieman. 'M'zab community, Algeria, North Africa: its planning and architectural aspects – past, present and future', MA thesis, The University of Arizona, 1988.

Brigid Ann Starkey. 'State, culture and foreign policy: exploring linkages in the Muslim world (Egypt, Iran, Algeria, Indonesia)', PhD thesis, University of Maryland College Park, 1991.

Hollins McKim Steele, Jr. 'European settlements versus Muslim property: the foundation of colonial Algeria, 1830-1880', PhD thesis, Columbia University, New York, 1965.

A. M. Tacherifte. 'The effectiveness of rural development planning in Algeria: a case study of administrative factors', PhD thesis, Sheffield Univrsity, England, 1984.

A. Taleb. 'The Algeran emigration to France: a sociological study of the background, origin and present difficulties', PhD thesis, Essex University, England, 1987.

Susan Rosemary Tarrow. 'Re-reading Albert Camus: politics and fiction', PhD thesis, Cornell University, 1980.

B. Tayebi. 'Responsibility for economic injuries to aliens, with special reference to Algerian practice', LL M thesis, Queen's University, Belfast, Northern Ireland, 1982.

C. Tekfi. 'Design of a computer information system for the Algerian national archives', PhD thesis, City University, England, 1990.

B. Temagoult. 'An examination of espiest courses in Algerian universities and the design of an EST (English for science and technology) course for science technology students', PhD thesis, University of Wales, Cardiff, 1986.

M. Tighezza. 'Work stress and coping strategies: a study of perceived stress among production workers in an Algerian glass works', PhD thesis, University of Surrey, England, 1987.

Rachid Tlemcani. 'State and revolution in Algeria: an approach to the study of state-formation in post-colonial society', PhD thesis, Boston University, 1984.

Spencer Coakley Tucker. 'The Fourth Republic and Algeria', PhD thesis, University of North Carolina, Chapel Hill, North Carolina, 1966.

Ahmad S. Turkistani. 'News exchange via Arabsat and news values of Arab television news people (Algeria, Kuwait, Saudi Arabia, Tunisia)', PhD thesis, Indiana University, 1988.

Stuart Hope Van Dyke, Jr. 'French settler politics during the Algerian war, 1954-1958', PhD thesis, University of Chicago, 1980.

Ena Cecilia Vulor. 'The North African reality in the work of Albert Camus: rereading "L'Etranger", "La Peste", "L'Exile et le Royaume" from a colonial perspective', PhD thesis, Cornell University, 1994.

Paul Ernest Wehr. 'Local leadership and problems of rural development in Algeria', PhD thesis, University of Pennsylvania, 1968.

S. Yassia. 'Development planning and project generation and selection processes in the Algerian public sector', MPhil thesis, Lancaster University, England, 1988.

Ahmad Yazdanpanah. 'The impact of oil price on food security in Algeria, Iran and Saudi Arabia: cointegration, vector-error correction model, dynamics and causality analysis', PhD thesis, Iowa State University, 1994.

L. Ydroudj. 'Modernization in Algeria and the quest of technology: a sociopolitical analysis of secondary education', MPhil thesis, University of Surrey, England, 1988.

G. Yielding. 'Active tectonics of the El-Asnam region (Algeria)', PhD thesis, Cambridge University, England, 1984.

H. Zaidi. 'Educational development in Algeria: the planning and implementation of a technological university in Algiers', PhD thesis, Sheffield University, England, 1984.

S. E. Zaimeche. 'Economic growth and consumer demand in Algeria 1962-1980', PhD thesis, Manchester University, England, 1989.

R. M. Zeffane. 'Organizational patterns in different societies: a comparative study of Algerian state-owned companies in a mono- and cross-national perspective', PhD thesis, UWIST, Wales, 1981.

L. Zerdani. 'Urban neighbourhoods in Algiers', MPhil thesis, Nottingham University, England, 1989.

Amine Zerhouni. 'The parallel market in Algeria: nature, causes and impacts', MA thesis, The American University, 1992.

Habiba Mounira Zerkine. 'The Federation of Elected Muslims of the Department of Constantine', PhD thesis, Georgetown University, 1984.

M. S. Zerouala. 'Architectural education in Algeria', PhD thesis, Newcastle University, England, 1986.

Abdelhamid Zoubir. 'American and Algerian writers: a comparative study examining the relation between literary language and national culture', PhD thesis, University of Essex, England, 1987.

The Country and Its People

1 **Algeria-Britain Academic Network Newsletter.**
  1992- . quarterly.
The newsletter of the Algeria-Britain Academic Network is co-ordinated by Keith Šutton (Department of Geography, University of Manchester, England) and Ahmed Aghrout (Department of Economics, University of Sétif, Algeria). It aims to keep members in touch with each other's research and publishing activities, gives notices and reports of relevant conferences and seminars, provides short reviews of books on Algeria, and lists the contents of relevant journals and edited books and essays.

2 **Algérie incertaine.** (Uncertain Algeria).
  Revue du Monde Musulman et de la Méditerranée, no. 65 (1993), 203p.
This special issue of the journal, prepared under the direction of Pierre Robert Baduel, offers an historical perspective on the place of Islam in Algerian society and discusses the role of the army and the Berber question. It also analyses the current political crisis and the obstacles to democratization and examines the policy of economic liberalization, and current demographic and cultural changes.

3 **Algérie: vers l'état islamique?** (Algeria: towards the Islamic state?).
  Peuples Méditerranéens, no. 52-53 (1990), 299p.
The entire issue, which appeared just after the sweeping success of the Front Islamique du Salut (FIS) in the June 1990 local elections, is devoted to articles on Algeria which together present a provocative and stimulating approach to understanding Algerian society and one which challenges existing concepts. It argues for the importance of an anthropological approach to the study of Algerian society and criticizes the past dominance of 'un économisme naïf'. The emphasis is on the previously ignored religious dimension. The twenty-one articles cover a range of political, social, cultural, linguistic and economic issues. English summaries of the articles are provided on p. 293-99.

4 **The Maghreb in the modern world: Algeria, Tunisia, Morocco.**
Samir Amin, translated by Michael Perl. Harmondsworth, England:
Penguin Books, 1970. 256p. 2 maps. bibliog.

Examines the impact of French colonization as it affected Algeria, Tunisia and
Morocco, and the principal changes which accompanied the establishment of the three
independent states. The description and analysis cover three different facets of
Maghreb society: the economic, the social and the political. It remains a valuable
reference work for the impact of French colonialism on Algeria and the difficulties
experienced by the newly independent state.

5 **Annuaire de l'Afrique du Nord.** (North African Yearbook).
Paris: Editions du Centre National de la Recherche Scientifique, 1962- .
annual.

An essential work of reference for all students of Algeria. In addition to detailed
articles on a variety of economic, political, social and cultural themes, each issue
contains a review of political, economic, social and cultural developments in Algeria
during the year, together with a chronology of political events, a list of legislation,
treaties, agreements and conventions, and the full text of major government
pronouncements. This publication also represents the most important single
bibliographical source on Algeria. Each issue contains extensive review articles
together with a comprehensive systematic bibliography of books and articles in
European languages and Arabic. References are listed not by country but by major
subject headings, which are further sub-divided – general references, politics, foreign
relations, economic questions, education and cultural life, social problems, and
emigration. Each issue contains over 1,000 references.

6 **Enjeux sahariens.** (Saharan issues).
Edited by Pierre Robert Baduel. Paris: Editions du CNRS, 1984. 442p.

A collection of articles encompassing the Saharan region as a whole but relevant to
Algeria, with the focus on modern times. Thematically the book is divided into
sections on political, economic and cultural perspectives, though the emphasis is on
political issues, especially the Western Saharan conflict. The substantial section on
Saharan socio-economic issues deals with both oasis agriculture and pastoral
nomadism in selected regions, examining whether nomadic pastoralists are doomed by
history to extinction. An important essay traces the evolution of Saharan images in
French popular novels.

7 **Contemporary North Africa: issues of development and integration.**
Edited by Halim Barakat. London: Croom Helm, 1985. 271p.

A thought-provoking overview of politics and society in North Africa arranged around
four broad themes – the Maghreb between East and West, including a review of the
cultural and intellectual circumstances of North African political élites pressured by
foreign and indigenous normative currents, and a discussion of US policy towards the
region; intraregional conflicts, including the impact of the Western Sahara conflict and
regional relationships; structural changes, including a case-study of Algeria to argue
that industrialization is indispensible to Third World development (the only
contribution devoted specifically to Algeria); and cultural dynamics.

8 **The making of contemporary Algeria, 1830-1987: colonial upheavals and post-independence development.**
Mahfoud Bennoune. Cambridge, England: Cambridge University Press, 1988. 323p. bibliog.

After a brief discussion of Algerian society and its economy before 1830, and of the socio-economic consequences of colonial development, the bulk of this work is devoted to a study of the political economy of post-independence development supported by a wealth of statistical data. It is argued that the rapid development of basic industries provides the only path by which Algeria and other countries in the Third World can hope to attain real independence and that this policy demands a degree of public participation that only a democratic government can generate. It includes discussions on the stagnation of agricultural production, urbanization and the housing crisis, public health, employment, and education and development. Bennoune ends by criticizing the economic policy adopted after the death of President Boumediène in this basic reference on post-independence Algeria.

9 **Between two fires.**
Index on Censorship, no. 4-5 (1994), p. 135-70.

A useful file on the crisis in Algeria following the military intervention in January 1992. The contributions include: Lyes Si Zoubir's account of the dangers encountered during a train journey from Algiers to Oran after Islamist militants had forbidden travel by train because there are no separate sections for men and women; Said Essoulami and Abdelkrim Zerouali on press censorship since the coup; Mohammed Harbi on the factions that divide Algeria's ruling establishment; an excerpt from an open letter to the Head of State from a schoolgirl encapsulating the agony and uncertainty in Algeria; and the last piece written by journalist, poet and novelist, Tahar Djaout, murdered in May 1993 in which he asks, 'What can be expected from a dialogue between parties whose social programmes are light years apart?' and attacks the High State Committee for its failure to determine a direction for Algeria.

10 **Algeria.**
Marlene Targ Brill. Chicago: Children's Press, 1993. 127p. maps.

Discusses the geography, history, people and culture of Algeria, and is aimed mainly at school children.

11 **State and society in independent North Africa.**
Edited by Leon Carl Brown. Washington, DC: The Middle East Institute, 1966. 332p. map. bibliog. (The James Terry Duce Memorial Series, vol. 1).

A collection of fifteen essays describing the political, social and economic setting of North Africa during the first decade of independence. This pioneering work remains a useful reference on the newly independent state of Algeria and its Maghreb neighbours.

12 **Bulletin of Francophone Africa.**
London: Maghreb Research Group, School of Languages, University of
Westminster, Spring 1992- . biannual.
Contains articles on Algeria on a wide range of subjects, including literature, culture,
history and social conditions.

13 **L'Algérie indépendante: bilan d'une révolution nationale.**
(Independent Algeria: evaluation of a national revolution).
Gérard Chaliand, Juliette Minces. Paris: François Maspero, 1972.
175p. bibliog. (Petite Collection Maspero).
One of the most perceptive studies of Algeria during the first decade of the country's
independence. It examines the political and economic problems which faced the new
state, the policies adopted by the new leadership to restructure the state and the
economy, and their impact of Algerian society and social classes.

14 **The Annual Register: a Record of World Events.**
Edited by Alan Day. London: Longman Cartermill, 1758- . annual.
Includes a short but authoritative analysis of political and economic developments in
Algeria and key events in international relations during the current year.

15 **Algeria: the revolution institutionalized.**
John P. Entelis. Boulder, Colorado: Westview Press; London: Croom
Helm, 1986. 239p. bibliog. (Profiles/Nations of the Contemporary
Middle East).
A useful reference work, which provides an assessment of political processes and the
political economy since the mid-1970s to the mid-1980s. 'Institutionalization' evokes
a sense of the stabilization achieved in the later Boumediène and early Chadli years, in
contrast to the turbulent political scene which prevailed in the 1960s, and also points
to a fading of the revolutionary *élan* which was sustained until the mid-1970s. After a
brief history of Algeria to independence, chapters cover: Islam, state secularization
and social problems; the political economy of development, including hydrocarbon
policy, development planning and the problems of the agricultural sector; the
dynamics of political life, political culture, structures, processes and power; and
foreign relations.

16 **State and society in Algeria.**
Edited by John P. Entelis, Philip C. Naylor. Boulder, Colorado:
Westview Press, 1992. 307p. bibliog.
Covers an important transitional period in Algeria's history, the end of the socialist
one-party system and the emergence of an altogether different, but as yet insubstantial,
political and economic system. The various authors critically assess the
democratization process in Algeria in the context of political, economic, social and
foreign policy changes in this basic reference work.

17 **Algérie, cultures et révolution.** (Algeria: cultures and revolution).
Bruno Etienne. Paris: Editions du Seuil, 1977. 333p. bibliog.

A penetrating analysis of the Algerian state, political system and society during the first fifteen years of independence. Etienne analyses the social composition of the Algerian ruling élite, the contradictions inherent in an approach to modernization which seeks to adopt Western technology without renouncing the Arab-Islamic cultural heritage, and the conflicts between technocrats and traditionalists.

18 **North Africa: nation, state and region.**
Edited by George Joffé. London: Routledge, 1993. 311p. bibliog.

Contains seventeen wide-ranging essays, the product of a university-sponsored conference on North Africa held in Britain in 1989. The historical period covered stretches from the 17th-century 'Barbary pirates' to the formation of the Maghreb Arab Union. However, the bulk of the contributions focus on the 20th century and directly or indirectly on the concept of the nation-state. The final section on the region today deals with the state, relations with the EU and the Maghreb Arab Union. Four contributions deal specifically with Algeria.

19 **Algeria: the challenge of modernity.**
Edited by Ali El-Kenz. Dakar, Senegal; London: Codesria Book Series, 1991. 310p.

A translation of *Algérie et la modernité*, published in 1989, and bringing together a valuable collection of essays on Algeria by Algerians. Contributions include: 'Towards and new approach to development' and 'Algerian society today: a phenomenological essay on the national consciousness' by Ali El-Kenz; 'Social-historical foundations of the contemporary Algerian state' by Mahfoud Bennoune; 'The Algerian population: between archaic values and modernity' by Abderrahmane Iles; 'Town and country planning: the challenge of modernity' by Mohamed Dahmani; 'Imbalances in the Algerian economy' by Rabah Abdoun; 'Algerian agriculture: balance sheet and prospects' by Slimane Bedrani; 'The worker, the prince and the facts of life' by Said Chikhi; 'Algerian companies at the intersection of the economy, the polity and the society' by Djillali Liabes; 'The right to information in Algeria: principles and realities' by Brahim Brahimi; and 'Algerian intellectuals: between identity and modernity' by Amin Khan.

20 **Algerian reflections on Arab crises.**
Ali El-Kenz, translated by Robert W. Stookey. Austin, Texas: Centre for Middle Eastern Studies, University of Texas, 1991. 133p.

This book is made up of five short chapters, originally given at conferences, in which the author, an astute observer, draws on the experience of his own country, Algeria, to try and explain the malaise which has befallen the Arab world as a whole. He investigates the role and shortcomings of the intelligentsia, the different crises to which his native Algeria is now subjected, the failure of nationalism, the nature of social scientific inquiry in the Arab world, and finally, Islam.

21 **North-west Africa: a political and economic survey.**
Wilfred Knapp. Oxford: Oxford University Press, 1977. 3rd ed.
453p. 5 maps. bibliog.

Chapter 2 (p. 51-173) of this useful reference work is devoted to Algeria and includes a survey of the country's geography and population, history and politics, the economy, armed forces and security, foreign relations, society and education. The section on history and politics provides a thorough chronological survey of events. The concluding chapter traces the development of North African literature, including the contribution of Algerian writers, from the pre-colonial period to modern times. The bibliography is surprisingly short and incomplete for a reference work of this type.

22 **Maghreb: les années de transition.** (Maghreb: the years of transition).
Edited by Bassma Kodmani-Darwish. Paris: Masson, 1990. 395p.
bibliog.

The product of a research programme initiated by the French Institute of International Relations following the signature of the treaty instituting the Arab Maghreb Union (UMA) in February 1989. Part 1 contains an analytic chapter on each of the five member states of the UMA and on three region-wide 'challenges': the rise of Islamist movements; the plight of the younger generation; and the likelihood of cooperation replacing the heretofore 'egocentric' national development strategies. Part 2 is organized around the theme of regional and international environments, and contains chapters on the Western Sahara dispute, the policies of major powers, France, the United States and the Soviet Union, towards the Maghreb, and Maghrebian relations with the larger Arab world, sub-Saharan Africa and Europe.

23 **L'état du Maghreb.** (The state of the Maghreb).
Edited by Camille Lacoste, Yves Lacoste. Paris: La Découverte, 1991.
572p. 17 maps. bibliog.

Contains short but authoritative articles on or relevant to Algeria. These cover a wide range of topics: geography, history, population and emigration, civilization, daily life, art and culture, politics and society, economy and employment and international relations. Many of the sections compare and contrast the five Maghreb countries (Algeria, Morocco, Tunisia, Libya and Mauritania) but there are also sections devoted to individual countries. Each section contains a short bibliography of key works and there is a selected bibliography at the end of the volume. This major reference work was prepared with the collaboration of 115 specialists on the Maghreb.

24 **North Africa: contemporary politics and economic development.**
Edited by Richard Lawless, Allan Findlay. London, Canberra: Croom
Helm; New York: St Martin's Press, 1984. 283p. 5 maps.

Includes two substantive chapters on Algeria. The first analyses political developments from independence to the death of Boumediène and the election of Chadli as president of the republic; the second focusses on economic development since independence and the contradictions arising from the emphasis on developing the heavy industrial sector. Detailed notes and references are found at the end of each chapter.

25 **Africa Contemporary Record. Annual Survey and Documents.**
Edited by Colin Legum.   London: Rex Collings, 1968/69- . annual.
A chapter in the country-by-country section reviews the political and economic developments in Algeria during the years concerned.

26 **The government and politics of the Middle East and North Africa.**
Edited by David E. Long, Bernard Reich.   Boulder, Colorado:
Westview Press, 1980. 472p. maps.
This edited volume aims to present a survey of the political situation in the Middle East and North Africa in the 1970s. Chapters are devoted to individual countries or groups of countries and follow a common approach – historical background, political environment, political structure, political dynamics and foreign policy, all considered from the perspective of mid-1979. The work includes a contribution on the Maghreb in general, Algeria, Morocco and Tunisia by John P. Entelis.

27 **Maghreb-Machrek.**
Paris: La Documentation Française, 1974- . quarterly.
Probably the most valuable journal for students of Algeria, containing regular and authoritative articles on a wide range of subjects but particularly on political and economic issues and foreign relations. It includes a useful chronology of key events and a review of new French-language publications on Algeria.

28 **Maghreb Review.**
London, 1976- . quarterly.
Contains regular articles on Algeria covering a wide range of subjects – history, politics, economy, society and culture – and also includes reviews of books on Algeria and lists of theses.

29 **The Middle East and North Africa.**
London: Europa Publications, 1948-1976- . annual.
A section on Algeria has been included since the eleventh edition (1964-65). It briefly describes the country's physical and social geography, traces its history and recent political developments, and presents a survey of the main sectors of the economy. The sections on recent political developments and on the economy are revised and updated every year. It also includes a statistical summary, and basic information on the government, diplomatic representation, judicial system, press, radio and television, banking, trade and industry, transport, tourism and education. The 1995 edition of this valuable work of reference contains a feature article on the current Algerian crisis by George Joffé, entitled 'Algeria: the failure of dialogue' (p. 3-13).

30 **Middle East Economic Digest.**
London, 8 March 1957- . weekly.
Commonly cited as MEED, this journal contains a regular section of short news items on the Algerian economy and in recent years has also included items on political developments and foreign relations. There are sometimes feature articles dealing with important economic or political events. An annual index is also published. It constitutes a basic reference in English on all sectors of the Algerian economy.

31 **Middle East International.**
London: 21 Collingham Road, 1971- . twice monthly.
Includes short articles on Algeria, mainly dealing with political issues but also foreign relations.

32 **Algeria: a country study.**
Edited by Harold D. Nelson. Washington, DC: United States Government Printing Office, 1985. 4th ed. 414p. maps. bibliog. (Foreign Area Studies of The American University).
The fourth edition of this periodically updated handbook is divided into five sections: historical setting; society and its environment; the economy; government and politics; and national security. In addition there is a country profile providing basic information and statistics.

33 **Quarterly Economic Review Annual Supplement – Algeria.**
London: Economist Intelligence Unit, 1970- . annual.
The annual supplement to the *Quarterly Economic Review* contains analyses of the Algerian economy and political developments, and is continued from *Quarterly Economic Review Algeria, Morocco* (1970). The *Quarterly Economic Review* provides up-to-date news items on the economy, including oil and gas, politics and foreign relations, and is particlarly useful.

34 **Islamism and secularism in North Africa.**
Edited by John Ruedy. Basingstoke, England: Macmillan Press, 1994. 298p.
This collection of essays deals with the interaction of the secular and the religious in the Maghreb states of Algeria, Morocco, Tunisia and Libya. It explores this interaction from the perspectives of anthropology, sociology, economics and political science, while at the same time placing the phenomena within an historical perspective. The book is divided into three parts. Part 1 deals with secular-Islamic encounters in an historical perspective; part 2 with the Islamist challenge *per se*; and part 3 with state responses to the Islamic revival. Five contributions deal specifically with Algeria, and the collection as a whole provides useful comparative data on the Islamist challenge and state responses in other Maghreb countries.

35 **The Maghreb in the 1990's: political and economic developments in Algeria, Morocco and Tunisia.**
C. Spencer. London: Brassey's, 1993. 64p. (Adelphi Papers, no. 274).
Includes a discussion of political and economic developments in Algeria during the 1990s.

36 **State and revolution in Algeria.**
Rachid Tlemcani. Boulder, Colorado: Westview Press; London: Zed Books, 1986. 220p. bibliog.
A broad survey and critique of Algeria's political and economic development from the eve of the French conquest to the mid-1980s by a Marxist scholar. The central theme is that Algeria today has not simply been shaped by the domination of external forces

in the colonial period and since. In addition, internal class relations have fundamentally influenced the modern Algerian state and those who wield power within it. It is argued that a bureaucratic petty bourgeoisie, whose origins go back to Ottoman times, came to control the Front de Libération Nationale. Its interests can be seen today in every sector of policy from agrarian reform to its clientalist alliance with the private sector, or from its takeover of the workers' self-management movement to its cultural and religious policies towards the Kabyles and Islamic fundamentalists.

37 Man, state and society in the contemporary Maghrib.
Edited by I. William Zartman.   London: Pall Mall Press, 1973. 531p. 2 maps. bibliog.

A collection of forty studies on the Maghreb arranged by subject matter rather than by country. The introductory section presents the general characteristics of the region, whereas part II ranges over the spectrum of values and attitudes, from traditional to modern. Part III reviews the same spectrum through the personalities of leading politicians and part IV presents the aggregate personalities of important élite groups. Part V deals with the political mechanisms through which leaders, groups and peoples interact, and the final part with the problems which the people of the Maghreb must solve if they are to control their environment. Twelve contributions are devoted specifically to Algeria, and the book remains a useful reference work for Algeria during the first decade of independence.

38 Polity and society in contemporary North Africa.
Edited by I. William Zartman, William Mark Habeeb.   Boulder, Colorado: Westview Press, 1993. 249p. bibliog.

The twelve contributions that make up this volume are organized into three sections: history and politics; society and economics; and foreign relations. Together they provide a comparative analysis and evaluate the complex social, economic and political changes that continue to challenge the governments and people of Algeria and its Maghreb neighbours. Topics covered include: the historical context; the second stage of state building; political parties; the alienation of urban youth; Islam and the state; demographic pressures and agrarian dynamics; economic crises and policy reform in the 1980s; local societies; the Arab Maghreb Union and prospects for North African unity; the Maghrebi states and the European Community; and the US and North Africa.

Tourism and Travel

39 **Maghreb: Tunisie, Algérie, Maroc.** (Maghreb: Tunisia, Algeria, Morocco).
   Henri de la Bastide.   Paris: Horisons de France, 1973. 264p. 5 maps. bibliog.

Includes a useful introductory guide to Algeria's history, society and culture. It identifies common features between Algeria, Tunisia and Morocco and highlights those distinctive aspects that set Algeria apart from its neighbours. It is lavishly illustrated with colour and black-and-white photographs.

40 **Algeria's tourist industry.**
   Gerald H. Blake, Richard I. Lawless.   *Geography*, vol. 57, no. 255, pt. 2 (1972), p. 148-52.

The authors examine the resource base for Algerian tourism and the development of the tourist industry since 1966.

41 **The Sahara.**
   René Gardi, translated from German by Ewald Osers, Henry Fox.
   London: Harrap, 1970. 149p. 3 maps.

René Gardi made six expeditions to the Sahara and presents a valuable study of the Sahara and its people. He writes about the discovery of the Sahara, its varied landscapes, vegetation and the wildlife of the desert, its people, the Tuareg, and their society. In addition, there are specialized essays by Karl Suter on the geography of the Sahara, by Alexander Wandeler on the animals of the region, and by Hans Rhotert on rock pictures. The book contains over 100 excellent colour photographs, each with an informative caption.

42 **Les guides bleus: Algérie.** (The Blue Guides: Algeria).
   Paris: Hachette, 1977. 614p. 30 maps.

Provides brief geographical and historical introductions, detailed itineraries, and descriptions of places of interest.

43   **L'Algérie aujourd'hui.** (Algeria today).
Jean Hureau.   Paris: Editions Jeune Afrique, 1974. 264p. 16 maps.
The first part of this guide presents a 'panorama' of Algeria, including short sections on the landscapes of its different regions, its mineral wealth and industries, society and history. The second part describes the most notable features of the country's major towns and cities. In the third part Hureau suggests a number of tourist itineraries and excursions and gives basic information for tourists. The work is well illustrated with over 100 good colour photographs.

44   **Maroc, Algérie, Tunisie.** (Morocco, Algeria, Tunisia).
Bernard Joliat.   Geneva: Nathan/Panoramic, 1977. 199p. 2 maps.
(Merveilles des Cinq Continents, no. 4).
An illustrated tourist guide to the Maghreb. The section on Algeria (p. 7-72) explores the country's varied landscapes and people, notably the Saharan territories, and is lavishly illustrated with colour photographs.

45   **Maiden voyages: writings of women travellers.**
Edited and with an introduction by Mary Morris, in collaboration with Larry O'Connor.   New York: Vintage Books, 1993. 438p.
A chronologically arranged anthology of travel narratives by women writers, which includes extracts from 'Through Algeria' by Mabel Sharman and 'Tamrart: thirteen days in the Sahara' by Eleanor Clark.

46   **Sahara.**
Kazuyoshi Nomachi.   Newton Abbot, England: Westbridge Books, 1978. 125p. map.
A lavish photographic record of the author's travels in the Algerian Sahara, northern Niger and southern Libya. It includes sixty-three excellent black-and-white and colour photographs, together with short diaries of the author's three trips into the Sahara. The introduction briefly describes the desert, its landscapes and its peoples.

47   **Lumières du M'zab.** (Lights of the Mzab).
Claude Pavard.   Paris: Editions Delroisse, 1974. 164p. 5 maps.
This illustrated guide to the M'zab describes the five cities which dominate this part of the central Algerian Sahara, the history and religious institutions of their inhabitants, the Mzabites, the distinctive architecture of their settlements and the contemporary changes affecting their society. The text is in French, English and Arabic.

48   **Algeria and the Sahara: a handbook for travellers.**
Valerie Stevens, Jon Stevens.   London: Constable, 1977. 305p. 2 maps.
Basically a tourist guide to Algeria and the Sahara, with practical advice and information for the visitor in search of beaches, museums, mosques or desert exploration. Forty suggested routes are described in detail, and the main towns and villages on every route are indexed.

49 The Sahara.

Jeremy Swift, with photographs by Pierre Boulat. Amsterdam: Time-Life International, 1975. 184p. map. bibliog.

This book is based on several journeys through the Sahara by the author, who carried out extensive field work in the region, living with Tuareg herdsmen. It focuses on the varied and often dramatic landscapes of this vast desert region, its geological history, vegetation, wildlife and its inhabitants, the nomadic herdsmen. It is lavishly illustrated with colour photographs.

50 Traveller's guide to North Africa.

London: IC Magazines, 1981. 191p.

An introductory guide to Algeria, and its neighbours with notes on food, health, crossing the Sahara and the significance of Islam in the region.

51 Forbidden sands: a search in the Sahara.

Richard Trench. London: John Murray, 1978. 197p. map.

An observant account of the author's travels through the western border region of the Algerian Sahara to Timbuktu in Mali. Trench draws on the observations of previous travellers to supplement and give depth to his narrative. The epilogue describes the changes that have occurred along Algeria's Saharan border with Morocco as a result of the war in the disputed territory of the Western Sahara.

52 Guide du Sahara. (Guide to the Sahara).

Bénédicte Vaes, Gérard Del Marmol, Albert d'Otreppe. Paris: Hachette-Guides de Voyage, 1991. 7th ed. 750p.

A reference work covering the Algerian Sahara with information on history, society and ethnography together with practical information for the traveller.

53 Among the Berbers of Algeria.

Anthony Wilkin. Westport, Connecticut: Negro Universities Press, 1970. Reprint of 1900 ed. 263p. map.

A popular record of the author's journey through the mountains of eastern Algeria, with a description of the region's Berber inhabitants, their history, ways of life and customs.

Descriptions et iconographie de la ville d'Alger au XVIe siècle.
See item no. 116.

Le tourisme au Maghreb: repères bibliographiques.
See item no. 859.

Geography and Geology

54 **Algeria, Morocco and Tunisia: oil pollution management for the southwest Mediterranean sea.**
Washington, DC: The World Bank, Project Document, 1994. 159p.

The principal objective of the Oil Pollution Management Project is to reduce the input of petroleum hydrocarbons into the international waters of the Mediterranean. The project consists of both national and regional elements. It includes: (a) enhancement of oil spill response capabilities in Algeria, Morocco and Tunisia; and elaboration of national and regional spill contingency plans; (b) provision of pollution monitoring mechanisms; (c) rehabilitation and expansion of reception facilities at key ports to receive oily ballast and bilge waters; (d) provision of floating equipment, tank trucks, dispersants' sprayers, skimmer booms, etc. for combatting oil spills; (e) training; and (f) technical and marketing studies to evaluate re-refining or alternative uses of recovery oily materials.

55 **Algeria, official standard names gazetteer.**
United States Board on Geographic Names.   Washington, DC:
Department of the Interior, 1972. 754p. map.

This gazetteer contains some 45,200 entries for places and features in Algeria. The entries include standard names approved by the Board and unapproved variant names, the latter being cross-referenced to the standard names. The basic name coverage corresponds to that of maps at the scale of 1:200,000 for the northern part and 1:500,000 or 1:1,000,000 for the southern third of Algeria. Entries include the names of first, second, and most third order administrative divisions, populated places of all sizes, various other cultural entries, and a variety of physical features.

56 **Water management in the Maghreb.**
Mahmood Ali Ayub, Ulrich Kuffner.   *Finance and Development* (June 1994), p. 28-29.

Argues that Algeria, Morocco and Tunisia are entering a critical phase and that at current demand levels available water resources will be almost completely used up within the next fifteen to twenty years. After examining the region's water management problems, the authors argue that an important policy shift is needed, one that focuses on the 'demand' side (promoting more desirable levels and patterns of water use) rather than on the 'supply' side (i.e. locating, developing and exploiting new sources). This approach follows the thinking outlined in the World Bank's new policy paper on managing water resources.

57 **Le Sahara dans le développement des états maghrébins.** (The Sahara in the development of the Maghreb states).
Jean Bisson. *Maghreb-Machrek*, no. 134 (1991), p. 3-27; *Maghreb-Machrek*, no. 135 (1992), p. 79-106.

This important study, in two parts, challenges the prevailing notion that the Maghreb Sahara is on the road to desertification, abandonment and depopulation. The author argues that on the contrary, Saharan societies are demonstrating great internal dynamism: new forms of urbanization, employment, agriculture and economic organization are gradually bringing the Sahara out of its isolation and could render the outlook encouraging if the constraints of a fragile environment are respected. Two thirds of the three million inhabitants of the Maghreb Sahara live in Algeria.

58 **Boundaries and state territory in the Middle East and North Africa.**
Edited by G. H. Blake, R. N. Schofield. Wisbech, England: Middle East and North African Studies Press, 1987. 177p.

Three chapters are relevant to Algeria: 'International boundaries and Arab state formation' by Bahgat Korany; 'Frontiers in North Africa' by George Joffé; and 'Maritime boundaries of the Middle East and North Africa' by Gerald Blake.

59 **Cambridge atlas of the Middle East and North Africa.**
Edited by Gerald Blake, John Dewdney, Jonathan Mitchell. New York: Cambridge University Press, 1988. 124p. 58 maps. bibliog.

Includes maps and an accompanying text which covers: the physical environment; history; ethnicity and language; religion; literacy and learning; population, urbanization and migration; agriculture; fishing; oil and gas; minerals; industry; tourism and trade; trading partners and trading associations; communications, railways, roads, ports and airways. It includes Algeria and the Maghreb states.

60 **L'Algérie, volontarisme étatique et aménagement du territoire.**
Jean-Claude Brulé, Jacques Fontaine. Tours, France: URBAMA, 1987. 2nd ed. 248p. bibliog. maps.

The first part of this work describes Algeria in 1985, and discusses, in turn, population, the major physical contraints, and the different sectors of the economy. Part two, the most original contribution, presents the different approaches to the organization of space from the Ottoman period, through 'l'éspace dualiste' of the colonial period to 'le projet d'intégration territoriale' of independent Algeria. Part three examines the current changes taking place – industrialization and urbanization, the restructuring of rural space, the stagnation in agricultural production and food shortages. This section also includes a discussion of deficiencies in the provision of health facilities, housing and water, and presents the emerging contours of the country's new regional geography.

61 **Le Sahara français.** (The French Sahara).
   Robert Capot-Rey. Paris: Presses Universitaires de France, 1953.
   546p. 18 maps. bibliog. (L'Afrique Blanche Française, Tome 2).

Although published just before the outbreak of the Algerian war of independence, this work remains a useful regional text on the Algerian Sahara during the period of French colonial rule. It includes sections on climate, relief and population, and examines nomadic society and pastoral migrations, village life and oasis cultivation, and cities and urban life. The final section discusses the development programmes initiated during the French occupation. For a comparison with the present-day situation in the Algerian Sahara, see Jean Bisson, *Le Sahara dans le développement des états maghrébins* (item no. 57).

62 **The changing geography of Africa and the Middle East.**
   Edited by Graham P. Chapman, Kathleen M. Baker. London; New York: Routledge, 1992. 269p.

Includes a contribution by George Joffé on 'The changing geography of North Africa: development, migration and the demographic time-bomb' (p. 139-64) which covers Algeria and its neighbours, Morocco, Tunisia, Libya and Mauritania.

63 **L'Algérie ou l'espace retourné.** (Algeria or the reversed space).
   Marc Côte. Paris: Flammarion, 1988. 362p. bibliog. maps. (Collection 'Géographes').

One of the first major geographical studies of Algeria to take account of the profound economic and social changes that have occurred since independence. Against the background of the profound impact of colonial rule on the organization of Algerian space, the author examines the construction of a 'nouvel espace algérien'. The characteristics of rural, urban and industrial space are all examined at both the national and local level.

64 **L'Afrique du Nord.** (North Africa).
   Jean Despois. Paris: Presses Universitaires de France, 1964.
   622p. 21 maps. bibliog. (Pays d'Outre-Mer Colonies, Empires, Pays Autonomes, Quatrième Serie: Géographie 1).

A systematic treatment of the geography of the Maghreb with sections on the physical features, historical evolution, ecological structure and impact of French colonization. The final section describes the geographical personality of each country. Although the approach used is now regarded as 'traditional', the work remains a useful reference on the geography of Algeria under French colonial rule. It should be consulted in conjunction with the more recent publication, *Le Maghreb: hommes et espaces*, edited by Jean-François Troin (q.v.).

65 **Géographie de l'Afrique du Nord-Ouest.** (The geography of north-west Africa).
   Jean Despois, René Raynal. Paris: Payot, 1967. 570p. 43 maps. bibliog.

After a brief introduction to the region's physical and human geography, the authors provide major sections on each of the three countries – Algeria, Morocco and Tunisia

– together with a separate section on the Sahara. The section on Algeria describes in some detail the structure and relief, climate, vegetation, population and economy of each of the country's major regions. As more recent geographical studies of the Maghreb are mainly thematic, this remains a useful reference on the regional geography of Algeria at the end of French colonial rule.

66 **La Mitidja: décolonisation et espace géographique.** (The geographical implications of decolonization on the Mitidja Plain).
George Mutin.   Paris: Centre de Recherche et d'Etudes sur les Sociétés Méditerranéennes, 1977. 607p. 146 maps. bibliog.

An in-depth analysis of the changing agricultural economy of the Mitidja plain, south of Algiers, between 1966 and 1971, the first decade of independence. The impact of increased urbanization and industrialization on patterns of agriculture is assessed.

67 **La politique hydro-agricole de l'Algérie.** (Algeria's hydro-agricultural policy).
Jean-Jacques Perennes.   *Maghreb-Machrek*, no. 111 (1986), p. 57-76.

Traces Algeria's policies since independence for extending irrigated agricultural lands, the scale of investments made during the various development plans, the achievements realized in terms of the new dams constructed and irrigated zones equipped, and the major constraints facing policy-makers.

68 **The case of an indeterminate boundary: Algeria-Morocco.**
Anthony S. Reyner.   In: *Essays in political geography*.   Edited by C. A. Fisher.   London: Methuen, 1968, p. 242-51.

This article examines the historical background to the boundary dispute between Algeria and Morocco that erupted into warfare in 1963.

69 **Oasis du Sahara algérien.** (The oases of the Algerian Sahara).
M. Rouvillois-Brigol, C. Nesson, J. Vallet.   Paris: Institut Géographique National, 1973. 110p. 25 maps. bibliog. (Etudes de Photo-Interprétation, no. 6).

Brings together three studies illustrating the modes of Saharan land organization and irrigation south of the Mzab area, based on aerial photo-interpretation. The oases under study are Righ Wadi, Ouargla and Tamentit. The study includes reproductions of many of the aerial photographs.

70 **Le pays de Ouargla (Sahara algérien): variations et organisation d'un espace rural en milieu désertique.** (The Ouargla region [Algerian Sahara]: characteristics and organization of a rural settlement in a desert environment).
M. Rouvillois-Brigol.   Paris: Département de Géographie de l'Université de Paris-Sorbonne, 1975. 389p. 11 maps. bibliog. (Publication du Département de Géographie, no. 2).

This monograph on the Ouargla oasis discusses the social and economic development of the oasis and gives a detailed account of the land use and organization of the oasis settlement.

71   **The pre-Cambrian in North Africa.**
     H. M. E. Schurmann.   Leiden, Netherlands: Brill, 1974. 351p. 3 maps.
     bibliog.

A comprehensive study of evidence from cores and samples of the pre-Cambrian in
North Africa. Many Algerian sites are included in the analysis, particularly in north-
west Algeria and the Hoggar regions.

72   **Algeria: physical and human geography.**
     Keith Sutton.   *Encyclopaedia Britannica*, no. 24 (1993), p. 966-71.

A brief description of the main features of the country's physical geography –
structure and relief, drainage, soils, climate and plant and animal life – together with
notes on settlement patterns, population and demographic trends, the economy,
administration and social conditions, and cultural life.

73   **Water resource problems in Algeria.**
     Keith Sutton, Salah Zaimeche.   *Méditerranée* (France), no. 3-4 (1992),
     p. 35-43.

Explores two important aspects of the water question in Algeria: the destruction of
underground water resources through over-use and pollution; and the growing
shortage of water following droughts which may well portend climatic changes with
dramatic consequences for Algeria.

74   **Le Maghreb: hommes et espaces.** (The Maghreb: men and space).
     Edited by Jean-François Troin.   Paris: Armand Colin, 1985. 2nd ed.
     368p. 50 maps. bibliog.

Different specialists examine a range of geographical themes for the Maghreb region
(Algeria, Morocco and Tunisia) as a whole, including country case-studies: the
constraints and potential of the physical environment and its use by man; water
resources and national policies towards their development; population and
urbanization; agrarian structures, agricultural policies and food dependency;
industrialization; and regional and national space.

75   **The Mediterranean valleys: geological changes in historical times.**
     Claudio Vita-Finzi.   Cambridge, England: Cambridge University Press,
     1969. 140p. 17 maps. bibliog.

An attempt to discover how far the Mediterranean streams have modified their valleys
in the course of the last 2,000 years. Chapter four (p. 54-58) considers the evidence
from Algeria.

76   **Hydrogeology of the Albian formation, Algeria.**
     Robert Maurice Winn.   PhD dissertation, Texas Tech University,
     Lubbock, Texas, 1973. 108p. 6 maps. bibliog. (Available from
     University Microfilms, Ann Arbor, Michigan, order no. 73-23, 779).

An analysis of hydrogeological data on the surface and subsurface of the Albian
formation which outcrops in parts of northern Algeria and occupies a vast subsurface
extent in the Saharan zone. Special attention is paid to the analysis of the
characteristics of the Albian formation in the Saharan region.

North-west Africa: a political and economic survey.
See item no. 21.

The Middle East and North Africa.
See item no. 29.

Algeria: a country study.
See item no. 32.

The Sahara.
See item no. 41.

The limits of Utopia: Henri Duveyrier and the exploration of the Sahara in the 19th century.
See item no. 162.

Algeria: changes in population distribution 1954-66.
See item no. 266.

Population changes in Algeria, 1977-1987.
See item no. 268.

Population growth in Algeria, 1966-1977, with some comparisons from Tunisia.
See item no. 269.

Political changes in Algeria: an emerging electoral geography.
See item no. 469.

The Algerian law on air pollution control and the applicability of relevant common law principles to its reform.
See item no. 496.

African boundaries: a legal and diplomatic encyclopaedia.
See item no. 519.

Regional disparities and regional development in Algeria.
See item no. 610.

Oil and regional development: examples from Algeria and Tunisia.
See item no. 619.

Algeria: centre-down development, state capitalism, and emergent decentralization.
See item no. 621.

Industrialisation et urbanisation en Algérie.
See item no. 649.

Incidences géographiques de l'industrialisation en Algérie.
See item no. 655.

Industrialization and regional development in a centrally-planned economy – the case of Algeria.
See item no. 656.

The spatial structure of state-owned industry in the Oran region of Algeria.
See item no. 657.

The *centres de regroupement*: the French army's final legacy to Algeria's settlement geography.
See item no. 753.

The growth of Algiers and regional development in Algeria: contradictory themes.
See item no. 754.

The influence of military policy on Algerian rural settlement.
See item no. 755.

Vers un Maghreb des villes de l'an 2000.
See item no. 757.

The United States and Africa: guide to US official documents and government-sponsored publications on Africa: 1785-1975.
See item no. 841.

Progress in the human geography of the Maghreb.
See item no. 883.

Flora and Fauna

77 **Handbook of the birds of Europe, the Middle East and North Africa: the birds of the western Palearctic (Vol. 1: Ostrich to ducks; vol. 2 Hawks to bustards; vol. 3 Waders to gulls; vol. 4 Terns to woodpeckers; vol. 5 Tyrant flycatchers to thrushes; vol. 6 Warblers; vol. 7 Flycatchers to shrikes).**
Chief editor Stanley Cramp.   Oxford; London; New York: Oxford University Press, 1977– .

The main body of each volume consists of the species accounts which are divided into the following sections: field characteristics, habitat, distribution and population, movements, food, social pattern and behaviour, voice, breeding and plumages. It is illustrated by paintings showing plumage identifiable in the field, and flight patterns are illustrated where appropriate. The work includes Algeria and the rest of North Africa in its geographical coverage.

78 **Les sols d'Algérie.** (The soils of Algeria).
J. H. Durand.   Algiers: Gouvernement Général de l'Algérie, Direction du Service de la Colonisation et de l'Hydraulique, 1954. 244p. 9 maps. bibliog.

Examines the factors influencing soil formation, presents a classification of Algerian soils and discusses soil utilization and the problem of erosion. The work contains fifty-eight black-and-white illustrations. Though dated, it remains a useful reference on the subject.

79 **The birds of North Africa from the Canary Islands to the Red Sea.**
R. D. Etchécopar, François Hue, translated by P. A. D. Hollom, illustrated by Paul Barruel.   Edinburgh; London: Oliver & Boyd, 1967. 612p. 281 maps.

The book presents not so much a work of ornithological biogeography, but rather a practical, simple guide to the identification of birds, designed to help visitors to the region who are interested in its wildlife. The first guide of its type, it is illustrated with twenty-five half-tone and colour plates and many maps showing the distribution of the various birds illustrated in the text.

80   **Flore du Sahara.** (Flora of the Sahara).
Paul Ozenda.   Paris: Editions du CNRS, 1977. 2nd ed. 622p. 21 maps. bibliog.

A unique synthesis of existing knowledge about the vegetation of the northern and central Sahara. Part one examines climate and soils, the composition and origins of Saharan vegetation, the morphological and physiological adaptation of plants to unfavourable physical conditions and the influence of man on Saharan vegetation. Part two is a catalogue of individual plant types, giving detailed descriptions of each species together with numerous diagrams to facilitate identification.

81   **Nouvelle flore de l'Algérie et des régions désertiques méridionales.**
(New flora of Algeria and the southern desert regions).
P. Quézel, S. Santa.   Paris: Editions du CNRS, 1962-63. 2 vols. 42 maps.

A comprehensive survey of the vegetation of northern Algeria and the Sahara. The distinctive characteristics of each species are described and their distribution indicated. Many diagrams are included to permit easy identification. It remains a basic reference on the subject.

82   **Rural renovation in Algeria.**
Philip Stewart.   *Maghreb Review*, vol. 15, no. 1-2 (1990), p. 37-47.

Examines one of the most interesting attempts to carry out large-scale soil restoration which was launched in Algeria in 1960 and abandoned in 1965, three years after independence. The Rural Renovation Programme was founded on the idea of expanding the area of productive land, especially in the semi-arid zone, using revolutionary new methods of soil restoration. Estimated to cost between 12 and 15 billion new francs, the aim was to treat nearly half of northern Algeria. Only a series of pilot zones were completed and as a country-wide plan it was soon forgotton, though many elements were incorporated into the law governing the Agrarian Revolution of 1971.

83   **Change, the state and deforestation: the Algerian example.**
S. E. Zaimeche.   *Geographical Journal*, vol. 160, no. 1 (1994), p. 50-56.

Discusses how in the 1970s and 1980s, inappropriate government policies, fast-rising pressure on forest lands and administrative inefficiency led to widespread deforestation. As the country is embroiled in political turmoil in the early 1990s, and the people are fighting for survival under increasingly difficult conditions, the concept of salvaging the forests is being completely lost from sight. At the present rate of deforestation, Algeria's forests could be totally depleted within the next few decades.

84 The degradation of the Algerian environment through economic and social 'development' in the 1980s.

S. E. Zaimeche, K. Sutton. *Land Degradation and Rehabilitation*, no. 2 (1990), p. 317-24.

Algeria's natural environment is vulnerable and its ecosystems fragile. Once cleared, the country's woodlands and forests are slow to re-establish themselves and surface deposits are easily erodable. Soils were largely formed under past climatic conditions, and so cannot be restored naturally by present pedogenetic processes. This study seeks to demonstrate the dimensions of environmental degradation through observations and monitoring during the 1980s of Algeria's media, largely newspaper and television reports. Particular emphasis is placed on the growing environmental 'crisis' since 1988.

The Sahara.
See item no. 41.

Soils of Algeria.
See item no. 882.

Prehistory and Archaeology

85 **Le Bas-Sahara dans la préhistoire.** (The Low Sahara in prehistory).
Ginette Aumassip. Paris: Editions du CNRS, 1986. 612p.
The Low Sahara examined in this study is the vast depression of a half-million square
kilometres in southern Tunisia and north-eastern Algeria between the Atlas mountains
and the central highlands. Aumassip analyses virtually every known site in what has
been throughout prehistory an arid and thinly populated area. Pleistocene sites are
rare, though Lower, Middle and Upper Palaeolithic occupations are represented. The
vast majority of finds belong to the Epipalaeolithic and 'Neolithic' categories of
Holocene times.

86 **Les civilisations préhistoriques de l'Afrique du Nord et du Sahara.**
(The prehistoric civilizations of North Africa and the Sahara).
Gabriel Camps. Paris: Dion, 1974. 366p. 13 maps. bibliog.
This book traces the prehistory of North Africa and the Sahara from Palaeolithic times
to the end of the Neolithic period. It remains a basic reference work on the subject.

87 **Current research and recent radiocarbon dates from Northern
Africa.**
Angela E. Close. *Journal of African History*, no. 21 (1981), p. 147-67;
no. 25 (1984), p. 1-24; no. 29 (1988), p. 145-76.
A series of three articles reporting on recent archaeological research and new
chronometric (primarily radiocarbon) dates from North Africa. Several of the sites
discussed are from Algeria, especially from the Saharan provinces.

88 **The search for the Tassili frescoes: the story of the prehistoric
rock-paintings of the Sahara.**
Henri Lhote, translated by Alan Houghton Brodrick. London:
Hutchinson, 1959. 236p. 4 maps.
Describes the discovery of the Tassili rock paintings of the Algerian Sahara – one of
the greatest museums of prehistoric art in the world – and their contribution to our

understanding of the ancient populations of the Sahara, the different types of people who swept over the desert in successive waves, foreign influences and changes in fauna and climate. There are over a hundred colour and black-and-white illustrations.

89 **The North African stones speak.**
Paul Mackendrick.   London: Croom Helm, 1980. 434p. 14 maps.
bibliog.

Discusses the archaeology and cultural history of the Maghreb from prehistoric times to the Arab invasion of the region. Each country is considered separately in a chronological manner. Archaeological sites and finds are described with reference to their contribution to the socio-economic history of the region outlined.

90 **L'art rupestre préhistorique des massifs centraux sahariens.**
(Prehistoric rock art of the central Saharan massifs).
Alfred Muzzolini.   Oxford: BAR, 1986. 369p. (Cambridge
Monographs in African Archaeology, no. 16).

The basic aim of this study is to establish a chronology of the art in the Acacus and Tassili regions of the Algerian Sahara. Following useful summaries of past environments and of previous schools of thought about Saharan art, and a discussion of the ambiguity of absolute (radiocarbon) dates so far obtained, the author analyses the various groups of paintings and engravings. Method of classification is by the use of the concept of *noyaux*, cores or bundles of elements based on major discriminant criteria, to identify regional 'schools'.

Berbères aux marges de l'histoire.
See item no. 278.

History

General

91 History of the Maghrib.
Jamil M. Abun-Nasr. Cambridge, England: Cambridge University
Press, 1975. 2nd revised ed. 422p. 6 maps. bibliog.
Traces the history of Algeria, Morocco, Tunisia and Libya from the mercantile empire
of Carthage to their independence from European colonial rule in the 20th century.

92 A history of the Maghrib in the Islamic period.
Jamil M. Abun-Nasr. Cambridge, England: Cambridge University
Press, 1987. 455p. maps. bibliog.
This book represents an extensive revision of the author's earlier *History of the
Maghrib* (q.v.). The chapters on the pre-Islamic Maghreb have been deleted and most
of those covering the mediaeval and early modern periods have been rewritten and
expanded. Some new material has been added to the chapters on the colonial period
and the book concludes with a short epilogue on the post-colonial experiences of the
Maghreb states. Of special interest is the author's new appreciation of the quality of
Berber resistance to the Islamic conquest and of schismatic Islam for the evolution of
Maghrebi history. More space is devoted to important economic and to certain social
factors. There is a reconsideration of the relationship of state and society in Ottoman
Algeria.

93 Modern Algeria: a history from 1830 to the present.
Charles-Robert Ageron, translated and edited by Michael Brett.
London: C. Hurst & Co., 1991. 174p. maps. bibliog.
A revised and translated edition of *Histoire de l'Algérie contemporaine* (9th edition,
1990) by the doyen of French historians of the colonial period. The book is not so
much a history of the colonized as a masterful examination of the colonizers,
particularly with regard to the complicated, contradictory and often hostile
relationship between the métropole, local French administrators and the European

colon community. It places the onus for the terrible Algerian war squarely on the settler population and maintains that the single-party state, created after eight years of carnage, was the unnecessary consequence of revolution. A special feature of this edition is that Ageron takes his narrative up to the local elections in Algeria in 1990.

94 Banditry in Islam.
David M. Hart.   Wisbech, England: Middle East and North African Studies Press, 1987. 96p. bibliog.

Applies Marxist historian Hobsbawm's theory of banditry to case-studies in Algeria, Morocco and Pakistan. Hobsbawm's theory proposes that banditry is a result of political, social and economic unrest and that it is more appropriately referred to as a political protest.

95 History of North Africa: Tunisia, Algeria, Morocco: from the Arab conquest to 1830.
Charles-André Julien, edited and revised by R. Le Tourneau, translated by John Petrie, edited by C. C. Stewart.   London: Routledge & Kegan Paul, 1970. 446p. 11 maps. bibliog.

An English translation of the second French edition of *Histoire de l'Afrique du Nord*, published in 1961. The book traces the history of Algeria, Tunisia and Morocco from the Arab conquest of the Maghreb in the 7th century AD to the eve of the European conquest. It examines the rise of the great Berber empires, the Almoravids and the Almohads, and the establishment of Turkish rule in Algeria and Tunisia during the period 1516-1830. A new French edition appeared in 1986.

96 The history of the Maghrib: an interpretive essay.
Abdallah Laroui, translated from the French by Ralph Manheim. Princeton, New Jersey: Princeton University Press, 1977. 431p. 2 maps. bibliog. (Princeton Studies on the Near East).

The work presents a critical review of existing histories of the Maghreb. It sets out not so much to retrace the region's history as such, but rather attempts to determine what the attitude of a Maghrebi concerned with his future should be towards his past as a whole. The period under discussion stretches from classical times to the impact of European colonialism.

97 North Africa 1800-1900: a survey from the Nile valley to the Atlantic.
Magali Morsy.   London: Longman, 1984. 356p.

The book attempts to explain the factors which led to European colonial expansion into North Africa and the counter movements which it generated there. The author maintains that North Africa, from the Nile valley to the Atlantic, constitutes a single entity and that the divisions between Egypt and the Maghreb came into being only in the colonial period, a concept which some historians would dispute. The work is valuable in highlighting the fact that for a meaningful assessment of the important developments in the history of the region in the 19th century, it is necessary to investigate their impact not only on the élite but on society as a whole.

98 **Modern Algeria: the origins and development of a nation.**
John Ruedy. Bloomington, Indiana: Indiana University Press, 1992.
290p. maps. bibliog.
A survey of Algeria's history from the beginning of the Ottoman era up to the military intervention of January 1992, which brought to an end the democratic experiment initiated in the late 1980s. The central thesis of this important new reference work is that until the colonial era, the Algerian region was fragmented by regional, tribal, sectarian and linguistic divisions. The Ottomans, although creating a unified polity, played on these divisions to maintain their dominance. French colonial rule shattered those fragmented structures, eventually making it possible for new nationwide institutions to emerge.

Algeria: the revolution institutionalized.
See item no. 15.

North-west Africa: a political and economic survey.
See item no. 21.

The Middle East and North Africa.
See item no. 29.

Algeria: a country study.
See item no. 32.

Berbères aux marges de l'histoire.
See item no. 278.

Classical period

99 **La résistance africaine à la romanisation.** (African resistance to Romanisation).
Marcel Benabou. Paris: François Maspero, 1976. 635p. 5 maps.
bibliog.
Presents a new approach to the impact of Roman rule on the North African provinces, focusing on the different forms of native resistance to the Roman presence. Part one examines the military problems and the effectiveness of the native revolts; part two traces the different forms of cultural resistance to Roman rule, and the native influences on Roman civilization in its African provinces.

100 **La civilisation de l'Afrique romaine.** (The civilization of Roman Africa).
Gilbert Charles-Picard. Paris: Libraires Plon, 1959. 406p. 3 maps.
bibliog. (Civilisations d'Hier et d'Aujourd'hui).
This book, which remains a useful introduction to the Roman provinces of North Africa, describes the administration of the provinces, population, economic life, social classes, urban life, customs and art.

101 **Les Vandales et l'Afrique.** (The Vandals and Africa).
Christian Courtois. Aalen, Germany: Scientia Verlag, 1964. Reprint
of 1955 Paris edition. 455p. 19 maps. bibliog.
The basic reference on the end of Roman rule in North Africa and the short period of
Vandal occupation. Courtois examines the origins of the Vandals, the situation in the
Roman provinces of Africa at the time of the Vandal invasion, the political structure
of the Vandal state, and the Berber kingdoms which emerged in those areas outside
Vandal control in the 5th and 6th centuries.

102 **The mosaics of Roman North Africa: studies in iconography and
patronage.**
Katherine M. D. Dunbabin. Oxford: Clarendon Press, 1978. 303p.
2 maps. bibliog. (Oxford Monographs on Classical Archaeology).
The author attempts to place North African mosaics within the wider context of
mosaic production in the rest of the Roman Empire, and concentrates on a study of the
classes of subject matter used on the figured mosaics. These are discussed with special
emphasis on those mosaics which were used to serve a particular function, either
connected with the social and civic interests of those who commissioned them, or with
religious or superstitious purposes. There are over 200 black-and-white and colour
plates. The book includes many examples of mosaics from sites in Algeria.

103 **Approches du Maghreb romain.** (Approaches to the Roman
Maghreb).
Paul-Albert Février. Aix-en-Provence, France: Edisud, 2 vols. 1990.
One of the most recent and comprehensive studies of Rome's North African provinces
by a former Professor of Archaeology at the University of Algiers.

104 **The Donatist Church: a movement of protest in Roman North
Africa.**
W. H. C. Frend. London: Oxford University Press, 1952. 360p.
3 maps. bibliog.
A basic reference on the Donatist movement, a schismatic Christian movement, in the
North African provinces during the late Roman Empire. This study examines the type
of society in which Donatism flourished. It tries to relate the Donatist movement to the
religious background of the Berbers in prehistoric times and in the early centuries of
the Roman occupation, and to examine whether there are links between Donatism and
Islam in North Africa. It also asks how far Donatism and other movements of
Christian dissent in the late Roman Empire contributed towards the permanent
cleavage in faith between peoples of the northern and southern shores of the
Mediterranean.

The North African stones speak.
See item no. 89.

Berbères aux marges de l'histoire.
See item no. 278.

A history of the Jews in North Africa: Volume I. From antiquity to the sixteenth century.
See item no. 285.

Myth and metrology: the early trans-Saharan gold trade.
See item no. 627.

Mediaeval period

105 **The Muslim invasion and the ruin of North African Christianity.**
K. Baus. In: *History of the Church.* Edited by H. Jedin, J. Dolan.
Vol. 2 *The imperial Church from Constantine to the early middle ages*,
by K. Baus, et al. London: Burns & Oates, 1980, p. 612-14.
Discusses the effects of the Muslim invasion of North Africa in the 7th century AD on
North African Christianity.

106 **L'Espagne catalane et le Maghrib aux XIIIe et XIVe siècles.**
(Catalan Spain and the Maghreb during the 13th and 14th centuries).
Charles-Emmanuel Dufourcq. Paris: Presses Universitaires de
France, 1966. 588p. map. bibliog.
The most detailed study of this period in Algeria's history, which describes the
tortuous commercial and diplomatic relations between the Christian kingdoms of
Spain and the Muslim states of the Maghreb. Chapter five deals specifically with the
kingdom of the 'Abd al Wadids (western Algeria) and the important gold trade centred
on the town of Tlemcen.

107 **The adventures of Ibn Battuta, a Muslim traveler of the 14th
century.**
Ross E. Dunn. London: Croom Helm, 1986. 357p. 12 maps. bibliog.
Presents a survey of the whole *Rihla* of Ibn Battuta, a Moroccan traveller, as presented
by Ibn Juzayy. The chapters follow each stage of the *Rihla*, commencing in Tangier
and ending in Mali. A concluding chapter assesses the literary merits of the work and
the part played by Ibn Juzayy. The whole *Rihla* may be viewed as a comment on the
Muslim world in the early 14th century as seen through the eyes of a Maghrebi, and
large sections of the book are specifically concerned with Maghrebi lands and their
rulers, cities and scholars of note. For example, chapters one and two are concerned
with Tangier, Algeria and Tunisia, and chapter twelve, the journey home, is in part
concerned with Algeria and Morocco.

108 **General history of Africa III. Africa from the seventh to the eleventh century.**
Edited by M. El Fasi, assistant editor I. Hrbek.   Paris: UNESCO; London: Heinemann; Berkeley, California: University of California Press, 1988. 869p.

Includes the following sections relevant to the Maghreb and Algeria: 'The conquest of North Africa and Berber resistance' by H. Monès (p. 224-45); 'The independence of the Maghreb' by M. Talbi (p. 246-75); 'The role of the Sahara and Saharians in relationships between north and south' by T. Lewicki (p. 276-313); and 'The Almoravids' by I. Hrbek and J. Devisse (p. 336-66).

109 **Medieval Muslim government in Barbary until the sixth century of the hijra.**
J. F. P. Hopkins.   London: Luzac, 1958. 148p.

A series of essays discussing what is known about various aspects of the government and administration of North Africa from the Muslim conquest in the 8th century until the 13th century.

110 **Ibn Khaldun: the birth of history and the past of the Third World.**
Yves Lacoste, translated by David Macey.   London: Verso Editions; New York: Schocken Books, 1984. 214p.

In a work first published in 1966, Lacoste analyses Ibn Khaldun's study of the political and social conditions of the Maghreb during the 14th century. Lacoste disputes the generally accepted 'myth of the Arab invasion' which attributes the crisis in mediaeval North Africa to the gradual invasion by nomadic tribes from the east. He also examines the significance of '*asabiyya*' or tribal solidarity as a key concept in Ibn Khaldun's study of '*umran*' or human association or culture. The author sees Ibn Khaldun's work as a major contribution to the study of the underlying causes of underdevelopment.

111 **The Almohad movement in North Africa in the twelfth and thirteenth centuries.**
Roger Le Tourneau.   Princeton, New Jersey: Princeton University Press, 1969. 126p. map.

A concise study of the rise and fall of the Almohad Empire which ruled over the Maghreb, including Algeria, and Spain, in the 12th and early 13th centuries.

112 **The Muslim conquest and settlement of North Africa and Spain.**
Abdulwahid Dhanun Taha.   London; New York: Routledge, 1989. 280p. bibliog. (Exeter Arabic and Islamic Series, no. 3).

The early history of Islam in North Africa and Spain is buried under a mass of legend and misinformation. The author's principal aim is to sort out the details of the early settlement by Muslims, both Arab and (newly converted) Berber, of the new territories of the extreme West. Despite the title, the work mainly concerns Spain; North Africa is studied essentially as providing the path to the peninsula and much of the manpower for the conquest. Part one covers the conquest and the earliest settlements, while the second part deals with the period of the governors dependent on North Africa and Damascus up to the establishment of effective local independence in the peninsula in AD 756.

A history of the Maghrib in the Islamic period.
See item no. 92.

History of North Africa: Tunisia, Algeria, Morocco: from the Arab conquest to 1830.
See item no. 95.

Berbères aux marges de l'histoire.
See item no. 278.

A history of the Jews in North Africa: Volume I. From antiquity to the sixteenth century.
See item no. 285.

Berbers and blacks: Ibadi slave traffic in eighth century North Africa.
See item no. 630.

Ottoman period

113 **The prisoners of Algiers: an account of the forgotten American-Algerian war 1785-1797.**
H. G. Barby. London: Oxford University Press, 1966. 343p. bibliog.

The story of the crew of an American schooner captured by Algerian pirates in the late 18th century and purchased as slaves by the Dey of Algiers. It describes their captivity in Algiers and the long and difficult negotiations to secure their release, including the first peace treaty between the United States and the Algiers Regency signed in September 1795.

114 **Les renégats et la marine de la Régence d'Alger.** (Renegades and seapower in the Regency of Algiers).
Pierre Boyer. *Revue de l'Occident Musulman et de la Méditerranée* (France), no. 39 (1985), p. 93-106.

Boyer discusses Christian renegades of Mediterranean origin, who in the 16th century made Algiers a pirate capital, holding political power in the city but making little contribution to technical progess. During the 17th century, although no longer politically dominant, a new breed of renegades originating from the Atlantic countries introduced new round vessels, giving Algerian piracy a second wind and bringing great prosperity. This prosperity disappeared along with the renegades during the 18th century.

115   **The Mediterranean and the Mediterranean world in the age of Philip II.**
Fernand Braudel, translated by Siân Reynolds.   London: Collins, 1972. 2 vols. 38 maps. bibliog.
One of the most important historical works on the Mediterranean region. It focuses on the second half of the 16th century, considers the Mediterranean as a physical unit, analyses the region's economies and societies, its overlapping civilizations, war, piracy, politics and people. Though Braudel's views have been challenged, this work remains a basic reference on North Africa during this period and on the region's relations with the rest of the Mediterranean lands and also includes an excellent account of Muslim privateering and the brilliant age of Algiers.

116   **Descriptions et iconographie de la ville d'Alger au XVIe siècle.**
(Descriptions and iconography of the city of Algiers in the 16th century).
Federico Cresti.   *Revue de l'Occident Musulman et de la Méditerranée* (France), no. 34 (1982), p. 1-22.
During the 16th century, knowledge of Algiers was spread throughout Europe by numerous descriptions and illustrations. The various authors and usually anonymous engravers show a town becoming more and more prosperous through trade and privateering. It developed from a small provincial port into an impregnable fortress and the capital of the central Maghreb. By 1600 it had reached a size that would not change until the 19th century.

117   **Ottoman North Africa and the Dutch Republic in the seventeeth and eighteenth centuries.**
Alexander H. DeGroot.   *Revue de l'Occident Musulman et de la Méditerranée* (France), no. 39 (1985), p. 131-47.
Describes how relations between the Dutch Republic and the Ottoman provinces of Algiers, Tunis and Tripoli during the 17th and 18th centuries were concerned primarily with war and trade. Treaties made in the 1620s during the Dutch struggle against Spain gained the Dutch freedom of action in the western Mediterranean, and joint Dutch-Ottoman action against the Spanish was planned. Later treaties were more concerned with trade and the freeing of Dutch captives from Barbary corsairs.

118   **Merchant friars in North Africa; the trade in Christian captives.**
Ellen G. Friedman.   *The Maghreb Review*, vol. 12, no. 3-4 (1987), p. 94-98.
At the beginning of the 13th century, a number of religious orders dedicated to the redemption of captives were instituted in Spain. This article shows how these orders combined the function of merchant-ransomers with religious concerns. Throughout the 17th century and even into the 18th century the intensification of the activities of the Maghrebian corsairs was accompanied by the expansion of the ransoming activities of the friars. The friars encounted their greatest difficulties in Algiers because of the heavy dependence of the regency's economy on ransom payments.

119 **Spanish captives in North Africa in the early modern age.**
Ellen G. Friedman. Madison, Wisconsin: The University of
Wisconsin Press, 1983. 242p. bibliog.

A study dedicated to piracy and Barbary corsair warfare which covers the period from
the last quarter of the 16th century to the end of the 18th century. It draws on original
archival sources to examine the effect that this prolonged state of undeclared warfare
had on Spanish society. The first part is dedicated to the captives and their captors and
the second to the description of life in captivity. The third deals with redemption;
procedure; the role of the Trinitarian and Mercedarian orders; the support of the State;
sources of ransom money; and the manner in which negotiations were carried out in
North Africa. Although centred on the Spanish side of the conflict, the book throws
new light on the North African situation *vis-à-vis* the economic role performed by the
European slaves and the dependence of the rulers on foreign currency obtained from
ransoms, both of which explain many aspects of their system of government. It also
shows that the principal motive of the North African offensive against Spain was not
religious but economic.

120 **The forgotton frontier: a history of the sixteenth-century
Ibero-African frontier.**
Andrew C. Hess. Chicago; London: University of Chicago Press,
1978. 278p. 4 maps. bibliog.

Challenges Braudel's (q.v.) vision of the unity of Mediterranean civilization and
argues that during the 16th century there was a separation of the Mediterranean world
into different, well-defined cultural spheres which produced a new segregation of
Mediterranean life. Hess seeks to substantiate this view by examining the relations
between Hapsburg Spain and Ottoman North Africa along their common frontier.

121 **Le miroir: aperçu historique et statistique sur la Régence d'Alger.**
(The mirror: historical and statistical survey of the Algiers Regency).
Hamdan Khodja. Paris: Sindbad, 1985. 319p. (Collection 'L'Histoire
décolonisée' de 'La Bibliothèque arabe').

Hamdan Khodja (1772-1842) was a wealthy and uniquely cosmopolitan member of
the Turkish governing élite overthrown by the French conquest of Algeria in 1830.
This volume was originally published in Paris in 1833 and was long out of print. It is
one of only three pre-1870 Algerian Muslim commentaries on Algerian society and
the capture of Algiers and the only indigenous work contemporary with the conquest.
This republished version includes a colonialist critique published in 1834 and
Hamdan's response. Part one of the book focuses on the customs and social
organization of Berbers, Arab bedouins and the urbanites of Algiers, and on the
structure and workings of the Turkish régime. In part two the author details his
observations of the French capture of Algiers and the events that followed.

122 **America's captive freemen in North Africa: the comparative
method in abolitionist persuasion.**
Lotfi Ben Rejeb. *Slavery & Abolition* (Great Britain), vol. 9, no. 1
(1988), p. 57-71.

Describes the use by abolitionists of the enslavement of free Americans by the
Barbary states in the late 18th and early 19th centuries as a way of attacking the
American enslavement of blacks.

123 **Algiers in the age of the corsairs.**
William Spencer. Norman, Oklahoma: University of Oklahoma
Press, 1976. 184p. map. bibliog.

This book is devoted to the rise of Algiers as the dominant maritime power in the western
Mediterranean region in the 16th and 17th centuries, when it was the headquarters of the
most successful arm of the Ottoman fleet. The author examines the government of the
city and Regency of Algiers, the structure of Algerian society, the resources and revenues
of the corsair state and its foreign relations. He points to the significant contribution of
the Regency to North African development during the Corsair Age, a period terminated
by the French conquest in 1830.

124 **Pour une nouvelle approche des relations Ottomano-Arabo-Africaines.** (For a new approach to Ottoman-Arab-African relations).
Abdeljelil Temimi. *Revue d'Histoire Maghrébine* (Tunisia), vol. 11,
no. 35-36 (1984), p. 179-82.

The Maghreb under the Ottomans formed the link between sub-Saharan Africa and the
Mediterranean. The article shows how diplomatic and commercial connections with
the kingdoms of Black Africa set in motion a two-way process of social and
intellectual exchange which was broken by colonialism. African minorities lived
peacefully in the Ottoman regencies and benefited from religious tolerance.

125 **Arguments for the conquest of Algiers in the late eighteenth and
early nineteenth centuries.**
Ann Thomson. *Maghreb Review* (Great Britain), vol. 14, no. 1-2
(1989), p. 108-18.

The French expedition against Algiers in 1830 followed half a century of argument in
favour of the colonization of North Africa, particularly the regency of Algiers. These
arguments are studied here to help clarify the deeper motivations behind the French
expedition. They were put forward by a fairly wide range of writers representing
divergent points of view and are more varied than is generally supposed. Some of the
arguments concern North Africa or 'Barbary' in general, but there is a tendency to
show a particular interest in Algiers, the most powerful and intractable of the Barbary
states.

126 **Barbary and enlightenment: European attitudes towards the
Maghreb in the eighteenth century.**
Ann Thomson. New York: E. J. Brill, 1987. 173p. bibliog.

This book is not strictly speaking a conventional history of the Maghreb in the century
leading up to the French invasion, nor is it a study of the relations between the
'Barbary states' and the European powers, but rather an attempt to chart the changing
contours of European views on North Africa in a period that stretches from the end of
the 17th century to the beginnings of French colonialism in the region. Thomson
examines the manner in which changed perceptions of Barbary and Islam in the early
decades of the 18th century under the influence of the French Enlightenment proved to
be only a transition between the ancient prejudices nourished by Christian Europe in
the preceding centuries and the aggressive and expansionist imperialism that came to
dominate European thinking in the wake of the French invasion. The new hostility is
ascribed to the scourge of piracy which revived the old Christian prejudices against
the Barbary corsairs. It was also exploited by the champions of colonial expansion to

justify the French government's policy of outright aggression and commerical exploitation, thus paving the way for Charles X's occupation of Algiers.

127 **Les corporations de métiers à Alger à l'époque ottomane.** (The trade guilds in Algiers during Ottoman times).
Houari Touati. *Revue d'Histoire Maghrébine* (Tunisia), vol. 14, no. 47-48 (1987), p. 267-92.

The article examines an unpublished manuscript, *Kitab Qanun al-Jaza'ir 'Ala 'l-Aswaq* (Book of Algerian law on markets) which contains 17th- and 18th-century regulations, laws and protocols concerning trade guilds. It reveals that in the 17th century, fifty-seven guilds were operating in Algiers. The guilds were supervised by a secretary, who represented them in dealings with the government. Strict regulations governed their activities, in work and pleasure, and the guilds functioned as economic, social, religious and ethical units, protecting their members' interests and guaranteeing security and status.

128 **Saint Vincent de Paul et l'expédition contre Alger du chevalier Paul, corsaire de Toulon.** (St Vincent de Paul and the expedition against Algiers by the chevalier Paul, corsair of Toulon).
Guy Turbet-Delof. *Africa* (Italy), vol. 41, no. 1 (1986), p. 128-37.

The money raised by Vincent de Paul and his Lazarists in 1657-58, which was thought to have been to finance the military expedition of the chevalier Paul against Algiers, was in fact intended to pay the debts of Jean Barreau, the French representative in Algiers, who had been arrested and imprisoned. Only when other finance was not forthcoming for the expedition was some money provided. The whole affair should be seen not as the result of the pressures in France for war against the Turks, but in the context of rivalries between different missionary orders in North Africa.

129 **On the eve of colonialism: North Africa before the French conquest 1790-1830.**
Lucette Valensi, translated by Kenneth Perkins. New York: Africana Publishing Company, 1977. 120p. map. bibliog.

Remains an important reference on Algeria immediately before the onset of French colonial rule. The book examines the pre-colonial history of Algeria and its neighbours, Morocco and Tunisia. It identifies a distinctive society which blended the characteristics of its pre-Islamic Berber and conquering Arab Muslim populations before the impact of colonialism disrupted their political and economic systems. It protrays a long-neglected civilization and corrects important misconceptions.

130 **Documents inédits sur un épisode de la lutte entre l'Algérie et le Maroc à la fin du XVIIème siècle.** (Unpublished documents concerning an episode in the struggle between Algeria and Morocco at the end of the 17th century).
Chantal de la Veronne. *Cahiers de Tunisie* (Tunisia), vol. 29, no. 3-4 (1981), p. 607-20.

The author describes the conflict between Algeria and Morocco in 1695-96 and prints the text of two letters concerning it from the Bey of Algiers, El-Haj Ahmed, to the governor of Oran, dated September 1696, preserved in the Archivo Historico Nacional, Madrid.

A history of the Maghrib in the Islamic period.
See item no. 92.

History of North Africa: Tunisia, Algeria, Morocco: from the Arab conquest to 1830.
See item no. 95.

Modern Algeria: the origins and development of a nation.
See item no. 98.

The French image of Algeria: its origin, its place in colonial ideology, its effects on Algerian acculturation.
See item no. 155.

The British in Barbary through the records of an English church in Algiers.
See item no. 176.

Colonialism and after: an Algerian Jewish community.
See item no. 283.

A history of the Jews in North Africa: Volume II. From the Ottoman conquests to the present time.
See item no. 286.

Migration, commerce and community: the Mizabis in eighteenth and nineteenth century Algeria.
See item no. 288.

Sufism in Africa in the seventeenth and eighteenth centuries.
See item no. 316.

Between Cairo and the Algerian Kabylia: the Rahmaniyya *tariqa*, 1715-1800.
See item no. 322.

The servants of the mosques.
See item no. 330.

Alms and arms: the combative saintliness of the Awlad Sidi Shaykh in the Algerian Sahara, sixteenth-nineteenth centuries.
See item no. 335.

Manuel des institutions algériennes de la domination turque à l'indépendance. Tome premier – la domination turque et le régime militaire 1518-1870.
See item no. 504.

Le commerce caravanier au Maghreb et ses mutations au course de l'ère précoloniale.
See item no. 625.

Changes in political succession, marital strategies and 'noble'/'vassal' relations in precolonial Ahaggar.
See item no. 763.

Le legs des Ottomans dans le domaine artistique en Afrique du Nord.
See item no. 818.

The central Ottoman archives as a source for Arab history.
See item no. 835.

Les sources Ottomanes: une source inépuisable pour l'analyse de la société, l'économie et la démographie de l'Algérie moderne.
See item no. 836.

Note sur les 'bulletins d'information' des 'recueils factices' de la bibliothèque municipale de Bordeaux relatifs au Maghreb (1664-1690).
See item no. 839.

Bibliographie des publications de G. Turbet-Delof relatives au Maghreb.
See item no. 862.

Petit supplément bibliographique pour servir à l'histoire du Maghreb.
See item no. 885.

Colonial period

131 **La personnalité de l'Emir Abdelkader dans les écrits algériens et français: analyse critique.** (Personality of Emir Abdel Kader in Algerian and French writings: a critical analysis).
Zakia Abdurahim. *Revue d'Histoire Maghrébine* (Tunisia), vol. 15, no. 49-50 (1988), p. 105-08.
Investigates the apparent contradiction implicit in French and Algerian biographies of Abdel Kader working from a bibliography of selected lives written between 1830 and 1983, and measuring the public and private facets of his character against political fact. Abdurahim suggests reasons for the dominance of certain personality traits in French and Algerian lives respectively, and attempts to redress the balance between them. Abdel Kader was a brilliant guerrilla commander and diplomat who organized resistance to the French conquest.

132 **Reductions in officer numbers and relations between army and nation: the example of the French army in 1815 and 1945.**
Claude d'Abzac-Epezy. *War and Society* (Australia), vol. 7, no. 2 (1989), p. 1-14.
This publication examines the differences and similarities between the two great reductions in numbers in the French army officer corps in 1815 and 1945. It argues

that after 1945, the redundant officers stood alone in a nation sick of war and defeat, and these officers were in a precarious financial state. There was no identification between nation and officer corps, and the latter turned inward, to explode in frustration and rage after the decision in 1961 to grant independence to Algeria.

133 **L'Association des Etudiants Musulmans Nord Africains en France durant l'entre-deux-guerres. Contribution à l'étude des nationalismes maghrébins.** (The Association of North African Muslim Students in France between the two world wars: contribution to the study of Maghrebian nationalisms).
Charles-Robert Ageron. *Revue Française d'Histoire d'Outre-Mer* (France), vol. 70, no. 1-2 (1983), p. 25-56.

Between the two World Wars the Association of North African Students in France condemned French colonialism and promoted Maghrebian unity based on a common Arab-Muslim culture. The association played an important role in training cadres for the political struggle that led to independence between 1956 and 1962.

134 *L'Etoile Nord-Africaine* **et le modèle communiste: éléments d'une enquête comparative.** (The Etoile Nord-Africaine and the Communist model: elements of a comparative study).
Charles-Robert Ageron. *Cahiers de Tunisie* (Tunisia), vol. 29, no. 3-4 (1981), p. 199-236.

Compares the doctrines and actions of the Algerian nationalist Etoile Nord Africaine movement with those of the French Communist Party between 1926 and 1939.

135 **The colonial harem.**
Malek Alloula, translated by Myrna Godzich, Wlad Godzich.
Minneapolis: University of Minnesota Press, 1986; Manchester, England: Manchester University Press, 1987. 157p.

First published in French in 1981, this is an illustrated diatribe against the European appropriation of Algerian women through the medium of postcards issued early in the 20th century. Until well into the 1920s, postcards discharged the documentary-cum-propaganda function of recording events and local activities as well as scenery and personalities. In doing so they filled a gap left by newspapers which were slow to adapt to the age of photographs. They served as an illustrated journal of the progress of civilization.

136 **Le décret Crémieux et l'insurrection de 1871 en Algérie.** (The Crémieux decree and the insurrection of 1871 in Algeria).
Richard Ayoun. *Revue d'Histoire Moderne et Contemporaine* (France), no. 35 (January-March 1988), p. 61-87.

The Crémieux decree of 24 October 1870 declared that Algerian Jews were henceforth considered citizens of France with full rights. It has previously been widely believed that the promulgation of this decree caused the Arab insurrection of early 1870 because Algerian Muslims were largely anti-Semitic and resented the new status accorded to Jews. Various contemporary interpretations of the causes of the insurrection are examined before the Crémieux decree is relegated to a decidedly minor or secondary position. The true cause of the insurrection should be seen as the attempt of Muslim tribal leaders to reassert their traditional privileges and rights in an Algeria weakened by the transfer of French military personnel back to France.

137 **Algériens et Tunisiens dans l'Empire Ottoman de 1848 à 1914.**
(Algerians and Tunisians in the Ottoman Empire from 1848 to 1914).
Pierre Bardin. Paris: Editions du CNRS, 1979. 271p. bibliog.
(Groupe de Recherches et d'Etudes sur le Proche Orient, Aix-en-Provence).

The study is divided into three parts. Part one briefly describes the Algerian and Tunisian colonies in the Ottoman Empire at the end of the 19th century and then examines in detail the situation of Algerians living in Syria and the political activities of the French in that province. Part two examines the emigration of Algerians to Syria between 1888-98. Part three deals with the emigration of Algerians and Tunisians to the Ottoman provinces between 1909-14, the causes of these population movements and their implications for French policy towards Turkey.

138 **French North Africa: the Maghreb between two world wars.**
Jacques Berque, translated by Jean Stewart. London: Faber & Faber, 1967. 422p. map.

A study of North Africa between the two World Wars, during the apparent apogee of French imperialism. It analyses the vices and contradictions of this stage of North African colonization and concludes that what appeared to be the triumph of colonial achievement was in fact the beginning of its downfall.

139 **La politique américaine en Afrique du Nord pendant la deuxième guerre mondiale.** (American policy in North Africa during World War II).
Juliette Bessis. *Revue de l'Occident Musulman et de la Méditerranée* (France), no. 36 (1983), p. 147-61.

Faced with the political problems of Algeria, Tunisia and Morocco after 1940, the United States was caught between a principled support for an end to colonialism, the imperatives of *realpolitik*, and the alliance with France, leading to often confused and contradictory policies in both Algeria and Tunisia. American sympathy, however, for nationalist aspirations served to counterbalance Axis propaganda promising independence; the US disapproved of the strong attachment to colonialism shown by all French political forces. The major concern of the United States came to be preventing the nationalist movements from falling into the Soviet orbit.

140 **La France en Algérie au XIXe siècle – l'insurrection de 1871.**
(France in Algeria in the 19th century – the insurrection of 1871).
Ahcène Bey. *Revue Historique des Armées* (France), no. 1 (1992), p. 15-23.

Argues that inherent social and cultural differences between the Algerians and the French, together with the occurrence of natural disasters and famine, the decline of French prestige in the Franco-Prussian war, and administrative and judicial changes benefiting French colonists in Algeria, brought about the insurrection of 1871 led by Muhammad al-Hajj al-Muqrani. The revolt swept across most of the country, involving over 200,000 Algerians. However, the insurrection failed because it was poorly organized and the rebels did not receive much-needed reinforcements and munitions from outside. For the rebels, the revolt had disastrous consequences, including the destruction of their agriculture and villages and the loss of their lands.

141 **The impact of Thomas-Robert Bugeaud and the decree of 9 June 1844 on the development of Constantine, Algeria.**
Philip Brebner. *Revue de l'Occident Musulman et de la Méditerranée* (France), no. 38 (1984), p. 5-14.

The decree of Bugeaud, governor-general of Algeria, ordered in June 1844 that the 'native' and European areas of Constantine should be kept separate. Europeans were excluded from the old city and Constantine preserved as a city with an Arab majority. However, the Arabs were effectively imprisoned within the limits of the pre-colonial settlement and Constantine became the scene of bad race relations and anti-Semitism among the colonists.

142 **Legislating for inequality in Algeria: the Senatus-Consulte of 14 July 1865.**
Michael Brett. *Bulletin of the School of Oriental and African Studies,* vol. 51, no. 3 (1988), p. 440-61.

The Senatus-Consulte of 1865 sought to remedy the problem of the application of French and Muslim law in Algeria by defining the 'native' Algerian Muslim as a French subject but not a French citizen unless he renounced his rights and duties under Islamic law. After the French conquest of 1830 the scope of Islamic law gradually eroded, being confined to civil matters and largely to the urban population. The new act ascribed an inferior status to the Muslim population, but defined that inferiority as a product of Islam, a strategy later strongly criticized by some legal commentators.

143 **Intellectual history in a culture under siege: Algerian thought in the last half of the 19th century.**
Allan Christelow. *Middle Eastern Studies,* vol. 18, no. 4 (1982), p. 387-99.

The author indicates how little we know about what Algerians thought in the period between the surrender of Abd al-Qadir (Abdel Kader) in 1847 and the first stirrings of nationalism under Messali Hajj and Abd al-Hamid Ben Badis in the 1920s. Algerian Muslim intellectual life in the colonial period was concentrated in three cities, Tlemcen, Algiers, and Constantine, of which the latter was Algeria's most vital intellectual centre. Several case-studies are presented, representing the concerns of different generations, from those who grew up under Ottoman rule to those who felt more severely the impact of French policies of cultural assimilation. These include: Muhammad al-Shadhli, one of the first Algerian scholars to visit France; Hasan Ben Brihmat and al-Makki Ben Badis, two of the most distinguished figures of the second generation; Abd al-Qadir al-Majjawi, the son of a prominent Tlimsani scholar born in exile; and Masa'ud al-Jabari who became involved in an alleged conspiracy to coordinate Algerian and Tunisian resistance efforts.

144   **Oral, manuscript, and printed expressions of historical consciousness in colonial Algeria.**
Allan Christelow.   *Africana Journal*, no. 15 (1990), p. 258-75.
Examines three different sources which provide expressions of Algerian attitudes toward colonial France in the early 20th century to show how the form of an attitude changes its tone. Oral expression tends to be the most flexible while manuscript sources are shown to be the most tradition-bound. Printed documents, especially ones in a colonial society, are the most conscious of their audience and tend to be conservative in tone.

145   **Ritual, culture and politics of Islamic reformism in Algeria.**
Allan Christelow.   *Middle Eastern Studies* (Great Britain), vol. 23, no. 3 (1987), p. 255-73.
This article studies the interaction between religion and politics in Algeria and discusses whether the interaction resulted in revolutionary political religion that challenged the status quo. It covers the period 1931-57, from the emergence of the Association of Reformist 'Ulama until its dissolution by the French, and considers the characters and roles of three important reformist leaders. The position in Algeria is set against the historical context of French colonization, which had separated church from state, leading to a study of Islamic education through the free schools begun by the Reformist 'Ulama in 1931.

146   **Rebel and saint: Muslim notables, populist protest, colonial encounters (Algeria and Tunisia, 1800-1904).**
Julia A. Clancy-Smith.   Berkeley, California: University of California Press, 1994. 370p. 9 maps. bibliog. (Comparative Studies on Muslim Societies, no. 18).
Examines the relationship of Sufi élites to popular protest, or collective action, and the specific roles that provincial and religious leaders played in rebellions directed against the French colonial régime in Algeria.

147   **France and Algeria: the problem of civil and political reform, 1870-1920.**
Vincent Confer.   Syracuse, New York: Syracuse University Press, 1966. 148p. bibliog.
This remains an important study of the middle years of French power in Algeria, a period when French civilian control had at last been established in the country and when French legislators and administrators sought to determine what civil and political rights should be conferred on the non-European residents of the Algerian *départements*. This was the moment when Muslim Algerians and the metropolitan French approached a balance of mutual respect which might have facilitated the way for harmonious political evolution. How and why it was not given a favourable opportunity in the years from 1911 to 1920 is the theme of the book.

148　**Some of ULTRA's poor relations in Algeria, Tunisia, Sicily and Italy.**
Noel Currier-Briggs. *Intelligence and National Security* (Great Britain), vol. 2, no. 2 (1987), p. 274-90.

Describes the author's experiences as a member of a cryptanalysis unit working alongside an intercept unit in the Mediterrean theatre of operations in 1942-43. The unit broke German hand cyphers and provided significant operational intelligence to the Allied forces in North Africa.

149　**Abd al-Qadir and the Algerians: resistance to the French and internal consolidation.**
Raphael Danziger.　New York; London: Holmes & Meier, 1977. 300p. 2 maps. bibliog.

This book traces the military and diplomatic resistance of the Algerians, led by Amir Abd al-Qadir (Abdel Kader), to the French conquest of Algiers in 1830 until the final victory of the French forces in 1847. In tracing the events of these seventeen years, this account emphasizes the immense practical achievements of Abd al-Qadir and presents a vivid multi-dimensional portrait of the Algerian leader.

150　**Abd al-Qadir ('Abd al-Qadir al-Jaza'iri) and Abd al-Rahman ('Abd al-Rahman al-Filali, Sultan of Morocco): religious and political aspects of their confrontation (1843-1847).**
R. Danziger.　*Maghreb Review,* no. 6 (1981), p. 27-35.

Examines some of the religious and political aspects of Abd al-Qadir's (Abdel Kader) stay in Morocco from November 1843 to September 1845, and from July 1846 to December 1847. The religious issues resulted from the rivalry between two leaders with strong claims to religious legitimacy: Abd al-Qadir, regarded in Algeria as *Amir al-Mu'minin* (Commander of the Faithful), who led the *jihad* or holy war against the French infidels; and Abd al-Rahman, who, as the duly chosen sultan, was the Imam and *Amir al-Mu'minin* in Morocco.

151　**Diplomatic deception as a last resort: Abd al-Qadir's oblique pleas to the French and the British 1846-1847.**
Raphael Danziger.　*Maghreb Review,* no. 4 (1979), p. 126-28.

Having failed to obtain support from the British, the Americans and the Ottomans against the French, or to persuade the French to cease the war against him on favourable terms, Abd al-Qadir (Abdel Kader) resorted to stratagems. In August 1846 one of his agents informed the French Consulate in Tangier that Abd al-Qadir was contemplating a takeover of the Moroccan throne and requesting France not to intervene. No such takeover was planned and the purpose of the move appears to have been to induce the French to cease their activities against his presence in Morocco. In November 1847 another of his agents approached the British Consul in Tangier stating that the French had offered him military aid if he took the Moroccan throne on the understanding that he did not become pro-British. Both moves ended in failure but are used to illustrate Abd al-Qadir's diplomatic skill as both consuls were taken in by his stratagems.

152   **From alliance to belligerency: Abd al-Qadir in Morocco 1843-1847.**
Raphael Danziger. *Maghreb Review*, vol. 5, no. 2-3 (1980), p. 63-73.
Danziger deals with the Amir Abd al-Qadir's (Abdel Kader) forced presence in
Morocco from November 1843 to September 1845 and from July 1846 to December
1847, when he used its territory as a shelter from and staging base against the French
army in Algeria. He attempts to trace the causes for and stages of the deterioration in
the relations between Abd al-Qadir and the Moroccan Sultan Abd al-Rahman, from a
virtual alliance to open belligerency.

153   **Durham et Tocqueville sur la colonisation libérale.** (Durham and
Tocqueville on liberal colonization).
Stephane Dion. *Journal of Canadian Studies* (Canada), vol. 25, no. 1
(1990), p. 60-77.
Compares Alexis de Tocqueville's writings about Algeria and John George Lambton,
1st Earl of Durham's report on Canada, stressing the similarity of ideas that the two
famous liberal colonialists shared in spite of the very different contexts. Trying to
justify, from a political as well as a moral point of view, the assimilation of the
colonized people, Tocqueville and Durham sought to conciliate colonial enterprise
with the values of universal liberalism.

154   **Hors-la-loi, violence rurale et pouvoir colonial en Algérie au debut
du XXe siècle: les frères Boutouizerat.** (Outlaws, rural violence and
colonial power in Algeria in the early 20th century: the Boutouizerat
brothers).
Abdelkader Djeghloul. *Revue de l'Occident Musulman et de la
Méditerranée* (France), no. 38 (1984), p. 37-45.
Although it had its origins in a village feud, the short-lived bandit career of the
Boutouizerat brothers in southern Algeria in 1915 led to the mobilization of
considerable armed forces. Increased taxation in the countryside and a flood of
rumours and prophecies about the First World War caused increased rural violence. In
this context, the brothers' refusal to submit became symbolic of resistance to the state.
Djeghloul argues that this kind of violence represents the intermediary stage between
early resistance to conquest and later nationalist movements.

155   **The French image of Algeria: its origin, its place in colonial
ideology, its effects on Algerian acculturation.**
Dorothea N. Gallup.   PhD dissertation, University of California, Los
Angeles, 1973. 588p. bibliog. (Available from University Microfilms,
Ann Arbor, Michigan, order no. 74-3971).
A study of French views of Algeria during the pre-colonial and colonial periods.
French images of Algeria from the 16th to the 19th centuries are based on religious
sources and accounts of various travellers and diplomats, while for the colonial period
the writings of the military and the settlers in Algeria provide the main source
material. The Algerian reaction to the French presence is studied through popular
Algerian literature of the 19th century, while fiction, journalism and political literature
of the 20th century allow study of the assimilation process of a French-educated élite.

156 **The violent decade.**
Frank Gervasi.   New York: Norton, 1989. 629p.
Author and correspondent Gervasi recounts his career, covering the Second World
War and the years immediately preceding it. During the war, he reported on the Allied
campaigns in North Africa, including Algeria, and in southern France.

157 **The passing of French Algeria.**
David C. Gordon.   London: Oxford University Press, 1966. 246p.
bibliog.
Traces the development of Algeria's identity from the centenary of French Algeria in
1930 to the overthrow of Ben Bella by Boumediène in 1965. Gordon analyses how the
vision of French Algeria faded, to be replaced by a militant nationalist ideology which
could not deny that part of Algeria's personality has remained French.

158 **Nationalisme et anti-impérialisme: la place du Maghreb dans la
stratégie Soviétique au cours des années vingt.** (Nationalism and
anti-imperialism: the place of the Maghreb in Soviet strategy in the
1920s).
Mohieddine Hadhri.   *Cahiers de Tunisie* (Tunisia), vol. 29, no. 3-4
(1981), p. 307-34.
This article discusses Soviet and Comintern policy toward anti-colonial movements in
the Maghreb from 1917 to 1925, showing how these movements seemed to confirm
the Leninist theory of colonial revolution.

159 **Albert Camus and the colonial question in Algeria.**
Alec G. Hargreaves.   *Muslim World*, vol. 77, no. 3-4 (1987),
p. 164-74.
Examines the reasons why Camus failed to comment on the question of his homeland,
Algeria, from 1956 to his death in 1958. In fact, his comments on the Algerian
situation had been muted since 1945. The main reason was Camus' knowledge that the
Muslim community had turned away from assimilation with France. Camus also never
came to terms with the racial divisiveness sustained by the political structure of his
homeland.

160 **Two ladies of colonial Algeria: the lives and times of Aurelie
Picard and Isabelle Eberhardt.**
Ursula Kingsmill Hart.   Athens, Ohio: Ohio State University Press,
1987. 140p. bibliog. (Monographs in International Studies, Africa
Series, no. 49).
Hart examines the interactions of two European women with colonial Algerian
Muslim society. Picard married into the leadership of a Sufi order, was sympathetic to
French interests in North Africa, and became a pillar of colonial society. Eberhardt,
the daughter of a Russian exile living in Switzerland, married a low ranking Algerian
officer after embracing Islam, and became critical of French policies in the region. On
Isabelle Eberhardt see also Annette Kobak's *Isabelle: the life of Isabelle Ederhardt*
(New York: Knopf, 1989. 272p.).

161   **A French colonial controversy: Captain Roudaire and the Saharan sea, 1872-83.**
Michael J. Heffernan.   *The Maghreb Review*, vol. 13, no. 3-4 (1988), p. 145-60.

A study of the life and works of Captain Roudaire, a surveyor in the French *Armée d'Afrique*, who was the architect of an ambitious project to create an immense inland sea in the Algerian and Tunisian Sahara. Inspired by the work of de Lesseps in the isthmus of Suez, he proposed to flood a series of saline depressions straddling the border between Algeria and Tunisia by means of a complex system of canals. The project provoked considerable controversy in scientific and colonial circles during the early Third Republic and provides an insight into the shifting relationship between French science and the politics of French colonialism.

162   **The limits of Utopia: Henri Duveyrier and the exploration of the Sahara in the 19th century.**
Michael Heffernan.   *Geographical Journal* (Great Britain), vol. 155, no. 3 (1989), p. 342-52.

The life and work of Henry Duveyrier (1840-92), the distinguished French geographer and explorer, is discussed in this article. He was committed to peaceful contact between Europe and Africa and was influenced by Saint-Simonian philosophy. After 1870 his utopian beliefs brought him into conflict with more agressive French imperialists. His life reveals both the centrality of geographical knowledge to the development of European colonial theory, and the complex and shifting nature of the European colonial mind in the 19th century.

163   **The Parisian poor and the colonization of Algeria during the Second Republic.**
Michael J. Heffernan.   *French History* (Great Britain), vol. 3, no. 4 (1989), p. 377-403.

Examines the French government's plan to send unemployed Parisians to colonize Algeria following the insurrection of June 1848. The project failed because of insufficient planning, funding and administration, which reflected a fundamental confusion over the colonies' role and purpose. Ultimately this episode reflected the ambiguity and short-sightedness of early French colonial policy.

164   **The French conquest of Algiers, 1830: an Algerian tradition.**
Alf Andrew Heggoy.   Athens, Ohio: Ohio University, Center for International Studies, 1986. 92p. bibliog. (Monographs in International Studies, Africa Series, no. 48).

Provides English translations of four texts selected from the corpus of songs, poems and stories by Algerian storytellers and poets, *jawwal* and *meddah* (itinerant poets, minstrels) recounting and commenting on the French conquest and rule in Algeria, 1830-1930. Three of the texts are accounts of the French conquest of Algiers in July 1830. The fourth comments on this event, but is a more general evaluation of the 'French achievements in Algeria'. It is composed of testimonies recorded from a number of sheikhs from the town of Blida and its region around 1910. All of the texts were originally published in French between 1853 and 1930. The translations are accompanied by introductory and concluding essays that provide some historical background, and an overview of various theoretical and methodological issues involved in the use of oral traditions by historians of Algeria. The work demonstrates the wealth and variety of information to be found in Algerian oral tradition and its potential value as a source for the study of Algerian history.

165 Agency Africa: Rygor's Franco-Polish network and Operation Torch.

John Herman. *Journal of Contemporary History* (Great Britain), vol. 22, no. 4 (1987), p. 681-706.

Major-General Rygor Slowikowski's Franco-Polish intellgence network – Agency Africa (Agency Rygor) – proved a valuable adjunct to the American Office of Strategic Services (OSS) in connection with Operation Torch, 1942.

166 France and Islam. The Haut Comité Méditerranéen and French North Africa.

William A. Hoisington, Jr. In: *North Africa: nation, state and region.* Edited by George Joffé. London; New York: Routledge, 1993, p. 78-90.

Underlines how French colonial politicians failed to understand the nature of popular rejection of assimilation into France and the French 'Mission civilisatrice'. It was this rejection throughout French North Africa that not only made the development of national movements of independence possible, but also set the scene, ultimately, for Maghrebi assumptions of a regional identity that were eventually to surface in the creation of the Maghreb Arab Union.

167 Histoire de l'Algérie contemporaine: la conquête et les débuts de la colonisation (1827-1871). (History of contemporary Algeria: the conquest and the beginning of colonization, 1827-1871).

Charles-André Julien. Paris: Presses Universitaires de France, 1964. 632p. 6 maps. bibliog.

This lengthy volume examines in great detail the French conquest of Algiers and the progress of the military occupation of the northern coastlands of Algeria. It describes the campaign against the Algerian nationalist leader, Abdel Kader, the consolidation of military rule, military administration and the first colonization schemes. It constitutes a basic reference work on the first decades of French rule in Algeria.

168 The impact of the French conquest of Algeria on Morocco (1830-1912).

Mohammed Kenbib. In: *North Africa: nation, state and region.* Edited by George Joffé. London; New York: Routledge, 1993, p. 34-48.

In this article, Kenbib focusses on Moroccan reactions to the French occupation of western Algeria, particularly to the consequences of Morocco's defeat at the battle of Isly in 1845. He suggests that after the initial Moroccan response in support of Emir Abdel Kader, the presence of a large body of Algerian immigrants on Moroccan territory between 1845 and 1912 caused a political alienation between the two communities and the growth of a more modern sense of secular nationalism.

169 **Algerian nationalism and the Allied military strategy and propaganda during the Second World War: the background to Sétif.**
Mohamed Khenouf, Michael Brett. In: *Africa and the Second World War*. Edited by David Killingray, Richard Rathbone. Basingstoke, England: Macmillan, 1986, p. 258-74.

A short study of the effects of the Anglo-American presence on Algerian nationalism after the November landings of 1942 as the background to the violence which erupted in Sétif in May 1945.

170 **Arms and the man: Abd el-Kader.**
John King. *History Today*, (Britain), no. 40 (August 1990), p. 22-28.

Argues that Emir Abdel Kader, leader of a revolt against the French in western Algeria until his defeat in 1847, may have received clandestine shipments of arms from the British, who wanted to prevent French expansion into Morocco.

171 **A study in radio propaganda broadcasts in French from North and West African radio stations, 8 November 1942-14 December 1942.**
Paul J. Kingston. *Revue d'Histoire Maghrébine* (Tunisia), vol. 11, no. 33-34 (1984), p. 127-41.

Covers BBC monitoring reports, offering an insight into aspects of early attempts by the Allies at ideological reeducation of a population in favour of Vichy's Révolution Nationale. Contrasts appear between French North African broadcasts and those of the Radiodiffusion Nationale Française (RDN), which dominated broadcasting in metropolitan France. Though under indirect German control, the RDN was not a puppet like the Nazi Radio Paris, but represented the Free French radio network. Stations covered include Radio Algiers.

172 **One Spanish military mission to Algiers (1844-45).**
Victor Morales Lezcano. *Revue d'Histoire Maghrébine* (Tunisia), vol. 12, no. 37-38 (1985), p. 48-52.

As a result of growing concern in Spain about the French occupation of Algeria, a military mission was sent to Algiers in 1844, ostensibly to follow the efforts of the French to overcome the resistance led by Abdel Kader in the west of the country. The mission provided the Spanish army with an invaluable insight into the methods being used to subdue Algeria and encouraged a renewal of Spanish curiosity about the past and present of North African societies. The papers of the two members of the mission, Lieutenant Colonel Crispin Jiminez de Sandoval and Captain Antonio Madero y Vivero, are of interest for the history of the western Ottoman Empire and European colonial rivalries.

173 **State building failure in British Ireland and French Algeria.**
Ian Lustick. Berkeley, California: Institute of International Studies, University of California, 1985. 119p. bibliog. (Research Series, no. 63).

Analyses the causes which contributed to Britain and France's inability to retain Ireland and Algeria respectively within their political domain. Lustick stresses the role played by the settlers from the metropolitan country in frustrating attempts to incorporate indigenous élites into the local power structure, and the need to integrate a study of state formation with theories of imperialism and decolonization.

174 **Le gouvernement du Front Populaire et la poussée nationaliste au Maghreb (1936-1937).** (The government of the Popular Front and nationalist pressure in the Maghreb, 1936-37).
Samya el-Mechat. *Revue d'Histoire Maghrébine* (Tunisia), vol. 11, no. 33-34 (1984), p. 85-91.

Swept along by the impetus of the Popular Front, Maghreb nationalists were persuaded that all desired reforms would be put into effect and informed A. Julien, the secretary-general of the Haut Comité Méditerranéen, of their claims. He was known to be sympathetic toward the nationalist cause. The idea of separatism had been fostered since the decision by Governor General Le Beau to insure public order and enforce respect for the security of citizens and their property. This did not prevent the nationalist parties from pursuing action, including the Communist Party, the Society of the Ulemas and Messali Hadj's North African Star.

175 **North Africa in the strategy and politics of the Axis powers, 1936-1943.**
Helmut J. F. Mejcher. *Cahiers de Tunisie* (Tunisia), vol. 29, no. 3-4 (1981) p. 629-48.

Discusses aspects of German and Italian policy in North Africa between 1936 and 1943, including the question of German war aims in North Africa and the fate of Hajj Muhammad Amin al-Husseini's campaign for the independence of North Africa at the hands of Italy and Germany in 1942-43.

176 **The British in Barbary through the records of an English church in Algiers.**
Alan G. Munro. *Maghreb Review* (Great Britain), vol. 13, no. 3-4 (1988), p. 183-90.

A discussion of the plaques installed in Holy Trinity Anglican church in Algiers by Robert Lambert Playfair, British consul-general from 1867 to 1896, as sources for the British role in North-west Africa from the late 16th century.

177 **Notes on French expansion in the Mediterranean during the nineteenth and twentieth centuries.**
André Nouschi. *Mediterranean Historical Review* (Great Britain), vol. 1, no. 1 (1986), p. 86-99.

Examines French colonial policy in the Mediterranean region from the time of the first expedition to Algiers in 1830 to Algerian independence in 1962. The French did not originally intend to colonize Algeria, but French soldiers and many non-French Europeans soon settled there. The French legal and educational systems became dominant in the region, and they played a role in inspiring the nationalist movements that eventually overthrew the French colonial system.

178 **Rural North East Algeria 1919-1938.**
Thomas Park. *Peasant Studies*, vol. 15, no. 2 (1988), p. 117-28.
Park critically reviews Johan H. Meuleman's 'Le Constantinois entre les deux guerres mondiales. L'évolution économique et sociale de la population rurale' (The Constantinois district between the two world wars. The economic and social evolution of the rural population) (1985), which studies the north-eastern Algerian department of Constantine between the two world wars and demonstrates that deterioration in the economic position of the peasantry there was a direct result of French colonial policy.

179 **Les étudiants algériens de l'université française, 1880-1962.**
(Algerian students of French university education, 1880-1962).
Guy Perville. Paris: Editions du CNRS, 1984. 346p. bibliog.
Examines the educational and socialization experiences of Algeria's élite stratum of Muslim university students and intellectuals during the pre-independence period (1880-1962) and the impact these experiences have had on the country's ambivalent cultural identity. The work is organized along three major themes: the development of Muslim students in the period leading to the beginning of the war of independence in 1954; the role of such students during the revolutionary war with a special focus on the activities of the student union (UGEMA) during that struggle; and an analysis of the ideological orientations of Muslim intellectuals in the years 1906-62. Perville shows how French educational policies disrupted Algerian cultural development by bifurcating society into two polar extremes, a Gallicized, Western-oriented élite cut off from and alien to the mass of illiterate and poorly educated Arabs and Berbers.

180 **The dark side of Beau Geste – the conquest of the Sahara.**
Douglas Porch. *Proceedings of the Annual Meeting of the Western Society for French History*, no. 10 (1984), p. 219-30.
A study of the military strategy and tactics of Theodore Pein and Henri Laperrine, who were jointly responsible for the French conquest of the west-central Sahara in the late 19th and early 20th centuries. Conventional historiography ascribed the conquest to the ingenious adaptability of native fighting traditions and the inspired use of native troops in the service of France. A closer look reveals unimaginative and fortuitous policies originating in Europe, not North Africa, and succeeding only by dogged and dishonest persistence.

181 **The archives of *Algérie imaginaire*.**
David Prochaska. *History and Anthropology* (Great Britain), vol. 4, no. 2 (1990), p. 373-420.
Reveals how the picture postcards of colonial Algeria, known as 'scenes and types', produced in the first three decades of the 20th century, presented stereotyped images of 'typical' Algerians in standardized 'exotic' contexts. The images were strongly influenced by the tradition of Orientalist painting and by the 19th-century idea of the 'picturesque', showing a static, unhistorical world as contrasted with the 'progressive' world of the French colonizers.

182 **Making Algeria French and unmaking French Algeria.**
David Prochaska. *Journal of Historical Sociology* (Great Britain),
vol. 3, no. 4 (1990), p. 305-28.

The making of colonial Algeria is viewed as a classic case of settler colonialism and the formation by the First World War of a distinctive colonial society and culture. Whereas the Algerians tend to view 'Algérie Algérienne' as the successful result of an unbroken tradition of resistance to the French throughout the colonial period, here the unmaking of 'Algérie Française' is presented in a manner which illuminates the historically contingent nature of Algerian nationalism by tracing over time the multiple and divergent strands of which it was composed.

183 **Making Algeria French: colonialism in Bône, 1870-1920.**
David Prochaska. New York: Cambridge University Press; Paris:
Maison des Sciences de l'Homme, 1990. 328p. bibliog.

This study of French settler colonialism in the Algerian port city of Bône, now Annaba, concentrates on the formative decades of settler society and culture between 1870 and 1920. After an overview of Bône in 1830, and a survey of French rule from 1830 to 1870, it describes in turn the town's economic, social, political and cultural history to the end of the First World War. The author argues that in making Bône a European city in the 19th and early 20th centuries, the settlers effectively blocked social evolution, attempted to contain history, and thereby precluded any genuine *rapprochement* with the Algerians in the 20th century.

184 **La vérité sur la mort de Darlan.** (The truth about the death of
Darlan).
Philippe Ragueneau. *Historama* (France), no. 23 (1986), p. 20-27.

A personal account of the assassination in Algiers on 24 December 1942 of Admiral Darlan, Commander-in-Chief of the French Armed Forces. Ragueneau maintains that the assassin, Fernand Bonnier de la Chapelle, was acting according to orders from the Count of Paris, although the elimination of Darlan benefited all the political forces then in play in North Africa; de Gaulle, Pétain and the Allied forces.

185 **L'émigration ouvrière italienne dans le Maghreb et les
répercussions algériennes après la constitution du comité
d'entr'aide des mineurs italiens du groupe de 'Il Minatore' (1907).**
(Italian labour migration to North Africa and its effects in Algeria after the formation of the Italian miners' self-help committee by the group from 'Il Minatore' [1907]).
Romain Rainero. *Cahiers de Tunisie* (Tunisia), vol. 29, no. 1-2
(1981), p. 83-99.

From an almost complete collection of *Il Minatore*, a miners' political weekly published in Tunis and distributed in Tunisia and Algeria from February to August 1907, this article discusses the syndicalist and socialist movement started by Italian immigrant workers, emphasizing the solidarity of the Italians with their Arab co-workers.

186 **British attitude to the French conquest of Algeria 1830-71.**
Joelle Redouane. *Maghreb Review*, vol. 15, no. 1-2 (1990), p. 2-5.
The article demonstrates that when Algiers fell to the French on 5 July 1830 Britain bowed to the inevitable but that her resentment was slow to disappear. However, Britain did not respond to the Algerians' appeals, even when the press praised Abdel Kader, the leader of the resistance. By 1850-51 British opinion had changed and French rule was formally acknowledged. The image of the Algerians was soon to deteriorate when Algiers became a wintering resort for British invalids in the 1860s. Moreover, the country's economic importance to the British still seemed uncertain, although some producers in Algeria were hoping for British participation. When the great insurrection of 1871 took place, the British, far from resenting the conquest of Algeria by France, came to approve of it. For more details about the British and Algeria during the period of French colonial rule see Joelle Redouane's doctoral thesis 'Les Anglais et l'Algérie 1830-1930' (The English and Algeria 1830-1930) (Thèse de doctorat unique d'histoire contemporaine soutenue à Rennes II, France, 1988).

187 **Irish in Algeria 1830-1930.**
Joelle Annie Redouane. *Éire-Ireland*, vol. 21, no. 4 (1986), p. 3-10.
Discusses the impact made by Irish immigrants to Algeria on the British community there between 1830 and 1930. Despite several schemes to attract Irish labour, few Irish settlers actually stayed. A few notable personalities are mentioned in some detail.

188 **La présence anglaise en Algérie de 1830 à 1930.** (The English presence in Algeria from 1830 to 1930).
Joelle Redouane. *Revue de l'Occident Musulman et de la Méditerranée* (France), no. 38 (1984), p. 15-36.
Explains that there were few English people in Algeria between 1830 and 1853, but that the Second Empire saw the establishment of an English colony formed by rich convalescents wintering in Algiers. In addition, the first British investments in colonial Algeria were made during this period. Anglo-Algerian trade developed during the 1890s, but winter residents still formed the basis of a self-contained English colony that had little contact with either the French or the Arabs and was based at Mustapha. Anglo-Algerian trade declined after 1918, and the crash of 1929 put an end to the colony.

189 **Le Cardinal Lavigerie 1825-1892: l'église, l'Afrique et la France.**
(Cardinal Lavigerie 1825-1892: the Church, Africa and France).
François Renault. Paris: Fayard, 1992. 698p. bibliog.
A biography of Lavigerie who was Cardinal Archbishop of Algiers. The book includes an interesting discussion of the problem of 're-establishing' and expanding the Catholic Church in North Africa. It shows how missionary activity in Kabylia mistakenly hoped to excavate and build upon some residual Berber Christianity, and how attempts to extend missionary work to the Sahara suffered from faulty appreciations of Tuareg politics.

190 **Economic motives and French imperialism: the 1837 Tafna Treaty as a case study.**
Richard A. Roughton. *Historian*, vol. 47, no. 3 (1985), p. 360-81.

Political and military interpretations have usually been employed by historians to explain the French conquest and colonization of Algeria. However, Roughton argues that economic conditions significantly influenced French policy in Algeria during the 1830s with advocates of Marseilles' commercial interests supporting colonization as beneficial to all of France. French concern for cost and commercial profits, coupled with disagreements over how to make Algeria profitable, led to various policy shifts. These shifts are examined through the Treaty of Tafna as French commercial interests were continually thwarted in Algeria.

191 **Algerian landownership and rural leadership, 1860-1940: a quantitative approach.**
Peter von Sivers. *Maghreb Review*, vol. 3, no. 2 (1979), p. 58-62.

Points out that very little empirical work exists which traces the transformation of Algerian social structures prior to the First World War. The social history of the political upper stratum of Algerians, the rural notables who fulfilled administrative functions in French services, is practically unknown. Even though the charge of political insignificance might possess merits, it is argued that the Algerian notables were not economic midgets. The landed and agricultural wealth represented by the political upper stratum allowed its members to wield considerable economic influence. This article investigates the evolution of this politically weak but economically powerful body of notables from the decisive angle of personal income.

192 **Insurrection and accommodation: indigenous leadership in eastern Algeria 1840-1900.**
Peter von Sivers. *International Journal of Middle East Studies*, no. 6 (1975), p. 259-75.

Surveys the changing status, both political and socio-economic, of three notable families of the Constantinois – the Banu Gana, the Bu Akkaz and the Banu Shanaf – over a sixty-year period. In tracing relations between these groups, as well as their relations with the French authorities, the author identifies three significant and distinct phases, ranging from Banu Gana aristocratic hegemony (1839-54) through a period of fierce interclan rivalry (1854-79) and ending in accommodation accompanied by a general decline in the actual political influence held by any one of the three families.

193 **The French stake in Algeria, 1945-1962.**
Tony Smith. Ithaca, New York; London: Cornell University Press, 1978. 199p. map. bibliog.

This book interprets French policy in Algeria from the end of the Second World War until Algerian independence in 1962. It examines the French stake in Algeria and confronts the question of why French disengagement proved so difficult.

194 **Screening 'Torch': Allied counter-intelligence and the Spanish threat to the secrecy of the Allied invasion of French North Africa in November 1942.**
Denis Smyth. *Intelligence and National Security* (Great Britain), vol. 4, no. 2 (1989), p. 335-56.

British and American preparations for the invasion of Morocco and Algeria in November 1942, Operation Torch, included concern that Spanish and German intelligence agents would learn the secret. German observers and scientific sensors provided very accurate information on shipping in the Strait of Gibraltar and military activity on Gibraltar itself.

195 **Les mémoires de Messali Hadj: aspects du manuscrit original.**
(Memoirs of Messali Hadj: aspects of the original manuscript).
Benjamin Stora. *Revue de l'Occident Musulman et de la Méditerranée* (France), no. 36 (1983), p. 75-101.

Examines and discusses the differences between the manuscript of Messali Hadj's memoirs, which covers the period 1898-1938, and the published version (1982). The vast manuscript is written in the discursive, circular style of an Arab folktale and also contains long quotations from newspaper articles, although Messali mainly relies on memory. Some of the major themes include Messali's religious outlook, his view of the colonial régime in Algeria, the relations between Arab nationalism and the French Left in the 1920s and 1930s, and the experience of Arab workers in France.

196 **Messali Hadj; pionnier du nationalisme algérien, 1898-1974.**
(Messali Hadj: pioneer of Algerian nationalism, 1898-1974).
Benjamin Stora. Paris: L'Harmattan, 1987. 304p. (Histoire et Perspectives Méditerranéennes).

A profile of the Algerian nationalist leader, Messali Hadj (Hadj Ali Abdel Kader), who founded the Etoile Nord-Africaine in 1926 which from the outset pursued a nationalist and radical programme including the independence of Algeria and the withdrawal of French troops. His striking characteristics are seen as his independence and his deep-seated commitment to liberty.

197 **Thomas-Robert Bugeaud, France and Algeria, 1784-1849: politics, power and the good society.**
Antony Thrall Sullivan. Hamden, Connecticut: The Shoe String Press, 1983. 216p. bibliog.

Bugeaud was Governor-General and Commander-in-Chief of French forces in Algeria from 1841 to 1847. The focus here is on Bugeaud's attempts to use Algeria to profit rural France, and his efforts to convert both French soldiers and Muslim warriors into settlers and peasants. The work emphasizes the importance of the savage North African war of the 1840s in changing Bugeaud from a supporter of Centrism and *le juste milieu* to an extremist and advocate of unrestricted military violence.

198   **The Europeanized Algerians and the emancipation of Algeria.**
Salah al Din al Zein el-Tayib.   *Middle Eastern Studies* (Great Britain),
vol. 22, no. 2 (1986), p. 206-35.

Europeanized Algerians were politically active from about 1911, and they all belonged to the liberal professions, were educated in France, and initially pressed for assimilation into France. This solution was eventually rejected, but the group continued to press for French citizenship and a separation of religion and state. After the Second World War the predominant form of relationship advocated changed, moving through repudiation of assimilation, to self-rule, autonomy, federation, statehood and finally full independence.

199   **French scientific expeditions to Africa during the July Monarchy.**
Maxine Taylor.   *Proceedings of the Annual Meeting of the Western
Society for French History*, no. 16 (1989), p. 243-52.

Studies the extent to which the July Monarchy controlled the Regency of Algiers by examining scientific expeditions to North Africa in the early 19th century. Unlike exploration in the Pacific, which followed navy and merchant marines, the scientific conquest of North Africa occurred simultaneously with the network of soldiers and entrepreneurs who were also discovering the continent for the first time. The data collected by these 'scientists' was not only used to further science but used and retained by the French government in 'the best interests of France'.

200   **L'Algérie politique: histoire et société.** (Political Algeria: history and
society).
Jean-Claude Vatin.   Paris: Presses de Fondation Nationale des
Sciences Politiques, 1983. rev. ed. 389p. bibliog.

Focuses on the impact of French domination on Algerian society from1830 to 1962 in order to provide the background essential to understanding contemporary Algeria. Vatin argues that Algeria was a society in the process of constructing a nation in 1830. The colonial conquest dealt a telling blow to that process, but Vatin shows how Algerian society absorbed this shock and then undertook its own reconstruction. He claims that by forcing Algerians off their own land and onto colonial estates, the *colons* triggered the very adaptations that eventually produced a coherent nationalist movement. There are thoughtful analyses of the assimilationist and Islamic currents of protest against the colonial order. The revised edition contains an essay discussing major writings on Algerian history that appeared between 1974 and 1982.

201   **Front populaire, front national: the colonial example.**
Irwin M. Wall.   *International Labor and Working Class History*,
no. 30 (1986), p. 32-43.

The author distinguishes between two types of alliance embraced by the French Communist Party during the 1930s. The popular front strategy called for an alliance with other elements on the Left to pursue certain goals, including the liberation and self-determination of people in French overseas territories like Algeria. The national front strategy called for alliance with any non-fascist group and sought strong ties between the French and their overseas peoples to prevent fascist incursions into the outlying entities. The strategies were conflicting, but the national strategy prevailed and replaced that of the popular front.

202 **OSS and Operation Torch.**
David A. Walker. *Journal of Contemporary History* (Great Britain),
vol. 22, no. 4 (1987), p. 667-79.

Operation Torch was the name given to the Allied landings in North Africa beginning in November 1942. The American Office of Strategic Services (OSS), set up in July 1942, helped to prepare the way for this operation by collecting military intelligence. They also carried out extensive investigation of the motives of the Vichy French occupying the area. Their military work bore fruit, but their anticipated success in winning French neutrality did not come about.

203 **La franc-maçonnerie française et les Algériens musulmans
(1787-1962).** (French freemasonry and the Muslim Algerians,
1787-1962).
Xavier Yacono. *Anales de Historia Contemporanea* (Spain), no. 6
(1987), p. 103-25.

Despite the apparent contradiction of their respective religions, Catholics, Protestants, Jews and Muslims sometimes became freemasons. In Algeria, French freemasons sometimes confused Muslim religious brotherhoods with masonic lodges, but freemasonry itself attracted individual Muslims, notably Abdel Kader, as the 'supreme religion of brotherhood'.

204 **The rise and fall of the movement of Messali Hadj in Algeria,
1924-1954.**
Janet Dorsch Zagoria. PhD dissertation, Columbia University, New
York, 1973. 381p. bibliog. (Available from University Microfilms, Ann
Arbor, Michigan, order no. 74-12,775).

A study of the Messalist movement, one of the four branches of the Algerian nationalist movement in the period prior to 1954. It was the largest, most radical branch of that movement, being the only one with a substantial mass following and an explicit commitment to independence and had a leader of unusual qualities. Yet Messali not only failed to take Algeria to independence, but he was pushed aside at the crucial moment. His movement virtually collapsed in 1954 when the Algerian war of liberation began.

The Maghreb in the modern world: Algeria, Tunisia, Morocco.
See item no. 4.

**The making of contemporary Algeria, 1830-1987: colonial upheavals and
post-independence development.**
See item no. 8.

State and revolution in Algeria.
See item no. 36.

A history of the Maghrib in the Islamic period.
See item no. 92.

Modern Algeria: a history from 1830 to the present.
See item no. 93.

North Africa 1800-1900: a survey from the Nile valley to the Atlantic.
See item no. 97.

Modern Algeria: the origins and development of a nation.
See item no. 98.

Le miroir: aperçu historique et statistique sur la Régence d'Alger.
See item no. 121.

Arguments for the conquest of Algiers in the late eighteenth and early nineteenth centuries.
See item no. 125.

Barbary and enlightenment: European attitudes towards the Maghreb in the eighteenth century.
See item no. 126.

Algeria – rebellion and revolution.
See item no. 229.

Insurgency and counterinsurgency in Algeria.
See item no. 232.

La migration Européenne en Algérie au XIXe siècle: migration organisée ou migration tolérée?
See item no. 270.

The Jews of North Africa during the Second World War.
See item no. 273.

A propos du pogrom de Constantine (Août 1934).
See item no. 276.

L'affirmation identitaire berbère à partir de 1900, constantes et mutations (Kabylie).
See item no. 279.

The Algiers riot, January 1898.
See item no. 280.

Colonialism and after: an Algerian Jewish community.
See item no. 283.

Three Kabyles and French assimilationism: Ait Ahmed, Feraoun, and Ibazizen.
See item no. 284.

A history of the Jews in North Africa: Volume II. From the Ottoman conquests to the present time.
See item no. 286.

Islam and state expansion in Algeria: nineteenth-century Saharan frontiers.
See item no. 287.

Migration, commerce and community: the Mizabis in eighteenth and nineteenth century Algeria.
See item no. 288.

Muslim responses to French imperialism: an Algerian Saharan case study.
See item no. 289.

Opposing aspects of colonial rule in this century to 1930: the unusual case of the Beni Mzab.
See item no. 292.

Le développement politique en Algérie: étude des populations de la région du M'Zab.
See item no. 294.

The Tijaniyya: a sufi order in the modern world.
See item no. 315.

Islam, politics and social movements.
See item no. 317.

A rereading of Islamic texts in the Maghreb in the nineteenth and early twentieth centuries: secular themes or religious reformism?
See item no. 318.

Algerian Islam in a time of transition c. 1890-c. 1930.
See item no. 319.

An Islamic humanist in the 20th century: Malik Bennabi.
See item no. 320.

Political ends and means of transport in the colonial North African pilgrimage.
See item no. 321.

In the eye of the beholder: sufi and saint in North Africa and the colonial production of knowledge, 1830-1900.
See item no. 323.

Cultural resistance and religious legitimacy in colonial Algeria.
See item no. 325.

'Abd Al-Qadir Al-Jaza'iri and Islamic reform.
See item no. 326.

The denunciation of mysticism as a bulwark against reason – a contribution to the expansion of Algerian reformism 1925-1939.
See item no. 328.

The servants of the mosques.
See item no. 330.

Le réformisme musulman en Algérie de 1925 à 1940 – essai d'histoire religieuse et sociale.
See item no. 331.

The Algerian ulamas, 1919-1931.
See item no. 333.

The role of the ulama in the Algerian revolution: 1945-1954.
See item no. 334.

Alms and arms: the combative saintliness of the Awlad Sidi Shaykh in the Algerian Sahara, sixteenth-nineteenth centuries.
See item no. 335.

The ulama and Islamic renaissance in Algeria.
See item no. 336.

My life story: the autobiography of a Berber woman.
See item no. 339.

Origins of the Algerian proletariat.
See item no. 342.

Le café maure. Sociabilité masculine et effervescence citoyenne (Algérie XVIIe-XXe siècles).
See item no. 345.

Women in Middle Eastern history: shifting boundaries in sex and gender.
See item no. 355.

The decline of tribal organisation in the Souf (S.E. Algeria).
See item no. 356.

The emergence of classes in Algeria: a study of colonialism and socio-political change.
See item no. 360.

Old and new élites in North Africa: the French colonial impact in comparative perspective.
See item no. 364.

Les classes moyennes au Maghreb.
See item no. 373.

The political and the religious in the modern history of the Maghrib.
See item no. 421.

Islamic law: social and historical contexts.
See item no. 488.

Career patterns of late nineteenth century Algerian Muslim magistrates.
See item no. 490.

An inquiry into the origins of the Algerian medjlis crisis of 1858.
See item no. 491.

Muslim law courts and the French colonial state in Algeria.
See item no. 492.

Orientalism, colonialism, and legal history: the attack on Muslim family endowments in Algeria and India.
See item no. 502.

Manuel des institutions algériennes de la domination turque à l'indépendance. Tome premier – la domination turque et le régime militaire 1518-1870.
See item no. 504.

Administration et tribu chez les Nemencha (Algérie) au XIXe siècle.
See item no. 505.

Etre caid dans l'Algérie coloniale.
See item no. 506.

Les bureaux arabes dans l'Algérie de la conquête.
See item no. 507.

Qaids, captains, and colons: French military administration in the colonial Maghrib, 1844-1934.
See item no. 509.

Indigenous administrators in Algeria, 1846-1914: manipulation and manipulators.
See item no. 511.

French and Algerian identities from colonial times to the present: a century of interaction.
See item no. 535.

Le commerce caravanier au Maghreb et ses mutations au course de l'ère précoloniale.
See item no. 625.

British trade with Algeria in the nineteenth century: an ally against France?
See item no. 628.

The development of commercial agriculture in Algeria, 1830-1970.
See item no. 670.

Land policy in colonial Algeria: the origins of the rural public domain.
See item no. 672.

La dépossession des fellahs (1830-1962).
See item no. 673.

Terroirs et sociétés au Maghreb et au Moyen Orient.
See item no. 681.

Patterns of emigration, 1905-1954: 'Kabyles' and 'Arabs'.
See item no. 708.

Vers un syndicalisme national en Algérie (1946-1956).
See item no. 721.

Contribution du syndicalisme au mouvement de libération nationale en Oranie (Ouest Algérien) 1945-56.
See item no. 726.

Interest groups and decolonization: American businessmen and organised labour in French North Africa.
See item no. 727.

Immigrants and political activists: Algerian nationalists in France, 1945-54.
See item no. 729.

Doctrine et action syndicales en Algérie.
See item no. 730.

The landscape of colonialism: the impact of French colonial rule on the Algerian settlement pattern, 1830-1987.
See item no. 742.

Changes in political succession, marital strategies and 'noble'/'vassal' relations in precolonial Ahaggar.
See item no. 763.

The nomads of Algeria under French rule: a study of social and economic change.
See item no. 767.

Les intellectuels et le pouvoir: Syrie, Egypte, Tunisie, Algérie.
See item no. 769.

Instituteurs algériens, 1883-1939.
See item no. 770.

French influence on North African education 1880-1962: an introduction.
See item no. 773.

Polémiques autour du premier Grand Prix littéraire de l'Algérie. La situation des lettres algériennes en 1921.
See item no. 783.

Le mouvement intellectuel et littéraire à la fin du XIXe et au debut du XXe siècle.
See item no. 784.

Le Grand Prix littéraire de l'Algérie (1921-1961).
See item no. 790.

Un romancier de l'identité perturbée et de l'assimilation impossible: Chukri Khodja.
See item no. 796.

Algeria and its history: colonial myths and the forging and decontructing of identity in pied-noir literature.
See item no. 799.

Colonial writers between the wars.
See item no. 801.

Location and identity: reflections in three pied-noir novels, 1949-1959.
See item no. 802.

Naissance du cinéma algérien.
See item no. 814.

La politique culturelle de l'Algérie.
See item no. 816.

Aspects de l'artisanat en Afrique du Nord.
See item no. 817.

Algerian theatre and protest.
See item no. 826.

Affrontements culturels dans l'Algérie coloniale: écoles, médecines, religion, 1830-1880.
See item no. 827.

The army at Vincennes: archives for the study of North African history in the colonial period.
See item no. 830.

La guerre d'Algérie par les documents. Vol. 1 L'Avertissement: 1943-1946.
See item no. 832.

Une lettre de l'Emir Abdelkader datée de 1880 aux archives de Sidi bel-Abbes.
See item no. 833.

Bibliographie raisonnée sur l'émir Abdelkader.
See item no. 863.

War of Independence

205 The question.
Henri Alleg, translated by John Calder. London: Calder, 1958. 98p.

A testimony by the French editor of *L'Alger Républicain*, a newspaper which was banned in September 1955. Alleg was arrested by the French authorities and tortured to make him reveal who had hidden him.

206 Algeria before the United Nations.
Mohamed Alwan. New York: Speller, 1959. 114p. bibliog.

A brief history of the arguments and deliberations on the Algerian problem at the United Nations, and the actions taken by the UN Assembly. The position taken up by various countries and the proposals put forward are described. Appendices contain the voting record and the resolutions.

207 Algeria: anticolonial war.
Djamila Amrane. In: *Female soldiers – combatants or non-combatants? Historical and contemporary perspectives.* Edited by Nancy Loring Goldman. Westport, Connecticut: Greenwood Press, 1982, p. 123-35.

Discusses the role played by women during Algeria's struggle for independence.

208 Des femmes dans la guerre d'Algérie: entretiens. (Women in the Algerian war: interviews).
Edited by Danièle Djamila Amrane-Minne. Paris: Karthala, 1994. 218p.

The author, who participated in the War of Independence and was imprisoned, presents interviews with thirty women, including some of European origin, who also participated in the struggle for independence.

209 French politics and Algeria. The process of policy formation 1954-1962.
William G. Andrews. New York: Appleton-Century-Crofts, 1962. 204p. chronology.

A study of the French constitutional system in operation, its policy-making machinery and its responsiveness to press and public opinion. The author analyses its weaknesses and describes how the inability to deal with the Algerian problem led to the fall of the Fourth Republic and continued to trouble de Gaulle's Fifth Republic up to the time of the Evian negotiations.

210 **Djamila Boupacha. The story of the torture of a young Algerian girl which shocked liberal French opinion.**
Simone de Beauvoir, Gisèle Halimi, translated by Peter Green. New York: Macmillan; London: Deutsch with Weidenfeld & Nicolson, 1962. 246p.

This book chronicles Boupacha's attempt to have her torturers indicted in the face of the complicity and connivance of the authorities in Algeria.

211 **La gauche chrétienne et la guerre d'Algérie.** (The Christian Left and the Algerian war).
Renée Bédarida, commentary by Jacques Julliard and André Mandouze. *Cahiers de l'Institut d'Histoire du Temps Présent* (France), no. 9 (1988), p. 89-104.

Opposed to nationalist French Catholics, a Catholic Left supported Algerian independence movements and urged a policy of decolonization of the country. Although such persons also supported the independence of Indochina, Morocco and Tunisia, they were most radical and demanding about Algeria. The intransigence of the government and most public opinion of France pushed the Catholic Left away from a vision of Algerian economic development in free association with France and toward a vision of complete separation of the two nations.

212 **Law and the Algerian revolution.**
Mohammed Bedjaoui. Brussels: International Association of Democratic Lawyers, 1961. 260p. map.

Examines the status of the Algerian state and the provisional government in international law as recognized by the international community and embodied in the principles of the United Nations.

213 **The Algerian problem.**
Edward Behr. Harmondsworth, England: Penguin Books, 1961; London: Greenwood Press, 1976. 252p. 2 maps. bibliog.

A succinct and readable account of the history of French involvement in Algeria, and the background to and unfolding of the war of liberation, up to the negotiations at Evian.

214 **The gangrene.**
Abdel Kader Belhadj, Bechir Boumaza (and others), translated by Robert Silvers. New York: Lyle Stuart, 1960. 96p.

This book exposes the torture of Algerians in France by the DST (*Direction de Surveillance Territoire*), the Paris security police, during the War of Independence. The original French edition was seized by the French police and the book was condemned by the French government as 'a tissue of lies and Communist propaganda'.

215 **Le protestantisme français et la guerre d'Algérie.** (French
Protestantism and the Algerian war).
Pierre Bolle. *Cahiers de l'Institut d'Histoire du Temps Présent*
(France), no. 9 (1988), p. 47-59.

Surveys texts issuing from the Reformed Church of France and the Protestant
Federation of France on the Algerian War of Independence. The religious leadership
did not hesitate to condemn the police use of torture or to organize relief efforts on
behalf of refugees, but reluctance to allow politics to enter church deliberations
sometimes led to an uncomfortable silence. Their foremost concern was the desire for
peace and justice.

216 **Algerian voices.**
Richard M. Brace, Joan Brace.   Princeton, New Jersey: Van Nostrand,
1965. 233p.

The sequel to *Ordeal in Algeria* (see below). The book is based on conversations in
Tunis with members of the provisional government of Algeria in 1961 and early 1962.
It continues the story of Algeria's struggle for independence and seeks to understand
and explain the actions of the Algerian nationalists.

217 **Ordeal in Algeria.**
Richard M. Brace, Joan Brace.   Princeton, New Jersey: Van Nostrand,
1960. 401p.

A detailed political history and analysis of the progress of the insurrection in Algeria
up to 1960. It also contains a good section on the background to the revolt and the
history of Algeria between the two World Wars.

218 **The Algerian war on the French stage.**
David Bradby. *French Cultural Studies*, vol. 5, pt. 2, no. 14 (June
1994), p. 179-89.

Despite the politicization of the French theatre in the 1960s, it was not until the 1980s
that certain French playwrights decided to write about the Algerian war – most of
them dealing with it from the distance of a whole generation. Four plays are selected
for consideration – by Bernard-Marie Koltès, Daniel Lemahieu, Eugène Durif and
François Bourgeat – all of which were staged in the period 1988-92. In one way or
another all represent an attempt to come to terms with the legacy of the war as it
affects French society today.

219 **Anglo-Saxon attitudes: the Algerian War of Independence in
retrospect.**
Michael Brett. *The Journal of African History*, vol. 35, no. 2 (1994),
p. 217-35.

The English-language literature on Algeria, generated by the Algerian war and
continuing down to the present, forms an intellectual as well as linguistic tradition
apart from the much more voluminous literature in French. Despite the involvement of
French and North African writers who have published in English, it is largely a
creation of outsiders looking at the country from British and North American points of
view, according to current fashions. The War of Independence remains central to its

concerns as the great transformer of a colonial into a national society, however that is to be understood. Most judgements have been based on the outcome and the political, social and economic performance of the régime, considered as good or bad. Since the death of Boumediène in 1978 they have tended to be unfavourable. Their largely secular analyses, however, have been called into question since 1988 by the rise of political Islam which has called for a reappraisal of the whole subject of the war and its consequences. The footnotes include useful references to books and articles on the War of Independence.

220 **Colonialism and violence: Camus and Sartre on the Algerian war, 1945-58.**
John P. Chesson. *Maghreb Review*, vol. 15, no. 1-2 (1990), p. 16-30.
Events leading up to the French exodus from Algeria can be regarded in two ways. Either conflict was inevitable, the necessary result of a system which was doomed to fail; or, the French in Algeria failed to seize increasingly rare opportunities to enact reforms which might have produced a stable, equitable system of government in Algeria. These two interpretations of France's colonial adventure in Algeria were highlighted by the dispute between Jean-Paul Sartre and Albert Camus over the nature of colonialism and the role of extreme violence in waging war. Sartre opted for the former interpretation, and his rendering of revolutionary Marxism sought to bring about that cartharsis. Camus favoured the latter approach; however his philosophy, embodied in his appeal for a civilian truce, failed to appreciate the realism inherent in that view. Camus' faith in the future of French Algeria caused him to overestimate French willingness to export democracy and to understate the extent to which hostilities might render impossible any negotiated settlement.

221 **De Gaulle et l'Algérie**. (De Gaulle and Algeria).
Jean Daniel. Paris: Editions du Seuil, 1986. 279p.
A selection of Jean Daniel's regular articles in *L'Express* from 1958 to 1962. Daniel, a *pied-noir* and friend of Camus, was one of a group of prominent international journalists covering the Algerian war. He was among the first to sense that de Gaulle would astonish those who had rushed him to power on 13 May 1958 by his ingratitude and his commitment to Algerian self-determination.

222 **Abdel Nasser et la révolution algérienne.** (Abdel Nasser and the Algerian revolution).
Mohamed Fathi Al Dib. Paris: L'Harmattan, 1986. 440p. (Histoire et Perspectives Méditerranéennes).
The author, who was President Nasser of Egypt's adviser on North African affairs during the Algerian War of Independence, presents previously unpublished documents and evidence on Nasser and the Algerian revolution.

223 **A dying colonialism.**
Frantz Fanon, translated by Haakon Chevalier. New York: Grove Press, 1967; Harmondsworth, England: Penguin Books, 1970. 160p.
Fanon examines the way in which the colonial situation distorts even the relationship between doctor and patient in hospital. He demonstrates how the requirements of the revolutionary war altered the standard mores of the Algerian family and redefined relationships between its members.

224 Toward the African revolution.

Frantz Fanon, translated by Haakon Chevalier. London: Writers and Readers, 1980. new ed. 197p.

A collection of Fanon's articles, political essays and notes written during the most active period of his life. Most of them appeared in various reviews, and a large number in *El Moudjahid*, the principal organ of the Front de la Libération Nationale (FLN). He was a militant in the Algerian revolutionary organization, for which he became an apologist and propagandist, relentlessly attacking the colonial system and all that it entailed. He constantly linked the fate of the Algerian revolution with that of the continent as a whole.

225 The wretched of the earth.

Frantz Fanon, translated by Constance Farrington. Harmondsworth, England: Penguin Books, 1983. reprint. 255p.

In this penetrating analysis of the nationalist anticolonial movements of Asia and Africa in the 20th century, Fanon exposes the economic and psychological degradation of imperialism and charts the way forward to a socialist revolution. This is a study of the Algerian war, written by a practising psychiatrist working in the country.

226 La guerre d'Algérie: la fin des secrets et le secret d'une guerre doublement nationale. (The Algerian war: the end of secrets and the secret of a twofold national war).

René Gallissot. *Mouvement Social* (France), no. 138 (1987), p. 69-107.

Surveys various historical works published from 1960 to 1986 on the Algerian war (1954-62) and suggests an array of new interpretations, mainly connected with social history, that explain most major problems, both in France and in Algeria. An English summary is provided.

227 The political roles of Islamic women: a study of two revolutions – Algeria and Iran.

Barbara Glendora Gates. PhD thesis, The University of Texas at Austin, 1987. 377p. bibliog.

Gates points out that much of the material written on revolutions focuses on men. Women are treated, if at all, as part of the stage on which the drama is acted out rather than as coparticipants with men. They are preceived as being fought for and fought over, but not as fighters themselves. This work examines the political roles of Islamic women and their participation in the development, execution and the after-effects of the revolutions in Algeria and Iran. It defines the nature, level and degree of women's participation and then examines the factors encouraging women's participation in the two revolutions.

228 Frantz Fanon: a critical study.

Irene L. Gendzier. New York: Pantheon Books, 1973. 270p.

A biography of Fanon, and study of the evolution of his ideas on the colonial system and violent decolonization in the context of his own life and work in Algeria.

229 **Algeria – rebellion and revolution.**
Joan Gillespie. New York: Praeger, 1960; London: Benn, 1960.
191p. 3 maps. bibliog.
Concentrates on the rise of Algerian nationalism, its historical antecedents and the
nature of the relationship between *colons* and Muslims. The conduct and aims of the
insurrection are also analysed.

230 **Challenging De Gaulle: the OAS and the counterrevolution in
Algeria, 1954-1962.**
Alexander Harrison. New York: Praeger, 1989. 192p.
The author utilizes interviews with former members of the Organisation de l'Armée
Secrète (OAS), together with a range of unpublished material, to present a history of
an organization formed by rebellious French army officers and right-wing *colons*
which was committed to violent resistance to de Gaulle's negotiations with the
Algerian nationalist and opposition to the country's independence from France. It
demonstrates the vast differences which existed between the diffferent branches of the
organization which was far from cohesive. The result of factionalism was often
disastrous. This is essentially a history written from 'below', from the standpoint of
the ordinary foot-soldier and sector commander within the organization. Harrison
emphasizes those 'cult heroes' who are little known to the general public and attempts
to explain the reasons for their actions.

231 **La 7e wilaya: la guerre du FLN en France, 1954-1962.** (The 7th
wilaya: the FLN's war in France, 1954-1962).
Ali Haroun. Paris: Seuil, 1986. 522p.
Ali Haroun, one of the leaders of the Front de Libération Nationale's Fédération de
France, presents his evidence about the activities of the FLN in France during the War
of Independence.

232 **Insurgency and counterinsurgency in Algeria.**
Alf Andrew Heggoy. Bloomington, Indiana: Indiana University
Press; London: Indiana University Press, 1972. 266p. 8 maps. bibliog.
A study of the growth and political development of nationalism in Algeria leading to
the insurrection in 1954. The effectiveness of insurgency and counterinsurgency
techniques employed by both sides is discussed. The study ends in 1958, when the
struggle moved into the realm of politics.

233 **Wolves in the city: the death of French Algeria.**
Paul Henissart. New York: Simon & Shuster, 1970; London: Rupert
Hart-Davis, 1971. 481p. bibliog.
An account of the final period of the war, from the time when opposition to de
Gaulle's policy of self-determination for Algeria went underground, to the granting of
independence in 1962.

234   **A savage war of peace: Algeria 1954-1962.**
Alistair Horne.   London: Macmillan, 1987. new ed. 606p. 2 maps.
bibliog.
The seminal work in English on the War of Independence, which provides a detailed
study of the background and underlying causes of the revolt, tracing each stage of the
conflict.

235   **Revolutionary terrorism: the FLN in Algeria, 1954-1962.**
Martha Crenshaw Hutchinson.   Stanford, California: Hoover
Institution Press, 1978. 178p. map. bibliog.
Algeria was a classic case of revolutionary, nationalist terrorism against a colonial
power. This case-study examines the FLN's motivation for its reliance on terrorism,
the way in which FLN terrorism worked, and its success and failure in terms of the
political ends it accomplished. The relationship between terrorism and the FLN's
ultimate victory in the struggle for Algerian independence is also examined.

236   *Le Monde* **and the Algerian war during the Fourth Republic.**
Mohammed Khane.   In: *French and Algerian identities from colonial
times to the present: a century of interaction.*   Edited by Alec G.
Hargreaves, Michael J. Heffernan.   Lewiston, Idaho; Queenston,
Canada; Lampeter, Wales: The Edwin Mellon Press, 1993, p. 129-48.
Challenges the view that *Le Monde* championed opposition to French colonial policy
during the Algerian war. Khane argues that the paper was far more conservative than
its own later propaganda would lead one to imagine and that it was certainly not in the
forefront of the struggle for decolonization. *Le Monde's* journalists had a moderating
effect on French public opinion about Algeria. Contrary to its reputation for fearless
impartiality and objectivity, the paper in fact defended an indefensible status quo
during the first phase of the Algerian war.

237   **The French Communist Party and the Algerian war.**
Danièle Joly.   London: Macmillan, 1991. 199p. bibliog.
An assessment and evaluation of policies of the Parti Communiste Française (PCF)
towards the question of Algeria during the War of Independence. The particular focus
is the debate on Algeria within the PCF, especially the divergences between the
party's official political line and a possible 'opposition'. The first three chapters set
the scene by examining the particular nature of the relationship between France and
Algeria, the PCF's heritage on the colonial question and the role of the international
situation in the formulation of PCF policies. The next three chapters examine three
main axes of discussion within the Party about the Algerian war: the relationship
between Algeria and France and the Party's concept of the French nation; the PCF's
analysis of the Algerian Liberation Movement and the controversy over its definition
of the Algerian nation; and the Party's response to France's military involvement in
Algeria, the most openly challenged of its policies.

238   **De Gaulle and Algeria, 1940-1960: from Mers el-Kebir to the
Algiers barricades.**
Michael Kettle.   London: Quartet, 1993. 666p. maps. bibliog.
An account of the Algerian war and General de Gaulle's role in the conflict.

239 **Partiality and biases: the coverage of the Algerian Liberation War (1954-1962) by Al-Ahram and Le Monde.**
Mohamed Kirat. *Gazette: International Journal for Mass Communication Studies* (Netherlands), vol. 44, no. 3 (1989), p. 155-75.
Argues that the use of both a manipulative and a market model to analyse the treatment of the Algerian conflict by two prominent non-Algerian newspapers – *Al-Ahram* (Egypt) and *Le Monde* (France) – reinforces the thesis that foreign news coverage tends to follow the path of the foreign policy of the news organization's home country. Although the directionality and orientation of their coverage differed, both *Al-Ahram* and *Le Monde* offered biased, partial coverage without thorough explanation and in-depth analysis.

240 **The students' contribution to the internationalization of the Algerian national question, 1955-1961.**
Badra Lahouel. *Revue d'Histoire Maghrébine* (Tunisia), vol. 14, no. 45-46 (1987), p. 91-101.
Algerian students joined the national struggle for independence by forming the Union Générale des Etudiants Musulmans Algériens, which supported the National Liberation Front (FLN), in 1955. Algerian students were active in soliciting international support for their cause among student organizations elsewhere, and eventually, in 1960, they succeeded in persuading the French student organization, the Union Nationale des Etudiants Français, to join the Algerian cause.

241 **St Michael and the dragon: a paratrooper in the Algerian war.**
Pierre Leulliette, translated by Tony White. London: Heinemann, 1964. 270p.
The story of three years of French Army operations in Algeria, 1954-57, told by a member of the rank and file. The book was banned in France when originally published in 1961.

242 **The Algerian war and the one of indivisible French Republic.**
John P. Loughlin. In: *French and Algerian identities from colonial times to the present: a century of interaction.* Edited by Alec G. Hargreaves, Michael J. Heffernan. Lewiston, Idaho; Queenston, Canada; Lampeter, Wales: The Edwin Mellen Press, 1993, p. 149-60.
The Algerian war was waged on the French side on the principle of an indissoluble union between France and Algeria. France lost the war, and in so doing, this sacred principle suffered a severe blow. It was the committed and more extreme regionalists in France who learned the lesson from this defeat. The Algerian war gave an important impetus to the more uncompromising tendencies within the regionalist movement and eventually brought about a significant modification of the official, centralizing doctrine of French republicanism.

243 **Torture, the role of ideology in the French-Algerian war.**
Rita Maran. New York: Praeger, 1989. 214p. bibliog.
Analyses the ideology of the 'mission civilisatrice'(civilizing mission) in relation to torture used by the French state during the Algerian War of Independence 1954-62.

244 **Nationalism and new states in Africa from about 1935 to the present.**
Ali A. Mazrui, M. Tidy. London: Heinemann, 1984. 402p.
This volume includes an account of the Algerian War of Independence on p. 123-31.

245 **The FLN, Islam and Arab identity.**
André Nouschi. In: *French and Algerian identities from colonial times to the present: a century of interaction.* Edited by Alec G. Hargreaves, Michael J. Heffernan. Lewiston, Idaho; Queenston, Canada; Lampeter, Wales: The Edwin Mellen Press, 1993, p. 111-28.
Examines two particular issues of central concern both to the insurgents of the Front de Libération Nationale (FLN), who began the quest for independence, and to the members of the Conseil National de la Révolution Algérienne who brought that quest to a conclusion – Islam and Arab culture. Nouschi points out that despite the reference to Islam in its first proclamation, the FLN had not informed the *ulema* (religious scholars) of the decision to mount its anti-colonial offensive in 1954. At first the *ulema* retained a strategic distance from the FLN and it was not until the beginning of 1956 that they associated themselves directly with the FLN. The relationship between the FLN and Islam remained complex. Supporters of a secular constitution within the FLN lost the argument. As a pioneering anti-colonial force, the FLN had to accept that the most powerful and compelling cultural and moral code which could replace the colonial order was that provided by Islam.

246 **The Algerian insurrection 1954-62.**
Edgar O'Ballance. London: Faber & Faber, 1967. 220p. 3 maps. bibliog.
A factual account of the course of the war, giving a broad outline of the political background, the sequence of events and the international setting. Contrary to widely-held belief, the insurrection was started by a small group of rebels and the outcome was far from inevitable.

247 **L'insertion internationale du FLN algérien (1954-1962).** (The Algerian National Liberation Front [FLN] and international politics, 1954-62).
Guy Perville. *Relations Internationales* (France), no. 31 (1982), p. 373-86.
Examines the steps taken by the FLN to enter into international politics from its inception in 1954 until Algerian independence in 1962. The creation of an Algerian provisional government in 1958, and its success in building domestic support, paved the way for FLN progress at the international level. The article reviews the stages in the international acceptance of the provisional government and argues that such acceptance was rarely unconditional or unlimited. The decision of other nations to recognize the FLN as the legitimate representative of the Algerian people and state normally represented neither friendship nor sympathy with FLN goals but expedience or national interests.

248 **The politics of torture: Algeria as a crucial instance.**
Edward Peters. *Dissent*, vol. 32, no. 3 (1985), p. 305-09.
A short history of the use of torture in European colonies, particularly Algeria. It
concludes that European torturers did not learn the practice from indigenous people,
but that it flourished naturally in the absence of strict controls against it.

249 **The Fourth Republic 1944-1958.**
J.-P. Rioux. Cambridge, England: Cambridge University Press; Paris:
Maison des Sciences de l'Homme, 1987. 531p.
An English translation of *La France de la Quatrième République* (Paris, 1980-83). For
a discussion of the early stages of the Algerian war see Chapter 14, 'The Algerian
snare' (p. 253-84).

250 **La guerre d'Algérie dans l'histoire des intellectuels français.** (The
Algerian war in the history of French intellectuals).
Jean-Pierre Rioux. *Cahiers de l'Institut d'Histoire du Temps Présent*
(France), no. 10 (1988), p. 21-35.
The intellectuals of France responded to the Algerian War of Independence and their
own government's attempts to suppress Algerian independence movements in the
shadow of their shame over the Dreyfus affair. Many of their attitudes were
insufficiently critical and amounted to mere conformism.

251 **The war in Algeria.**
Jules Roy, translated by Richard Howard. New York: Grove Press,
1961; Westport, Connecticut: Greenwood Press, 1975. 128p.
This essay was written after a visit to Algeria in 1960 by the author, who was born and
raised there. He is bitterly critical of the French settlers and French Army, but tries to
understand the situation in Algeria from all sides. The book was an attempt to open
people's eyes to events in Algeria and put an end to the war.

252 **La réaction de la presse et de l'opinion publique américaines à la
politique du gouvernement Eisenhower envers la Révolution
Algérienne.** (The reaction of the American press and public opinion to
the Eisenhower government's policy toward the Algerian revolution).
John Ruedy. *Revue d'Histoire Maghrébine* (Tunisia), vol. 13,
no. 41-42 (1986), p. 116-37.
During the Algerian War of Independence, the *New York Times* generally supported
the policy of the American government, opted for reasons of state over anticolonial
principle, and backed France, though urging a peaceful solution. To the right, the
National Review advocated a more vigorous pro-colonial policy against communism
and Arabism, while to the left the *New Republic* and trade union leaders were pro-
Algerian. The *Jewish Commentary* published remarkably little about Algeria, and the
Catholic *Commonweal* and Protestant *Christian Century* urged Americans to persuade
France to change its policies.

253 **Algérie et Vietnam.** (Algeria and Vietnam).
David L. Schalk. *Cahiers de l'Institut d'Histoire du Temps Présent*
(France), no. 10 (1988), p. 245-52.

Compares the role of France in the Algerian War of Independence to that of the
United States in the war in Vietnam, including the repercussions in domestic politics
and the revolt of students and intellectuals. This issue of the journal is devoted to
papers from a round table on *The Algerian War and French Intellectuals*, held on 22
April 1988.

254 **War and the ivory tower: Algeria and Vietnam.**
David L. Schalk. New York: Oxford University Press, 1991. 258p.

A comparative history of French intellectuals responding to the Algerian war and
American intellectuals responding to the Vietnam war. The author is most concerned
with showing how intellectuals in France and the United States, during their nations'
respective wars without victory, left the 'Ivory Tower' for a state of committed
political engagement. The story is told through a modestly narrow frame. Schalk
presents the French side through a sympathetic account of Albert Camus' struggle to
find a role for France and for himself in Algeria, a supportive summary of anti-war
articles in *Esprit*, and a respectful look at Jean-Paul Sartre and *Les Temps modernes*
(Modern times).

255 **Lieutenant in Algeria.**
Jean-Jacques Servan-Schreiber, translated by Ronald Mathews. New
York: Knopf, 1957; London: Hutchinson, 1958; London: Greenwood
Press, 1977. 206p.

Provides the memoirs of Servan-Schreiber's personal experiences during six months'
service in Algeria in 1956. This book gives a good idea of how French Army officers
felt about army policy, and the kind of political pressure in Algeria at the time.

256 **Intellectuals and decolonization in France.**
Paul Clay Sorum. Chapel Hill, North Carolina: University of North
Carolina Press, 1977. 305p. bibliog.

A study of the writings of French intellectuals about the problems of decolonization
after the Second World War. It discusses their criticisms of France's colonial policies,
the alternative policies they suggested, their reactions to the issues connected with
decolonization, and the arguments they used to justify their position. Chapter five,
'Terror in Algeria' (p. 105-50), examines the climax of French decolonization, the
Algerian war and the moral dilemma that Algeria presented for the intellectuals.
Chapter six, 'The New Resistance' (p. 151-78), discusses those French intellectuals
who actively aided the Algerian nationalists.

257 **Guerre d'Algérie. La récupération des héritages de mémoires.** (The
Algerian war: misappropriation of the legacy of memories).
Benjamin Stora. *Cahiers d'Histoire* (France), vol. 31, no. 3-4 (1986),
p. 357-67.

Despite the impact on French society of the Algerian War of Independence, neither
the nearly three million veterans nor the repatriated French *pied noir* settlers have

expressed a collective memory of their experiences. On the Algerian side, oral history collection took place under the auspices of the government, and could thus be suspected of some subjectivity. Two television productions, *Guerre d'Algérie, mémoire enfouie d'une génération* (The Algerian war, buried memory of a generation) (1982) and *Serkadji, mes soeurs* (Serkadji, my sisters) (1985), on an Algerian women's prison, expressed a spontaneous collective memory. The authenticity of the memory of an event is distorted whenever it is invoked to serve the needs of a policy, power, or cause operating in the present.

258 **The war without a name: France in Algeria, 1954-1962.**
   John Talbott.   London: Faber, 1981. 318p.

The analysis focuses on changes in French political life, the character of de Gaulle, on the press and literary pressure groups in Paris rather than on the military action within Algeria. Increased opposition to and revelations about torture in Algeria are accompanied by a detailed treatment of the writings of Simon and others and of their impact on French political opinion. The events leading up to de Gaulle's accession to power and the manner in which he brought about the changes in attitude in France to permit firstly direct negotiations with the FLN and then a settlement largely on their terms, are dealt with in some detail.

259 **Le silence du fleuve.** (The silence of the river).
   Anne Tristan.   Paris: Association au Nom de la Mémoire, 1991. 135p.

Contains recollections about the massacre of Algerian workers in Paris by the French police after arrests made during a peaceful demonstration on 17 October 1961 during Algeria's struggle for independence. Some of the bodies were thrown into the River Seine, other buried in unmarked graves. Details of the police action were covered up for almost thirty years.

260 **Torture: cancer of democracy: France and Algeria 1954-62.**
   Pierre Vidal-Naquet, translated by Barry Richard.   Harmondsworth,
   England: Penguin Books, 1963. 179p. bibliog.

Describes how the use of torture by the French authorities became common practice, and then institutionalized, during the Algerian war. The author discusses the moral corruption of police, army and state officials both in Algeria and in France, and the need to conceal it from the public.

261 **Fanon and Africa: a retrospect.**
   Derek Wright.   *Journal of Modern African Studies* (Great Britain),
   vol. 24, no. 4 (1986), p. 679-89.

Writing in the context of the Algerian War of Independence during the last decade of his life, Frantz Fanon attempted to traumatize the French Left and indict Western colonialism in favour of Black nationalist and Pan African goals. However, his prescription of revolution as a unifying force in Africa was flawed by his failure to foresee the divisiveness of ethnic and social factors. Revolutionary peasants did not transform Algeria after the departure of the French, and contrary to Fanon's prediction, the Algerian revolution did not remake Black Africa.

Modern Algeria: a history from 1830 to the present.
See item no. 93.

The passing of French Algeria.
See item no. 157.

Les étudiants algériens de l'université française, 1880-1962.
See item no. 179.

Les pertes algériennes de 1945 à 1962.
See item no. 272.

Operation 'oiseau bleu', 1956. Géostratégie et ethnopolitique en montagne kabyle.
See item no. 290.

The rise of Algerian women: cultural dualism and multi-party politics.
See item no. 369.

La mise en place des institutions algériennes.
See item no. 404.

The F.L.N., in Algeria: party development in a revolutionary society.
See item no. 426.

Revolution and political leadership: Algeria, 1954-1968.
See item no. 451.

The FLN: French conceptions, Algerian realities.
See item no. 456.

Foreign relations of the United States, 1955-1957. Vol. 18: Africa.
See item no. 531.

French and Algerian identities from colonial times to the present: a century of interaction.
See item no. 535.

Les regroupements de la décolonisation en Algérie.
See item no. 740.

The *centres de regroupement*: the French army's final legacy to Algeria's settlement geography.
See item no. 753.

Who remembers the sea.
See item no. 792.

Images of the Algerian war: French fiction and film, 1954-1962.
See item no. 793.

Thinking the unthinkable: the generation of meaning in French literary and cinema images of the Algerian war.
See item no. 794.

Naissance du cinéma algérien.
See item no. 814.

Algerian theatre and protest.
See item no. 826.

Some useful French depositories for the study of the Algerian revolution.
See item no. 831.

La guerre d'Algérie par les documents. Vol. 1 L'Avertissement: 1943-1946.
See item no. 832.

The Algerian war of words: broadcasting and revolution.
See item no. 846.

Books on the Algerian revolution in English: translations and Anglo-American contributions.
See item no. 867.

Population

262 **Un siècle de transition démographique en Afrique Méditerranéenne 1885-1985.** (A century of demographic change in Mediterranean Africa, 1885-1985).
Philippe Fargues. *Population* (France), vol. 41, no. 2 (1986), p. 205-32.
Reassesses demographic statistics for Algeria and Egypt, demonstrating that the declining rate of mortality antedated the colonial government and coincided with the onset of economic growth. The secular, upward trend in birth rates has reversed.

263 **Essai de reconstitution de la pratique contraceptive en Algérie durant la periode 1967-1987.** (A study of contraceptive practice in Algeria 1967-1987).
Ali Kouaouci. *Population* (France), vol. 48, no. 4 (1993), p. 859-84.
The Algerian National Fertility Survey is the first significant attempt to assess the spread of contraceptive practice in different groups of the population, broken down by age, duration of marriage, parity and environment. Questions were designed to show how contraceptive behaviour evolved over time, and the motivation behind it, i.e. spacing compared to stopping. It is shown that this type of behaviour developed even before the value of birth regulation was acknowledged by politicians, and that it had become accepted in the population in spite of religious opposition.

264 **L'indispensable maîtrise de la croissance démographique en Algérie.** (The obligatory control of demographic growth in Algeria).
Djilali Sari. *Maghreb-Machrek*, no. 129 (1990), p. 23-46.
The rate of demographic growth in Algeria is one of the highest in the world. The population has doubled in twenty years, from 11 million to 23 million inhabitants and 55.9 per cent of Algerians are under twenty years of age. Meeting needs in terms of housing, food, water, education and employment has posed crucial problems. This article asks whether Algeria will be able to cope with 31 or 34 million inhabitants at the end of the decade. The Algerian authorities practised a resolutely natalist policy

until 1974 and although this position was modified after 1974, it was not until 1980 that programmes were implemented with a view to controlling demographic growth. Sari concludes that these programmes remain inadequate and do not meet the needs that the situation demands.

265 Studies in African and Asian demography: CDC Annual Seminar, 1990.

Cairo: Cairo Demographic Center, 1991. 971p. (Research Monograph Series, no. 20).

Includes a chapter on 'Population projections by age and sex for Algeria, 1987-2022'.

266 Algeria: changes in population distribution 1954-66.

Keith Sutton.   In: *Populations of the Middle East and North Africa – a geographical approach.*   Edited by J. I. Clarke, W. B. Fisher.
London: University of London Press, 1972, p. 373-403.

A geographical analysis of the results of the 1966 Algerian census of population, which examines regional variation in population change in the intercensal period 1954-66.

267 Household census data from Algeria: its content and potentiality.

Keith Sutton.   *The Maghreb Review*, vol. 6, no. 3-4 (1981), p. 45-48.

The 1977 population census of Algeria offers researchers a rather unique collection of data because the results are available at the levels of each household and individual. The researcher can therefore make a precise study of a single village or of an urban quarter, or can extract large samples without the problems of generalization that result from the use of data aggregated to the level of communes or *arrondissements*. The range of information available from the Algerian census is described and demonstrated for two villages, a *centre de regroupement* and an agrarian reform village.

268 Population changes in Algeria, 1977-1987.

K. Sutton, M. Nacer.   *Geography*, vol. 75, no. 4 (1990), p. 335-47.

The Algerian population census of 1987 reveals that previous inter-censal trends between 1966 and 1977 have not always been continued. Coastal urban poles have decelerated in their growth and the primacy of Algiers has not been strengthened. A belt of the interior High Plains region has shown strong acceleration, again a marked reversal of earlier trends. In part this may reflect success for a regional planning strategy but other such policies may need to be re-evaluated in the light of these 1977-87 population trends. Particular emphasis is given to the unexpectedly slow growth rate of the coastal metropolises and especially the appearance of 'inner city' population decline in central Algiers.

269 Population growth in Algeria, 1966-1977, with some comparisons from Tunisia.

Keith Sutton.   *The Maghreb Review*, vol. 5, no. 2-4 (1980), p. 41-50.

The first results of the delayed 1977 census of Algeria permit an up-dated analysis of national and regional trends in its population geography. After considering several basic parameters of Algeria's population as revealed by the census, this article focusses first on the high population growth rate and reviews the limited approach to family planning taken by the government. Comparisons with Tunisia, with its more active population policy, suggest a divergence between the demographies of the two countries. Regional population growth is then examined, revealing considerable variation, towards which the contribution of urbanization is discussed.

270 **La migration Européenne en Algérie au XIXe siècle: migration organisée ou migration tolérée?** (European migration to Algeria in the 19th century: organized or tolerated migration?)
Emile Temine. *Revue de l'Occident Musulman et de la Méditerranée* (France), no. 43 (1987), p. 31-45.

Recent studies of European migration to Algeria after the French conquest of 1830 permit an evaluation of the relative importance of state-supported and uncontrolled immigration. The original French project to attract colonists from Germany and Switzerland was an almost complete failure, and uncontrolled immigration from Spain, Malta and Italy became more and more important. Much of this was originally seasonal migration, especially from southern Spain, and the French authorities were suspicious or hostile toward both Spanish and Maltese. However, the lack of an alternative eventually combined with the cheap labour and low expectations of these migrants caused a change in attitude.

271 **Fertility in Algeria: trends and differentials.**
Jaques Vallin. In: *Women's status and fertility in the Muslim world.* Edited by J. Allman. London: Praeger, 1978, p. 131-51.

An analysis of changes in fertility and the relationship between socio-economic variables and fertility differentials.

272 **Les pertes algériennes de 1954 à 1962.** (Algerian losses from 1954 to 1962).
X. Yacono. *Revue de l'Occident Musulman et de la Méditerranée* (France), no. 34 (1982), p. 119-34.

Algerian population losses between 1954 and 1962 have been subject to estimates varying from 200,000 to three million people. A comparison with other conflicts shows that the higher figures are to be discarded. The results of the 1962 referendum cannot be used as a basis for deduction as the figures are not exact, but the study of demographic evolution and census returns makes it possible to propose, as being the most valid, a figure of approximately 300,000.

Algérie incertaine.
See item no. 2.

North-west Africa: a political and economic survey.
See item no. 21.

Polity and society in contemporary North Africa.
See item no. 38.

Le Sahara dans le développement des états maghrébins.
See item no. 57.

L'Algérie, volontarisme étatique et aménagement du territoire.
See item no. 60.

Le Sahara français.
See item no. 61.

The changing geography of Africa and the Middle East.
See item no. 62.

Infant and juvenile mortality at Algiers: results of a survey organized by WHO and the Ministry of Public Health in 1974-75.
See item no. 375.

La géopolitique de la démographie méditerranéenne.
See item no. 582.

Le Grand Maghreb et l'Europe: enjeux et perspectives.
See item no. 583.

L'avenir de l'espace méditerranéen.
See item no. 587.

Demographic Yearbook.
See item no. 732.

Urban growth and housing policy in Algeria: a case study of a migrant community in the city of Constantine.
See item no. 738.

Algeria.
See item no. 751.

The growth of Algiers and regional development in Algeria: contradictory themes.
See item no. 754.

The influence of military policy on Algerian rural settlement.
See item no. 755.

Vers un Maghreb des villes de l'an 2000.
See item no. 757.

Progress in the human geography of the Maghreb.
See item no. 883.

Minorities

273 **The Jews of North Africa during the Second World War.**
Michel Abitbol, translated by Catherine Tihanyi Zentelis. Detroit:
Wayne State University Press, 1989. 212p.

Includes an examination of the experiences of Algerian Jews during the Second World
War when the Vichy government repealed the Crémieux decree of 1870 by which they
had become French citizens, and restricted admission of Jews to the university.

274 **The Mzab.**
E. A. Alport. In: *Arabs and Berbers: from tribe to nation in North
Africa.* Edited by Ernest Gellner, Charles Micaud. London:
Duckworth, 1973, p. 141-52.

A study of the origins of the inhabitants of the Mzab, a heterdox Muslim group, the
history of their settlement in the central Algerian Sahara, and the social structure of
their cities.

275 **Une correspondance entre le rabbin Isaac Morali et le
commandant Armand Lipman.** (Corresondence between the Rabbi
Isaac Morali and Commander Armand Lipman).
Robert Attal. *Revue des Etudes Juives* (France), vol. 144, no. 1-3
(1985), p. 145-67.

Reproduces ten letters from Rabbi Isaac Morali of Algiers to his friend Armand
Lipman in Versailles, illustrating aspects of the life of the Jewish community in
Algiers between 1928 and 1932.

276 **A propos du pogrom de Constantine (Août 1934).** (Concerning the pogrom at Constantine, August 1934).
Richard Ayoun. *Revue des Etudes Juives* (France), vol. 144, no. 1-3 (1985), p. 181-86.

Describes in detail the anti-Jewish violence in the Constantine region, Algeria, between the 3 and 6 August 1934, and considers the question of premeditation.

277 **Les Juifs de Mostaganem.** (The Jews of Mostaganem).
Norbert Bel-Ange. Paris: L'Harmattan, 1990. 300p. (Histoire et Perspectives Méditerranéennes).

A study of the role of the Jewish community in the development of the western Algerian town of Mostaganem. Bel-Ange examines the history, economy and cultural and religious life of the community.

278 **Bèrberes aux marges de l'histoire.** (Berbers on the fringes of history).
Gabriel Camps. Paris: Editions des Hespérides, 1980. 350p. map.

The author examines the political structures of the Berber world, its social organization, and its beliefs, and draws attention to the marked diversity which distinguishes the varied and far-flung Berber communities. After a discussion of the real and legendary origins of the Berbers, Camps proceeds to introduce the little known peoples of the Maghreb in the Proto-historic, the Classical and the Islamic periods, assessing the significant role which they played. He contrasts this with the profound impact of foreign culture on the Berbers: Punic, Roman, Byzantine and Arab. The cosmological and theological beliefs of the Berbers are examined and the work concludes with the perennial elements in Berber cultures: the alphabets, artistic skills, ways of organizing their communities and the role of women in society. The text is accompanied by a wide range of photographs and drawings.

279 **L'affirmation identitaire berbère à partir de 1900, constantes et mutations (Kabylie).** (Berber affirmation of identity since 1900, continuities and changes [Kabylia]).
Salem Chaker. *Revue de l'Occident Musulman et de la Méditerranée* (France), no. 44 (1987), p. 13-33.

Discusses how the first manifestations of Berber consciousness in Kabylia in the early 20th century were purely cultural, the Berberist movement becoming politicized only in the 1930s and 1940s. Conflicts between Arabs and Berbers within the Algerian nationalist movement were followed by resistance and repression after independence and the promulgation of the false idea that Berber consciousness was deliberately created by French colonialism.

280 **The Algiers riot, January 1898.**
Alan D. Corré. *The Maghreb Review*, vol. 5, no. 2-4 (1980), p. 74-78.

A translation of a poem entitled 'The story of the destruction of Algiers', composed in colloquial Algerian Judeo-Arabic and published by the Imprimerie Express of Algiers in 1898. It provides insights into the anti-Jewish riots which spread to Algiers in January 1898 at a time when the notorious Dreyfus affair was being played out in Paris and further fuelled the fires of anti-Semitic sentiment.

281 **Traditionalism through ultra-modernism.**
Jeanne Favret. In: *Arabs and Berbers: from tribe to nation in North Africa.* Edited by Ernest Gellner, Charles Micaud. London: Duckworth, 1973, p. 307-24.

Attempts to interpret two rural rebellions in Algeria which occurred in the early years of independence, one in the Aurès Mountains and the other in Kabylia, both Berber-speaking regions.

282 **Islam: state and society.**
Edited by Klaus Ferdinand, Mehdi Mozaffari. London: Curzon; Riverdale, Maryland: The Riverdale Company, 1988. 219p. bibliog.

This collection of theoretical essays and country case-studies includes one contribution on Algeria, 'Culture and minorities in the Arabo-Islamic identity of Algeria' by Tuomo Melasuo.

283 **Colonialism and after: an Algerian Jewish community.**
Elizabeth D. Friedman. South Hadley, Massachusetts: Bergin & Garvey, 1988. 170p. bibliog.

Describes the history and present-day conditions of a Jewish community in Batna, Algeria and, after 1962, in France. The changing status of Jews from an oppressed minority to a privileged stratum in colonial Algeria is addressed. This ethnographic study also explores the difficulties faced by the community following their decision to leave Algeria at the termination of French rule there and their adaptation to a new life as immigrants in France.

284 **Three Kabyles and French assimilationism: Ait Ahmed, Feraoun, and Ibazizen.**
Alf Andrew Heggoy, Claude C. Sturgill. *Proceedings of the Annual Meeting of the Western Society for French History*, no. 13 (1986), p. 294-301.

The speakers of Kabyle, a Berber language, made up over a quarter of the population of 19th-century Algeria. They resisted French military occupation and colonization longer than other Algerians and organized the first revolts against French rule. This study looks at the careers of three French-educated Kabyle intellectuals – Ait Ahmed, Mouloud Feraoun and Augustin Ibazizen – examining their different responses to French assimilationist policies. Their attitudes varied from pro-French assimilationism to radical support for independence movements, from fighting in the French army, or fighting against the French army, to pacifism.

285 **A history of the Jews in North Africa: Volume I. From antiquity to the sixteenth century.**
H. Z. Hirschberg. Leiden, Netherlands: E. J. Brill, 1974. 2nd rev. ed. 518p. 4 maps. bibliog.

Traces the history of the Jewish communities in the Maghreb from the classical period to the 16th century, when the region came under Turkish rule. The work, translated from Hebrew, examines their position under Muslim rule, analysing the nature of Jewish society, the forms of Jewish communal organization and their economic and spiritual life.

286   A history of the Jews in North Africa: Volume II. From the
      Ottoman conquests to the present time.
      H. Z. Hirschberg, edited by Eliezer Basham, Robert Attal.   Leiden,
      Netherlands: E. J. Brill, 1981. 2nd rev. ed. 362p. bibliog.

This second volume of Hirschberg's study, also translated from Hebrew, takes up
where the first left off, in the mid-16th century and traces the history of the North
African Jewish communities to the Second World War. The author divides the region
into its conventional geographic areas (Algeria, Morocco, Tunisia and Triplotania,
[Libya]) and recounts the story of the Jewish communities in each.

287   Islam and state expansion in Algeria: nineteenth-century Saharan
      frontiers.
      Donald C. Holsinger.   In: *Islamism and secularism in North Africa*.
      Edited by John Ruedy.   Basingstoke, England: Macmillan, 1994,
      p. 3-21.

This essay focusses on one Saharan community – the Mzab, inhabited by Ibadi
Muslims – as it adapted to the new challenges brought on by the French occupation
and expansion in Algeria. It explores ways in which a self-consciously 'Islamic'
community coped with the challenges of state encroachment during the 19th century.
Holsinger concludes that the experience of the Mzab in the 19th century illuminates
the nature and significance of imperialism and state expansion for Muslim Algerians.
This oasis community was severely shaken by the turbulence of shifting state
frontiers, but survived tattered but intact. Not all Algerian groups were as fortunate.

288   Migration, commerce and community: the Mizabis in eighteenth
      and nineteenth century Algeria.
      Donald C. Holsinger.   *Journal of African History*, no. 21 (1980),
      p. 61-74.

Examines the Mzabi (the Ibadi communities of the Mzab in the Algerian Sahara)
commercial dispersion by sketching the historical background to settlement in the
Mzab, pointing out some of the salient features of their economic system, and tracing
the history of their northern dispersion. The article also describes the organization of
Mzabi corporations in Algerian cities, and discusses the relation of an Ibadi reformist
ethic to Mzabi commercial success.

289   Muslim responses to French imperialism: an Algerian Saharan
      case study.
      Donald C. Holsinger.   *International Journal of African Historical
      Studies*, vol. 19, no. 1 (1986), p. 1-15.

Faced with the disruption of their economic ties to the Mediterranean coast in the mid-
19th century by advancing French imperialism, the isolated community of Ibadi
Muslims occupying the five oasis towns of the Mzab in the Sahara succeeded in
adapting to changing power realities in the Sahara and in preserving their unique way
of life.

290 **Operation 'oiseau bleu', 1956. Géostratégie et ethnopolitique en montagne kabyle.** (Operation 'blue bird', 1956: geostrategy and ethnopolitics in the Kabyle mountains).
C. Lacoste-Dujardin. *Revue de l'Occident Musulman et de la Méditerranée* (France), no. 41-42 (1986), p. 167-93.

Operation Blue Bird, 1956, was an attempt to create an anti-Front de Libération Nationale (FLN) force among the Berbers of the Iflissen mountains. It failed completely and was in fact used by members of the FLN to gain arms and supplies. It was carried out using the advice of ethnologists, seeking to exploit supposed divisions between ethnic groups and hostility between Berbers and Arabs. However, their view was unhistorical, taking little account of social change during the colonial period, and based on an idea of an ancient, static and 'traditional' Berber society.

291 **The reproduction of colonial ideology: the case of the Kabyle Berbers.**
M. Lazreg. *Arab Studies Quarterly*, no. 5 (1983), p. 380-95.

Argues that the 'Kabyle myth' – the emphasis placed on the difference between Arabs and Berbers expressed as a fundamental difference in origins, religious feelings and language – provided an ideological framework within which a Kabyle élite was able to articulate racial awareness as the foundation of a quest for power. The reproduction of the myth was made possible not only by the rise of a Kabyle élite trained in Orientalist thought, but also by the failure of the Algerian government to address the multifaceted issue of cultural dependency.

292 **Opposing aspects of colonial rule in this century to 1930: the unusual case of the Beni Mzab.**
Jon Marks. In: *North Africa: nation, state and region.* Edited by George Joffé. London; New York: Routledge, 1993, p. 59-69.

Leaders of resistance against France in the 19th century have since independence been lauded as early nationalist heroes. However, not all resistance movements felt it necessary to promote 'national' aims and they were often more successful when based on more particularist values. Among the groups most successful at achieving their aims were those with relatively limited objectives, such as the Ben Mzab or Mozabites who articulated their opposition to aspects of French rule in ethnic and religious terms, specific to a well-defined group.

293 **Formation des cités chez les populations sédentaires de l'Algérie: Kabyles du Djurdjura, Chaouia de l'Aouras, Beni Mezab.**
(Formation of towns among the sedentary populations of Algeria: Kabyles of the Djurdjura, Chaouia of the Aourès [Aurès], Beni Mezab [Mzab]).
Emile Masqueray, introduction by Fanny Colonna. Aix-en-Provence, France: Edisud, 1983. 374p. (Archives Maghrébines).

The re-publication of an important study which originally appeared in 1886. After detailed descriptions of traditional Berber institutions in Kabylia, the Aurès Mountains and the Mzab, the author compares Berber settlements and ancient Rome. His work contributed significantly to future anthropologists analysing social structures in the

Maghreb. The introduction by Fanny Colonna places Masqueray in the context of late 19th-century Algerian political and intellectual circles, and outlines and discusses some of the basic notions contained in this study.

294 **Le développement politique en Algérie: étude des populations de la région du M'Zab.** (Political development in Algeria: study of the populations of the Mzab region).
Baelhadj Merghoub. Paris: Armand Colin, 1972. 175p. 2 maps. bibliog. (Etudes Maghrébines, no. 10).

Examines the traditional political systems of the Mzabite communities of the Algerian Sahara, the tensions resulting from French colonial rule, and their efforts to maintain traditional institutions in the face of the centralizing policies of the independent Algerian state.

295 **Berbers in distress.**
Susan Morgan. *The Middle East*, no. 235 (June 1994), p. 20-21.

Morgan analyses the attitudes of the secular opposition parties, the Front of Socialist Forces (FFS) and the Assembly for Culture and Democracy, both of which have a strong Berber constituency, towards the Islamists. She argues that in Kabylia, Berberism and the sense of cultural identity have channelled the discontent of young people who face the same problems as those in the rest of the country. She predicts that the longer the authorities delay in bringing democracy, the greater the risk of Berber radicalization will be.

296 **The Berbers in Arabic literature.**
H. T. Norris. London; New York: Longman, 1982. 280p.

Examines the history, religion, language and literature of the Berber peoples of North Africa as they are presented in Arabic works, including those of Berber scholars, from the early Middle Ages to the present day.

297 **The Berbers in the Algerian political elite.**
William B. Quandt. In: *Arabs and Berbers: from tribe to nation in North Africa.* Edited by Ernest Gellner, Charles Micaud. London: Duckworth, 1973, p. 285-303.

An analysis of why Algeria managed to avoid conflicts rooted in ethnic particularism during the years of independence.

298 **Algerian socialism and the Kabyle question.**
Hugh Roberts. Norwich, England: University of East Anglia, School of Development Studies, 1981. 376p. 7 maps. bibliog. (Monographs in Development Studies, no. 8).

The author challenges existing academic views which treat the Kabyles as simply one among a number of ethnic groups with which the emerging nation-state has to contend. While accepting that one of the main oppositions which characterize contemporary Algerian politics is that between the nation-state and the various ethnic groups, he argues that the Kabyle question is not of this kind. The Kabyles are not merely an ethnic group like the rest and as a consequence they are not merely in opposition to the nation-state but to the régime in power.

299 The economics of Berberism: the material basis of the Kabyle question in contemporary Algeria.
Hugh Roberts. *Government and Opposition*, vol. 18, no. 2 (Spring 1983), p. 218-35.

An attempt to explain the recrudescence of 'Berberism' in the 1970s and its development from élites impregnated with French culture into a popular force with a firm base, not merely among exiles but within Kabylia itself. Roberts argues that the answer is the combination of the Algerian government's socialist economic policy and Arabist cultural policy which have posed a unique threat to the Kabyle middle class in general and the Kabyle bourgeoisie in particular. Because ties of kinship and clientele continue to transcend with ease the emerging class distinctions, popular support can be mobilized in defence of what is, at its base, a bourgeois interest. It is this interest which constitutes the material basis of popular Berberism today.

300 Towards an understanding of the Kabylie question in contemporary Algeria.
Hugh Roberts. *The Maghreb Review*, vol. 5, no. 5-6 (September-December 1980), p. 115-24.

In the light of the demonstrations that erupted in Kabylia in 1980, the so-called 'Tizi Ouzou Spring', the author examines the nature of the Kabyle question and its evolution, the present form of the Kabyle question, notably the demand for official recognition of the Berber language and their opposition to the Arabization of education and public administration. He also discusses the predicament of Berberist assimilationism and the three main tendencies of the Berberist movement: the 'cultural-pluralist' position; the 'Amazigh revivalists'; and the liberal-democratic tendency.

301 The unforeseen development of the Kabyle question in contemporary Algeria.
Hugh Roberts. *Government and Opposition*, no. 17 (1982), p. 312-34.

The growth of popular Berberism in Kabylia, articulating widespread opposition to the government's Arabization policy and the demand for official recognition of the Berber language, went unnoticed by outside observers until 1980. It had been visible since at least 1974 but could not be accommodated by prevailing conceptions of Berber society in general or of Kabyle history in particular. Between 1955 and 1957 the Kabyle community had come to constitute the central core of the nation-in-arms. Since independence Kabyles in government have held purely honorary posts or have been technocrats devoid of any popular following. The particularist sentiment which has developed in reaction to official cultural policy has thus tended to find expression outside the formal political system and in opposition to it.

302 **The Jews of Arab lands in modern times.**
Norman A. Stillman. Philadelphia: Jewish Publication Society, 1991.
632p. bibliog.
Part one examines the history of North African and Middle Eastern Jewish
communities in the 19th and 20th centuries. The effects and extent of European
encroachment, the influence of Zionism, anti-Semitism and nationalist ideologies, and
the impact of the Second World War are discussed, together with a description of the
emigration of various Jewish communities to Israel.

Algérie incertaine.
See item no. 2.

Lumières du M'zab.
See item no. 47.

Among the Berbers of Algeria.
See item no. 53.

Le décret Crémieux et l'insurrection de 1871 en Algérie.
See item no. 136.

Language, social relations and intellectual production in Algeria.
See item no. 304.

Arabization and the Kabyle language and cultural issues in Algeria.
See item no. 307.

**A thesorus of African languages: a classified and annotated inventory of
the spoken languages of Africa, with an appendix on their written
representation.**
See item no. 309.

Culture et enseignement en Algérie et au Maghreb.
See item no. 310.

Berber demands for linguistic rights in Algeria.
See item no. 312.

The conversion of the *mrabtin* in Kabylia.
See item no. 332.

My life story: the autobiography of a Berber woman.
See item no. 339.

Algeria 1960.
See item no. 343.

The women's movement: history and theory.
See item no. 344.

Les classes moyennes au Maghreb.
See item no. 373.

Human rights in the Western Arab world: fertile ground.
See item no. 427.

***Glasnost* the Algerian way: the role of Berber nationalists in political reform.**
See item no. 440.

Berbers and blacks: Ibadi slave traffic in eighth century North Africa.
See item no. 630.

Berbèrité et émigration Kabyle.
See item no. 697.

Patterns of emigration, 1905-1954: 'Kabyles' and 'Arabs'.
See item no. 708.

La sémantique au service de l'anthropologie: recherche méthodologique et application à l'étude de la parenté chez les Touaregs de l'Ahaggar.
See item no. 761.

Changes in political succession, marital strategies and 'noble'/'vassal' relations in precolonial Ahaggar.
See item no. 763.

A note on the formation of the Kel Ahaggar drum-groups in the 18th century and the meaning of 'Imuhag'.
See item no. 764.

The Tuareg: people of the Ahaggar.
See item no. 765.

Ecology and culture of the pastoral Tuareg with particular reference to the Tuareg of Ahaggar and Ayr.
See item no. 766.

Prolégomènes à une étude critique de la littérature judéo-maghrébine d'expression française.
See item no. 797.

Mémento pour les juifs d'Afrique du Nord.
See item no. 809.

An uncertain heritage: Berber traditional architecture in the Maghreb.
See item no. 822.

Reflections on a Kabyle pot: Algerian women and the decorative tradition.
See item no. 828.

Etudes touarègues: bilan des recherches en sciences sociales. Institutions- chercheurs- bibliographie.
See item no. 864.

Language

303 The relation of French and English as foreign languages in Algeria.
A. Allaoua.   PhD thesis, University of Glasgow, Scotland, 1990.

Examines the conflicts over national language planning by analysing how the policy of Arabization affected the status of French in Algeria in the long-term and how educated Algerians reacted to the use of French and English. The thesis also discusses the socio-linguistic issues related to the maintenance of French and the possibility of a shift towards English, especially in science and technology.

304 Language, social relations and intellectual production in Algeria.
Fanny Colonna.   *Review of Middle East Studies*, no. 4 (1991),
p. 107-20.

Colonna examines the present state of the language situation in Algeria which is dominated by the tensions which exist between the Arabic language and culture on the one hand and the French language and culture on the other. To these is added the tension between both languages and cultures and the Berber cultural claim for recognition. This article investigates the relationship between these three cultures on intellectual production, especially scientific intellectual production.

305 Language and identity.
Charles F. Gallagher.   In: *State and society in independent North Africa*.   Edited by Leon Carl Brown.   Washington, DC: Middle East Institute, 1966, p. 73-96.

A study of the linguistic dilemma of the newly independent Maghreb states, focussing in particular on the continuing importance of the French language, the progress of Arabization and the problem of cultural identity.

306   **Arabisation et politique linguistique au Maghreb.** (Arabization and
      linguistic policy in the Maghreb).
      Gilbert Grandguillaume.   Paris: Maisonneuve et Larose, 1983. 214p.
      bibliog. (Islam d'Hier et d'Aujourd'hui, no. 19).

One of the most important assessments and analyses of the Arabization issue as it has
affected Algeria and its Maghreb neighbours since they achieved independence. The
book makes clear that many contemporary controversies surrounding Arabization have
their roots in the past and that Arabization must not be seen as a singular cultural
experience. Arabization policies have often been political or economic in their origins
and their impact. After a long oppressive economic and cultural dependence on
colonialist France, all three countries proceeded to Arabize as part of a statement of
independence. For a shorter discussion of some of these issues in English see the
author's chapter entitled 'Language and legitimacy in the Maghreb' in *Language
policy and political development*, edited by Brian Weinstein (Norwood, New Jersey:
Ablex Publishing, 1990).

307   **Arabization and the Kabyle language and cultural issues in
      Algeria.**
      Alf Andrew Heggoy.   *Africana Journal*, no. 15 (1990), p. 292-304.

The Algerian government officially decreed a single language policy for the country in
1973. The Kabyle-speaking Berbers, who comprise 20 per cent of the population,
demanded linguistic and cultural equality in opposition to assimilation but their
protests failed. The author traces the history of the formal study of Berber culture
since the 19th century and shows the long-term conflict between Arabs and Berbers.

308   **The ambiguous compromise: language, literature, and national
      identity in Algeria and Morocco.**
      Jacqueline Kaye, Abdelhamid Zoubir.   London; New York:
      Routledge, 1990. 150p. bibliog.

Citing francophone examples of literary and oral traditions of Algeria and Morocco,
the authors argue that there are radical differences and conflicts between the two
traditions. They illustrate the dilemma of language-defining national characteristics
and question why post-colonial writers continue to utilize the language of their
oppressors.

309   **A thesorus of African languages: a classified and annotated
      inventory of the spoken languages of Africa, with an appendix on
      their written representation.**
      M. Mann, D. Dalby, et al.   London: Zell, for the International African
      Institute, 1988. 325p.

Includes a discussion of the Berber language.

310   **Culture et enseignement en Algérie et au Maghreb.** (Culture and
      education in independent North Africa).
      Abdulla Mazouni.   Paris: Maspero, 1969. 242p.

A discussion of the political nature of the relationship between language and national
culture. The end of colonialism in Algeria posed distinct problems for the new

nationalist government which wished to accent the Islamic heritage and Arabic language of the majority of Algerians, in reaction to the imposition of a foreign culture. Extra complications arose as the Berbers, an important minority of the country's population, tended to resist the enforced Arabization of teaching and national cultural life. The practical problems posed by bilingualism, the Arabization of teaching and research and the conflict with the Berber cultural tradition are examined, especially in the light of university education.

311 **Amateur theatre in Algeria: choice and use of language.**
    Z. Siagh. *International Journal of the Sociology of Language*, no. 87 (1991), p. 71-86.

The evolution of street theatre, forum theatre and amateur theatre in Algeria are closely linked to the struggle for independence while since independence they have become the scene of struggle and the expression of Algerian youths from modest backgrounds. Analysing the discourse of actors during rehearsals and the languages used, as well as the theatrical production, the author explores whether or not the language used in the theatre differs from the social use of language and also compares the ideology of this type of theatre to the official ideology *vis-à-vis* these languages.

312 **Berber demands for linguistic rights in Algeria.**
    Mala Tabory, Ephraim Tabory. *Plural Societies* (Netherlands), vol. 16, no. 2 (1986), p. 126-60.

Considers language policy in Algeria since 1962, noting the increasing efforts to emphasize Arabic as the single national language. The Berbers have struggled to have their language taught and accepted, which has resulted in protests and violent demonstrations, but no change of government policy.

313 **The impact of the French colonial heritage on language policies in independent North Africa.**
    Rachida Yacine. In: *North Africa: nation, state and region.* Edited by George Joffé. London; New York: Routledge, 1993, p. 221-32.

Examines the way in which the language debate has influenced the process of nation-building in Algeria, Morocco and Tunisia. Yacine concludes that the conflict-prone, complex linguistic situation in the Maghreb has prevailed in spite of the efforts undertaken since independence to bring about a change in the situation inherited from the colonial period. There is a need for a reassessment of the policies adopted and for a different approach which will take into consideration the contextual features of the three countries. Not accounting for contexts, and neglecting other language alternatives while planning language policy has generated consequences which, after a decade, have made the linguistic issue in the Maghreb as problematic and highly controversial as before.

Algérie: vers l'état islamique?
See item no. 3.

Towards an understanding of the Kabyle question in contemporary Algeria.
See item no. 300.

The unforeseen development of the Kabyle question in contemporary Algeria.
See item no. 301.

Algeria's battle of two languages.
See item no. 436.

L'école algérienne de Ibn Badis à Pavlov.
See item no. 772.

Nouveaux enjeux culturels au Maghreb.
See item no. 819.

La communication inégale: l'accès aux média dans les campagnes algériennes.
See item no. 849.

Religion

314 I was an Algerian preacher.
Said Abouadaou, translated and edited by W. N. Heggoy.   New York:
Vantage Press, 1971. 92p. map.
The autobiography of a Kabyle, describing his conversion and his work as an
evangelical preacher in the first half of the century, told mostly in his own memoirs,
with additions from the mission annals, and other missionaries who knew him. Native
missionaries who had apostasized faced particular hostility among their own people,
but in the end he won respect for his hard work and personal goodness. The editor has
added a prologue, and epilogue, a survey article and some translations of native
proverbs and parables which Abouadaou used in his teaching.

315 The Tijaniyya: a sufi order in the modern world.
Jamil M. Abun-Nasr.   London; New York; Toronto: Oxford
University Press, 1965. 204p. map. bibliog. (Middle Eastern
Monographs, no. 7: under the auspices of the Royal Institute of
International Affairs).
Investigates the doctrines of one of the Sufi orders – the Tijaniyya, founded in Algeria
shortly before the French conquest – as they are revealed in its social and political
history. The story of the Tijaniyya offers an example of the dilemma which faced the
Sufi orders during the French period. Anxious to preserve their hold over their
followers, they cooperated closely with the colonial masters, but their association was
detrimental to the Tijaniyya's prestige in society and gave their opponents grounds for
condemning them on both religious and political grounds.

316 Sufism in Africa in the seventeenth and eighteenth centuries.
Louis Brenner.   *Islam et Sociétés au Sud de Sahara* (France), no. 2
(1988), p. 80-93.
A report on nine workshop papers which examine the development of Sufi ideas and
organization in North and Sudanic Africa in the 17th and 18th centuries in an attempt
to improve the understanding of the contribution of Sufism to the movements of

renewal and reform that swept over North Africa and the entire Islamic world during the 18th and 19th centuries. Particularly noteworthy was the increased reliance on a highly structured *tariqa* (brotherhood), which allowed a charismatic visionary leader to place himself in the vanguard of political and religious change.

317 **Islam, politics and social movements.**
Edited by Edmund Burke III, Ira M. Lapidus. Berkeley, California: University of California Press; London: Tauris, 1988. 320p. bibliog.

After two introductory chapters on 'Islamic political movements: patterns of historical change' and 'Islam and social movements: methodological reflections' by the editors, the following case-studies include three essays on Algeria: 'Rural uprisings as political movements in colonial Algeria, 1851-1914' by Peter von Sivers; 'Saints, Mahdis, and arms: religion and resistance in nineteenth century North Africa' by Julia Clancy-Smith; and 'The transformation of a saintly lineage in the northwest Aures mountains (Algeria): nineteenth and twentieth centuries' by Fanny Colonna.

318 **A rereading of Islamic texts in the Maghreb in the nineteenth and early twentieth centuries: secular themes or religious reformism?**
Khalifa Chater. In: *Islamism and secularism in North Africa.*
Edited by John Ruedy. Basingstoke, England: Macmillan Press, 1994, p. 37-51.

In reaction to European penetration, Maghreb rulers resorted to *fatwas* issued by *ulema* to legitimate their actions and especially the innovations that they envisioned. The initiatives to revise and call into question well-established norms and values were part of a determined movement to read and reinterpret religious texts, and represented a renaissance in Muslim thought. They clearly showed Western secular influences and thus actual, if not formal, secular tendencies. Chater presents an analysis of the reform dynamic and its different ideological threads through the study of state *fatwas* from Algeria, Morocco and Tunisia.

319 **Algerian Islam in a time of transition c. 1890-c. 1930.**
Allan Christelow. *The Maghreb Review*, vol. 8, no. 5-6 (1983), p. 124-30.

Examines the relationship between Islam and the colonial state in the late 19th and early 20th centuries. The analysis is concerned primarily with cities and with urban notables, for it was in this milieu that religious edifices and offices, at least the ones controlled by the state, were concentrated and where the most important changes took place.

320 **An Islamic humanist in the 20th century: Malik Bennabi.**
Allan Christelow. *The Maghreb Review*, vol. 17, no. 1-2 (1992), p. 69-83.

A survey of the thought and works of Malik Bennabi, one of the most prolific religious and philosophical essayists of 20th-century Algeria, whose works are known in the Middle East and Europe as well as North Africa. His works touch on several domains of critical concern to the student of modern Arab and Islamic thought. He was a deeply religious man, dedicated to revitalizing Islam so that Muslims might effectively meet the challenge of the 20th century. He was also a sharp and often critical observer of nationalist politics and politicians. He explored the relationship between Islamic civilization and both modern science and the other major civilizations of the world.

321 **Political ends and means of transport in the colonial North African pilgrimage.**
Allan Christelow. *The Maghreb Review*, vol. 12, no. 3-4 (1987), p. 84-89.

The author points out that the pilgrimage to Mecca (*hajj*) presented a dilemma for the French colonial authorities in North Africa. France sought to be liberal in her religious policy but feared the potential of the *hajj* for stirring up Pan-Islamic and anti-colonial feelings. The study deals mainly with Algeria, where the interference of the colonial state in religious affairs was the most far-reaching. It examines how the *hajj* was conducted, what problems of a practical order were encountered, and how the *hajj* changed during the period of French domination.

322 **Between Cairo and the Algerian Kabylia: the Rahmaniyya *tariqa*, 1715-1800.**
Julia A. Clancy-Smith. In: *Muslim travellers: pilgrimage, migration, and the religious imagination.* Edited by Dale F. Eickelman, James Piscatori. London: Routledge, 1990, p. 200-13.

This study of the Rahmaniyya religious order in Algeria during the late 18th century concerns the shifting balance between local, regional, and wider bases for religious authority. It combines attention to the biography of the movement's founder, regional politics, and social history to explain why new networks of religious authority arose during this period. It demonstrates the way in which the founder gained adherents during his travels at a time of political uncertainty. The individual act of self-assertion that such visits represented also enhanced a sense of solidarity which sustained the new brotherhood. On the founder of the Rahmaniyya order see Clancy-Smith's chapter 'The man with two tombs: Muhammad ibn 'Abd al Rahman, founder of the Algerian Rahmaniyya 1715-1798', in *Manifestations of sainthood in Islam*, edited by G. M. Smith, C. W. Ernst (Istanbul: Isis Press, 1993, p. 147-69).

323 **In the eye of the beholder: sufi and saint in North Africa and the colonial production of knowledge, 1830-1900.**
Julia Clancy-Smith. *Africana Journal*, no. 15 (1990), p. 220-57.

Surveys 19th-century French writing about marabouts and sufi brotherhoods. These authors represented three different traditions in the French sociology of Islam – government officials, travellers and academics. All three carried out their studies from the perspective of a colonial power that was interested in understanding the sources of opposition to that power. The growth of an official 'canon' on North African Islam is traced.

324 **Algérie: continuité d'une religion du peuple?** (Algeria: the continuity of a peoples' religion?)
Edited by Fanny Colonna. *Maghreb-Machrek*, no. 135 (1992), p. 37-78.

Three short articles are presented, all devoted to an aspect of religion that has been rarely discussed. In 'Passion and irony in the city. Annaba, from ribat to reformism',

Leila Babès explains the long history of the relationship between emotion and reason in the Maghreb tradition, using as an illustration a Muslim saint long revered in the city of Annaba. Smail Hadj Ali comments on the officially-sponsored 'First National Zaouias Seminar' held in Algiers in May 1991 and the reaction of the press to this 'return to the past'. Ugo Colonna analyses one aspect of the activities of the Pères de la Compagnie de Jésus in the Kabyle mission (1830-80) through their correspondence and demonstrates that in the eyes of the Jesuits of the Counter Reformation, the late 19th-century Islam of the brotherhoods in Algeria seemed to be a religion of ignorance and an obstacle to progress.

325 Cultural resistance and religious legitimacy in colonial Algeria.

Fanny Colonna. *Economy and Society*, vol. 3, no. 3 (Aug. 1974), p. 233-52.

Examines the part played by religious forces in the resistance to colonialism in Algeria, in particular those religious movements with conspicuous political roles.

326 'Abd Al-Qadir Al-Jaza'iri and Islamic reform.

David Commins. *Muslim World*, vol. 78, no. 2 (1988), p. 121-31.

A brief study of Abdel Kader's contribution to the Syrian intellectual scene during his exile in Damascus from 1855 to 1883 and in particular of the development of reformist tendencies in his thought. Also considered is Abdel Kader's association with French freemasonry which could have been motivated by its power and influence or a belief that its proclamation of universal brotherhood would influence French dealings with Muslims on the basis of respect rather than superiority.

327 Habous et ministères des habous en Afrique du Nord depuis les indépendances. (Habous and ministries of habous in North Africa since independence).

Maghreb, no. 48 (Nov.-Dec. 1971), p. 39-44.

The section on Algeria describes the functions of the Ministry of Habous, or religious endowments, which was renamed the Ministry of Original Education and Religious Affairs in 1970. The ministry is responsible for the construction and maintenance of mosques and other religious buildings, the training of imams (religious leaders), the organization of the pilgrimage to Mecca, religious education and the promotion of Arab/Islamic culture and values.

328 The denunciation of mysticism as a bulwark against reason – a contribution to the expansion of Algerian reformism 1925-1939.

Ludmilla Hanischi. *The Maghreb Review*, vol. 11, no. 5-6 (1986), p. 102-06.

Attempts to explain the origin and spread of Islamic reformism in Algeria, against the background of socio-economic development, and to investigate the extent to which the elements of this doctrine were an appropriate answer to the social problems of that time.

329 **Algériennes entre islam et islamisme.** (Algerian women between Islam and Islamism).
Djedfiga Imache, Inès Nour. Aix-en-Provence, France: Edisud, 1994. 160p.

Presents the results of an survey of 200 female Algerian students divided into two groups, those who wear the *hijab* (head cover) and those who do not. They give their perceptions on the roles of men and women, on the mixing of the sexes and on marriage for example. The work offers new insights into women's acceptance or rejection of Islamist views.

330 **The servants of the mosques.**
Baber Johansen. *The Maghreb Review*, vol. 7, no. 1-2 (1982), p. 23-31.

Johansen analyses documents in the Algerian National Archives which include lists of salaried persons employed in the Hanafite mosques of Algiers between 1811 and 1814 and in 1836 and compares the information available to Hanafite legal theory as developed from the 11th century onwards.

331 **Le réformisme musulman en Algérie de 1925 à 1940 – essai d'histoire religieuse et sociale.** (Muslim reformism in Algeria from 1925 to 1940 – an essay in religious and social history).
Ali Merad. The Hague, Paris: Mouton, 1967. 472p. 3 maps. bibliog.

Examines the creation and expansion of the Islamic reformist movement against the background of Algerian Muslim society, and Sufism during the interwar period. Its religious doctrine and moral, social, cultural and political ideals are analysed. It remains one of the basic reference works on the subject.

332 **The conversion of the *mrabtin* in Kabylia.**
Hugh Roberts. In: *Islam et politique au Maghreb.* Edited by Ernest Gellner, Jean-Claude Vatin, et al. Paris; Aix-en-Provence, France: Editions du CNRS, 1981, p. 101-25.

Describes the traditional status and functions of maraboutic (saintly) families in Kabylia and seeks to explain how some of these families have succeeded in preserving their prestigious position in the period since independence despite the process of modernization which has tended to erode the material basis of traditional maraboutism. Roberts argues that many of the most flourishing maraboutic families owe their present position to the dexterity with which they have exchanged traditional roles for modern ones, thus acquiring a new lease of life for their special status. Others have found a continuing need for their traditional services because of the problems, especially for women, which modernization generates. The chapter concludes that in the future relatively few of these families will be able to preserve their privileged status.

333 **The Algerian ulamas, 1919-1931.**
Belkacem Saadallah. *Revue d'Histoire Maghrébine*, no. 2 (July 1974), p. 138-50.

A study of the Algerian reformist movement, the factors which contributed to its development after the First World War, and the contribution of the *ulama* (religious scholars) to Algerian nationalism.

334 **The role of the ulama in the Algerian revolution: 1945-1954.**
Fahd Abdullah al-Semmari. *Jusur: The UCLA Journal of Middle Eastern Studies*, no. 2 (1986), p. 83-102.

Explores the contributions of the Islamic reform movement led by the *ulama* (religious scholars) to Algerian nationalism during the period 1945-54.

335 **Alms and arms: the combative saintliness of the Awlad Sidi Shaykh in the Algerian Sahara, sixteenth-nineteeth centuries.**
Peter von Sivers. *The Maghreb Review*, vol. 8, no. 5-6 (1983), p. 113-23.

Argues that the history of the Awlad Sidi Shaykh, the descendents of the saint Sidi Shaykh living in the southwestern Algerian Sahara, is essentially the history of the tribalization of a community implanted under different demographic circumstances by the saintly founder. The author traces the steps of this tribalization process in which alms for education were turned into arms for controlling the almsgivers.

336 **The ulama and Islamic renaissance in Algeria.**
Salah el Din el Zein el-Tayib. *American Journal of Islamic Social Sciences*, vol. 6, no. 2 (1989), p. 257-88.

A discussion of the activities of the *ulama* (religious scholars) in the social and religious fields. The Association of Algerian Ulama, founded in 1931, established schools where Arabic and the doctrines of Islam were taught. The French colonial authorities claimed the right to approve schools and the teaching of Islam and Arabic, which the association refused to concede, and their teaching produced a cultural revival that paved the way for political separation from France.

Algérie incertaine.
See item no. 2.

Algérie: vers l'état islamique?
See item no. 3.

Islamism and secularism in North Africa.
See item no. 34.

Polity and society in contemporary North Africa.
See item no. 38.

The Donatist Church: a movement of protest in Roman North Africa.
See item no. 104.

Ritual, culture and politics of Islamic reformism in Algeria.
See item no. 145.

Rebel and saint: Muslim notables, populist protest, colonial encounters (Algeria and Tunisia, 1800-1904).
See item no. 146.

Abd al-Qadir ('Abd al-Qadir al-Jaza'iri) and Abd al-Rahman ('Abd al-Rahman al-Filali, Sultan of Morocco): religious and political aspects of their confrontation (1843-1847).
See item no. 150.

Le Cardinal Lavigerie 1825-1892: l'église, l'Afrique et la France.
See item no. 189.

The FLN, Islam and Arab identity.
See item no. 245.

Migration, commerce and community: the Mizabis in eighteenth and nineteenth century Algeria.
See item no. 288.

Women in Middle Eastern history: shifting boundaries in sex and gender.
See item no. 355.

Gender and politics in Algeria: unravelling the religious paradigm.
See item no. 361.

Algeria's democracy between the Islamists and the elite.
See item no. 380.

L'Algérie par ses islamistes.
See item no. 383.

From nationalism to revolutionary Islam.
See item no. 387.

The Islamic movement in North Africa.
See item no. 389.

L'islamisme au Maghreb: la voix du Sud.
See item no. 390.

La mobilisation islamiste et les élections algériennes du 12 juin 1990.
See item no. 391.

Islam and power.
See item no. 397.

Algeria.
See item no. 399.

Political Islam in Algeria: the nonviolent dimension.
See item no. 409.

Religion

The Islamic threat: myth or reality?
See item no. 410.

Islam et politique au Maghreb.
See item no. 417.

Islam and the West.
See item no. 418.

The political and the religious in the modern history of the Maghrib.
See item no. 421.

The politics of Islamic revivalism: diversity and unity.
See item no. 423.

Les islamistes algériens face au pouvoir.
See item no. 430.

Islamism and Islamists: the emergence of new types of politico-religious militants.
See item no. 431.

Le Maghreb face à la contestation islamiste.
See item no. 437.

The challenge of radical Islam.
See item no. 442.

Identity, politics and women: cultural reassertions and feminisms in international perspective.
See item no. 443.

Authority in Islam from Muhammad to Khomeini.
See item no. 448.

Islam in the political process.
See item no. 450.

From radical mission to equivocal ambition: the expansion and manipulation of Algerian Islamism, 1979-1992.
See item no. 457.

Radical Islamism and the dilemma of Algerian nationalism: the embattled Arians of Algiers.
See item no. 459.

Les frères et la mosquée: enquête sur le mouvement islamiste en Algérie.
See item no. 461.

Continuities and discontinuities in the Algerian confrontation with Europe.
See item no. 463.

Taking up space in Tlemcen. The Islamist occupation of urban Algeria.
See item no. 471.

Islam et état au Maghreb.
See item no. 473.

Muslim law courts and the French colonial state in Algeria.
See item no. 492.

L'islam religion de l'état, comme principe constitutionnel: reflexions sur le cas algérien.
See item no. 499.

Orientalism, colonialism, and legal history: the attack on Muslim family endowments in Algeria and India.
See item no. 502.

Migrant Muslim women in France.
See item no. 695.

Le mouvement intellectuel et littéraire à la fin du XIXe et au debut du XXe siècle.
See item no. 784.

Affrontements culturels dans l'Algérie coloniale: écoles, médecines, religion, 1830-1880.
See item no. 827.

Essai de bibliographie sélective et annotée sur l'Islam maghrébin contemporain: Maroc, Algérie, Tunisie, Libye (1830-1978).
See item no. 879.

Social Organization and Social Change

337 **L'enfant illégitime dans la société musulmane.** (Illegitimate children in Muslim society).
Nadia Ait-Zai. *Peuples Méditerranéens*, no. 48-49 (1989), p. 113-22.
The narrow interpretation by Algerian lawmakers of the *hadith*, or tradition, 'A child belongs to the bed' is accountable for the legal inexistence of children born out of wedlock. The Algerian family, conscious that illegitimate births defy social values, seeks to save its honour by keeping news of such a birth from spreading and brings pressure to bear on the mother to forsake, abandon or kill the baby. The state has not measured up to this situation, neither providing social services for single mothers, nor passing laws taking into account the child's interests. An English summary appears on p. 331.

338 **Algerian women in development: a case study of the shantytowns in Annaba.**
Hadda Fawria Allali. PhD thesis, Boston University, 1988. 348p.
bibliog.
Addresses the socio-economic position of women within different historical periods to understand the disparate aspects of gender inequalities as Algerian society moved from pre-colonial to colonial and post-colonial situation. The empirical research focusses on shantytown women in Annaba as a case-study, examining gender stratification within three communities: Sidi Salem, Cité Seybouse and Bou Hamra. Allali discusses work division and gender relations within the home and in the workplace, where the research focusses on gender-based differentials in salary, training and promotion, as well as attitudes towards, and experience in, work.

339 **My life story: the autobiography of a Berber woman.**
Fadhma A. M. Amrouche, translated by Dorothy S. Blair. New Brunswick, New Jersey: Rutgers University Press, 1989. 221p.
Originally published in 1968, this book recounts phases of Amrouche's life, beginning with her childhood in a convent in Algeria and a French Catholic orphanage, to her

marriage and birth of seven children. The unequal treatment of women is a major theme, as is the difficulty of life under French colonial rule. The author shows the meanings found in poetry of her native Kabyle homeland; seven poems follow the main text.

340 Algerian women confront fundamentalism.

Karima Bennoune. *Monthly Review*, no. 46 (1994), p. 26-39.

Based on interviews with Algerian women in 1992, 1993 and February 1994. The author reports on violence by 'Muslim fundamentalists' against women activists, working women, and women who refuse to wear the veil.

341 Class structuration and economic development in the Arab world.

Mahfoud Bennoune, Imane Hayef. *Journal of Asian and African Studies* (Netherlands), vol. 21, no. 1-2 (1986), p. 44-65.

An analysis of the growth of authoritarian régimes in Egypt and Algeria in the light of Marxist theory. The author argues that historically Arab states lacked economic classes so when pushed by Western governments to develop economically, they created 'structures of power'.

342 Origins of the Algerian proletariat.

Mahfoud Bennoune. *MERIP Reports*, no. 94 (February 1981), p. 5-13, p. 32.

Argues that the genesis of the Algerian working class occurred in the devastated urban centres during the first period of the French conquest. The French colonization of Algeria aimed, from beginning to end, at continually constricting the economic base of the native population. By expropriating the indigenous producers, they were transformed into a modern, colonized proletariat. Shortly after the introduction of the French capitalist system into Algeria, the native socio-economic formation based on small commodity production was intentionally dismantled and restructured in line with superimposed capitalist production relations.

343 Algeria 1960.

Pierre Bourdieu, translated by Richard Nice. Cambridge, England: Cambridge University Press; Paris: Editions de la Maison des Sciences de l'Homme, 1979. 158p.

Presents in translation three of Bourdieu's essays, previously published in French. The first and most important essay, entitled 'The disenchantment of the world' is a shortened version of *Travail et travailleurs en Algérie* (Work and workers in Algeria), first published in 1963, presenting the findings of ethnographic and statistical studies carried out in Algeria between 1958 and 1961. Two further essays are added: 'The sense of honour' on the sentiment of honour in Kabyle society; and 'The Kabyle house or the world reversed'.

344 **The women's movement: history and theory.**
Edited by J. de Bruijn, L. D. Derksen, C. M. J. Hoeberichts.
Aldershot, England; Brookfield, Vermont: Avebury, Ashgate Pub. Co., 1993. 215p. bibliog.
This collection of essays includes a number of case-studies, one of which is on 'Images of women. Stepmothers and motherless girls in narratives from Kabylia, Algeria: oral and written productions' by Daniela Merolla.

345 **Le café maure. Sociabilité masculine et effervescence citoyenne (Algérie XVIIe-XXe siècles).** (The Algerian Moorish cafe: male sociability and exuberant citizenship: Algeria in the 17th-20th centuries).
Omar Carlier. *Annales: Economies, Sociétés, Civilisations* (France), vol. 45, no. 4 (1990), p. 975-1,003.
Examines the social functions, especially those that affected male behaviour, of Moorish cafes in Algeria, focussing on changes brought about by such influences as colonialism and modernization.

346 **State and gender in the Maghreb.**
Mounira Charrad. *Middle East Report*, no. 163 (March-April 1990), p. 19-24.
A study of the different policies adopted in regard to family law and women's rights in Algeria, Morocco and Tunisia from the time of national independence to the mid-1980s. The author argues that in explaining changes in women's rights, it is necessary to consider the process of state formation and to relate state to gender. The article briefly examines Islamic law and women's legal status and women's rights after independence. In Algeria from the time of independence until 1984 there were several attempts to reform family law but it was held hostage to political cleavages in the ruling establishment. Despite Algerian leaders repeatedly expressing their interest in changing family law to increase women's rights, the long-awaited Family Code adopted in 1984 remained faithful to the principles of the Maleki legal school of Sunni Islam.

347 **Clientalism in Algeria.**
Bruno Etienne. In: *Patrons and clients in Mediterranean societies.*
Edited by Ernest Gellner, John Waterbury. London: Duckworth, 1977, p. 291-307.
Examines the hypothesis that clientalism in Algeria assists the integration into national life of marginal and periperal populations having their own system of values.

348 **Middle Eastern Muslim women speak.**
Edited by E. W. Fernea, B. Q. Bezirgan. Austin, Texas; London: University of Texas Press, 1977. 402p. map. bibliog.
Two chapters of this volume are devoted to Algeria. There is an interview with Jamilah Buhrayd, a heroine of the War of Independence, which deals with her role and that of other women in the insurrection (p. 251-62); and translated excerpts from Fadéla M'rabet's *Les Algériennes*, discussing the status of women five years after

independence and the continuing hold of traditional ways, in spite of the revolution's lip service to emancipation (p. 319-58).

349 **Women and the family in the Middle East: new voices of change.**
Edited by E. W. Fernea. Austin, Texas: University of Texas Press, 1985. 368p. bibliog.

Includes essays on Algeria by novelist Assia Djebar entitled 'A forbidden glimpse, a broken sound' (from *Women of Algiers in their apartment* [q.v.]), translated by J. M. McDougal (p. 337-50), and by Fatiha Akeb and Malika Abdelaziz entitled 'Algerian women discuss the need for change' (p. 8-23).

350 **Nationalité et citoyenneté: les femmes algériennes et leur droits.**
(Nationality and citizenship: Algerian women and their rights).
M. Gadant. *Peuples Méditerranéens*, no. 44-45 (1988), p. 293-337; p. 344-45.

The state, in its efforts to control modernization, has imposed models of the militant, working woman who remains, above all, a mother and wife. This subordination to the family confers nationality on women while depriving them of citizenship, an ambiguity incorporated in the legal code. The historical phases of the modernization of the family are analysed together with the difficulties facing Algerian feminism in a society undergoing crisis – a society where the family is a refuge and the state partly founds its legitimacy on keeping women out of the political sphere. An English summary is provided on p. 344-45.

351 **Women of the Mediterranean.**
Edited by Monique Gadant, translated by A. M. Berrett. London: Zed Press, 1986. 196p.

An English translation of *Femmes de la Méditerranée*, originally published in 1983 as no. 22-23 of *Peuples Méditerranéens*. This series of country case-studies, includes 'Fatima, Ouardia and Malika: contemporary Algerian women' by Monique Gadant and 'Neighbourhood relations and social control: the role of women in Maghrebian communities in southern France' by Sossie Andezian and Jocelyne Streiff-Fenart. There is also an essay on the Draft law on the status of persons in Algeria.

352 **Human development and adolescent studies in Algeria.**
Zoubida Guernina. Aldershot, England; Brookfield, Vermont: Avebury, 1994. 281p. bibliog.

Presents the results of a cross-sectional study examining the distribution of behaviour problems among a sample of Algerian adolescents and their association with factors such as age, sex, type of school, bilingualism, parents' level of education and the pupils' level of achievement.

353 **L'élite dirigeante et la genèse de l'entrepreneur industriel au Maghreb: 'l'exemple algérien'.** (The ruling élite and the origins of the industrial entrepreneur in the Maghreb: the Algerian example). M'hammed Ibnolmobarek. *Revue d'Histoire Maghrébine* (Tunisia), vol. 11, no. 35-36 (1984), p. 137-52.

Despite its socialist rhetoric, the ruling élite in Algeria has since 1968 favoured the emergence of an entrepreneurial bourgeoisie in the sectors of light industries and service industries while keeping a state monopoly on heavy industry. Law and policies have favoured employers rather than trade unions and the course of labour disputes has shown the connivance between the élite and the bourgeoisie. The overwhelming economic importance of the state sector prevents private capital from mounting any challenge to the hegemony of the ruling élite.

354 **Women without men: gender and marginality in an Algerian town.** W. H. M. Jansen. Leiden, Netherlands: E. J. Brill, 1987. 301p. map. bibliog.

A study of poor women who are widowed, divorced or orphaned – women without men – based on fieldwork carried out in 1981-82 in a fast growing town in northern Algeria. These women are among the most destitute of their sex and disturb the social order. They are described at their often despised and demeaning work – in the bathhouses, as washers of the dead mediating life and death, as religious intermediaries who facilitate communication between women and the supernatural, as assistants in fertility and birth, and working black magic. In all these activities, women defy the gender hierarchy that would place them in seclusion. Their daughters are the first to replace them as workers outside the home in public service and professional careers; they have an edge over other girls in education because they do not have men to keep them in seclusion. Such women are paving the way for the liberation of women in Algeria.

355 **Women in Middle Eastern history: shifting boundaries in sex and gender.** Edited by Nikki R. Keddie, Beth Baron. New Haven, Connecticut; London: Yale University Press, 1991. 355p.

This collection of case-studies includes one contribution on Algeria by Julia Clancy-Smith entitled 'The house of Zaineb: female authority and saintly succession in colonial Algeria'.

356 **The decline of tribal organisation in the Souf (S. E. Algeria).** Nico Kielstra. *Revue de l'Occident Musulman et de la Méditerranée* (France), no. 45 (1987), p. 11-24.

The article points out that secular tribal organization was very weak in the Souf area in the pre-colonial period but became more prominent between 1860 and 1890 when tribal leaders could act as intermediaries with external authorities. The French colonial authorities, however, failed to understand that neither secular nor religious leaders constituted an established hereditary aristocracy and that leadership was unstable and based on shifting alliances. As a result, traditional authority declined despite the French attempt to maintain it.

357 **Algerian women since independence.**
Peter R. Knauss. In: *State and society in Algeria.* Edited by John P. Entelis, Phillip C. Naylor. Boulder, Colorado: Westview Press, 1992, p. 151-69.

Surveys women's status in Algeria since independence, concluding that during the whole of the post-colonial period women have been disillusioned with the many promises of dramatic change made by the all-male political leadership following the visible role played by Algerian women in the War of Independence. Knauss contends that patriarchal traditions were revived and reinforced in Algeria by the severity of the trauma of French colonialism. He argues that the 1983 Family Code further ensconces patriarchal and traditionalist values and practices. The chapter concludes with preliminary assessments of the status of Algeria's feminist movement and the new challenge posed by the growing strength of Islamism.

358 **The persistence of patriarchy: class, gender, and ideology in twentieth century Algeria.**
Peter R. Knauss. New York: Praeger, 1987. 176p. bibliog.

Suggests that though patriarchy had lost its economic base under colonial, agrarian capitalism, it continued to thrive in the revolutionary and post-revolutionary periods because it provided Algerians with a sense of identity. In the same way, Islam became the beleaguered symbol for a separate Algerian identity. Successful in mobilizing all classes against colonial rule, this ideology became an obstacle to social change in the hands of the nationalist leaders after independence. Knauss argues that Algerian women, who ought to have been liberated after independence, became the principal victims of this ideology.

359 **The eloquence of silence: Algerian women in question.**
Marnia Lazreg. New York: Routledge, 1994. 270p. bibliog.

This work describes how Algerian women, primarily Arabophone and illiterate, were structurally marginalized by both colonial and native societies, yet used the weight of their silent physical presence to play an important role in the revolution.

360 **The emergence of classes in Algeria: a study of colonialism and socio-political change.**
Marnia Lazreg. Boulder, Colorado: Westview Press, 1976. 252p. bibliog.

Seeks to determine the impact of colonialism on the evolution of social classes in Algeria from 1830 to the present, and to analyse the relationship between classes and political and economic development.

361 **Gender and politics in Algeria: unravelling the religious paradigm.**
Marnia Lazreg. *Signs*, vol. 15, no. 4 (1990), p. 755-80.

Algerian women were active during the War of Independence yet the National Liberation Front took few steps to improve women's conditions when opportunities were available to do so. In the 1984 Family Code, male authority in marriage, divorce and child custody was reaffirmed. This article argues that the reasons for this should not be sought in a religious paradigm, but in the social and political interactions and secular values which took on moral overtones during the conflict. In 1989 Algerian women were becoming their own 'visible advocates' for a new order.

362 Studies in power and class in Africa.
Edited by I. L. Markovitz. New York: Oxford University Press, 1987. 415p. maps. bibliog.

Includes an essay on 'Algerian women's access to power 1962-1985' by A. Lippert (p. 209-32).

363 Tradition and the veil: female status in Tunisia and Algeria.
S. E. Marshall, R. G. Stokes. *Journal of Modern African Studies*, no. 19 (1981), p. 625-46.

The authors examine the sharply different state policies towards female status in Tunisia and Algeria. Tunisia's régime has vigorously undermined traditional Islamic constraints on women whereas Algeria's leadership has reaffirmed Islamic traditions restricting women to a subordinate domestic role. They argue that these differences can best be explained as outcomes of the differing political contingencies facing the élites of Tunisia and Algeria.

364 Old and new elites in North Africa: the French colonial impact in comparative perspective.
Clement Henry Moore. In: *Les influences occidentales dans les villes Maghrébines à l'époque contemporaine, Etudes méditerranéennes* 2. Aix-en-Provence, France: Editions de l'Université de Provence, 1974, p. 17-37.

An extremely useful comparative study of the impact of colonialism on the old élites of Algeria, Morocco and Tunisia, the new élites created by the French educational system and the degree of social mobilization.

365 La guerre des femmes. Magie et amour en Algérie. (The war of the women. Magic and love in Algeria).
Nedjima Plantade. Paris: La Boîte à Documents, 1988. 184p. bibliog.

This unique study, carried out into the female domain in Kabylia, explores marriage, amorous and sexual rivalries and the practices of sexual magic. It argues that the 'magie d'amour' is more important in 'sexualité sociale' than 'sexualité biologique'.

366 Both right and left handed: Arab women talk about their lives.
Bouthaina Shaaban. London: The Women's Press, 1988. 242p.

A series of interviews with women, profiling women in Lebanon, Syria, Palestine and Algeria. The interviews are essentially life stories that focus on specific experiences and relationships, such as marriage, political involvement, education, work and family relations. Many of the interviews are with women active politically in movements ranging from the Syrian and Algerian anti-colonial struggles to women in the *Amal* movement in Lebanon.

367 'Hassiba Ben Bouali, if you could see our Algeria': women and public space in Algeria.
Susan Slyomovics. *Middle East Report,* no. 192 (January-February 1995), p. 8-13.

For complex historical, economic and religious reasons, both women and men in Algeria subscribe to economic and spatial arrangements that reinforce the legitimacy of women's lower status. Today, many women in the social and intellectual élite, such as university students, profess fervent Muslim faith but reinterpret Islam's idea of women. It is precisely the protected status symbolized by the veil that encourages them to believe that they will be able to compete in the male public world. However, these new and supposedly Islamic conceptions of women's role are not supported by the Front Islamique du Salut. More remarkably, the Islamist leadership's attitudes conform to legislation put in place after independence by the Front de Libération Nationale. The factions now struggling for power in Algeria are in fundamental ideological agreement that women's social freedom must be severely restricted.

368 The Republic of cousins: women's oppression in Mediterranean society.
Germaine Tillion, translated by Quintin Hoare. London: Al Saqi Books, 1983. 181p.

First published in French in 1966 as *Le harem et les cousins.* The author, a distinguished French ethnologist with wide experience of Algeria, argues that the origin of women's oppression has nothing to do with Islam, but can be traced to ancient times and the beginning of patrilineal society, itself a product of the beginning of agriculture. She argues that it was endogamy (the practice of marrying within the lineage) that set the stage for the oppression of women within patrilineal society, long before the rise of Islam. Endogamy, 'the republic of cousins', kept property (land and animals) within the lineage and protected the economic and political interests of the men.

369 The rise of Algerian women: cultural dualism and multi-party politics.
R. Tlemcani. In: *Women and development in the Middle East and North Africa.* Edited by Joseph G. Jabbra, Nancy W. Jabbra. Leiden, Netherlands: E. J. Brill, 1992, p. 69-81.

During the Algerian struggle for national liberation (1954-62), nationalist leaders proudly proclaimed that women, as men's equals, would occupy key positions in the modern state building process in Algeria's post-independence period. This original commitment to share political power at all levels has been expressly emphasized since Algeria gained independence. Almost three decades after independence, women's enjoyment of political rights has been insignificant and progress for women has been largely minimal. The rise of the Islamist movement in the 1980s and the crisis of the rentier state caused by the fall in oil prices have added pressure to maintain the traditional position of women in the home. This article focuses on the specific problems experienced by Algerian women and analyses some of the factors which have inhibited women's emancipation in Algeria.

370   **Women in Islamic societies: social attitudes and historical perspectives.**
Edited by Bo Utas.   Brooklyn, New York: Olive Branch Press, 1988. 259p.

Surveys the role of women in several states including Algeria. Utas addresses relationships to men, education, sexuality, responsibilities, and female honour as defined by Islamic societies.

371   **Le code algérien de la famille.** (The Algerian Family Code).
Hélène Vandevelde.   *Maghreb-Machrek*, no. 107 (1985), p. 52-64.

Presents extracts from the controversial and long-awaited Family Code of 1984, together with an analysis of its main features. Vandevelde emphasizes the patriarchal character of the new legislation by examining its provisions about marriage, the family and divorce. On the background to this controversial legislation, see also the author's article entitled 'Où en est le problème du code de la famille en Algérie?' (*Maghreb-Machrek*, no. 97 [1982], p. 39-54).

372   **'I am living in a foreign country here': a conversation with an Algerian 'hittiste'.**
Meriem Vergès.   *Middle East Report,* no. 192 (January-February 1995), p. 14-17.

A short but fascinating interview with an Algerian hittiste, 'Abd al-Haq, one of the young desocialized, unemployed men who hang out on the streets in the cities, leaning against the walls (heit). Not all the young have found salvation with the Front Islamique du Salut (FIS), nor an outlet for their despair in religion. In the shadow of the FIS, 'Abd al-Haq exemplifies the fragile category of 'in-betweens' who go back and forth between cannabis and the mosque. For them ideological commitment is problematic. Individual resistance, escape into some imaginary compensation, search for a life elsewhere, and longing to get out remain their strategies for circumventing reality.

373   **Les classes moyennes au Maghreb.** (The middle classes in the Maghreb).
Abdelkader Zghal, et al.   Paris: Editions du CNRS, 1982. 388p.

This collection of essays includes two general articles: on the middle classes and development in the Maghreb by A. Zghal; and on the concept of social class, its use and application in 'undeveloped societies' by A. Sayad. Articles on Algeria include contributions: by C.-R. Ageron on the middle classes of colonial Algeria; by R. Weexsteen analysing spatial structures – social structures in pre-colonial, colonial and contemporary Algeria; by H. Sanson on the 'middle classes' in the Algerian strategy of the National Charter; and by D. Holsinger on internal migration and the middle classes in Algeria – the case of the Mzabites.

Algérie: vers l'état islamique?
See item no. 3.

The Maghreb in the modern world: Algeria, Tunisia, Morocco.
See item no. 4.

Annuaire de l'Afrique du Nord.
See item no. 5.

Enjeux sahariens.
See item no. 6.

The making of contemporary Algeria, 1830-1987: colonial upheavals and post-independence development.
See item no. 8.

State and society in independent North Africa.
See item no. 11.

L'Algérie indépendante: bilan d'une révolution nationale.
See item no. 13.

Algeria: the revolution institutionalized.
See item no. 15.

Algérie: cultures et révolution.
See item no. 17.

Algeria: the challenge of modernity.
See item no. 19.

North-west Africa: a political and economic survey.
See item no. 21.

Algeria: a country study.
See item no. 32.

State and revolution in Algeria.
See item no. 36.

Man, state and society in the contemporary Maghrib.
See item no. 37.

Polity and society in contemporary North Africa.
See item no. 38.

Le miroir: aperçu historique et statistique sur la Régence d'Alger.
See item no. 121.

The colonial harem.
See item no. 135.

Algerian landownership and rural leadership, 1860-1940: a quantitative approach.
See item no. 191.

Algeria: anticolonial war.
See item no. 207.

The political roles of Islamic women: a study of two revolutions – Algeria and Iran.
See item no. 227.

111

Berbères aux marges de l'histoire.
See item no. 278.

Algériennes entre islam et islamisme.
See item no. 329.

The conversion of the *mrabtin* in Kabylia.
See item no. 332.

Gender and politics in Algeria: unravelling the religious paradigm.
See item no. 361.

Les enjeux politiques et symboliques de la lutte des femmes pour l'égalité entre les sexes en Algérie.
See item no. 379.

Islamism and feminism: Algeria's 'rites of passage' to democracy.
See item no. 392.

Women and democracy in Algeria.
See item no. 403.

Jeunesse: sport et politique.
See item no. 411.

Les communistes algériens et l'émancipation des femmes.
See item no. 414.

L'état-relais à partir de l'exemple algérien: la transnationalisation à l'oeuvre sous le modèle de l'état national.
See item no. 415.

Islamism and Islamists: the emergence of new types of politico-religious militants.
See item no. 431.

Identity, politics and women: cultural reassertions and feminisms in international perspective.
See item no. 443.

Taking up space in Tlemcen. The Islamist occupation of urban Algeria.
See item no. 471.

Political elites in Arab North Africa – Morocco, Algeria, Tunisia, Libya and Egypt.
See item no. 481.

Modernization: Islamic law.
See item no. 486.

Muslim law courts and the French colonial state in Algeria.
See item no. 492.

Administration et tribu chez les Nemencha (Algérie) au XIXe siècle.
See item no. 505.

Etre caid dans l'Algérie coloniale.
See item no. 506.

North Africa: regional tensions and strategic concerns.
See item no. 552.

Bâtisseurs et bureaucrates: ingénieurs et société au Maghreb et au Moyen Orient.
See item no. 593.

Le capitalisme d'état algérien.
See item no. 614.

Le complexe sidérurgique d'El-Hadjar: une expérience industrielle en Algérie.
See item no. 652.

Industriels algériens.
See item no. 653.

Algeria's agrarian transformation.
See item no. 669.

La dépossession des fellahs (1830-1962).
See item no. 673.

Migrant Muslim women in France.
See item no. 695.

Urban growth and housing policy in Algeria: a case study of a migrant community in the city of Constantine.
See item no. 738.

La sémantique au service de l'anthropologie: recherche methodologique et application à l'étude de la parenté chez les Touaregs de l'Ahaggar.
See item no. 761.

The nomads of Algeria under French rule: a study of social and economic change.
See item no. 767.

Essai sur l'université et les cadres en Algérie.
See item no. 771.

Women and the process of educational democratization in the Arab world: the case of Algeria.
See item no. 775.

Veil of shame: the role of women in the contemporary fiction of North Africa and the Arab world.
See item no. 781.

Le mouvement intellectuel et littéraire à la fin du XIXe et au debut du XXe siècle.
See item no. 784.

Women of Algiers in their apartment.
See item no. 795.

A wife for my son.
See item no. 798.

Desperate spring: lives of Algerian women.
See item no. 808.

Reflections on a Kabyle pot: Algerian women and the decorative tradition.
See item no. 828.

La communication inégale: l'accès aux média dans les campagnes algériennes.
See item no. 849.

Social Services, Health and Welfare

374 **Médecins et protection sociale dans le monde arabe.** (Doctors and social security in the Arab world).
Edited by B. Curmi, S. Chiffoleau. Beirut; Amman, Jordan: Centre d'Etudes et de Recherche sur le Moyen Orient Contemporain, 1993. 283p. (Cahiers du CERMOC, no. 5).

Includes three articles on doctors and the health service in Algeria: 'Positions et pratiques des médecins dans le système de soins algérien' (Conditions and practices of doctors in the Algerian care system) by F. Z. Belhocine and M. Belhocine on p. 57-65; 'Systèmes de protection en matière de santé en Algérie (Security systems on health matters in Algeria) by M. F. Grangaud on p. 67-82; 'Médecine, recherche et protection sociale: le cas algérien' (Medicine, research and social security: the Algerian case) by R. Waast on p. 83-99.

375 **Infant and juvenile mortality at Algiers: results of a survey organized by WHO and the Ministry of Public Health in 1974-75.**
World Health Statistics Quarterly, no. 34 (1981), p. 44-63.

An analysis of the results of a survey carried out in Algiers by the World Health Organization and the Algerian Ministry of Public Health into the sensitive subject of infant and juvenile mortality.

376 **The Institut Technologique de la Santé Publique, Constantine, Algeria: preparing health personnel for Algeria.**
Comité Pedagogique. In: *Personnel for health care: case-studies of educational programmes.* Edited by F. M. Katz, T. Fülöp. Geneva: World Health Organization, 1978, p. 19-30. (Public Health Papers, no. 70).

Outlines the aims and nature of education programmes for health team training in the Institut Technologique de la Santé Publique in the city of Constantine.

377 **Systèmes de santé and de protection sociale dans le monde arabe: Algérie.** (Systems of health and social welfare in the Arab world: Algeria).
Maghreb-Machrek, no. 138 (1992), p. 115-16.
A short account explaining the complexities of the social security and national health systems in Algeria, the problems of funding the national health service and the expansion of private health care.

378 **The private life of Islam.**
Ian Young. London: Allen Lane, 1974. 307p.
This book is based on the diary which the author, a British medical student, kept during a summer spent in a provincial maternity hospital in Kabylia. It describes a series of medical nightmares, the incompetence of the Bulgarian doctors and the lack of concern of the Algerian authorities. Many of the comments on the problems which beset the Algerian health service are valid, but the work shows little real understanding of Algerian society.

The making of contemporary Algeria, 1830-1987: colonial upheavals and post-independence development.
See item no. 8.

UN Statistical Yearbook.
See item no. 734.

Affrontements culturels dans l'Algérie coloniale: écoles, médecines, religion, 1830-1880.
See item no. 827.

Politics

379 **Les enjeux politiques et symboliques de la lutte des femmes pour l'égalité entre les sexes en Algérie.** (Symbolic and political issues in Algerian women's struggle for sexual equality).
Rabia Abdelkrim. *Peuples Méditerranéens*, no. 48-49 (1989), p. 257-78; p. 334.

Algerian women's determination to achieve emancipation, a determination that can be based on a democratic movement, has encountered an Islamist movement that has grown rapidly since 1988. The Front Islamique du Salut (FIS) has clearly voiced its intentions to send women back into the home and condemned the mixing of the sexes. The author asks whether the alternative for women is between laicism or religious fascism. There is an English summary on p. 334.

380 **Algeria's democracy between the Islamists and the elite.**
Lahouari Addi. *Middle East Report*, no. 175 (March-April 1992), p. 36-38.

Argues that Algeria's experience over the previous three years has shown that in a Muslim land the process of democratization gives rise to currents which seek to destroy it. However, neutralizing these currents by force entails halting the democratization process and enclosing society in repression. Society can escape that enclosure only if Islam is depoliticized, if it no longer serves as a political resource in the struggle for power.

381 **L'Algérie et la démocratie.** (Algeria and democracy).
Lahouari Addi. Paris: La Découverte, 1994. 240p.

A very lucid analysis of the origins of Algerian Islamism and populism. It examines: whether the democratization of power is possible, and under what conditions; whether the political wing of the Islamist movement can be trusted; and the risks involved in the integration of the Front Islamique du Salut in the democratic process.

382 **L'affaire Mécili.** (The Mécili affair).
Hocine Ait-Ahmed. Paris: La Découverte, 1989. 260p.

A passionate denununciation by the leader of the Front des Forces Socialistes (FFS) of the French and Algerian states for their part in the assassination in Paris on 7 April 1987 of Ali-André Mécili, a lawyer and leading member of the FFS.

383 **L'Algérie par ses islamistes.** (Algeria by its Islamists).
Mustafa Al-Ahnaf, Bernard Botiveau, Frank Frégosi. Paris: Karthala, 1991. 328p. bibliog.

An introduction to the ideology of the different tendencies that make up Algerian Islamism. The authors present and comment on a selection of texts from the political/religious press on a wide range of subjects – politics, economy, education and culture, violence, women and the family, France and the West – together with portraits of key personalities in the movement and descriptions of the most important organizations. These are preceded by a short history of Algerian Islamism since the birth of the the national movement.

384 **Algeria, assassination in the name of religion.**
London: Article 19, 1993. 14p. (Censorship News, no. 31).

Since the cancellation of national elections in January 1992, Algeria has been gripped by violence which continues to escalate. Radical Islamic groups are now targeting for the assassination of prominent public figures, journalists, writers and intellectuals known for their opposition to the activities of the Islamist movement. Press freedom also continues to be curtailed by the authorities under the emergency regulations which were introduced to combat the violence.

385 **Algeria, deteriorating human rights under the state of emergency.**
New York: Amnesty International USA, 1993. 16p.

A short account of the deterioration in human rights in Algeria since a state of emergency was declared early in 1992. This is one of a number of reports prepared by Amnesty International detailing human rights abuses in Algeria by the security forces and the Islamist militants since the military coup in January 1992.

386 **Liberalism in Northern Africa.**
Lisa Anderson. *Current History*, vol. 89, no. 546 (1990), p. 145-48; p. 174-75.

Although North African rulers and dominant-party élites were slow to loosen their grip or promote policies that would weaken their power, there were signs during the 1980s that they would permit modest experiments with political liberalization – particularly to enlist support for unpopular economic reforms.

387 **From nationalism to revolutionary Islam.**
Edited by Said Amir Arjomand. Albany, New York: State University of New York Press; London: Macmillan, 1984. 256p. bibliog.

One of the essays is devoted to an analysis of incipient Islamic traditionalism in Algeria, 'National integration and traditional rural organization in Algeria 1970-80: background for Islamic traditionalism?' by Peter von Sivers (p. 94-118).

388 **Le parti selon la Charte Nationale Algérienne.** (The party according to the Algerian National Charter).
Jean-Louis Bernelas, Patrick Lecomte. *Maghreb-Machrek*, no. 75 (1977), p. 60-68.
Analyses the institutional and political consequences of the principles embodied in the National Charter of 1976 and its implications for the single party, the Front de Libération Nationale (FLN).

389 **The Islamic movement in North Africa.**
François Burgat, William Dowell. Austin, Texas: University of Texas Press, 1993. 310p. bibliog. (Middle East Monograph Series, no. 10).
This work is a revised and translated version of Burgat's *L'islamisme au Maghreb: la voix du Sud* (q.v.). This revised version in English includes new material gathered by Burgat from 1989 to 1992 and including events in Algeria through the summer of 1992.

390 **L'islamisme au Maghreb: la voix du Sud.** (Islamism in the Maghreb: the voice of the South).
François Burgat. Paris: Editions Karthala, 1988. 307p.
Argues that Islam's activist political form is no mere rejection of all things Western but, instead, constitutes an authentic 'voice of the South' – an articulation of cultural and political identity rooted in historical experience and religious expression. In the early chapters, the author distinguishes Islamism from its historical and contemporary competitors, identifies the various political, military, and cultural forces that have transformed Islam as a faith into Islamism as a militant political doctrine, and examines the modalities and instrumentalities of Islamic discourse and action including the role of the mosque, the university, political writings, and violence. Three chapters are devoted to the evolution of political Islam in Algeria and its neighbours, Morocco, Libya and Tunisia. A thirty-page chronology on the emergence of the Islamic current in the region ending with the October 1988 riots in Algeria is appended.

391 **La mobilisation islamiste et les élections algériennes du 12 juin 1990.** (Islamist mobilization and the Algerian elections of 12 June 1990).
François Burgat with Jean Leca. *Maghreb-Machrek*, no. 129 (1990), p. 5-22.
Investigates the political significance of the June 1990 local elections in which the Front Islamique du Salut won a sweeping victory. The article argues that the Islamist movement, as much a product of history as the dogmas it embraces, is being shaped by forces whose capacity to develop in accordance with the country's social, economic and political realities should not be underestimated.

392 **Islamism and feminism: Algeria's 'rites of passage' to democracy.**
Boutheina Cheriet. In: *State and society in Algeria.* Edited by John
P. Entelis, Phillip C. Naylor. Boulder, Colorado: Westview Press,
1992, p. 171-215.

Examines the developments that led to the emergence of Islamism and feminism as
serious political and social protagonists in Algeria. The representation of women as
guardians of tradition has further strengthened Islamist and conservative claims as to
the proper role and status of women in Algerian society, a status formalized in the
1984 Family Code. Paradoxically, the promulgation of this code also provoked the
emergence of an outspoken feminist movement. The tensions and discontinuities
characterizing Islamist-feminist relations are analysed, and the dynamics linking these
movements to the centralized state in the context of Algeria's evolving democratic
political system are also examined.

393 **The resilience of Algerian populism.**
Boutheina Cheriet. *Middle East Report*, no. 174 (January-February
1992), p. 9-14; p. 34.

The process of political democratization and economic liberalization in Algeria is far
from being a neat rupture with the one-party system, as the same actors are monitoring
the process – the army, the presidency and the politbureau of the FLN party. At the
same time, there is a propensity within Algerian public opinion to favour a millennial
solution to the economic and social problems facing the country. Hence the
formidable popularity of Islamist discourse, particularly that dispensed by the Front
Islamique du Salut, which has explicitly rejected democracy as alien and divisive.

394 **The American periodical press and Ahmed Ben Bella.**
J. J. Cooke, A. A. Heggoy. *Muslim World*, vol. 61, no. 4 (October
1971), p. 293-302.

Analyses the ambivalent and often hostile attitides towards Ben Bella, the first
president of the Algerian republic (1963-65), and his policies which have been
adopted by leading journals of the American periodical press.

395 **After the storm: the changing military balance in the Middle East.**
Anthony H. Cordesman. Boulder, Colorado: Westview Press;
London: Mansell, 1993. 817p. bibliog.

North Africa is one of the five regions into which the Middle East is divided.
Cordesman presents an overview of the military situation in the region, arms transfers
and weapons proliferation, and examines trends in arms sales and the military status of
individual countries. The conclusion summarizes the military problems of each region.

396 **The military forces of the Maghrib: the next decade.**
A. H. Cordesman. *RUSI and Brassey's Defence Yearbook*, no. 96
(1986), p. 227-53.

A discussion of the military forces of the Maghreb countries, including Algeria, over
the next decade.

397 **Islam and power.**
Edited by A. S. Cudsi, Ali E. Hillal Dessouki. Baltimore, Maryland: Johns Hopkins University Press; London: Croom Helm, 1981. 204p. bibliog.

Includes an essay by J.-C. Vatin on 'Religious resistance and state power in Algeria' (p. 119-57).

398 **Le drame algérien, un peuple en otage.** (The Algerian drama, a people held hostage).
Paris: La Découverte, 1994. 226p.

A collection of essays by journalists and academics aimed at the general public written in an attempt to 'demystify' both the Islamist movement in Algeria and the military régime which took power in January 1992. The authors argue that the régime in power is neither civilian, secular nor democratic and practises blind repression in order to ensure that the 'political-military mafia' can continue to enjoy their privileges. State terrorism feeds that of the Islamist militants.

399 **Algeria.**
M.-J. Deeb. In: *Religion and politics: a world guide.* Edited by S. Mews. Harlow, England: Longman, 1989, p. 6-9.

A brief discussion on Islam and politics in Algeria.

400 **Islam and the state in Algeria and Morocco: a dialectical model.**
Mary-Jane Deeb. In: *Islamism and secularism in North Africa.* Edited by John Ruedy. Basingstoke, England: Macmillan, 1994, p. 275-87.

Proposes a dialectical model to explain the successes and failures of Islamist movements in the Maghreb. Deeb's thesis is that the more pluralistic the state, the less developed the Islamic challenge will be and that the more the modernizing state succeeds in incorporating Islamic traditions and institutions into its programmes, the more successful that challenge will be. Thus Islamism is most successful in Algeria, the most authoritarian state and one that is explicitly secular, and least so in Morocco, which has long permitted a limited expression of dissent and which has always projected itself as an Islamic state.

401 **World encyclopedia of political systems and parties.**
Edited by G. E. Delury. New York: Facts on File, 1987. 2nd ed. 1,440p.

Includes a section on Algeria by D. E. Spiro and K. J. Perkins (p. 12-18).

402 **Transition to democracy in Algeria.**
Bradford Dillman. In: *State and society in Algeria.* Edited by John P. Entelis, Philip C. Naylor. Boulder, Colorado: Westview Press, 1992, p. 31-51.

Dillman surveys and interprets the most important political changes in Algeria since 1988, stressing that these changes must be seen in the context of the severe economic crisis since 1985 and the October 1988 riots. He argues that political changes from 1988 to 1991 were so enormous as to undermine many previous assumptions about Algerian politics. The chapter focuses on the multiple levels at which democratization was taking place during this period – in the government (reformers versus hard-liners), within the economic sphere (public versus private), between parties (secularists versus Islamists), within parties, and among groups in civil society.

403 Women and democracy in Algeria.
Dalila Djerbal, Louisa Ait Hamou.   *Review of African Political Economy*, no. 54 (1992), p. 106-25.
Explores the growth of the women's movement in Algeria in the context of the intertwined processes of democratization and the rise of Islamic fundamentalism. The authors acknowledge that women are themselves divided along 'traditionalist' and 'modernist' lines, but argue that it is only through increased democratization that fuller participation by women in society can be achieved.

404 La mise en place des institutions algériennes. (The establishment of Algeria's institutions).
Jean-Claude Douence.   Paris: Fondation Nationale des Sciences Politiques (Centre d'Etudes des Relations Internationales), 1964. 68p. bibliog.
A useful work which examines the nature of the Evian Accords which established Algeria's independence from France, and the struggle for power during the first months of independence. It includes a detailed chronology of political events in 1962.

405 The second battle of Algiers.
Khalid Duran.   *Orbis*, vol. 33, no. 3 (1989), p. 403-21.
Discusses the riots in Algeria in early October 1988 in which over 500 people were killed. The causes of the riots, their lack of leadership and President Chadli's reforms are discussed in some detail.

406 Comparative politics of North Africa: Algeria, Morocco, and Tunisia.
John P. Entelis.   Syracuse, New York: Syracuse University Press, 1980. 196p. map. bibliog. (Contemporary Issues in the Middle East).
A comparison of the contemporary political systems of Algeria, Morocco and Tunisia, each analysed in terms of its post-independence politics, political culture and ideology, political processes, political economy and foreign policy.

407 Elite political culture and socialization in Algeria: tensions and discontinuities.
John P. Entelis.   *Middle East Journal*, vol. 35, no. 2 (1981), p. 191-208.
In Algeria it is only in the relatively small, 'modernized' sector and its even smaller élite component that political culture and ideology are meaningful categories of analysis. Algerian political culture reflects the impact of both general cultural values and of recent historical experiences, especially the War of Independence, on the men

who have assumed leadership positions in the state. From both these environments has emerged a conflictual political culture where intra-élite hostility and mistrust predominate. Algerian politicians often behave, and expect others to behave, as if they are constantly manoeuvring and scheming to acquire more power.

408 **Islam, democracy, and the state: the reemergence of authoritarian politics in Algeria.**
John P. Entelis. In: *Islamism and secularism in North Africa.*
Edited by John Ruedy. Basingstoke, England: Macmillan Press, 1994, p. 219-51.

Focusses on the 1992 military coup in Algeria, which overthrew the Chadli government and annulled the results of the first round of legislative elections won by the Front Islamique du Salut (FIS) in December 1991. Entelis argues that the FIS had inaugurated a political discourse consistent with Algeria's culture, history and experience, but that discourse represented a challenge that was unacceptable to the military, which had always been the mainstay of Algeria's authoritarian system.

409 **Political Islam in Algeria: the nonviolent dimension.**
John P. Entelis. *Current History*, vol. 94 (January 1995), p. 13-17.

Argues that the principal Islamist opposition group in Algeria, the Front Islamique du Salut (FIS) is non-violent but that pressure from violent fringe groups and the repressive policies of the military-backed government has brought the movement to a crossroads. With its leaders Abassi Madani and Ali Benhadj under house arrest, thousands of FIS militants imprisoned in desert camps, and government death squads killing or intimidating FIS supporters, the movement has become increasingly radicalized. Entelis maintains that at a time when moderate Islamists represent the best hope for a non-violent transition to democracy, moderate FIS leaders have been forced underground or abroad by a régime determined to impose 'law and order' at any cost. He claims that the FIS is now pursuing a strategy of political pressure and armed coercion in the hope that the military dimension will be put aside once the democratic process is restarted.

410 **The Islamic threat: myth or reality?**
John L. Esposito. New York: Oxford University Press, 1992. 262p. bibliog.

Provides an account of the differences in the organization and ideologies of contemporary Islamist movements, followed by a number of country case-studies and a description of Islamist opposition movements in North Africa, including Algeria. The conclusion focusses on the policy implications of misreading the Islamic resurgence.

411 **Jeunesse: sport et politique.** (Youth: sports and politics).
Youssef Fates. *Peuples Méditerranéens*, no. 52-53 (1990), p. 57-72; p. 294-95.

Sports have developed enormously in Algeria, where 70 per cent of the population is under thirty years old, not only as a way of organizing young people and keeping them busy, but also as a means of educating them politically and obtaining their support for the FLN's plans for a socialist society. However, the soccer stadium has also been the learning ground for political protest. As the only tolerated space and emotional outlet in a single-party state, it has attracted youths who oppose the established order. A factor in the October 1988 uprising was the failure of the régime's policies towards the country's youth. An English summary is provided on p. 294-95.

412 **Les élections législatives algériennes. Résultats du premier tour – 26 décembre 1991.** (The Algerian legislative elections. Results of the first round – 26 December 1991).
Jacques Fontaine. *Maghreb-Machrek*, no. 135 (1992), p. 155-65.
A detailed analysis of the first round of the 1991 legislative elections with comparisons with the pattern of voting during the local elections in 1990. Fontaine points to the fact that although the Front Islamique du Salut won 188 of the 430 contested seats, they actually won the support of less than a quarter of registered voters. He also notes the collapse of the Front de Libération Nationale, the former single party, and the weak performance of the so-called democratic parties, with the exception of the Front des Forces Socialistes. The article includes maps illustrating the distribution of votes for the FIS, FLN and FFS and of abstentions.

413 **Les élections locales algériennes du 12 juin 1990.** (The local elections in Algeria on 12 June 1990).
Jacques Fontaine. *Maghreb-Machrek*, no. 129 (1990), p. 124-40.
A detailed analysis of the results of the 1990 local and regional elections held in June 1990. It identifies the areas of influence of the principal parties and compares the results of the communal and departmental elections. It also highlights the fact that control of 90 per cent of towns of more than 20,000 inhabitants, containing some 9 million inhabitants and including the four major cities (Algiers, Oran, Constantine and Annaba) was won by the Front Islamique du Salut, but that the Islamists were less successful in the smaller towns.

414 **Les communistes algériens et l'émancipation des femmes.** (Algerian Communists and women's emancipation).
Monique Gadant. *Peuples Méditerranéens* (France), no. 48-49 (1989), p. 199-228.
Faithful to their position since the 1940s, Algerian Communists reasserted the equality of men and women a few weeks after independence, a position close to that stated in the Tripoli Charter in 1962. The analysis of texts published since then shows that the Algerian Communist Party has tried to have women join as activists or wives of activists. In conformity with Party orthodoxy, the question of women's emancipation is subordinated to the progress of productive forces and the establishment of socialism; feminism is rejected. Because they do not want to shock religious opinion, Algerian communists, though claiming to be Marxist-Leninist, do not refer to any Marxist author when dealing with women's issues but rather to religious authorities. An English summary is provided on p. 333.

415 **L'état-relais à partir de l'exemple algérien: la transnationalisation à l'oeuvre sous le modèle de l'état national.** (The state as a relay [the case of Algeria]: transnationalization at work in the model of the nation-state).
René Gallissot. *Peuples Méditerranéens* (France), no. 35-36 (1986), p. 247-56.

Although state nationalism is the legitimating ideology of Algeria, the state is a place where a powerful process of transnationalization is at work. The state acts as a relay both through social management, which swells the number of wage earners in the tertiary sector, and through the provision of public assistance to the population, most of which has been drawn into a process of urbanization.

416 **L'obsession unitaire et la nation trompée: la fin de l'Algérie socialiste.** (Unitary obsession and the nation betrayed: the end of socialist Algeria).
Lisa Garon, preface by Jacques Zylberberg. Montreal: Les Presses de l'Université de Laval, 1993. 278p. bibliog.

This study, by a Canadian political scientist, examines the period from independence to the violent disturbances in October 1988 which signaled the end of the rule of the single party. Garon seeks to answer two major questions: how the FLN-state maintained its hold for nearly thirty years; and how the self-proclaimed heir of the War of Independence succeeded in destroying all forms of political, cultural and religious opposition.

417 **Islam et politique au Maghreb.** (Islam and politics in the Maghreb).
Edited by Ernest Gellner, Jean-Claude Vatin. Paris: Editions du CNRS, 1981. 374p.

A collection of articles from a round-table seminar at the Centre de Recherches et d'Etudes sur les Sociétés Méditerranéennes at Aix-en-Provence in 1979. Of particular interest are contributions by Jean-Claude Vatin on 'The state and Islam in Algeria', and by Jean-Robert Henry on 'Muslim law and the structure of the modern state in Algeria: the colonial heritage'.

418 **Islam and the West.**
Salame Ghassan. *Foreign Policy*, no. 90 (Spring 1990), p. 22-37.

Argues that the Islamist trend can no longer be ignored by leaders in the Muslim world or in the West. Islamists in such countries as Algeria and Egypt have been successfully pressuring their secular governments gradually to implement *sharia* (Islamic law) as they plan more direct challenges to the secular régimes in power. Although they do not constitute a monolithic entity and do not all condone the violence of more radical groups, they do believe that their current leaders have failed to challenge the threat of Western secularist ideas, have failed to liberate Palestine, and have come to rely more on foreign support to remain in power.

419 **L'Algérie dans la tourmente.** (Algeria in turmoil).
Juan Goytisolo. Paris: La Nuée Bleue, 1994. 100p. bibliog.

One of the best books on the current Algerian crisis. It explains the roots of the tragedy that has engulfed Algeria since the military intervention in January 1992, examines the evolution of Algerian society since independence in 1962, and discusses the string of errors made by the country's political leaders. During the summer of 1994 the author travelled extensively in regions and quarters held by the Islamist militias and describes their aspirations and organization. He also records the violence of the régime's military repression.

420 **The F. F. S., on Algerian opposition to a one-party system.**
Alf Andrew Heggoy. *African Historical Studies*, vol. 2, no. 1 (1969), p. 121-40.
Describes the Front of Socialist Forces (FFS), the organized opposition to Ben Bella, which appeared in 1963. Translations of some of the party's political tracts are appended.

421 **The political and the religious in the modern history of the Maghrib.**
Abdelbaki Hermassi. In: *Islamism and secularism in North Africa*.
Edited by John Ruedy. Basingstoke, England: Macmillan Press, 1994, p. 87-99.
The political and bureaucratic élites in the Maghreb managed to impart a certain authority to the state system beginning in the 19th century; state authority was justified by the exigencies of survival and efficiency in the modern world. However, there arose cultural reactions tied to religious movements that were characterized more by resistance and protest than by adaptation. A dialectic emerged between a logic of adjustment and a logic of resistance that marked all the major stages of modern history, even though that dialectic took slightly different forms during the different stages, from the pre-colonial period to the present. Despite the gradual secularization of the state, paralleled by an equally gradual decline in religious institutions and ideas, Islamic protest attempted to win back space in the cultural and judicial spheres, and the states made concessions to religion as they tried to gain symbolic legitimacy and to break up Islamist opposition.

422 **Human Rights Watch World Report.**
Washington, DC; New York: Human Rights Watch, 1987- . annual.
The volume is organized by regional divisions. The entry on each country describes human rights development, the ability of various human rights organizations to carry out monitoring, US policy towards the country and the division's work there. The Middle East Watch division includes Algeria.

423 **Algeria: a revolution that failed. A political history since 1954.**
Arslan Humbaraci. London: Pall Mall, 1966. 295p. 2 maps. bibliog.
A study of Algeria under Ben Bella (president of Algeria from 1962-65) – his programmes, politics and methods, and the reasons for his downfall.

424 **The politics of Islamic revivalism: diversity and unity.**
Edited by Shireen T. Hunter. Bloomington, Indiana: Indiana
University Press, 1988. 303p. bibliog.

An introduction on 'The Islamic revival: catalysts, categories, and consequences', by
the editor, is followed by country case-studies, which include essays on Algeria by
Mohammad Arkoun (p. 171-86); Morocco by Henry Munson, Jr; and Tunisia by
Norma Salem.

425 **Politics and government in the Middle East and North Africa.**
Edited by Tariq Y. Ismael, Jacqueline S. Ismael. Miami: Florida
International University Press, 1991. 570p. bibliog.

The volume begins with an introduction on history, religion, economic, social and
ethnic geography and the development of the region's nationalisms. The rest of the
work is devoted to country chapters which identify the important and special
determinants of the politics and government in each country. A single chapter by
Bahgat Korany is devoted to Algeria, Morocco and Tunisia.

426 **The F. L. N., in Algeria: party development in a revolutionary
society.**
Henry F. Jackson. London: Greenwood Press, 1977. 244p. map.
bibliog.

An examination of the Front de Libération Nationale from revolution to independence.
Jackson describes the party's internal structure and the role it played during the
insurrection, and later Ben Bella's attempts to use it as a means of social mobilization
and development in a single-party state.

427 **Human rights in the Western Arab world: fertile ground.**
George Joffé. In: *The Middle East and Europe: an integrated
communities approach.* Edited by Gerd Nonneman. London:
Federal Trust for Education and Research, 1992, p. 213-17.

A study of the emergence of independent human rights organizations in Algeria and
the other Maghreb countries that can affect government action. It argues that outside
pressure must continue if the human rights picture in each country is to continue to
improve. The question of minorities, such as the Berbers, can in part be seen as an
extension of the human rights issue, as the most frequent way of disadvantaging
minorities is in terms of their access to universal standards of protection for their
human rights.

428 **Algeria's crisis intensifies: the search for a civic pact.**
Arun Kapil. *Middle East Report,* no. 192 (January-February 1995),
p. 2-7; p. 28.

Examines the possible consequences of the abrupt termination by the military-led
régime of 'dialogue' with its Islamist opponents. Kapil argues that the banned Front
Islamique du Salut (FIS) is characterized by multiple centres of decision and frequent
power struggles. Since the FIS leaders lack the means to challenge the armed
extremists by force, it is suggested that they may be content to let the army do the task
for them. Kapil speculates about the likely contours of a deal between the army and

the FIS and the possible role of the 'democrats'. He concludes that the future of Algeria is Islamist but asks whether it will be an Islamism which imposes its model on all of society or one that is obliged to cede some space to those who do not share its vision.

429 Algeria's elections show Islamist strength.
Arun Kapil. *Middle East Report*, no. 166 (September-October 1990), p. 31-36.

A perceptive analysis of the sweeping victory of the Front Islamique du Salut in the June 1990 local and regional elections.

430 Les islamistes algériens face au pouvoir. (The Algerian Islamists face the power).
Aissa Khelladi. Algiers: Editions Alfa, 1992. 203p.

The author, a well-informed Algerian journalist, argues that a religious lobby, which favoured evolution of the Islamist movement, operated quietly within the Front de Liberation Nationale (FLN) and that the régime, anxious to keep total control over society, pursued a zealous policy of Islamization. Islamists in Algeria drew most of their ideas from abroad and neglected the outstanding works of indigenous thinkers such as Malek Bennabi. Yet they built their strength on the failures of the FLN régime whose leaders are blamed for using Islamic ideology to legitimize their rule and for attempting to produce a synthesis between Islam and socialism that was bound to fail. The Islamists, appealing to the underprivileged, succeeded in their mobilization campaign, although the Front Islamique du Salut lacked a coherent programme.

431 Islamism and Islamists: the emergence of new types of politico-religious militants.
Séverine Labat. In: *Islamism and secularism in North Africa*. Edited by John Ruedy. Basingstoke, England: Macmillan Press, 1994, p. 103-21.

Presents an in-depth analysis of the origins and evolution of the various components of Algeria's Front Islamique du Salut (FIS), arguing that the FIS is not a cohesive movement and that, notably, it is distinguished by a wide chasm between those who insist upon a totally Islamic policy and those willing to work within a more pluralistic system. The study concludes that there are now two groups whose divergences on the issues of the Algerian nation-state and the distinction between the religious and the political seem irreconcilable.

432 Algerian socialism: nationalism, industrialization and state-building.
Jean Leca. In: *Socialism in the Third World*. Edited by Helen Desfosses, Jacques Levesque. New York; Washington, DC; London: Praeger, 1975, p. 121-60. (Praeger Special Studies in International Politics and Government).

Argues that Algerian political culture is characterized by two basic features – populism and segmentarity – and that it is precisely the combination of these two aspects that allows the Algerian system to function.

433 **L'Algérie politique: institutions et régime.** (Algeria's political organization: institutions and régime).
Jean Leca, Jean-Claude Vatin. Paris: Presses de la Fondation Nationale des Sciences Politiques, 1975. 501p.

One of the most important and detailed analyses of the Boumediène régime and the country's political institutions during that period (1965-78). The evolution of institutions of central and local govenment and their functioning are described, and the régime's ideology and strategy examined.

434 **Algérie: politique et société.** (Algeria: politics and society).
Jean Leca, Remy Leveau, Abdelkader Djeghloul, Arun Kapil.
Maghreb-Machrek, no. 133 (July-September 1991), p. 89-138.

A valuable dossier analysing the political crisis in Algeria in mid-1991, six months before the military take-over. After an introduction by Jean Leca, Remy Leveau looks at the two key actors in the crisis, the Front Islamique du Salut (FIS) and the army. Abdelkader Djeghloul places the events of mid-1991 against the background of the process of democratization initiated after the violent disturbances of October 1988. Arun Kapil examines in turn the political programmes of the three political parties which make up the Islamist movement in Algeria: the FIS; Mouvement de la Société Islamique (HAMAS); and the Mouvement de la Nahda Islamique (MNI). Attached documents include the programme of prime minister Ghozali's government, and press interviews by leading politicians.

435 **Reflections on the state in the Maghreb.**
Remy Leveau. In: *North Africa: nation, state and region.* Edited by George Joffé. London; New York: Routledge, 1993, p. 247-65.

Investigates the actual nature of the state in the three Maghreb countries (Algeria, Morocco and Tunisia) in terms of colonial influences and the threats to its survival since independence. Leveau emphasizes that the nascent Islamist movements do not necessarily threaten the North African state, particularly if they are prepared to participate in the democratic process. He argues that the innate role of Islamic values inside the region should make moderate political Islam a peculiarly appropriate vehicle for pluralistic political systems in the future in what he terms the 'arbitrator state'.

436 **Algeria's battle of two languages.**
Abdeslam Maghraoui. *Middle East Report*, no. 192 (January-February 1995), p. 23-26.

Argues that the political contest in Algeria in the early 1990s is more than a disagreement about power sharing, economic policies or the distribution of social goods. A fundamental dispute, generally repressed because of the formidable repercussions it entails, involves what language should be used to discuss these issues – language in the sense of authoritative interpretation and representation of the material world. All parties to the conflict seem to believe that the privileging of one language at the expense of the other ultimately implies unconditional political surrender. Both the established order and the Front Islamique du Salut doubt and reject each other's languages as a legitimate medium to engage in a dialogue.

437 **Le Maghreb face à la contestation islamiste.** (The Maghreb faced
with the Islamist challenge).
Paris: Le Monde diplomatique, 1994. 100p. (Manière de Voir, no. 24).

In this collaborative work, a number of French specialists, including Eric Rouleau,
Gérard Grizbec, Lahouari Addi, Mohammed Arkoun, Jacques Berque and François
Burgat, offer their interpretations of the Algerian crisis provoked by the intervention
of the army in January 1992, and examine the nature of the Islamist challenge in
Algeria and the approach to the problem adopted by its neighbours, Tunisia and
Morocco. The study concludes that the stability of the region is not only threatened by
the Islamist challenge but points out that the still unresolved question of the Western
Sahara, the lack of interest of some Western European countries in the Maghreb, and
the region's poverty are also factors which induce instability.

438 **L'Algérie des illusions. La révolution confisquée.** (Illusory Algeria:
the confiscated revolution).
T. M. Maschino, Fadéla M'rabet. Paris: Laffont, 1972. 289p.

A description of Algeria ten years after independence, illustrated by many examples
from daily life. The authors, a naturalized Frenchman and his Algerian wife, denounce
the ways in which the benefits of a self-styled socialist revolution have been
confiscated by a rising new class which has made a mockery of the hopes of Algerians
in the first years of independence.

439 **Ahmed Ben Bella.**
Interviewed by Robert Merle, translated by Camilla Sykes. New
York: Walker; London: Joseph, 1967. 160p.

An account of Ben Bella's life and career as told by himself in a series of taped
interviews recorded and edited by Robert Merle. It provides an insight into the
character and personality of the first President of Algeria and his own view of his
achievements.

440 *Glasnost* **the Algerian way: the role of Berber nationalists in
political reform.**
Salem Mezhoud. In: *North Africa: nation, state and region.* Edited
by George Joffé. London; New York: Routledge, 1993, p. 142-69.

Argues that since the early 1970s the Berber movement has been the main source of
popular opposition to the Algerian régime, first under Boumediène and then under
Chadli Bendjedid. The author claims that the Berberists are for a large part responsible
for forcing the Chadli régime to recognize the pluralism inherent in Algerian society
at a cultural level and, implicitly, at a political level as well. The Berber Cultural
Movement was remarkable because it mobilized a very large proportion of the
population, not just in Kabylia, but among most Kabyles elsewhere in the country and
abroad, and it led a sustained struggle for two entire decades.

441 **The Middle East military balance: a comprehensive data base and in-depth analysis of regional strategic issues.**
Jerusalem: Jerusalem Post; Boulder, Colorado: Westview Press, 1983- . annual.

After a discussion of major strategic developments in the region, there follows a section on individual countries, including Algeria.

442 **The challenge of radical Islam.**
Judith Miller. *Foreign Affairs*, no. 72 (Spring 1993), p. 43-56.

Argues that governments and individuals concerned with human rights, democracy and pluralism must not be complacent about the rise of militant Islamic movements in most Middle Eastern countries. Miller claims that Islam is incompatible with democratic values, as evidenced by the continued oppression of women and minorities in Muslim societies. Unfortunately, because Islamic groups are now the best organized opposition in many states, free elections seem likely to produce militant Islamic régimes that are actually inherently anti-democratic. The actions of Islamic groups in Algeria are discussed together with steps that could be taken by the Clinton administration to promote democracy in the Middle East.

443 **Identity, politics and women: cultural reassertions and feminisms in international perspective.**
Edited by Valerie M. Moghadam. Boulder, Colorado: Westview Press, 1994. 472p.

One of the three parts into which the study is divided focusses on country case-studies and includes a chapter by Alya Baffoun on 'Feminism and Muslim fundamentalism: the Tunisian and Algerian cases'.

444 **Algeria after the explosion.**
Robert A. Mortimer. *Current History*, vol. 89, no. 546 (1990), p. 161-64; p. 180-82.

The government of President Chadli Bendjedid began a difficult task of political reconstruction after the Algiers riots of October 1988 exposed serious cleavages in Algerian society and the ruling National Liberation Front.

445 **Algeria: the clash between Islam, democracy, and the military.**
Robert A. Mortimer. *Current History*, vol. 92, no. 570 (1993), p. 37-41.

Argues that Algeria stands divided against itself as two essentially authoritarian solutions – one military and the other theocratic – battle for supremacy while secular democrats agonize over the narrow space left to them.

446 **Islam and multi-party politics in Algeria.**
Robert Mortimer. *Middle East Journal*, vol. 45, no. 4 (1991), p. 575-93.

Examines the transition from one-party to multi-party politics and the local elections of June 1990, analysing the configuration of army, state and society that led to the declaration of martial law in June 1991. The author argues that the new mode of relating state and society in Algeria became overheated as the prospect of parliamentary elections approached but concludes that despite the political crisis in mid-1991, Algeria has the capacity to move forward toward a stable system of multi-party politics.

447 **The politics of reassurance in Algeria.**
Robert A. Mortimer. *Current History*, vol. 84, no. 502 (1985), p. 201-04; p. 228-29.

Mortimer argues that during the early 1980s Algeria's President Chadli Bendjedid, in contrast to his radical and aggressive predecessor, Houari Boumediène, practised a policy of moderate reform at home, while seeking to reassure and conciliate Algeria's neighbours.

448 **Authority in Islam from Muhammad to Khomeini.**
Mehdi Mozaffari. *International Journal of Politics*, vol. 16, no. 4 (1986-87), p. 1-129.

Examines Islam as a political system, analysing the original Medina model of authority and power, the later Shi'i model, and nine contrasting contemporary models, including Algeria. The article shows how the uses of power are rooted in, or justified by, Islamic theories of power, and discusses the tensions between religious and secular authority.

449 **Algeria. The politics of a socialist revolution.**
David B. Ottaway, Marina Ottaway. Berkeley, California; Los Angeles: University of California Press, 1970. 290p. map. bibliog.

A political history of the first five years of independent Algeria. The book describes Ben Bella's attempt to create a 'socialist revolution' and his failure. Boumediène's new style of government after the army coup in 1965 is also discussed.

450 **Islam in the political process.**
Edited by J. P. Piscatori. Cambridge, England: Cambridge University Press, 1983.

Includes an essay by Jean-Claude Vatin on 'Popular puritanism versus state reformism: Islam in Algeria' (p. 98-121).

451 **Revolution and political leadership: Algeria, 1954-1968.**
W. B. Quandt. Cambridge, Massachusetts; London: MIT Press, 1969. 295p. bibliog.

Traces the evolution of political thinking among Algerian leaders from liberals to revolutionaries. Quandt discusses the emergence of power-groupings and élites in the struggle against France and the nature of political leadership exercised in independent Algeria by Ben Bella and Boumediène.

452 **Algeria between eradicators and conciliators.**
Hugh Roberts. *Middle East Report* (July-August 1994), p. 24-27.

Since June 1992 two tendencies have been confronting one another within the Algerian power structure – those who favour a strategy of brutal suppression of the

Islamist movement (les éradicateurs) and those who argue that a compromise must be negotiated if the state is to be preserved (les conciliateurs). If a full descent into open civil war is to be avoided, it will be through a bargain of some kind between the Islamist movement and the state. This bargain can either be at the expense of democracy, or it can be to the advantage of democracy by permitting a return to the electoral process.

453 The Algerian bureaucracy.

Hugh Roberts. *Review of African Political Economy*, no. 24 (May-August 1982), p. 39-54.

Algeria has a form of 'state capitalism' and thus the role of the bureaucracy is crucial. Analysing it as a bureaucracy, and in the context of the working of the Algerian state, Roberts reveals that the relationships between it and a bourgeois class with a separate existence are mediated through and by other features that affect the 'rationality' of the Algerian bureaucracy. Religion plays an important role, not one that dictates the pattern of politics as in some Islamic countries, but as an ideological and legitimating link with the people. The pursuance of personal benefits and traditional obligations through the bureaucratic system limits its effectiveness in pursuing policy goals, however. Patronage in turn feeds into a pattern of factions that rend the bourgeoisie, thus limiting its emergence as a national class, and also the bureaucracy, thus further imparing its efficacy.

454 Algeria's ruinous impasse and the honourable way out.

Hugh Roberts. *International Affairs*, vol. 71, no.2 (1995), p. 247-67.

Examines the nature of the continuing conflict within Algeria. The article considers in detail and rejects the main elements of the official French position on the conflict. The author suggests that an accurate analysis of its component factors and of recent attempts at moves towards a resolution indicates that a valid, internally achieved solution is by no means impossible. For this to happen, he argues, the army needs to reconsider its position as the depository of popular sovereignty, which it can no longer sustain, and France needs to cease its covert obstruction of such initiatives as the 1995 Rome platform put forward by all the main opposition groups.

455 Doctrinaire economics and political opportunism in the strategy of Algerian Islamism.

Hugh Roberts. In: *Islamism and secularism in North Africa.* Edited by John Ruedy. Basingstoke, England: Macmillan Press, 1994, p. 123-47.

Highlights the absence of a coherent economic vision on the part of the Front Islamique du Salut (FIS) and its willingness to ally itself with the reformist policies of the Bendjedid government for the sake of sharing in power.

456 The FLN: French conceptions, Algerian realities.

Hugh Roberts. In: *North Africa: nation, state and region.* Edited by George Joffé. London; New York: Routledge, 1993, p. 111-41.

Argues that both the radical Islamist and the Berberist movements are important and impressive but none the less remain a secondary factor in Algerian politics, whereas the Front de Libération Nationale (FLN) is fundamental and central to Algerian politics. Roberts suggests that to describe and explain the FLN by means of a framework of interpretation constructed out of French political conceptions is to misconceive the FLN, and that the FLN has been repeatedly misconceived in the existing literature on Algeria.

457 **From radical mission to equivocal ambition: the expansion and manipulation of Algerian Islamism, 1979-1992.**
Hugh Roberts. In: *Accounting for fundamentalisms: the dynamic character of movements.* Edited by Martin E. Marty, R. Scott Appleby. Chicago: University of Chicago Press, 1994, p. 428-89. (The Fundamentalism Project: American Academy of Arts and Sciences).

One of the most detailed studies in English on the rise of the Front Islamique du Salut. It examines the nature of Algerian Islamism before the formation of the FIS in February 1989 and then discusses the strategic perspective of the new party, its organization and leadership, the nature of its constituency and the content and especially the ordering of priorities within its discourse and propaganda. Roberts argues that the dramatic expansion of Algerian Islamism cannot be explained solely in terms of economic, social and ideological factors. The dynamic of this development has been largely political and requires an appreciation of Algeria's political history to understand it. Divisions within the Islamist movement have been secondary to the divisions within the state apparatus and the politico-military that staffs it. The latter has largely determined the expansion and subsequent contraction of Algerian Islamism. While the author does not doubt the sincerity of the convictions of Algeria's Islamists, he maintains that they have been easily manipulated by the state, a relationship that has implications for other Muslim countries.

458 **The politics of Algerian socialism.**
Hugh Roberts. In: *North Africa: contemporary politics and economic development.* Edited by Richard Lawless, Allan Findlay. London, Canberra: Croom Helm; New York: St Martin's Press, 1984, p. 5-49.

The relationship between state and society in Algeria has gone through four distinct phases since independence. After a period of incessant factional turmoil under Ben Bella, which was not brought to an end until 1967, this relationship was one of authoritarian and technocratic élitism in which the construction of state institutions and the public sector of the economy had no place for popular participation. However, in late 1971 the Boumediène régime suddenly embarked upon an audacious strategy of popular mobilization around an extremely ambitious programme of radical social policies. Since the death of Boumediène the state has settled down into an essentially conservative role in relation to society. His followers have been purged from government and his successors are content to administer the system in routine fashion, having no changes of substance to propose.

459 **Radical Islamism and the dilemma of Algerian nationalism: the embattled Arians of Algiers.**
Hugh Roberts. *Third World Quarterly*, special issue on 'Islam and Politics', vol. 10, no. 2 (1988), p. 556-89.

Traces the continuity between the Islamist movement and the Islamic reform movement of Ben Badis and examines the origins of Algerian Islamism. Despite the suppression of Al Qiyam – the association seen as the precursor of the later radical Islamist movement – following Boumediène's *coup d'état* in June 1965, a revival of Islamist agitation occurred in the mid-1970s in reaction to the left turn in government policy, and in conjunction with the government's Arabization programme. The crisis in the Algerian state and in its nationalist project on the death of Boumediène in October 1978 resulted in the rapid development of the Islamist movement. Its tendency to employ violence distinguishes it from all of its rivals. Under President Chadli the Islamist movement was at first allowed to develop in order to intimidate the student left and the Berberists.

460 **A trial of strength: Algerian Islamism.**
Hugh Roberts. In: *Islamic fundamentalisms and the Gulf crisis.*
Edited by James Piscatori. Chicago: University of Chicago Press, 1991, p. 131-54. (Fundamentalism Project for the American Academy of Arts and Sciences).

This chapter briefly examines and contrasts the origins, leadership and political programmes of the Front Islamique du Salut (FIS), HAMAS and the Mouvement de la Nahda Islamique before discussing the Islamist movement in Algeria and the Gulf crisis of 1990-91. The author argues that the way in which Algerian public opinion reacted to the Gulf crisis forced the Islamist movement to choose between, on the one hand, important elements of its own doctrinal outlook and its connections with the Gulf monarchies, and on the other, its popular base. This choice was starkest in the case of the FIS, because of the size of the popular following that it had achieved in the June 1990 elections and the vested interest that it had acquired in preserving this. It was only natural that the FIS would go furthest in expressing the militancy of popular support for Iraq. In electoral terms the FIS appeared to be somewhat weakened by the Gulf crisis and produced an excess of self-confidence in President Chadli's entourage. The régime's drive to counteract the influence of the FIS resulted in confrontation between the FIS and the authorities in May and June 1991, culminating in the arrest of the FIS leaders Abassi Madani and Ali Benhadj.

461 **Les frères et la mosquée: enquête sur le mouvement islamiste en Algérie.** (The brothers and the mosque: investigation into the Islamist movement in Algeria).
Ahmed Rouadjia. Paris: Karthala, 1990. 309p.

Explains the origins and growth of the Islamist movement in Algeria from the 1970s, based on the author's research in the city of Constantine. He points in particular to the importance of mosque construction by the state and by private individuals, often local notables, and the Arabization of secondary education and some parts of the university system in the 1980s. He describes how the Islamists gradually took control of the mosques in Constantine, particularly those in the poor quarters, which became progressively 'chambres d'écho des contradictions sociales'.

462 **Grandeur et décadence de l'Etat algérien.** (The greatness and decline of the Algerian state).
Ahmed Rouadjia. Paris: Karthala, 1994. 406p.

A detailed analysis of the causes of the decay of the régime established by the Front de Libération Nationale (FLN) after independence and the growing strength of the

Islamist opposition. Rouadjia discusses the 'schizophrenic' ideology of the 'FLN-state', the practice of clientalism and corruption in the management of an essentially 'rentier' economy, the enrichment of the *nomenklatura* and those social groups associated with it to the detriment of the majority of the population, and the repressive role of the single party, the police and the army.

463 **Continuities and discontinuities in the Algerian confrontation with Europe.**

John Ruedy.   In: *Islamism and secularism in North Africa.*   Edited by John Ruedy.   Basingstoke, England: Macmillan Press, 1994, p. 73-85.

Argues that the recent emergence of Islam as a major political force in Algeria represents a surfacing of contradictions in the Algerian experience that have existed for centuries. These contradictions are primarily cultural and political in nature, but they are related to geography as well. Ruedy hypothesizes that the current conflict between the secular and the Islamic is but a new phase of an ongoing struggle between Mediterranean and interior Algeria.

464 **Algeria's return to the past. Can the FIS break the vicious cycle of history?**

Paul Schemm.   *Middle East Insight*, vol. 11, no. 2 (January-February 1995), p. 36-39.

Briefly traces the rise of the Islamist movement in Algeria, the goals and beliefs and of the Front Islamique du Salut (FIS) and its success in the municipal and legislative elections. It is argued that since the military coup in January 1992 the FIS has been seriously fragmented by the war and repression and is threatened by the military successes of the Armed Islamic Group (GIA). The author concludes that the challenges confronting the FIS are greater than at any time in its history. It would be tempting for the leadership to accede to the more radical elements in the front but, Schemm argues, the FIS cannot exclude the secular, French-educated élites from the future Algeria. Consensus, compromise and pluralism must be adopted so that the FIS becomes more than just the autocratic son of the FLN.

465 **Hope for Algeria? Renewed possibility for dialogue may end country's agony.**

Paul Schemm.   *Middle East Insight*, vol. 10, no. 6 (September-October 1994), p. 44-48.

An examination of the splits within the Islamist opposition in Algeria and their attitudes towards President Zéroual's call for renewed dialogue to end the civil war. It also looks at the attitudes of Western governments to the crisis.

466 **Islam and Islamic groups: a worldwide reference guide.**

Edited by Farzana Shaikh.   Harlow, England: Longman Current Affairs, 1992. 326p.

A country-by-country listing of Islamic organizations. Profiles of each organization include date of foundation, leadership, organizational structure, membership and aims. The section of Algeria (p. 10-15) includes a short discussion of Islam and the state since independence, followed by a listing of the major Islamic organizations.

467 **Neopatriarchy: a theory of distorted change in Arab society.**
Hisham Sharabi.   New York; Oxford: Oxford University Press, 1988.
196p. bibliog.

The author finds in neopatriarchy and its political expression, the neopatriarchal state, a product of Western modernization and its dual nefarious impact on the Arab world – dependency and underdevelopment. He sees in the four 'core countries' of the Arab world – Egypt, Syria, Iraq and Algeria – the emergence of neopatriarchal governments since the Second World War, a consequence of the seizure of power by petty bourgeois army officers and political party leaders. He argues that in many ways the neopatriarchal state is no more than a moderized version of the traditional patriarchal sultanate.

468 **Multi-party elections in Algeria: problems and prospects.**
Keith Sutton, Ahmed Aghrout.   *Bulletin of Francophone Africa*, no. 2
(1992), p. 61-85.

This article seeks to explain the political manoeuvres leading up to the December 1991 Algerian elections; to evaluate the results of what proved to be a partial election before the army coup prevented the decisive second round of voting; and to make some comparisons between the 1990 local and the 1991 national electoral patterns. Finally, it attempts to investigate the reasons why the democratic process was halted and to consider the future prospect of democracy in Algeria.

469 **Political changes in Algeria: an emerging electoral geography.**
Keith Sutton, Ahmed Aghrout, Salah Zaimeche.   *The Maghreb Review*, vol. 17, no. 1-2 (1992), p. 3-27.

The victory of the Front Islamique du Salut (FIS) in Algeria's first multi-party local elections in 1990 sent shock-waves through the Maghreb and into France. The 1980s' transition to multi-partism and the rise of Islamist political strength is examined. Socio-economic problems and serious riots in Algiers in 1988 were instrumental in these changes. The election results are analysed regionally and the question of whether the FIS could repeat their success in the 1991-92 national elections is addressed in terms of electoral bias, abstentions and the likelihood of anti-Islamist political alliances. Early FIS policy initiatives, difficulties experienced in administering local government and potential splits are considered as contributions to the question of whether Islam, democracy and modernization can co-exist in Algeria.

470 **The arduous democratization process in Algeria.**
Mohand Salah Tahi.   *Journal of Modern African Studies*, vol. 30,
no. 3 (1992), p. 397-419.

Describes the political reforms announced after the October 1988 riots, the new constitutional framework and electoral code, and the impact of the sweeping victory of the Front Islamique du Salut (FIS) in the June 1990 local elections. Tahi examines the events leading up to the decision to halt the general elections, the phenomenon of the FIS, and the challenge presented by the Kabyles, not only to the central authorities in Algeria but also to the Islamists. There is a short postscript on Boudiaf, the first head of the Higher Council of State.

471 **Taking up space in Tlemcen. The Islamist occupation of urban Algeria.**
Middle East Report, no. 179 (November-December 1992), p. 11-15.

An interview with urban sociologist Rabia Bekkar about her research in the town of Tlemcen in western Algeria. She provides a rare local perspective on the activities of the Front Islamique du Salut (FIS), which won the municipal elections in 1990. She also discusses the incorporation of the so-called 'charitable' neighbourhood associations by the FIS, its work among the young unemployed in the town, and the financial support the movement received from the local commercial bourgeosie.

472 **Anger and governance in the Arab world: lessons from the Maghrib and implications for the West.**
Mark Tessler. *The Jerusalem Journal of International Relations*, vol. 13, no. 3 (1991), p. 7-33.

Popular anger in the Arab world stems not so much from Islamist ideological anti-Westernism as from ordinary citizens' frustration at their own governments' autocratic and inequitable practices. In the case of Algeria, Morocco and Tunisia, recent moves in the direction of participatory government have so far seen little success and indications are that the crisis affecting these states and the rest of the Arab world will continue.

473 **Islam et état au Maghreb.** (Islam and the state in the Maghreb).
Mohamed Tozy. *Maghreb-Machrek*, no. 126 (1989), p. 25-46.

Uses a comparative approach to evaluate the role of religion in the political arena, both geographically and historically, in Algeria, Morocco and Tunisia since their independence. Despite the obvious differences between the political programmes put forward by each of the three régimes, Tozy notes that all three have passed through nearly identical stages in terms of their relations with Islam.

474 **Human rights abuses in Algeria: no one is spared.**
Edited by Andrew Whitley. New York: Human Rights Watch, 1994. 67p. bibliog.

Documents human rights abuses in Algeria since the military coup in January 1992 in a situation where ordinary civilians suffer violence from both the security forces and the Islamist militants.

475 **Islam, democracy and the West.**
Robin Wright. *Foreign Affairs*, no. 71 (Summer 1992), p. 131-45.

Wright's main argument in this article is that the second phase of Islamic resurgence in the past thirteen years provides a deep challenge and an enormous opportunity to the West. Unfortunately, the people of the United States and its Western allies have failed to understand that not all Muslims are fanatic extremists, so Western policy refuses to acknowledge or support Islamic democracies in the Middle East. In this context, 'the failed attempt at Islamic democracy in Algeria' is discussed.

476 **Yearbook on International Communist Affairs: Parties and Revolutionary Movements.**

Stanford, California: Hoover Institution Press, 1966- . annual.

Provides data on the organization, policies, activities and international contacts of communist parties and Marxist-Leninist movements throughout the world. Information is contained in country listings, grouped by geographic region, and a section on Algeria is included, dealing mainly with the Parti de l'Avant Garde Socialiste (Progressive Socialist Party).

477 **The Algerian army in politics.**

I. William Zartman. In: *Man, state and society in the contemporary Maghrib.* Edited by I. William Zartman. London: Pall Mall Press, 1973, p. 211-24.

A short analysis of the origins and evolution of the National People's Army (ANP) into a professional force. It distinguishes the political and military values that have been important to the professional leadership of the ANP and discusses the army's role as guardian of the revolution.

478 **The challenge of democratic alternatives in the Maghreb.**

I. William Zartman. In: *Islamism and secularism in North Africa.* Edited by John Ruedy. Basingstoke, England: Macmillan Press, 1994, p. 201-17.

Argues that the most important obstacle to democratization in North Africa is neither Islamic fundamentalism nor single-party authoritarianism, but the inability of the political systems to produce credible opposition parties capable of attracting voters, representing broad interests, and presenting alternative programmes. Instead, established single parties find themselves facing either small, narrow, inexperienced groups with no claim on the allegiance of large sectors of the population, or utopianist religious movements with no sense of the practical needs of govenment. The result is the perpetuation of authoritarian rule and the alienation of the electorate. The chapter examines political pluralism and the democratic alternative parties in each of the three Maghreb states, Algeria, Morocco and Tunisia.

479 **L'élite algérienne sous la présidence de Chadli Bendjedid.** (The Algerian élite under the presidency of Chadli Bendjedid).

I. W. Zartman. *Maghreb-Machrek*, no. 106 (1984), p. 37-53.

After a brief examination of the organization of the élite under the régime of President Boumediène, this article describes the successive stages whereby President Chadli consolidated his power. Lacking a national base, Chadli sought to strengthen his position through liberalization, coercion, control of the organizational structure of the single party, and changes to key military and political personnel. Zartman argues that Chadli's régime was dominated by a military élite. It followed a policy of pragmatic change and benefited from the divisions and isolation of the opposition.

480 **The military in the politics of succession: Algeria.**
I. William Zartman. In: *The military in African politics.* Edited by
John W. Harbeson. New York: Praeger, 1987, p. 21-45.
Examines the role of the military in the succession following the death of President
Boumediène and the appointment of Chadli Bendjedid to the presidency.

481 **Political elites in Arab North Africa – Morocco, Algeria, Tunisia,
Libya and Egypt.**
Edited by I. W. Zartman. London: Longman, 1982. 273p.
An analysis of the political élites in each country, current political conditions and
possible future developments. An introductory chapter by the editor presents a brief
overview of current élites in all five countries, noting such characteristics as socio-
economic background, educational experience and institutional structure, and then
goes on to discuss élite dynamics. The chapter on Algeria by John P. Entelis notes the
relatively smooth transfer of power to the presidency of Chadli Bendjedid following
the death of Boumediène in 1978 and argues that although effective power remains in
the hands of a relatively small core élite, Algeria has begun a process of successful
political institutionalization.

482 **The painful transition from authoritarianism in Algeria.**
Yahia H. Zoubir. *Arab Studies Quarterly*, vol. 15, no. 3 (1993),
p. 83-110.
Examines political developments in Algeria since the bloody riots of October 1988
and the process of democratization that followed. Zoubir argues that the authoritarian
rulers allowed a liberalization of the system, hoping that it would enable them to
'extracate' themselves from the catastrophic socio-economic and political crisis
caused by the bankrupt system they had imposed for three decades. The process has
been arduous due to the violence which has pervaded it and to the resistance of the old
rulers to surrendering their power. The author argues that notwithstanding the
willingness of some forces within the régime to initiate genuine democratization of the
system, the main objective of democratization, in fact, was a scheme orchestrated by
particular clans inside the régime to preserve their rule and hegemony. The primary
question is how to modernize a neopatriarchal society, dominated by emerging forces
which have used religion for political purposes but who accord little or no toleration
to democtratic values.

Algérie incertaine.
See item no. 2.

Algérie: vers l'état islamique?
See item no. 3.

Annuaire de l'Afrique du Nord.
See item no. 5.

Contemporary North Africa: issues of development and integration.
See item no. 7.

**The making of contemporary Algeria, 1830-1987: colonial upheavals and
post-independence development.**
See item no. 8.

Between two fires.
See item no. 9.

State and society in independent North Africa.
See item no. 11.

L'Algérie indépendante: bilan d'une révolution nationale.
See item no. 13.

The Annual Register: a Record of World Events.
See item no. 14.

Algeria: the revolution institutionalized.
See item no. 15.

Algérie: cultures et révolution.
See item no. 17.

Algeria: the challenge of modernity.
See item no. 19.

North-west Africa: a political and economic survey.
See item no. 21.

Maghreb: les années de transition.
See item no. 22.

Africa Contemporary Record. Annual Survey and Documents.
See item no. 25.

The government and politics of the Middle East and North Africa.
See item no. 26.

The Middle East and North Africa.
See item no. 29.

Middle East Economic Digest.
See item no. 30.

Algeria: a country study.
See item no. 32.

Quarterly Economic Review Annual Supplement – Algeria.
See item no. 33.

Islamism and secularism in North Africa.
See item no. 34.

The Maghreb in the 1990's: political and economic developments in Algeria, Morocco and Tunisia.
See item no. 35.

State and revolution in Algeria.
See item no. 36.

Man, state and society in the contemporary Maghrib.
See item no. 37.

Polity and society in contemporary North Africa.
See item no. 38.

Modern Algeria: a history from 1830 to the present.
See item no. 93.

Modern Algeria: the origins and development of a nation.
See item no. 98.

The passing of French Algeria.
See item no. 157.

L'affirmation identitaire berbère à partir de 1900, constantes et mutations (Kabylie).
See item no. 279.

The reproduction of colonial ideology: the case of the Kabyle Berbers.
See item no. 291.

Le développement politique en Algérie: étude des populations de la région du M'Zab.
See item no. 294.

Berbers in distress.
See item no. 295.

The Berbers in the Algerian political elite.
See item no. 297.

Algerian socialism and the Kabyle question.
See item no. 298.

The economics of Berberism: the material basis of the Kabyle question in contemporary Algeria.
See item no. 299.

Towards an understanding of the Kabyle question in contemporary Algeria.
See item no. 300.

The unforeseen development of the Kabyle question in contemporary Algeria.
See item no. 301.

The conversion of the *mrabtin* in Kabylia.
See item no. 332.

Algerian women confront fundamentalism.
See item no. 340.

Class structuration and economic development in the Arab world.
See item no. 341.

Algerian women since independence.
See item no. 357.

The emergence of classes in Algeria: a study of colonialism and socio-political change.
See item no. 360.

Gender and politics in Algeria: unravelling the religious paradigm.
See item no. 361.

The rise of Algerian women: cultural dualism and multi-party politics.
See item no. 369.

Le multipartisme à l'algérienne.
See item no. 494.

Algérie: l'interruption du processus électoral. Respect ou déni de la Constitution?
See item no. 497.

North Africa: regional tensions and strategic concerns.
See item no. 552.

Meddling while Algeria burns.
See item no. 554.

The development of the UMA and integration in the western Arab world.
See item no. 575.

The politics of economic reform in the Middle East.
See item no. 592.

Bâtisseurs et bureaucrates: ingénieurs et société au Maghreb et au Moyen Orient.
See item no. 593.

The rentier state.
See item no. 594.

From central planning to market economy: a study of the political economy of changes in Algerian industrial development.
See item no. 598.

Workers' self-management in Algeria.
See item no. 599.

Privatization and liberalization in the Middle East.
See item no. 604.

The menace and appeal of Algeria's parallel economy.
See item no. 605.

Le capitalisme d'état algérien.
See item no. 614.

Economic adjustment in Algeria, Egypt, Jordan, Morocco, Pakistan, Tunisia, and Turkey.
See item no. 616.

Privatization and democratization in Algeria.
See item no. 617.

Development and the state in post-colonial Algeria.
See item no. 622.

The political economy of Maghribi oil: change and development in Algeria and Libya.
See item no. 623.

Algeria and the politics of energy-based industrialization.
See item no. 648.

Industriels algériens.
See item no. 653.

Les intellectuels et le pouvoir: Syrie, Egypte, Tunisie, Algérie.
See item no. 769.

The United States and Africa: guide to US official documents and government-sponsored publications on Africa: 1785-1975.
See item no. 841.

Algeria: press freedom under the state of emergency.
See item no. 844.

Le pouvoir, la presse et les intellectuels en Algérie.
See item no. 848.

The Arab press: news media and political process in the Arab world.
See item no. 856.

Secret decree: new attack on the media in Algeria.
See item no. 857.

Constitution and Legal System

483 Algeria: revision of labour legislation.
Social and Labour Bulletin, no. 2 (June 1975), p. 105-06.
Presents the main points covered by a series of enactments adopted by the Algerian government on 29 April 1975, concerning general working conditions in the private sector, labour courts and tribunals, protection of wages, functions of the labour inspectorate, protection of trade union rights in private firms, joint disciplinary committees in private sector undertakings, and social welfare activities.

484 The Algerian constitution.
Middle East Journal, vol. 17, no. 4 (1963), p. 446-50.
An unofficial translation of the constitution adopted by the Algerian National Assembly on 28 August 1963 and approved by the Algerian people by an almost unanimous vote of 98.14 per cent in a referendum held on 8 September 1963.

485 Algeria.
Abraham Almany, Gisbert H. Flanz. In: *Constitutions of the countries of the world*. Edited by Albert P. Blaustein, Gisbert H. Flanz. Dobbs Ferry, New York: Oceana Publications, 1972, 44p.
The text of the Algerian Constitution, as voted by the National Constituent Assembly on 28 August 1963 and approved by the Algerian people on 8 September, is reproduced here, together with a constitutional chronology and an annotated bibliography.

486 Modernization: Islamic law.
J. N. D. Anderson, in consultation with N. J. Coulson. In: *Northern Africa: Islam and modernization*. Edited with an introduction by Michael Brett. London: Frank Cass, 1973, p. 73-83.
An examination of the reforms in the law of family relations and succession which have been introduced into the North African countries.

487 **Attack on justice.**
Index on Censorship, no. 4-5 (1994), p. 167-70.
A brief account of the harassment and persecution of judges and lawyers in Algeria since the upsurge of Islamist violence in 1992. Lawyers are a prime target for those who hold human rights in contempt in Algeria.

488 **Islamic law: social and historical contexts.**
Edited by Aziz Al-Azmeh. London: Routledge, 1988. 277p.
Brings together papers originally presented at a colloquium held at Exeter in 1985. They include an essay by Allan Christelow on 'The transformation of the Muslim court system in colonial Algeria'.

489 **The legal position of the Algerian woman under the Algerian family law code of 1984 in a comparative framework.**
M. Boumediene. LL M, Glasgow University, Scotland, 1990.
Examines the main controversial aspects of the Algerian family code of 1984 on the assumption that the code has not improved the legal position of Algerian women. The thesis compares the Algerian code with equivalents in other legal systems.

490 **Career patterns of late nineteenth century Algerian Muslim magistrates.**
Allan Christelow. *Maghreb Review*, no. 6 (1981), p. 36-39.
This article presents what can be reliably determined about the duration of a magistrate's career, upward mobility within the judicial hierarchy, geographical mobility within the country, and the correlation of the factors with place of origin. The period under discussion stretches from 1856, with the first serious attempts by the French to intervene in matters of judicial organization, to 1892, by which time the Algerian Muslim judicial system had won a secure place in the colonial order and had assumed the form and characteristics which it would carry into the 20th century.

491 **An inquiry into the origins of the Algerian medjlis crisis of 1858.**
Allan Christelow. *Revue d'Histoire Maghrébine*, vol. 6, no. 15-16 (July 1979), p. 35-51.
Criticizes the established view of the problems experienced by the Muslim judicial system created by the colonial administration in 1854, and seeks a new interpretation of the crisis which hit the *medjlis*, or courts of appeal, in Muslim civil litigation during 1858.

492 **Muslim law courts and the French colonial state in Algeria.**
Allan Christelow. Princeton, New Jersey: Princeton University Press, 1985. 311p. map. bibliog.
Christelow traces the development of the Islamic judicial system in Algeria under colonial rule, reviewing the major decrees affecting the organization of Muslim courts in the second half of the 19th century. For each decree the author considers the political context, the issues at stake, the goals of the French *colons* and the reactions of the Algerians. He shows how the French consolidated their domination over Algeria by gradually expanding their control over Muslim law courts and

manipulating the legal system in order to facilitate the French settlers' appropriation of land. Control over the Muslim judicial system was exerted through a process of bureaucratization and centralization. The analysis, which is restricted to northern Algeria, excluding Kabylia, is based on a wealth of archival sources, and provides clues to various aspects of Algerian society of the period, including marriage patterns, divorce rates and kinship structure. Detailed information is also provided about the social origins, career patterns and ideological positions of *qadis* (religious judges) and religious leaders.

493 **La constitution algérienne du 22 Novembre 1976.** (The Algerian constitution of 22 November 1976).
Bernard Cubertafond. *Maghreb-Machrek*, no. 75 (1977), 68-74.
An analysis of the major provisions of the new Algerian constitution, adopted in 1976.

494 **Le multipartisme à l'algérienne.** (Algerian multi-partism).
A. Djeghloul. *Maghreb-Machrek*, no. 127 (1990), p. 194-210.
Presents the text of the law of 5 July 1989 legalizing political parties, the background to the constitutional changes made following the October 1988 riots and details about each of the main political parties.

495 **L'évolution constitutionnelle de l'Algérie.** (Constitutional development of Algeria).
Baudouin Dupret. Louvain-le Neuve, Belgium: Centre d'Etudes et de Recherches sur le Monde Arabe Contemporain, 1991. 52p. (Cahiers, no. 85-6).
An overview of constitutional developments in Algeria since independence, together with the complete texts of the constitutions of 10 September 1963, 19 November 1976 and 23 February 1989.

496 **The Algerian law on air pollution control and the applicability of relevant common law principles to its reform.**
B. Guettaia. LL M, University of Warwick, England, 1989.
Analyses the Algerian legal and administrative framework aimed at controlling environmental pollution. The first part is devoted to legal issues and the second to administrative matters.

497 **Algérie: l'interruption du processus électoral. Respect ou déni de la Constitution?** (Algeria: stopping the electoral process. Respect for, or denial of, the constitution?)
Mohammed Harbi. *Maghreb-Machrek*, no. 135 (1992), p. 145-54.
Harbi, a historian and political activist, examines the constitutional implications of the resignation of President Chadli and the events which followed, based on articles which appeared in the press by specialists on the subject.

498 **Algérie, naissance d'une société nouvelle. Le text intégral de la Charte nationale adoptée par le peuple algérien.** (Algeria, birth of a new society: integral text of the National Charter adopted by the Algerian people).
Introduction by Robert Lambotte.   Paris: Editions Sociales, 1976. 352p.
The full text of the National Charter, approved by popular referendum in 1976. The introduction examines the political tensions which led up to the debate on the Charter.

499 **L'Islam religion de l'état, comme principe constitutionnel: reflexions sur le cas algérien.** (Islam state religion, as constitutional principle: reflections on the Algerian case).
Ali Merad.   *Maghreb Review*, vol. 6, no. 1-2 (1981), p. 1-9.
After a brief introduction on the relations between the state and Islam in Algeria during the French colonial period, the main part of this article is devoted to the period since independence and to the constitutional aspects of Islam, the national religion, and the State, as the expression of national sovereignty in Algeria.

500 **Social legislation in the contemporary Middle East.**
Edited by Laurence O. Michelak, Jeswald W. Salacuse.   Berkeley, California: University of California Institute of International Studies, 1986. 393p. (Research Series, no. 64).
Includes a chapter by J.-C. Vatin which examines the state apparatus and social legislation in the Maghreb, including Algeria.

501 **Some legal aspects of foreign investment in developing countries with particular reference to the situation in Algeria.**
F. Naimi.   LL M, Glasgow University, Scotland, 1989.
Part one examines the economic impact of foreign investment on recipient countries, whereas part two looks at the current situation of foreign investment under contemporary international law. In part three, Naimi focuses on some legal aspects of foreign investment in Algeria, analysing the investment climate in the Boumediène era when the activities of foreign companies operating in the country were not regulated by specific legislation dealing with foreign investment. The work examines the main improvements in Algeria's investment laws, especially under the political and economic reforms which followed the October 1988 riots. In part four some general conclusions are made with respect to the situation of joint venture law in Algeria and the current international law of foreign investment.

502 **Orientalism, colonialism, and legal history: the attack on Muslim family endowments in Algeria and India.**
David S. Powers.   *Comparative Studies in Society and History*, vol. 31, no. 3 (1989), p. 535-71.
Investigates the relationship between European colonial behaviour and the study of Islamic law through the specific historical cases of French Algeria and British India over the last two centuries. The colonial experience exerted a subtle influence on the emerging subject of Islamic legal studies, creating a conflict between Islamic law and the European settlers.

503   **An introduction to law in French-speaking Africa, volume 2. North Africa.**
Jeswald W. Salacuse.   Charlottesville, Virginia: Mitchie Company, 1975. 542p. map. bibliog.
This book is divided into three major parts, each devoted to one of the three North African countries. The section on Algeria deals with constitutional development, sources of the law, the judicial system, the law of persons, civil, commercial and land law, criminal law and procedure. It traces the historical background and legal developments in Algeria both before and since independence but emphasizes in particular the post-colonial period to 1973. It provides a valuable and comprehensive picture of the contemporary legal situation.

Legislating for inequality in Algeria: the Senatus-Consulte of 14 July 1865.
See item no. 142.

L'enfant illégitime dans la société musulmane.
See item no. 337.

State and gender in the Maghreb.
See item no. 346.

Algerian women since independence.
See item no. 357.

Islamism and feminism: Algeria's 'rites of passage' to democracy.
See item no. 392.

Islam et politique au Maghreb.
See item no. 417.

Manuel des institutions algériennes de la domination turque à l'indépendance. Tome premier – la domination turque et le régime militaire 1518-1870.
See item no. 504.

Les instruments juridiques de la politique algérienne des hydrocarbures.
See item no. 634.

Administration and Local Government

504 **Manuel des institutions algériennes de la domination turque à l'indépendance. Tome premier – la domination turque et le régime militaire 1518-1870.** (Manual of Algerian institutions from the period of Turkish rule to independence. vol. 1 Turkish rule and the military régime 1518-1870).
Claude Bontems. Paris: Editions Cujas, 1976. 564p. bibliog.

Describes the structure of central, regional and local government, and the principal public services during the period of Turkish rule. The work also examines the relations between the Algiers Regency and France before 1830 and the political situation during the early years of the French occupation. This is followed by a detailed study of the administrative reorganization of Algeria under French military rule and the new financial and legal institutions established. Bontems has provided a basic reference on the administrative organization of Algeria during the period 1518-1870.

505 **Administration et tribu chez les Nemencha (Algérie) au XIXe siècle.** (Administration and tribe among the Nemencha [Algeria] in the 19th century).
Colette Establet. *Revue de l'Occident Musulman et de la Méditerranée* (France), no. 45 (1987), p. 25-40.

An analysis of letters written between 1872 and 1890 by caids and sheikhs of the peoples of the Nemencha in south-eastern Algeria to French officials, which shows a growing bureaucratization in style and in the writers' role. The systematic use of particular terms, often in ways different from their original Arabic meanings, illustrates the desire of the French authorities to clarify and rationalize tribal society, with the result that the needs of the administration created an artificial idea of tribal organization.

506   **Etre caid dans l'Algérie coloniale.** (To be a caid in colonial Algeria).
       Colette Establet.   Paris: Editions du CNRS, 1991. 385p. (Sociétés
       Arabes et Musulmanes, no. 6).

An important study re-examining colonial history and society from the viewpoint of
the colonized. It is based on research on an important corpus of Arabic letters kept in
the Archives of Overseas France in Aix-en-Provence which were exchanged between
1872 and 1896 by the caids and sheikhs of the Nemenchas and the French officers who
headed the Arab bureau at Tebessa in north-east Algeria. In the first part of the study,
the author seeks to determine what type of native was selected by the French to carry
out their policies, and in the second part to understand better the caids' daily exercise
of power. The third part examines what caids had to gain from the position that they
sought so eagerly, showing that by 1890 the caids were acting mainly as policemen
and enforcers of the detailed native code developed by the French in 1881. Their
bureaucratization was a way of destroying old tribal ties and transforming Algerian
society.

507   **Les bureaux arabes dans l'Algérie de la conquête.** (The *bureaux
       arabes* in Algeria after the conquest).
       Jacques Frémeaux.   Paris: Denöel, 1993. 310p. bibliog.

A detailed study of the work of the 'bureaux arabes', which formed an essential
organization during the French conquest of Algeria, responsible for administering and
controlling the conquered population. It describes the daily activities of its officers
who were both oppressors of the Muslim population and at the same time their
defenders against the demands of the European settlers. This essential reference work
covers the early decades of French colonial rule in Algeria.

508   **The elections of February 5, 1967.**
       Nicole Grimaud.   In: *Man, state and society in the contemporary
       Maghrib*.   Edited by I. William Zartman.   London: Pall Mall Press,
       1973, p. 340-43.

A preliminary analysis of the results of the elections for the 676 communal councils,
and the social origins of the council members. These elections, the first popular
consultation after the military takeover in 1965, were intended to encourage popular
participation in the reconstruction of the Algerian state.

509   **Qaids, captains, and colons: French military administration in the
       colonial Maghrib, 1844-1934.**
       Kenneth J. Perkins.   New York; London: Africana Publishing
       Company, 1981. 278p. bibliog.

A study of the local military administrators – the Algerian Bureaux Arabes, the
Tunisian Service des Renseignements and the Moroccan Service des Affaires
Indigènes – who worked among the Arab and Berber tribes of the colonial Maghreb.
Military administration of the tribes began in Algeria in 1844 with the creation of the
Bureaux Arabes, three- or four-man teams intended to oversee tribal affairs, to supply
information to Algiers and to ensure that the orders of the central government were
obeyed. Yet they expanded their role and functions, naming tribal leaders, interpreting
and enforcing the law, arbitrating disputes as well as setting up schools and infirmaries

and introducing modern farming methods. The *colons* however saw these soldiers as competitors for political power, obstacles to their own ambitions and champions of the native population.

510 **Les institutions administratives du Maghreb: le gouvernement de l'Algérie, du Maroc et de la Tunisie.** (The administrative institutions of the Maghreb: the government of Algeria, Morocco and Tunisia).
Missoum Sbih. Paris: Hachette, 1977. 285p. bibliog.

The first comprehensive study of the entire administrative institutions of Algeria, Morocco and Tunisia. Part one examines the structure and organization of government, the functions of the ministries and the processes whereby government policies are formulated and implemented. Part two is devoted to the structure of local government and communal organizations, while part three looks at public office, and at the recruitment and career structure of civil servants.

511 **Indigenous administrators in Algeria, 1846-1914: manipulation and manipulators.**
Peter von Sivers. *The Maghreb Review*, vol. 7, no. 5-6 (1982), p. 116-21.

From an index of Algerian administrative tenures from the French conquest to the First World War (1830-1914), the author argues that the received picture of the decapitation of Algerian society during the 19th century has to be greatly modified. In fact, there is evidence of a strong historical continuity of the leading segments of Algerian rural society from Turkish times to the early 20th century, in spite of the multiple calamities of conquest, epidemics, colonization and rebellions. French efforts at recasting the Algerian rural élite, if not destroying it altogether, were eventually to no avail, as the élite survived quite vigorously. The French colonial officials may have successfully manipulated the Algerian élite through their control of the selection process, but the élite in turn successfully manipulated the French in order to maintain its monopoly of local power.

Medieval Muslim government in Barbary until the sixth century of the hijra.
See item no. 109.

La mobilisation islamiste et les élections algériennes du 12 juin 1990.
See item no. 391.

Les élections locales algériennes du 12 juin 1990.
See item no. 413.

Algeria's elections show Islamist strength.
See item no. 429.

Political changes in Algeria: an emerging electoral geography.
See item no. 469.

Taking up space in Tlemcen. The Islamist occupation of urban Algeria.
See item no. 471.

Foreign Relations

512 **Common regional policy for Algeria and Libya: from Maghrebi unity to Saharan integration.**
Noureddine Abdi. In: *Social and economic development of Libya.* Edited by E. G. H. Joffé, K. S. McLachlan. Wisbech, England: Middle East and North African Studies Press; Boulder, Colorado: Westview Press, 1982, p. 215-31.

Argues that until 1968 both Algeria and Libya were committed to a regionally integrated Maghreb on the common economic basis of the domination of agricultural exports. From 1968 onwards, the desire for regional dominance in both Libya and Algeria resulted from each state's realization of its importance as energy producers and exporters. Both states, it is argued, turned southwards to the Sahel, the region in which their expansionary ideas would be most likely to take root. After 1979 Algeria seems to have reconsidered its ideas of regional integration and to have returned to an emphasis on the Maghreb. Libya, however, remains committed to further interventions in a southwards direction.

513 **The Organisation of African Unity and Afro-Arab cooperation.**
Mario J. Azevedo. *Africa Today*, vol. 35, no. 3-4 (1988), p. 68-80.

Afro-Arab relations within the context of the Organization of African Unity (OAU) and the Arab League over the past twenty-five years have been largely shaped by the respective positions taken on the issue of Israel and the Palestinians and have at times disrupted cooperation between the states of North and sub-Saharan Africa.

514 **Soviet economic assistance to the less developed countries: a statistical analysis.**
Q. V. S. Bach. Oxford: Clarendon, 1987. 177p.

Includes a discussion of Soviet economic assistance to Algeria.

515 **French policy in North Africa.**
Paul Balta. *Middle East Journal*, vol. 40, no. 2 (1986), p. 238-51.

Balta argues that until 1985 France had no overall policy with regard to the Maghreb, operating instead with a series of bilateral policies. In 1985, the Ministry of Foreign Affairs called a meeting of its ambassadors to the Maghreb to establish a co-ordinated policy. French security and stategic interests in the area are examined in relation to French policies since 1958, particularly towards Algeria and also Morocco, which both presented special problems.

516 **Arms transfer as an instrument of Soviet policy in the Middle East.**
Alexander J. Bennett. *Middle East Journal*, vol. 39, no. 4 (1985), p. 745-74.

The former USSR was a major arms supplier to the Middle East but dependence on Soviet arms has not always been translated into political influence, and relations have been ruptured by Arab states if their autonomy has been threatened. This article divides recipients into three grades of dependence: exclusive – South Yemen, Afghanistan, Egypt, Syria and Algeria; primary – Iraq, Libya and North Yemen; and minimal – Iran, Kuwait, Lebanon, Jordan and Morocco. Bennett examines the patterns of these supplier-client relationships in relation to these grades of dependency and their effects on Soviet foreign policy and internal economics.

517 **Le Sahara Occidental: enjeu maghrébin.** (The Western Sahara: Maghrebian stake).
Abdelkhaleq Berramdane. Paris: Editions Karthala, 1992. 357p. bibliog.

Examines the role of the various international actors in the conflict over the Western Sahara, including that of Algeria. The author views the basic causes of the rupture between Algeria and Morocco as deriving from the former's geopolitical interests and the latter's quest for legitimization of a threatened throne. He concludes that given Algeria's current crisis, both Algeria and Morocco share an interest in a referendum in the Western Sahara that is favourable to Morocco.

518 **Algeria's policy toward France 1962-1972.**
Mohamed Bouzidi. PhD dissertation, University of Denver, Colorado, 1973. 232p. bibliog. (Available from University Microfilms, Ann Arbor, Michigan, order no. 73-28,521).

This study examines the domestic and foreign factors which accounted for Algeria's policy towards France, a policy characterized by Algeria's acceptance of dependence on France, even though the wartime FLN rejected such a policy and advocated total decolonization. It also shows how Algerian leaders solved the conflict between their wartime goal of total decolonization and their goal of economic development, which required the continuation of dependence on France. Following a lengthy introduction, devoted to the colonial legacy, Bouzidi deals first with the Ben Bella régime and then with that of Boumediène.

519 **African boundaries: a legal and diplomatic encyclopaedia.**
Ian Brownlie. London: C. Hurst, 1979. 1,355p. maps.
The chapters relevant to Algeria are: 'Algeria-Morocco' (p. 55-83); and 'Algeria and the Western Sahara' (p. 99-101). Each chapter includes sections on the general situation, texts of agreed alignments, legislative and administrative measures, current issues and references.

520 **The superpowers and the Maghreb: political, economic and strategic relations.**
Ahmed Salim Al-Bursan. PhD thesis, University of Durham, England, 1992.

A comprehensive examination of the relations between the United States and the Soviet Union and the Maghreb states. The author discusses the diplomatic, economic, military and cultural relations between the two superpowers and each of the Maghreb states (Algeria, Morocco, Tunisia and Libya), focussing mainly on the period since independence.

521 **Maghreb et Palestine.** (Maghreb and Palestine).
Jean-Paul Chagnollaud. Paris: Editions Sindbad, 1977. 259p.
Deals with the Algerian, Moroccan and Tunisian reactions to the Palestinian problem, the Balfour Declaration of 1917 and the October war of 1973.

522 **Le Maghreb et l'Afrique.** (The Maghreb and Africa).
Slimane Chikh. *Etudes Internationales* (Canada), vol. 17, no. 4 (1986), p. 801-36.

Chikh discusses the relationship between the Maghreb states and sub-Saharan Africa in the 1970s and early 1980s, indicating three major issues: how the Maghreb and the rest of Africa view colonialism, apartheid, neo-colonialism and imperialism; internal problems in both areas and their mutual effects on each other; and African unity, focussing on the Maghreb's relations with sub-Saharan Africa.

523 **Conflict in north-west Africa: the Western Sahara dispute.**
John Damis. Stanford, California: Hoover Institution Press, 1983. 214p. bibliog.
A detailed analysis of the Western Sahara dispute and of the implications of the failure to resolve it. Damis argues that the phosphate deposits of the Western Sahara are only a marginal factor in the Moroccan policy of claiming the disputed territory. Morocco's claim, opposed by Algeria, is an unquestioned and integral part of Moroccan nationalist ideology. Most observers believe that the resolution of the dispute lies in the more general resolution of the long-standing dispute between Morocco and Algeria.

524 **The Moroccan-Algerian conflict over the Western Sahara.**
John Damis. *Maghreb Review*, vol. 3, no. 2 (1979), p. 49-57.
Analyses the shifting aims, positions and strategies of the various parties during the phases of the Western Saharan dispute, with special emphasis on Algeria and Morocco.

525 Morocco and the Western Sahara.

John Damis. *Current History*, vol. 89, no. 546 (1990), p. 165-68; p. 184-86.

The author argues that prospects for a political settlement of the fifteen-year-old Western Sahara conflict between Morocco and the Polisario Front improved after mid-1987 as various concessions and accommodations between Morocco and Algeria – Polisario's main benefactor – removed many of the key obstacles.

526 United States relations with North Africa.

John Damis. *Current History*, vol. 84, no. 502 (1985), p. 232-34.

Includes a brief survey of US diplomatic, strategic and economic relations with Algeria during the late 1970s and early 1980s.

527 Libya's foreign policy in North Africa.

Mary-Jane Deeb. Boulder, Colorado: Westview Press, 1991. 203p.

Deeb makes two key propositions: that the further an opportunity or event is from the core interest area of North Africa, the more likely is it that Libyan foreign policy will be ideologically motivated; and conversely that the closer a situation is to Libya's area of core interests, the more likely it is that its foreign policy will be motivated by pragmatic geopolitical considerations. These propositions are then tested in a largely chronological treatment of contemporary foreign policy toward Algeria, Chad, Egypt, Morocco, Sudan, Tunisia and Western Sahara. The work contends that the principal Libyan motivation for the 1975 treaty with Algeria, seen as the most important alliance in North Africa in the 1970s, was to find an alternative to Egypt for regional protection. It reinforces the central theme that the Libyan state, despite Qadhafi's rhetoric, was, and remains, much more important to him than any form of Arab or African union.

528 The new nuclear threat.

John M. Deutch. *Foreign Affairs*, no. 71 (Fall 1992), p. 120-34.

Argues that the United States needs to make nuclear nonproliferation a higher priority and should make it clear that violation of the Nuclear Non-Proliferation Treaty would prompt sanctions, including the possibility of multilateral, or even unilateral, military action. Algeria is one of three cases discussed as examples of the difficulties of making progress on nonproliferation.

529 Conflict in Western Sahara: a study of Polisario as an insurgency movement.

B. Hacene Djaballah. Ann Arbor, Michigan; London: University Microfilms International, 1985. 248p. bibliog.

An analysis of the Polisario Front (Popular Frente Para la Liberacion de Saguia El Hamra y Rio de Oro), which seeks independence for the Sahawari people of Western Sahara, in terms of environment, organization and cohesion, popular support, external support and government response. The author attributes the growth and strengthening of the guerrilla movement between 1975 and 1982 to organizational cohesion and support from Algeria and Libya. The result has been to escalate an unwinnable war.

530　**Cuba's foreign policy in the Middle East.**
Damian J. Fernandez. Boulder, Colorado: Westview Press, 1988.
171p. bibliog. (Westview Special Studies on Latin America and the
Caribbean).

Documents Cuba's involvement in the Middle East, including North Africa, and
analyses its interaction with key regional actors. The first section reviews Cuba's
overall international affairs since 1959, outlining the shifting patterns of its foreign
policy. The second section focuses directly on the extent of Cuba's involvement in the
Middle East and the motives behind this involvement. The third section analyses the
implementation of Cuba's foreign policy country by country, including Algeria. The
fourth section is devoted exclusively to an examination of Cuban-Libyan relations.

531　**Foreign relations of the United States, 1955-1957. Vol. 18: Africa.**
Washington, DC: US Government Printing Office, 1989. 881p.

This work includes documentary material on US policy toward Algeria in the pre-
independence period, and US political and economic relations with Algeria's Maghreb
neighbours.

532　**Algeria and Socialist France.**
Nicole Grimaud. *Middle East Journal*, vol. 40, no. 2 (1986), p. 252-66.

The election of President Mitterrand in 1981 seemed to herald a new era in relations
between France and Algeria, but by 1985 these were in disarray. Problems were
caused by France's bilateral policies in the Maghreb, with each country expecting to
be treated as the principal partner, and by complex post-independence relations that
were an ambiguous mixture of paradoxes. The policies of de Gaulle, Pompidou and
Giscard d'Estaing toward Algeria are examined as a backdrop to the Mitterrand
presidency.

533　**La politique extérieure de l'Algérie.** (Algeria's foreign policy).
Nicole Grimaud. Paris: Editions Karthala, 1984. 366p. bibliog.

The first publication to survey exclusively Algerian foreign policy from 1962-78, this
remains the major work on the subject. It is organized into three parts, each relating to
Algerian external perspectives and policies: the relationship 'imposed' on Algeria by
its initial dependence on France and by superpower bipolarity; 'fraternal' relations
with the Maghreb and the Arab East; and the Algerian-led 'wished for' relations
between developing and developed nations. Grimaud provides particularly extensive
coverage of Algerian-French relations, and also a detailed discussion of Algeria's
policies towards its North African neighbours and the rest of the Arab world. The
chapters on Algeria and the Third World chronicle Algerian leadership initiatives
which culminated during the years 1973-75 when Algiers asserted and enjoyed its
greatest influence.

534　**Algeria and Libya and the Palestinian question.**
Saadallah A. S. Hallaba. *Search: Journal for Arab and Islamic
Studies*, no. 6 (1985), p. 46-62.

An examination of the foreign policy responses during the 1970s of Houari
Boumediène of Algeria and Muammar Qadhafi of Libya to the Arab-Israeli conflict
and the question of a homeland for Palestinian refugees.

535 **French and Algerian identities from colonial times to the present: a century of interaction.**
Edited by Alec G. Hargreaves, Michael J. Heffernan. Lewiston, Idaho; Queenston, Canada; Lampeter, Wales: The Edwin Mellen Press, 1993. 253p.

Attempts to illuminate the deep imprint which has been left on the collective and personal identities of those involved in the long and often tortuous relationship between France and Algeria. After a stimulating introduction by Jean-Robert Henry which reviews the 'mental universe' of Franco-Algerian relations, the volume is divided into three parts, each covering one of the key phases which have marked the social and psychological interplay between France and Algeria: the colonial period; the war of liberation; and the period since independence.

536 **Western Sahara: the roots of a desert war.**
Tony Hodges. Westport, Connecticut: Lawrence Hill & Company, 1983. 388p. 4 maps. bibliog.

Hodges discusses the origins and evolution of Morocco's territorial claims to Western Sahara, Mauritania and parts of the Algerian Sahara. He examines the shifts in Spanish policy, analyses Algerian attitudes to the Western Sahara problem and recounts the history of the UN and OAU action on the territory. The tensions between Algeria and Morocco during the long years of war between Polisario and Morocco are also covered.

537 **Soviet policy towards Algeria during the Ben Bella régime, 1962-1965.**
Jill Davis Khadduri. PhD dissertation, Johns Hopkins University, Baltimore, Maryland, 1970. 244p. bibliog. (Available from University Microfilms, Ann Arbor, Michigan, order no. 73-12,098).

This study reveals that the Soviet Union did not base its policy towards newly independent Algeria on the hope that Ben Bella's government would evolve into a régime dominated by a communist party and pursuing social and economic policies modelled on Soviet ones. Rather, the major basis for Soviet policy towards Algeria from 1962 to 1965 was to use Soviet friendship with Algeria to augment anti-American feeling in the Third World, and at the same time, to meet Chinese competition there.

538 **The limits of Soviet power in the developing world: thermidor in the revolutionary struggle.**
Edited by E. A. Kolodziej, R. E. Kanet. London: Macmillan, 1989.

Includes a contribution by I. W. Zartman on 'Soviet-Maghrebi relations in the 1980s' (p. 301-31) which discusses Soviet-Algerian relations.

539 **The foreign policy of Arab states: the challenge of change.**
Bahgat Korany, et al. Boulder, Colorado: Westview Press, 1991. 2nd ed. 461p.

This volume contains two general chapters by Bahgat Korany and Ali E. Dessouki on 'The global system and Arab foreign policies: the primacy of constraints' and 'Arab foreign policies in a changing environment', and one chapter by Bahgat Korany on Algeria, entitled 'From revolution to domestication: the foreign policy of Algeria'. The first edition of the book which appeared in 1984 contains a chapter by Bahgat Korany on 'Third Worldism and pragmatic radicalism: the foreign policy of Algeria' p. 79-118.

540   **Does France have a policy?**
       Chris Kutschera.   *The Middle East*, no. 239 (November 1994),
       p. 11-14.
Highlights some of the problems and contradictions that the current Algerian crisis presents for the French government and discusses the differences of opinion between French politicians on what French policy towards Algeria should be. The article focuses in particular on the differences between the French Interior Minister, Charles Pasqua and the Foreign Minister, Alain Juppé.

541   **Non-alignment and Algerian foreign policy.**
       Assassi Lassassi.   Aldershot, England: Avebury, 1988. 249p. bibliog.
Algeria has been one of the most active member states of the Non-Aligned Movement, especially during the 1970s when the developing states collectively used that organization to bid for significant reforms in the international system. This study reviews the origins of Algerian foreign policy during the wartime period as articulated by the FLN and provisional government. For the post-independence era of Algerian diplomacy, four topics are discussed – colonial problems; economic problems; the superpowers; and international organizations. The analysis ends in 1978.

542   **The United States and North Africa: a cognitive approach to foreign policy.**
       Azzedine Layachi.   New York: Praeger Publishers, 1990. 203p. bibliog.
Layachi applies a cognitive approach to the study of élite images in the foreign policy-making process, focusing on the way the decision-maker views and interprets the available information. Two relatively narrow case-studies are selected for detailed study, the controversy that developed in Washington in 1978-79 over the proposed arms sale to Morocco, and the twelve-year ordeal surrounding attempts to conclude a huge liquefied natural gas contract between Algeria and the US. The principal objective of both case-studies is to uncover the mental images of United States policy-makers towards North Africa in general, and Algeria and Morocco in particular. The author endeavours to determine whether these images had an impact on the policies and actions pursued throughout these complex and controversial disputes.

543   **The rise and demise of Third Worldism with special reference to Algeria.**
       R. Malley.   DPhil, Oxford University, England, 1991.
Discusses the evolution and demise of Third Worldism and draws on Algeria as a case-study. Part one describes the historical origins of Algerian Third Worldism. Part two shows that specific economic, political and international factors can account for the de-legitimation of the concept of Third Worldism as a means of interpretation and a principle of political organization. As a result of these developments, the Algerian régime, opposition movements and observers have gradually turned to different ideological assumptions. The mythology of historical process, reification of the

unanimous 'people' and celebration of the messianic providential state have been victims of the post-Third Worldism outlook.

544 **Le Maghreb dans le monde arabe: ou les affinités sélectives.** (The Maghreb in the Arab world: or selective relationships).
Edited by Hubert Michel, Jean-Claude Santucci. Paris: Editions du Centre Nationale de la Recherche Scientifique; Aix-en-Provence, France: Centre de Recherches et d'Etudes sur les Sociétés Méditerranéennes, 1987. 336p.

A thorough study of the role of North Africa in the rest of the Arab world. The first section deals with the 'myth' of Arab unity, and a range of subjects are covered in the second section, including: Arab economic integration; the evolution of Arab economies; industrial and financial systems along with the economic inequivalence of Mediterranean Arab nations; and the role of the Maghreb in inter-Arab migrations.

545 **Mohammed Yazid on Algeria and the Arab-Israeli conflict.**
Journal of Palestine Studies, vol. 1, no. 2 (1972), p. 3-18.

An interview with Mohammed Yazid, Algerian ambassador to Lebanon in the early 1970s. He is questioned on Algeria's position in the Arab-Israeli conflict and the possible lessons of Algeria's struggle for the Palestinian resistance.

546 **Algeria and the politics of international economic reform.**
Robert A. Mortimer. *Orbis*, vol. 22, no. 3 (1977), p. 671-700.

This article has two related objectives: to set forth the ideas and organizational activities which characterized Algeria's rise to leadership among Third World states; and to analyse what the Algerian experience reveals about the developing state's potential for greater power through collective action in the international system.

547 **Algerian foreign policy in transition.**
Robert A. Mortimer. In: *State and society in Algeria*. Edited by John P. Entelis, Philip C. Naylor. Boulder, Colorado: Westview Press, 1992, p. 241-66.

Examines Algerian foreign policy changes in the late 1980s under the impact of new societal pressures and shifts in the regional and global balance of power. As economic and social problems shook the very foundations of the régime's legitimacy, President Chadli Bendjedid's foreign policy increasingly stressed pragmatic business deals with southern Europe and diplomatic solidarity with the Palestinians. Mortimer concludes that declining means and domestic crises forced Algeria to retreat from the high-profile diplomacy of the Boumediène era to a more regionally-based policy, even as the Maghreb became caught up in the passions of the Gulf war.

548 **The Algerian revolution in search of an African revolution.**
Robert A. Mortimer. *Journal of Modern African Studies*, vol. 8, no. 3 (1970), p. 363-87.

Intended as a study in inter-African politics, this article examines the impact of Algeria's African policy upon the inter-African system and, to some extent, upon the Algerian political system.

549 **The Arab autumn of 1984: a case study of Soviet Middle East diplomacy.**
Larry C. Napper. *Middle East Journal*, vol. 39, no. 4 (1985), p. 733-44.

Argues that Soviet peace diplomacy in the Middle East has not been allocated significant resources, but that advances in influence have been made through bilateral political, economic and arms supply relationships. Against this background, the Soviets launched a political offensive in the spring of 1984, with agreement with Egypt on ambassadorial relations, the courting of Jordan, major diplomatic activity in South Yemen, and meetings with Yasser Arafat. This was followed by diplomatic activity in Algeria and a visit to Moscow by Syria's President Assad. All such activity was thrown into disarray by Jordan's hosting of the Palestine National Congress meeting in November 1984, which hastened the failure of the USSR's policy in courting the moderates and involving itself in the peace process.

550 **French-Algerian relations, 1980-1990.**
Phillip C. Naylor. In: *State and society in Algeria.* Edited by John P. Entelis, Phillip C. Naylor. Boulder, Colorado: Westview Press, 1992, p. 217-40.

Naylor claims that the decade 1980-90 encapsulates the entire post-colonial relationship between Algeria and France, alternating between periods of proximity and privilege with moments of alienation and hostility. He concentrates on two particularly controversial issues, the politics of natural gas and the politics of Algerian workers in France. Although such issues seemed at times to be on the verge of fracturing Algerian-French ties, the remarkable aspect of the 1980s, he maintains, was the way in which diplomats, politicians and technocrats on both sides managed to overcome short-term crises to maintain the basic integrity of the relationship. He concludes by examining the implications of the October 1988 riots and the rise of the Front Islamique du Salut for French-Algerian relations.

551 **Spain and France and the decolonization of Western Sahara: parity and paradox, 1975-87.**
Phillip C. Naylor. *Africa Today*, vol. 43, no. 3 (1987), p. 7-16.

Discusses how French and Spanish policy towards the disputed territory of the Western Sahara is controlled by each nation's foreign policy and economic relations with the other states of the Maghreb.

552 **North Africa: regional tensions and strategic concerns.**
Richard B. Parker. New York: Praeger, 1987. 2nd ed. 211p. bibliog. (A Council on Foreign Relations Book).

The author, a former American ambassador to Algeria, argues that the North African states have not received the attention they deserve in the United States. They have strategic and economic importance and are considerably closer to the vital interests of the USA in Europe than Iran, Afghanistan or the Levant, and the region's oil resources are far more accessible to Europe than those of the Gulf. However, the strategic importance of the North African states is not confined to their Mediterranean role; their control of access to Black Africa could also become critical. The work contains a general discussion of relations between North Africa and the major powers, together with a survey of each North African country. One chapter is devoted to the problem of the Western Sahara. A brief epilogue has been added, reviewing social, economic and political trends in North Africa between 1984, when the book was first published, and 1986. Parker underscores the region's socio-economic fragility in the mid-1980s and points to the close connections between economic and social uneasiness. Updated import-export statistics and figures on spiraling debt-service ratios are provided together with revised demographic data.

553 **Algerian-American relations (1962-1985): the study of Algeria's anti-imperialist foreign policy and its impact on Algerian-American relations.**
Seghir Rahmani. PhD thesis, Georgetown University, 1987. 548p. bibliog. (Available from University Microfilms International, Ann Arbor, Michigan).

Examines four main hypotheses: that the closer the links between the US and Morocco, or any other of Algeria's regional adversaries, the higher the degree of Algerian hostility towards the US; that the greater the historical differences between Algeria and the US, the less the likelihood for cooperation between the two; that the more irreconcilable the differences of outlook between Algeria and the US are on the issues of Third World liberation movements and search for a New International Order, the higher will be the level of conflict between them; and that the more economic cooperation with the US serves Algeria's economic developmental needs and interests, the greater the propensity for cooperation between them. The author finds that Algerian-American relations during the Ben Bella era fell within the confines of the 'politics of hostility' model. In contrast, Algerian-American relations during both the Boumediène and Chadli Bendjedid eras followed the pattern of the 'search for accommodation' model.

554 **Meddling while Algeria burns.**
Hugh Roberts. *Index on Censorship*, no. 4-5 (1994), p. 154-60.

Roberts argues that France is a major player in the current drama in Algeria and that it is the French veto on a political settlement that is prolonging Algeria's agony. The Algerian army is functioning more and more as a dependent appendage of the French defence establishment.

555 **The Saharan cul-de-sac and the responsibility of Polisario's intellectual sympathisers.**
Hugh Roberts. *Morocco: the Journal of the Society for Moroccan Studies, Occasional Papers*, no. 1 (1994), p. 85-96.

Much of the article is devoted to an analysis of Algeria's relations with Polisario, arguing that Algeria's support for Polisario is not an example of a general position of support for the right of self-determination, but rather an example of a general position of support for the inviolability of colonial frontiers. This general position is itself founded on the self-interest of the Algerian state, given the extremely arbitrary nature of its own Saharan frontiers.

556 **Polisario and Western Sahara.**
Brigitte Robineault. *International Perspectives* (Canada), vol. 17, no. 2 (1988), p. 14-16.

Describes the origins of the guerilla war between the Kingdom of Morocco and the Polisario Front, a national liberation movement representing the people of the Western Sahara. With Algeria's backing since 1973, the Polisario Front led the stuggle first against the Spanish and then against Moroccan forces. Algeria has been the principal diplomatic and military supporter of the Polisario, who are totally dependent on Algerian assistance. Attempts by the international organizations to resolve the conflict have failed, and the war, having reached a military stalemate, continues on the diplomatic front.

557 **Algeria and the June 1967 Arab-Israeli War.**
Richard A. Roughton. *Middle East Journal*, no. 23 (1969), p. 433-44.

An examination of Algeria's especially militant anti-Israeli stance in the Arab-Israeli War of June 1967 in the context of the country's recent violent historical experience as a French colony.

558 **Algerian socialism under Ben Bella and Boumedienne: the Soviet assessment.**
Carol R. Saivetz. *The Maghreb Review*, vol. 7, no. 3-4 (1982), p. 87-93.

Soviet interest in Algeria dates back to the mid-1950s when the FLN began its eight-year struggle to end French colonial rule. The Soviet Union proffered moral and some clandestine military support to the FLN; since then the Soviet-Algerian relationship has flowered. Of the 'progressive', non-industrial states with which the Soviet Union maintains relations, Algeria stands out as a major aid recipient and long-time friend. The author goes on to analyse Soviet writing about Algeria, especially its development programmes and to provide an insight into how the Soviet leadership views events in a 'progressive' state such as Algeria and, by extension, in other less developed countries as well. For a more detailed study on this subject see the author's PhD thesis, entitled 'Socialism and Egypt and Algeria, 1960-1973: the Soviet assessment' (Columbia University, 1979).

559 **Responses to the Gulf crisis in the Maghreb.**
David Seddon. *Review of African Political Economy*, no. 50 (1991), p. 70-74.

Governments in the Maghreb generally opposed the military offensive against Iraq while condemning the invasion and calling for withdrawal. Popular responses throughout the Maghreb were strongly in support of Iraq and against the war; huge demonstrations took place in Algeria, Tunisia and Morocco. Fuelled by widespread and growing political frustration and by deteriorating conditions, popular resentment at Western intervention in the region and in Arab affairs grew dramatically after the war started in January1991.

560 **India and the Maghreb Africa: a study of India's relations with Libya, Tunisia, Algeria and Morocco.**
Kulwant Singh. New Dehli: Bahri Publications, 1993. 130p. bibliog.

Compared with the considerable literature on Algeria's relations with Europe, especially France, there are few studies devoted to Algeria's relations with other Third World states, particularly individual countries. This publication, which discusses relations between India and Algeria and its Maghreb neighbours, is therefore particularly useful.

561 **Morocco's Saharan frontiers.**
Frank E. Trout. Geneva: Droz, 1969. 561p. 45 maps. bibliog.
(Bibliotheca Africana Droz, no. 1).

Examines the origins of the Algerian-Moroccan Saharan frontier and the dispute between the two countries over the north-western Sahara, from pre-colonial times to the early years of Algerian independence.

562 **Western Sahara: a foreign policy success waiting to happen.**
Carlos Wilson, Yahia Zoubir. *TransAfrica Forum*, vol. 6, no. 3-4 (1989), p. 27-39.

The authors discuss the conflict over the disputed Western Sahara between the Polisario Front (supported by Algeria) and Morocco (supported by Mauritania), noting the diplomatic efforts of the UN and Organization of African Unity to end the struggle.

563 **Foreign relations of North Africa.**
I. William Zartman. *Annals of the American Academy of Political and Social Sciences*, no. 489 (1987), p. 13-27.

Algeria and its North African neighbours occupy an 'island' and are therefore preoccupied above all by relations among themselves. Torn between the pressure to work together and to distinguish themselves from each other, they are caught up with the need to develop a sense of rank and relation among themselves and to carry their competition into the power vacuum of the poorer states that surround them. Relations with the Arab and African worlds are determined by the North African states' bids for leadership, their need for support on security issues, and their extension of intra-Maghreb relations onto the two wider fields. The same intra-Maghreb purposes guide their relations with Europe, especially France, and with the two superpowers.

564 **Ripe for resolution: conflict and intervention in Africa.**
I. William Zartman. New York: Oxford University Press, 1985. 260p.

The author uses the conflict between Algeria and Morocco over the Sahara as one of four case-studies in this examination of conflict resolution.

565 **Reactions in the Maghreb to the Gulf crisis and war.**
Yahia H. Zoubir. *Arab Studies Quarterly*, vol. 15, no. 1 (1993), p. 83-103.

Provides a brief overview of the situation prevailing in the Maghreb on the eve of the 1990-91 Gulf crisis, followed by reactions in the Maghreb to the crisis identified within four phases: the invasion of Kuwait; Western intervention; the war; and the aftermath and consequences of the war. In Algeria no party condoned the Iraqi occupation and annexation of Kuwait, but all the parties, the government and the masses were unanimous in their condemnation of the presence of foreign forces in the region. This represented in their eyes a more serious situation than Iraq's invasion of Kuwait. Algerians were convinced that the West's motivations for intervening in the region had little to do with genuine concern for international legality.

566   **Soviet policy in the Maghreb.**
      Yahia Zoubir.   *Arab Studies Quarterly*, vol. 9, no. 4 (1987),
      p. 399-421.
Reviews the aims and accomplishments of the USSR's foreign policy in North Africa since the 1960s, noting that the Soviet Union is increasingly perceived as a friendly power in the region.

Annuaire de l'Afrique du Nord.
See item no. 5.

Enjeux sahariens.
See item no. 6.

Contemporary North Africa: issues of development and integration.
See item no. 7.

The Annual Register: a Record of World Events.
See item no. 14.

Algeria: the revolution institutionalized.
See item no. 15.

North-west Africa: a political and economic survey.
See item no. 21.

Maghreb: les années de transition.
See item no. 22.

The government and politics of the Middle East and North Africa.
See item no. 26.

The Middle East and North Africa.
See item no. 29.

Middle East Economic Digest.
See item no. 30.

Quarterly Economic Review Annual Supplement – Algeria.
See item no. 33.

Polity and society in contemporary North Africa.
See item no. 38.

Boundaries and state territory in the Middle East and North Africa.
See item no. 58.

The case of an indeterminate boundary: Algeria-Morocco.
See item no. 68.

The prisoners of Algiers: an account of the forgotten American-Algerian war 1785-1797.
See item no. 113.

La politique américaine en Afrique du Nord pendant la deuxième guerre mondiale.
See item no. 139.

Nationalisme et anti-impérialisme: la place du Maghreb dans la stratégie Soviétique au cours des années vingt.
See item no. 158.

L'insertion internationale du FLN algérien (1954-1962).
See item no. 247.

La réaction de la presse et de l'opinion publique américaines à la politique du gouvernement Eisenhower envers la Révolution Algérienne.
See item no. 252.

After the storm: the changing military balance in the Middle East.
See item no. 395.

Comparative politics of North Africa: Algeria, Morocco, and Tunisia.
See item no. 406.

Human Rights Watch World Report.
See item no. 422.

The challenge of radical Islam.
See item no. 442.

The politics of reassurance in Algeria.
See item no. 447.

Algeria's ruinous impasse and the honourable way out.
See item no. 454.

A trial of strength: Algerian Islamism.
See item no. 460.

Hope for Algeria? Renewed possibility for dialogue may end country's agony.
See item no. 465.

Anger and governance in the Arab world: lessons from the Maghrib and implications for the West.
See item no. 472.

Islam, democracy and the West.
See item no. 475.

Regional economic union in the Maghreb.
See item no. 567.

Le grand Maghreb: des indépendances à l'an 200.
See item no. 569.

The present and future of the Maghreb Arab Union.
See item no. 570.

The Maghreb Arab Union and regional reconciliation.
See item no. 571.

La création de l'Union du Maghreb arabe.
See item no. 572.

Inter-Maghrebi relations since 1969: a study of the modalities of unions and mergers.
See item no. 573.

The development of the UMA and integration in the western Arab world.
See item no. 575.

The Western Arab world: background assessment.
See item no. 576.

Maghreb matters.
See item no. 578.

Regionalism and geopolitics in the Maghreb.
See item no. 579.

Maghrib unity: illusive or elusive?
See item no. 580.

Le Grand Maghreb Arabe: projet et perspectives.
See item no. 581.

La géopolitique de la démographie méditerranéenne.
See item no. 582.

Le Grand Maghreb et l'Europe: enjeux et perspectives.
See item no. 583.

La politique méditerranéenne de la CEE et les pays du Maghreb: un bilan.
See item no. 585.

L'avenir de l'espace méditerranéen.
See item no. 587.

The effects of E.E.C. enlargement on the Maghreb countries.
See item no. 588.

The EEC and the Mediterranean countries.
See item no. 589.

At the periphery: North Africa, the European Community and the end of the Cold War.
See item no. 590.

Soviet and Eastern European trade and aid in Africa.
See item no. 631.

Algeria – dramatic political change.
See item no. 633.

Les instruments juridiques de la politique algérienne des hydrocarbures.
See item no. 634.

The revolution of oil concessions in the Middle East and North Africa.
See item no. 635.

OPEC: the rise and fall of an exclusive club.
See item no. 639.

The African Petroleum Producers' Association: an oil regime with a limited future?
See item no. 641.

Revolution and evolution: the liquified natural gas contracts between the United States and Algeria.
See item no. 642.

La politique algérienne des hydrocarbures.
See item no. 644.

OPEC: twenty-five years of prices and politics.
See item no. 645.

Algeria and the politics of energy-based industrialization.
See item no. 648.

Algérie et route transsaharienne.
See item no. 686.

International migration and dependence.
See item no. 693.

Algerian emigration to France and the Franco-Algerian Accords of 1980.
See item no. 702.

Return migration to the Maghreb: people and policies.
See item no. 704.

The making of family identities among Franco-Algerian couples.
See item no. 716.

Interest groups and decolonization: American businessmen and organised labour in French North Africa.
See item no. 727.

The Algerian war of words: broadcasting and revolution.
See item no. 846.

United States foreign policy and the Middle East/North Africa: a bibliography of twentieth century research.
See item no. 880.

Maghreb Unity

567 **Regional economic union in the Maghreb.**
Ahmed Aghrout, Keith Sutton. *Journal of Modern African Studies* (Great Britain), vol. 28, no. 1 (1990), p. 115-39.
Until the 1980s, ideological, personal and economic rivalries split apart the independent states of the Maghreb. Moroccan-Algerian strife, including boundary disputes and a proxy war in the Western Sahara, had long minimalized prospects for Maghreb union. However, reconciliation treaties between Algeria and Tunisia in 1983, the winding down of the Western Sahara conflict, and above all the looming economic challenge provided by the expanding European Community finally launched Maghrebi cooperation in the form of the Union du Maghreb Arabe (UMA), founded in 1989.

568 **Le Maghreb dans le système régional et international: crises et mutations.** (The Maghreb in the regional and international system: crises and changes).
Saed Amrani, Najib Lairini. *Etudes Internationales* (Canada), vol. 22, no. 2 (1991), p. 339-56.
As the 1980s drew to a close in the Maghreb, old plans for unification were dusted off with the creation of the Arab Maghreb Union, an organization bringing together all five countries of North Africa: Algeria, Mauritania, Morocco, Tunisia and Libya. This article analyses this new dynamic of regional integration by emphasizing its significance, characteristics, scope and limits.

569 **Le grand Maghreb: des indépendances à l'an 2000.** (The Greater Maghreb: from independence to the year 2000).
Paul Balta. Paris: Editions La Découverte, 1990. 326p. bibliog.
Traces the evolution of the notion of a unified Maghreb from the early decades of the 20th century, and discusses each of the five member countries of the Union du Maghreb Arabe (UMA) together with the 'Sahrawi Arab Democratic Republic' which has constituted the single largest political stumbling block to union. The final sections return to the transnational perspective to debate issues relating to the union and its future.

570   **The present and future of the Maghreb Arab Union.**
Mohamed Chtatou.   In: *North Africa: nation, state and region.*
Edited by George Joffé.   London; New York: Routledge, 1993,
p. 266-87.

The author claims that the people of the Maghreb are determined to achieve the
historical dream of union. Their governments are, therefore, indirectly compelled to
succeed in this mission for fear of losing popular credibility and being swept away if
they do not. The countries of the Maghreb have the resources and the means to
achieve economic integration and unity, so there is no reason which should prevent
the success of this promising undertaking. By 1992 if the Maghreb is not sufficiently
strong, it will be crushed by the European giant looming on the horizon.

571   **The Maghreb Arab Union and regional reconciliation.**
John Damis.   In: *North Africa: nation, state and region.*   Edited by
George Joffé.   London; New York: Routledge, 1993, p. 288-96.

Examines the potential impact of the Maghreb Arab Union on the resolution of
regional disputes within North Africa. Damis concludes that in the short term the
union is likely to have only a limited effect on regional reconciliation; it has not so far
facilitated a resolution of the Western Sahara conflict, the Maghreb's most divisive
dispute. Over the past two years, progress toward the settlement of the Western Sahara
issue has been achieved in the context of Moroccan-Algerian *rapprochement.* The
union may encourage and facilitate Moroccan-Algerian co-operation in many aspects
of their bilateral relations, but it is unlikely to move these two states to resolve their
differences over the Western Sahara.

572   **La création de l'Union du Maghreb arabe.** (The establishment of the
Arab Maghreb Union).
Zakya Daoud.   *Maghreb-Machrek*, no. 124 (1989), p. 120-38.

Presents the text of the treaty establishing the Arab Maghreb Union between Algeria,
Morocco, Tunisia, Libya and Mauritania, signed at Marrakesh on 17 February 1989,
together with a commentary on the new union and a chronology of the main events
leading up to the Marrakesh treaty.

573   **Inter-Maghrebi relations since 1969: a study of the modalities of
unions and mergers.**
Mary-Jane Deeb.   *Middle East Journal*, vol. 43, no. 1 (1989),
p. 20-33.

This study is concerned first with determining the purposes of the various unions in
North Africa and whether they were the fulfillment of the dreams of the leaders of
those states or played a significant role in North African politics. Secondly, the study
examines the conditions under which such unions emerged and, thirdly the reasons for
their break up or dissolution. Finally, the reasons why some mergers materialize while
others fail to come to fruition are addressed.

574　North African union: fact or fantasy?
Lillian Craig Harris. *Arab Affairs*, vol. 1, no. 2 (Autumn 1990), p. 52-60.

An analysis of the background to the formation of the Arab Maghreb Union in February 1989, the motives for greater integration, and the potential and prospects for the union. Harris concludes that the success of the union is far from assured; however, economic cooperation could bring at least limited success and offer prospects of progress towards the resolution of regional conflicts and population pressures.

575　The development of the UMA and integration in the western Arab world.
George Joffé. In: *The Middle East and Europe: an integrated communities approach.* Edited by Gerd Nonneman. London: Federal Trust for Education and Research, 1992, p. 199-212.

Examines the status and prospects for development in the Maghreb world in the medium term. Joffé focusses in particular on relations with the EC in the light of the development of the Single European Market, the full integration of Spain and Portugal into the EC in 1995, and the changes in Eastern Europe. Particular attention is paid to economic, social and security issues, and generally to the potential of the Arab Maghreb Union (UMA) as an integrative political and economic regional framework. Finally the implications of the political reassertion of Islam in Algeria are examined.

576　The Western Arab world: background assessment.
George Joffé. In: *The Middle East and Europe: an integrated communities approach.* Edited by Gerd Nonneman. London: Federal Trust for Education and Research, 1992, p. 193-97.

Examines the history of regional cooperation in the Maghreb, the economic rationale for economic integration and the political differences which hinder Maghreb unity. The chapter concludes that the success or failure of the current moves towards regional cooperation depends almost entirely on the Maghreb's relations with Europe.

577　The gains from reserve pooling in the Maghreb.
Robinton Medhora. *The Maghreb Review*, vol. 17, no. 1-2 (1992), p. 55-68.

According to Medhora, no country of the proposed Maghrebi monetary union would have lost from a regional reserve pooling arrangement during the period 1972-89. By defining coverage as the rate of reserve holdings to reserve variability, the paper shows that by belonging to a regional reserve pool, each country would have enjoyed a higher level of coverage than it actually did. The gains are shown to be directly related to the degree of enhanced coverage that each country would have enjoyed in the pool. It is argued that such an arrangement has a better chance of success if it is part of a regional monetary union, rather than being implemented on its own, as this would minimize 'moral hazard'.

578 **Maghreb matters.**
   Robert A. Mortimer. *Foreign Policy*, no. 76 (1989), p. 160-75.
The creation of the Arab Maghreb Union in February 1989 calls for new US policy towards North Africa, which should focus on Algeria rather than Libya as the key factor and consider long-term regional interests. The recent espousal of the Greater Maghreb concept indicates regional economic cooperation, but also has political and diplomatic significance for settling the war between Morocco and the Polisario Front and for moderating the Libyan régime.

579 **Regionalism and geopolitics in the Maghrib.**
   Robert Mortimer. *Middle East Report*, no. 184 (September-October 1993), p. 16-19.
Argues that the obstacles facing the Arab Maghreb Union are both economic and political. In 1989 inter-Maghreb trade represented only 3 per cent of member-states' total trade, as compared with 40 per cent for the six original partners of the EEC. With economic underpinnings so fragile, the Union depends even more than other regional economic schemes upon the political will of the partners. In the turmoil of the 1990s that has not been the priority.

580 **Maghrib unity: illusive or elusive?**
   Phillip C. Naylor. *Africana Journal*, no. 15 (1990), p. 305-15.
Naylor provides a brief survey of the forces of both unity and disunity between Algeria and its North African neighbours in the 20th century.

581 **Le Grand Maghreb Arabe: projet et perspectives.** (The Greater Arab Maghreb: plan and perspectives).
   Pierre Rondot. *Afrique et l'Asie Modernes* (France), no. 143 (1984-85), p. 47-60.
Discusses past and present prospects for unity among the states of the Maghreb since the time of decolonization.

Contemporary North Africa: issues of development and integration.
See item no. 7.

Maghreb: les années de transition.
See item no. 22.

Polity and society in contemporary North Africa.
See item no. 38.

L'Association des Étudiants Musulmans Nord Africains en France durant l'entre-deux-guerres. Contribution à l'étude des nationalismes maghrébins.
See item no. 133.

France and Islam. The Haut Comité Méditerranéen and French North Africa.
See item no. 166.

Common regional policy for Algeria and Libya: from Magrebi unity to Saharan integration.
See item no. 512.

Libya's foreign policy in North Africa.
See item no. 527.

La politique extérieure de l'Algérie.
See item no. 533.

Algerian foreign policy in transition.
See item no. 547.

Foreign relations of North Africa.
See item no. 563.

Le Grand Maghreb et l'Europe: enjeux et perspectives.
See item no. 583.

Relations with the European Union

582   **La géopolitique de la démographie méditerranéenne.** (The
       geopolitics of Mediterranean demography).
       Bichara Khader.   Louvain-la-Neuve, Belgium: Centre d'Etudes et de
       Recherches sur le Monde Arabe Contemporain, 1990. 38p. (Cahiers,
       no. 74).
This brief work outlines recent demographic trends relevant to the Maghreb and its
relations with a unifying Europe.

583   **Le Grand Maghreb et l'Europe: enjeux et perspectives.** (The
       Greater Maghreb and Europe: issues and prospects).
       Bichara Khader.   Paris: Editions Publisud, 1992. 264p.
A well-documented overview of the changing economic relationship between Europe
and the Maghreb. Part one examines the challenges of economic development in the
Maghreb since the 1970s, the history of Euro-Maghrebi economic relations, the Arab
Maghreb Union and the possible impact of a unified Europe on the Maghreb's
economic fortunes. The author demonstrates how one-sided the economic interaction
between the Maghreb and European Union remains. Part two focusses on issues of
demography and migration, examining the problems associated with continuing
reliance of the Maghreb on Europe for access for its labourers.

584   **Les investissements de la CEE dans les pays du Maghreb: bilan et
       perspective.** (EEC investments in the Maghreb: balance sheet and
       outlook).
       Bichara Khader.   Louvain-la-Neuve, Belgium: Centre d'Etudes et de
       Recherches sur le Monde Arabe Contemporain, 1991. 54p. (Cahiers,
       no. 83-4).
Examines the financial relationship between Algeria, Morocco and Tunisia and the
European Community, concentrating on private investments and debt servicing.

Khader also considers available resources, including new forms of financing and the impact of the economic opening of Eastern Europe. Extensive tables, charts and graphs accompany the text.

585 **La politique méditerranéenne de la CEE et les pays du Maghreb: un bilan.** (The Mediterranean policy of the European Community and the Maghreb countries: a summary).
Bichara Khader. Louvain-la-Neuve, Belgium: Centre d'Etudes et de Recherches sur le Monde Arabe Contemporain, 1991. 26p. (Cahiers, no. 81).

Khader discusses the nature of Maghrebi-EEC commercial relations during the 1980s, and analyses the impact of EEC accords on the economic and social evolution of the Maghreb countries. The study concludes that the EEC is not promoting codevelopment, but rather is working to extend its influence over the southern Mediterranean states.

586 **The Maghreb and the Machreq countries.**
P. Mishalani. In: *The second enlargement of the EEC*. Edited by D. Seers, C. Vaitsas. London: Macmillan, 1982, p. 193-215.

A discussion of the impact of the accession of Spain, Portugal and Greece to the EEC on the Maghreb states and those of the Arab East.

587 **L'avenir de l'espace méditerranéen.** (The future of Mediterranean space).
Edited by Christopher Reynaud, Abdelkader Sid Ahmed. Paris: Editions Publisud, 1991. 990p.

A collection of papers based on a conference held in Montpellier, France in 1990, sponsored by Crédit Mutuel Méditerranéen. The articles examine the relationship between the European Community and North Africa in such areas as demography, politics, and economics, and in the broader context of North-South cooperation.

588 **The effects of E.E.C. enlargement on the Maghreb countries.**
Annette Robert. In: *European studies in development: new trends in European development studies*. Edited by J. de Bandt, P. Mandi, D. Seers. London: Macmillan, 1980, p. 49-62.

A paper originally presented at the 1978 European Association of Development Institutes' Conference in Milan. Robert provides an analysis of trading patterns of Greece, Spain, Portugal, Morocco, Algeria and Tunisia with the EEC, identifying similarities between exports, particularly in the agricultural sector. The accession of Spain, Portugal and Greece to the EEC will disfavour Maghreb countries, and increased EEC protectionism is likely to occur. This would have a damaging effect on the Maghreb countries as they currently depend on export to the EEC.

589 **The EEC and the Mediterranean countries.**
Edited by Avi Shlaim, G. N. Yannopoulos. London: Cambridge
University Press, 1976. 352p.
Includes both a discussion of EEC relationships with the Maghreb and an assessment
of EEC policies within the Mediterranean region as a whole.

590 **At the periphery: North Africa, the European Community and the
end of the Cold War.**
Dirk Vandewalle. *The Maghreb Review*, vol. 17, no. 1-2 (1992),
p. 28-41.
Focusses on a central dilemma in changing European-North African relations, the fact
that both sides have become interdependent to an extent where increased cooperation
has become unavoidable. However, this growing interdependence is highly unequal,
as it is increasingly favourable to the European Community. The Community has
recently dramatically increased bilateral and multilateral lending and aid to improve
local conditions, but European policy-makers have concluded that only internal
political and economic reform in the Maghreb can put a halt to a lingering crisis
between the local states and increasingly restive societies – a process they can hope to
promote but over which they have little concrete leverage.

Maghreb: les années de transition.
See item no. 22.

Polity and society in contemporary North Africa.
See item no. 38.

The present and future of the Maghreb Arab Union.
See item no. 570.

**The development of the UMA and integration in the western Arab
world.**
See item no. 575.

The Western Arab world: background assessment.
See item no. 576.

Economic
Development and
Economic
Liberalization

591 **Foreign debt and prospects for growth in Africa during the 1980s.**
Adebayo Adedeji. *Journal of Modern African Studies* (Great Britain),
vol. 23, no. 1 (1985), p. 53-74.
By the early 1980s Africa began to face a debt-servicing crisis in relation to its ability
to meet obligations accruing from its external debt. Most of Africa's foreign debt is
owed not by the poorer countries, but by the middle-to-upper-income and developing
states like Algeria and its neighbour Morocco.

592 **The politics of economic reform in the Middle East.**
Edited by Henri J. Barkey.   New York: St Martin's Press, 1992. 271p.
This volume is divided into three parts: 'Economic reform and political continuity';
'Economic reform and the politics of controlled change'; and 'Economic reform and
the politics of régime transformation'. Algeria is one of the case-studies included.

593 **Bâtisseurs et bureaucrates: ingénieurs et société au Maghreb et au
Moyen Orient.** (Builders and bureaucrats: engineers and society in the
Maghreb and Middle East).
Lyon, France: Maison de l'Orient Méditerranéen, 1990. 436p. bibliog.
A collection of conference papers examining the emergence of engineers as new
socio-political actors and their role in the developmental process in specific countries,
a subject that has been neglected by researchers. Topics covered include: the
organization of the profession; its recruitment, training and ideology; and its role in
technology transfer and choice of development strategies. Three contributions are
devoted to Algeria.

594 **The rentier state.**
Edited by Hazem Beblawi, G. Luciani.   London: Croom Helm, 1987.
240p. bibliog. (Nation, State and Integration in the Arab World, no. II).
Includes two contributions relevant to Algeria: 'Fiscal resources and budget financing
in the countries of the Maghreb (Algeria, Morocco, Tunisia, Libya and Mauritania)'

by Fathallah Oualalou and Larbi Jaidi (p. 172-93); and 'Political aspects of state building in rentier economies: Algeria and Libya compared' by D. Vandewalle (p. 159-71).

595 **Money, inflation and causality in a financially depressed economy – Algeria, 1970-88.**
Abdelkader Beltas, T. Jones. *Applied Economics*, vol. 25, no. 4 (1993), p. 473-80.

The objective of this paper is to replicate tests identifying the line of causality between money supply and the rate of inflation using Algerian data for the period 1970-88, and to provide new evidence for a developing economy. The results show that there is a very strong relationship between the money supply and the rate of inflation with the line of causation being unidirectional, that is from the money supply to inflation with no feedback effects.

596 **Inflation et chômage en Algérie: les aléas de la démocratie et de réformes économiques.** (Inflation and unemployment in Algeria: the risks of democracy and economic reform).
Abdellatif Benachenhou. *Maghreb-Machrek*, no. 139 (1993), p. 28-41.

Algeria experienced a continual rise in non-agricultural employment from 1954 to 1984, at wage levels higher than the growth in productivity. Oil revenues enabled them to subsidize the production of basic necessities and to import consumer goods easily. After 1984 inflation accelerated with the rise in prices of foodstuffs and an anticipation of a weakening of the dinar. At the same time the employment situation declined, affecting the educated and professionals, while income inequalities widened. This article seeks to discover how it will be possible to control inflation and improve production and productivity levels without going too far in reducing employment. Successive governments have hesitated on the appropriate methods to adopt and attempted several, often contradictory, economic policies.

597 **Planification et développement en Algérie 1962-1980.** (Planning and development in Algeria 1962-1980).
A. Benachenhou. Algiers: Presses de l'E. N. Imprimerie Commericale, 1980. 301p.

A basic reference on the economic policies of the Boumediène era. It examines: the theoretical basis for Algeria's development strategy, and the factors that led to the creation of a strong public sector; the Algerian experience of economic planning; and the planning and organization of the industrial, commercial and agricultural sectors. The author concludes with a discussion of the political economy of development, focussing on the social implications of Algeria's strategy and the policies introduced to try and correct some of the social problems – employment, housing, health – that had emerged.

598 **From central planning to market economy: a study of the political economy of changes in Algerian industrial development.**
Brahim Bouattia. *Review of Middle East Studies*, no. 6 (1993), p. 50-72.

Algeria proceeded from highly centralized socialist planning in the 1970s to a market economy model in the late 1980s. The economic restructuring introduced in the early 1980s is analysed here including the official justification given for the policy and the objectives sought. Bouattia goes on to study the socio-economic achievements and the second stage of the economic reforms introduced in the late 1980s and early 1990s. Finally the system of political economy is examined in an attempt to understand how the successive changes, which did not seriously threaten the relative political stability of the régime under the single party rule, were possible.

599 **Workers' self-management in Algeria.**
Ian Clegg. London: Allan Lane, Penguin Books, 1971. 249p. bibliog.

This book is concerned with a specific product of the Algerian revolution – the workers' committees which were set up in the summer of 1962 to manage the agricultural estates and factories of the colonial bourgeoisie. The committees were formalized as a system of economic development known as *autogestion* (self-management) and represent a chapter in the search for appropriate forms of revolutionary reorganization of the economy and society. Clegg attempts to analyse the self-management experience and the specific conditions surrounding and determining the conflicts and dilemmas over revolutionary authority in Algeria.

600 **La réforme économique algérienne: une réforme mal aimée?** (The Algerian economic reform: an unpopular reform?)
George Corm. *Maghreb-Machrek*, no. 139 (1993), p. 9-27.

Analyses the reforms undertaken between 1987 and 1990 and cut short in June 1991 by the fall of the Hamrouche government. President Chadli started decentralizing state economic structures, but it was primarily the sharp decline in oil revenues beginning in 1985 that led a team of reformers to design a step-by-step programme for economic transformation. Their actions are based on a view of the respective roles of the state, responsible for setting the rules, and of the economic actors, subject to regulation by market forces. They are coming up against a lethargic upper bureaucracy and external financial contraints.

601 **Algeria: the contradictions of rent-financed development.**
Hartmut Elsenhans. *The Maghreb Review*, vol. 14, no. 3-4 (1989), p. 226-48.

After a theoretical introduction examining the emergence of rent and its implication for the political structures of the Third World, and the contradictions in rent-financed development strategies, the author examines the Algerian example. He argues that the Boumediène presidency represented an attempt to break through to an egalitarian socialist strategy with an integrated economy based on mass consumption. Its contradictions led to a considerable part of the state-class abandoning that strategy and opting for a different one based on less state intervention, greater market control and the acceptance of increasing degrees of inequality. Both strategies and both segments of the state-class blocked each other until a crisis was reached which led to the popular revolt of 1988. The dominant segment of the Algerian state-class, under the leadership of President Chadli, opted for a strategy of deepening market relations and 'bourgeois' democracy.

602 **Contradictions in the Algerian development process: the reform of the public sector and the new approach to the private sector in industry.**
Hartmut Elsenhans. *The Maghreb Review*, no. 7 (1982), p. 62-72.
Tensions between production and consumption, inadequate investment, stagnation in agricultural production, a crisis in housing and an unsatisfactory rise in industrial production have all emerged in Algeria since the oil price rise in the early 1970s and have led to important government measures. The mode of regulation of the economy is changing: public enterprise is being restructured, economic incentives will become more important, the private sector in manufacturing will be encouraged and agricultural prices partially decontrolled.

603 **Le monde Arabe face à l'endettement: le cas des pays du Maghreb.**
(The Arab world running into debt: the case of the Maghreb countries).
Yves Gazzo. *Maghreb-Machrek*, no. 114 (1986), p. 30-43.
Discusses how Arab countries of north-west Africa have become progressively indebted due to a rapid population increase coupled with the economic shock of the crash in oil prices after the oil embargo.

604 **Privatization and liberalization in the Middle East.**
Edited by Iliya Harik, Denis J. Sullivan. Bloomington, Indiana: Indiana University Press, 1992. 249p.
This collection of country case-studies includes one contribution on Algeria by Dirk Vandewalle entitled 'Breaking with socialism: liberalization and privatization in Algeria'.

605 **The menace and appeal of Algeria's parallel economy.**
Deborah Harrold. *Middle East Report*, no. 192 (January-February 1995), p. 18-22.
One of the few articles in English on the important subject of the parallel economy in Algeria. Policies of centralized economic control and extremely uneven liberalization have contributed to the development of a large informal economy in Algeria, licit and illicit, linked to the formal economy but evading state accounting. This parallel economy has been estimated by some to be as much as 50 per cent of the official economy. Although the private sector statistically accounts for a low rate of investment, it produces a high rate of profit. Since only a minimum of such profits are declared, it represents substantial wealth outside state control, and has a strong interest in decreasing the state's dense network of administrative regulation. Invested in politics and society, this private wealth contributes to the social welfare organizations that undergird Islamist politics, and many may fund armed resistance to the state. One of the best studies in French is Ahmed Henni's *Essai sur l'économie parallèle: cas de l'Algérie* (Essay on the parallel economy: the case of Algeria), (Algiers: ENAG, 1991).

606 **Algeria: the contradictions of rapid industrialisation.**
Richard I. Lawless. In: *North Africa: contemporary politics and economic development*. Edited by Richard Lawless, Allan Findlay. London, Canberra: Croom Helm; New York: St Martin's Press, 1984, p. 153-90.

Traces the creation of an economic system dominated by state capitalism and examines the Algerian development strategy formulated in the mid-1960s which was built around two basic priorities: that of capital accumulation over consumption; and industrialization over the development of agriculture. Lawless argues that the priority given to industrial investment after 1966 increased the disparities and pressures existing between the development of industry and that of other sectors of the economy. Agriculture, housing, health and education all received inadequate investment, resulting in acute shortages of housing and community facilities, stagnant agricultural production and rising food imports.

607 **Le secteur privé en Algérie.** (The private sector in Algeria).
Jean Leca, Nicole Grimaud. *Maghreb-Machrek*, no. 113 (1986), p. 102-19.

A useful dossier on the place of the private sector in the Algerian economy in the early 1980s, especially in terms of employment and revenues, and the new policy adopted towards private national capital by the Central Committee of the FLN in December 1981. The authors present some extracts from the press debating the role of the private sector in Algeria and give the text of the legislation of 1982 relative to private investment.

608 **Algeria – a little late in the day.**
Susan Morgan. *The Middle East*, no. 235 (June 1994), p. 29-30.

A brief account of Algeria's economic problems and the difficulties facing the implementation of the IMF agreement of April 1994 which has been condemned by the Islamist opposition as 'impoverishing the masses'.

609 **Development and autonomy: the Algerian approach.**
Robert A. Mortimer. *TransAfrica Forum*, vol. 4, no. 2 (1987), p. 35-48.

Considers Algeria's efforts to achieve national development and retain its autonomy by restricting foreign investments and emphasizing self-reliance. Mortimer argues that Algeria has nonetheless remained tied to the international capitalist system by its trade in oil and natural gas to Europe and the United States.

610 **Regional disparities and regional development in Algeria.**
M'hamed Nacer, Keith Sutton. In: *The Socialist Third World. Urban development and territorial planning*. Edited by Dean Forbes, Nigel Thrift. Oxford: Basil Blackwell, 1987, p. 129-68.

Algeria's avowed socialism can be interpreted as state capitalism. The authors argue that perhaps more emphasis should be given to the Algerian Government's attempts to reduce socio-economic disparities through regional development policies. These policies are analysed in terms of their limited impact in reducing disparities, particularly in terms of the regional component of national plans. However, they ask whether this is true decentralization or just deconcentration. A mid-1980s programme of industrial development spread widely throughout the regions is described as evidence of deconcentration and the *plans communaux de développement* as evidence of the beginnings of decentralization.

611 **A comparative assessment of the development performances of Algeria and Tunisia.**
John R. Nellis. *Middle East Journal*, no. 37 (1983), p. 370-93.

Examines the development strategies of Algeria and Tunisia in the socio-economic as well as economic realm. Nellis considers to what extent the strategies differ and whether the capitalist-socialist distinction is valid and useful, comparing the post-independence socio-economic performances of the two states in order to determine which is better at achieving its development ends. He also examines the relationship between development performance and ideological orientation.

612 **Algeria's oil economy: liberation or neocolonialism?**
James A. Paul. In: *OPEC and the Middle East: the impact of oil on societal development.* Edited by Russell A. Stone. New York; London: Praeger, 1977, p. 225-47. (Praeger Special Studies in International Politics and Government).

A critical analysis of Algeria's development strategy. It concludes that with all its oil wealth and revolutionary rhetoric, Algeria remains a neo-colonial state, not a liberated society.

613 **Economic liberalization in the 1980s: Algeria in comparative perspective.**
Karen Pfeifer. In: *State and society in Algeria.* Edited by John P. Entelis, Phillip C. Naylor. Boulder, Colorado: Westview Press, 1992, p. 97-116.

Examines economic liberalization in the 1980s and places Algeria in the context of the recent region-wide trend toward reducing the central influence of the state as an economic agent. The external forces include the International Monetary Fund, private lenders, the World Bank and aid agencies, which connect new lending and the rescheduling of old debt under conditions of foreign exchange shortages to public policies, giving greater scope to the private sector and the adoption of free-market economics. The domestic forces analysed include local private capitalists and their colleagues within the state apparatus, whose critiques of central planning gained a wider hearing during the recessionary years of the early 1980s and from 1986 to 1990. The author questions whether free-market principles will restore economic growth with an equitable distribution of benefits.

614 **Le capitalisme d'état algérien.** (Algerian state capitalism).
Marc Raffinot, Pierre Jacquemot. Paris: François Maspero, 1977.
394p. bibliog. (Documents et Recherches d'Economie et Socialisme,
no. 9).

This work analyses in detail the Algerian development model and draws attention to
the negative social consequences – regional inequalities, unemployment and emigration.
It examines the expansion of the state sector since 1965 and the creation of a powerful
state bourgeoisie. The final section investigates worker self-management in agriculture
and the impact of the agrarian reform.

615 **The economic external relations of the Maghreb countries as seen
through their balance of payments during the 1977-86 decade.**
Abderrahman Robana. *The Maghreb Review*, vol. 14, no. 3-4 (1989),
p. 249-70.

Examines the external relations of Algeria, Morocco and Tunisia through an analysis
of each country's macro-economic conditions and the evolution of the balance of
payments during the decade 1977-86. This analysis focusses on trade, financing and
external debt. Common external factors are identified and some policy suggestions
presented.

616 **Economic adjustment in Algeria, Egypt, Jordan, Morocco,
Pakistan, Tunisia, and Turkey.**
Alan Roe, Jayanta Roy, Jayshree Sengupta. Washington, DC: World
Bank, 1989. 81p. (Economic Development Institute of the World Bank
Policy Seminar Report, no. 15).

Algeria is one of the case-studies used in four papers examining different aspects of
economic adjustment experiences. Topics discussed include: policies of economic
adjustment to correct external payments imbalances; external debt, inflation and the
public sector; the political management of economic adjustment and reform; and
foreign trade and industrial policy.

617 **Privatization and democratization in Algeria.**
Lynette Rummel. In: *State and society in Algeria.* Edited by John
P. Entelis, Phillip C. Naylor. Boulder, Colorado: Westview Press,
1992, p. 53-71.

Rummel examines the economics and politics of privatization, arguing that the
privatization policies undertaken by the Chadli régime and continued by his
successors are not the cause for much of the societally-based discontent in Algeria.
Economic reform is essential for political liberalism to take hold so that privatization
measures will have to be expanded and accelerated in the future.

618 **The economies of the Arab world: development since 1945.**
Yusif A. Sayigh. London: Croom Helm, 1978. 726p.

Written by one of the Arab world's leading economists, chapter twelve (p. 521-78)
examines Algeria's development strategy against the background of the French
colonial experience and discusses the prospects and problems of development.

619   **Oil and regional development: examples from Algeria and Tunisia.**
Konrad Schliephake, translated by Merrill D. Lyew.   New York;
London: Praeger, 1977. 203p. map. bibliog. (Praeger Special Studies in
International Economics and Development).

Aims to give detailed information on regional development, particularly that based on
hydrocarbons in Algeria and Tunisia, and on a more general level, to show the
mechanisms and regional effects generated by the oil industry under different
economic systems. Chapters three, six and ten are devoted to Algeria and examine the
evolution of the country's oil industry and development strategy, the effects of oil
production on the oil-producing regions and the regional effects of Algeria's oil-
processing industries.

620   **Self-management in Yugoslavia and the developing world.**
H. D. Seibel, U. G. Damachi.   London: Macmillan, 1982. 316p.

Chapter fifteen (p. 277-90) is devoted to 'Self-management and workers' participation
in Algeria: origins and development'.

621   **Algeria: centre-down development, state capitalism, and emergent
decentralization.**
Keith Sutton.   In: *Development from above or below? The dialectics
of regional planning in developing countries.*   Edited by Walter B.
Stohr, D. R. Fraser Taylor.   Chichester, England: John Wiley & Sons,
1981, p. 351-75.

Algeria's 1970s development strategy has essentially been a centre-down approach
with industrializing industries playing a central role. However, some beginnings of
development from below can be detected; these include regional development plans or
'special programmes' and *plans communaux* which sought to devolve decision-
making to the local level. In addition, the agrarian revolution of the 1970s contained
interesting attempts at introducing cooperative approaches to both agricultural
production and the supply of services. While going no further than calling this an
'evolving bottom-up strategy', this study sets that promotion of political
decentralization against the centralized development of a heavy industrial base which
dominated Algerian thinking.

622   **Development and the state in post-colonial Algeria.**
Rachid Tlemcani, William W. Hansen.   *Journal of Asian and African
Studies* (Netherlands), vol. 24, no. 1-2 (1989), p. 114-33.

Traces the history of the growth of statist economic development policy in Algeria,
which tied itself to the growth of heavy industry and was funded by Western
investments and high export prices for oil and gas. The article puts forward the
argument that these statist policies have suppressed revolutionary tendencies among
the people and created a rigid bureaucracy to enforce the policy of the ruling party.
Both the party and the bureaucracy have been threatened by recent economic
problems.

623   **The political economy of Maghribi oil: change and development in Algeria and Libya.**
Dirk Joseph Vandewalle.   PhD thesis, Columbia University, 1988.
317p. bibliog. (Available from University Microfilms, Ann Arbor, Michigan).

In the wake of rapidly growing oil and natural gas revenues, Algeria and Libya adopted a state capitalist strategy during the 1970s in order to minimize the dislocations caused by continued reliance on the international economy and, in the long run, to move toward more self-reliant local economies. In each country economic development implied certain political rearrangements: government ownership of all oil and natural gas reserves necessitated a strategy to allocate the assets generated by the sale of finite resources among different classes and interest groups. In this process the role of the state was crucial. In Algeria, a techno-bureaucratic élite, to which the state quickly lost control during the 1970s, was put in charge of development. By 1976 the inefficiencies of the public sector and the alignment of the techno-bureaucratic élite with an expanding private sector, led Algeria back toward a more market-oriented development strategy.

Algérie incertaine.
See item no. 2.

Algérie: vers l'état islamique?
See item no. 3.

The Maghreb in the modern world: Algeria, Tunisia, Morocco.
See item no. 4.

Annuaire de l'Afrique du Nord.
See item no. 5.

Enjeux sahariens.
See item no. 6.

The making of contemporary Algeria, 1830-1987: colonial upheavals and post-independence development.
See item no. 8.

State and society in independent North Africa.
See item no. 11.

L'Algérie indépendante: bilan d'une révolution nationale.
See item no. 13.

Algeria: the revolution institutionalized.
See item no. 15.

Algeria: the challenge of modernity.
See item no. 19.

North-west Africa: a political and economic survey.
See item no. 21.

Maghreb: les années de transition.
See item no. 22.

Africa Contemporary Record. Annual Survey and Documents.
See item no. 25.

The Middle East and North Africa.
See item no. 29.

Middle East Economic Digest.
See item no. 30.

Algeria: a country study.
See item no. 32.

Quarterly Economic Review Annual Supplement – Algeria.
See item no. 33.

The Maghreb in the 1990's: political and economic developments in Algeria, Morocco and Tunisia.
See item no. 35.

State and revolution in Algeria.
See item no. 36.

Man, state and society in the contemporary Maghrib.
See item no. 37.

Polity and society in contemporary North Africa.
See item no. 38.

Class structuration and economic development in the Arab world.
See item no. 341.

L'élite dirigeante et la genèse de l'entrepreneur industriel au Maghreb: 'l'exemple algérien'.
See item no. 353.

The emergence of classes in Algeria: a study of colonialism and socio-political change.
See item no. 360.

Liberalism in Northern Africa.
See item no. 386.

Comparative politics of North Africa: Algeria, Morocco, and Tunisia.
See item no. 406.

Doctrinaire economics and political opportunism in the strategy of Algerian Islamism.
See item no. 455.

Some legal aspects of foreign investment in developing countries with particular reference to the situation in Algeria.
See item no. 501.

Le Maghreb dans le monde arabe: ou les affinités sélectives.
See item no. 544.

North Africa: regional tensions and strategic concerns.
See item no. 552.

The gains from reserve pooling in the Maghreb.
See item no. 577.

Les investissements de la CEE dans les pays du Maghreb: bilan et perspective.
See item no. 584.

L'avenir de l'espace méditerranéen.
See item no. 587.

At the periphery: North Africa, the European Community and the end of the Cold War.
See item no. 590.

Oil, the Middle East, North Africa and the industrial states: developmental and international dimensions.
See item no. 637.

The role of the hydrocarbon sector in the Algerian development experience 1965-1985.
See item no. 643.

Algeria and the politics of energy-based industrialization.
See item no. 648.

Le complexe sidérurgique d'El-Hadjar: une expérience industrielle en Algérie.
See item no. 652.

Industrialization and regional development in a centrally-planned economy – the case of Algeria.
See item no. 656.

Aspects of the brain drain in Algeria.
See item no. 710.

Socialist management of entreprises in Algeria: participation and conflict.
See item no. 723.

The rise and demise of participative management in Algeria.
See item no. 724.

UN Statistical Yearbook.
See item no. 734.

The growth of Algiers and regional development in Algeria: contradictory themes.
See item no. 754.

La politique de l'emploi-formation au Maghreb, 1970-1980.
See item no. 768.

Essai sur l'université et les cadres en Algérie.
See item no. 771.

The United States and Africa: guide to US official documents and government-sponsored publications on Africa: 1785-1975.
See item no. 841.

Progress in the human geography of the Maghreb.
See item no. 883.

Trade

624 **Export promotion of non-hydrocarbon manufactured products from Algeria.**
L. Boukersi. PhD thesis, UMIST, Manchester, England, 1991.
Delineates domestic exporters' perceptions of export objectives, barriers and promotion techniques and examines how these objectives, barriers and promotion techniques vary by category of exporters (public and private) and by industry. The thesis also determines how foreign representatives view Algeria's manufactured export characteristics.

625 **Le commerce caravanier au Maghreb et ses mutations au cours de l'ère précoloniale.** (The caravan trade in the Maghreb and its changes during the pre-colonial era).
Khelifa Chater. *The Maghreb Review*, vol. 12, no. 3-4 (1987), p. 99-104.
The author points out that despite the growing dominance of trade with Europe, the caravan trade within the Maghreb and across the Sahara remained active during the course of the 19th century though it experienced profound changes. The article examines the caravan trade within the Maghreb and with sub-Saharan Africa during the 19th century

626 **The effects of protection in a capital-deficit-oil-exporting country: a case study of Algeria.**
A. Derbal. PhD thesis, Lancaster University, England, 1989.
Evaluates the impact of the government's commercial policies on the allocation of resources in the manufacturing sector. Derbal assesses Algeria's development strategy for industrialization between 1963 and 1985 with respect to the continuous use of tariffs, import controls and other market interventions to foster industrialization in a sheltered market, and argues that the industrialization objective was not well served. The policy of import substituting industrialization neither reduced the import

dependence of the economy, nor ensured a sustained growth of output. The main conclusions of this thesis are that the operation of the import control system distorted domestic prices and thus misallocated scarce domestic resources. This misallocation resulted in Algeria incurring a substantial net social cost. Furthermore, the trade restrictive régime gave rise to unproductive profit-seeking activities in the country.

627 **Myth and metrology: the early trans-Saharan gold trade.**
Timothy F. Garrard. *Journal of African History*, no. 23 (1982), p. 443-61.

Coins and weights provide evidence which throw light on the origins of the trans-Saharan gold trade. Such a trade does not seem to have existed before the end of the 3rd century AD, but from 296 to 311 an irregular gold coinage was issued at Carthage, and by the end of the the 4th century there were significant changes in the North African tax system to enable more gold to be collected. The *solidus*, a coin first issued in 312, provided the standard used for weighing gold-dust in the trans-Saharan trade, while copper, a major item of merchandise in that trade, was being imported to Jenne-Jeno by AD 400. This strongly suggests that the gold trade first assumed significance in the 4th century. The trade was evidently flourishing before the Arab conquest.

628 **British trade with Algeria in the nineteenth century: an ally against France?**
Joelle Redouane. *The Maghreb Review* (Great Britain), vol. 13, no. 3-4 (1988), p. 175-82.

During the 1830s and 1840s some Algerian traders looked to Britain for support in the face of economic overdependence on France. The little-known archives of the Algiers Chamber of Commerce indicate that they sought to promote Algerian exports to Britain above any other country, often to secure outlets other than those imposed by Paris. During the 1850s and 1860s they also encouraged British ships to call at Algerian ports and resisted the French navigation monopoly and tonnage duties.

629 **Le commerce extérieur de l'Algérie.** (Algeria's foreign trade).
Djilali Sari. *Maghreb-Machrek*, no. 88 (1980), p. 92-99.

Examines the structure of Algeria's foreign trade during the years 1970 to 1977, emphasizing that trade is essentially with the West and that hydrocarbons make up the bulk of exports. Sari looks briefly at the impact of industrialization of the country's foreign trade, at the decline in exports of agricultural products and the growing dependence on imported foodstuffs.

630 **Berbers and blacks: Ibadi slave traffic in eighth century North Africa.**
E. Savage. *Journal of African History*, no. 33 (1992), p. 351-68.

The origins of the slave trade from North Africa to the central Islamic regions lay in the Arab conquest. The demand for slaves still remained even after the end of the conquest and was a demand that North African merchants soon came to fill. Whatever the initial political and religious appeal of Ibadi opposition to the Arab conquest, the movement found its subsequent economic footing by meeting the ever-growing demand for labour with slaves from *Bilad-al-Sudan*. From the outset, this replacement was influenced strongly by Ibadi merchant-sheikhs until they made the slave trade a predominantly Ibadi monopoly from the mid-8th century onwards. The Ibadi community's wealth and security also provided the means for its emergence and expansion as a sect among the diverse Berber tribes, which was the beginning of their subsequent, far-flung network of trans-Saharan commerce.

631   **Soviet and Eastern European trade and aid in Africa.**
Baard Richard Stokke.   New York: Praeger, 1967. 326p. bibliog.
(Praeger Special Studies in International Economics and
Development).

An analysis of the economic relations between Africa and the centrally-planned economies since the mid-1950s. The section on Algeria considers commodity exchange with Eastern European countries, trade relations with them, and financial and technical assistance obtained from them.

The Middle East and North Africa.
See item no. 29.

Middle East Economic Digest.
See item no. 30.

Quarterly Economic Review Annual Supplement – Algeria.
See item no. 33.

L'Espagne catalane et le Maghrib aux XIIIe et XIVe siècles.
See item no. 106.

Le Grand Maghreb et l'Europe: enjeux et perspectives.
See item no. 583.

La politique méditerranéenne de la CEE et les pays du Maghreb: un bilan.
See item no. 585.

L'avenir de l'espace méditerranéen.
See item no. 587.

The effects of E.E.C. enlargement on the Maghreb countries.
See item no. 588.

The EEC and the Mediterranean countries.
See item no. 589.

At the periphery: North Africa, the European Community and the end of the Cold War.
See item no. 590.

Planification et développement en Algérie 1962-1980.
See item no. 597.

Development and autonomy: the Algerian approach.
See item no. 609.

Trade

The economic external relations of the Maghreb countries as seen through their balance of payments during the 1977-86 decade.
See item no. 615.

Trade routes of Algeria and the Sahara.
See item no. 690.

Le trafic commercial des ports maghrébins.
See item no. 691.

UN Statistical Yearbook.
See item no. 734.

Oil and Gas

632 **Arab Oil and Gas Directory 1994.**
Paris: The Arab Petroleum Research Center, 1994. 615p.
This yearbook provides information on reserves, exploration, production, transportation and the oil and gas industry in each country of the Middle East and North Africa, including Algeria. There are also chapters on the Organization of Petroleum Exporting Countries (OPEC) and the Organization of Arab Petroleum Exporting Countries (OAPEC).

633 **Algeria – dramatic political change.**
J. P. Audoux. *Energy Policy*, vol. 20, no. 11 (1992), p. 1,060-62.
Argues that an Islamic takeover in Algeria would undoubtedly result in the withholding of vitally-needed foreign investment in oil and gas development. The new economic reforms, announced by the present government, coupled with the debt rescheduling agreements, require a significant increase in Algeria's oil and gas revenues. Given generous economic aid and a major drive towards reform, the outlook for Algeria could be promising. Otherwise, the likelihood of Islamic rule could become greater, implying economic collapse, the repercussions of which would be felt throughout the European Community.

634 **Les instruments juridiques de la politique algérienne des hydrocarbures.** (The legal instruments of the Algerian hydrocarbon policy).
Madjid Benchikh. Paris: Librairie Générale de Droit et de Jurisprudence, R. Pichon et R. Durand-Auzias, 1973. 343p. bibliog. (Bibliothèque Africaine et Malgache, Droit, Sociologie, Politique et Economie, tome XX).
A study of the complex legislation governing the hydrocarbon resources of independent Algeria and the efforts of the Algerian government to adapt legislation

established by France during the colonial period to the development objectives of the new state. The second part examines Franco-Algerian cooperation in the development of Algerian oil and gas reserves and Algerian efforts to extend cooperation agreements to other oil-producing countries. This work constitutes an indispensible reference on the subject.

635 **The revolution of oil concessions in the Middle East and North Africa.**
Henry Cattan.   Dobbs Ferry, New York: Oceana Publications, for the Parker School of Foreign and Comparative Law, 1967. 173p.

Although not concerned specifically with Algeria, this work provides basic information (with many references to the Algerian case) on the development and ownership of oil. One section is devoted to the relations between France and Algeria *vis-à-vis* the oil industry.

636 **OPEC, its member states and the world energy market.**
John Evans.   Harlow, England: Longman Group, 1986. 703p.

A reference work on the Organization of Petroleum Exporting States (OPEC). It includes a section on the internal organization of OPEC and its operations, and another which surveys each of OPEC's member countries, including Algeria.

637 **Oil, the Middle East, North Africa and the industrial states: developmental and international dimensions.**
Edited by K. J. Gantzel, H. Mejcher.   Paderborn, Germany: Ferdinand Schoningh, 1984. 332p. (Internationale Gegenwart 6).

Includes two contributions on Algeria: 'A comparison of development in two oil-based economies: Algeria and Libya' by Mohammed Ben-Madani (p. 159-69); and 'Micro- and macro-regional effects of oil industry: national and international implications with cases from Algeria and Saudi Arabia' by K. Schliephake (p. 171-84).

638 **Le gaz naturel algérien.** (Algerian natural gas).
Maghreb-Machrek, no. 55 (1973), p. 21-34.

A discussion of Algeria's reserves and production of natural gas, the pipelines and liquefaction plants constructed since independence and the export market for Algerian gas.

639 **OPEC: the rise and fall of an exclusive club.**
Shukri M. Ghanem.   London; New York: Kegan Paul International, 1986. 243p.

A history of the Organization of Petroleum Exporting Countries (OPEC), of which Algeria is a member, from its rise to power in the 1960s and early 1970s and its decline since the 1973 oil embargo. It focusses upon the inherent differences between OPEC's members which led to the impotence of what began as a cohesive and effective body.

640 **The role of Algerian and Libyan oil and natural gas in Western energy supply.**
K. S. McLachlan, R. M. Burrell. In: *The Western Mediterranean: its political, economic and strategic importance.* Edited by Alvin J. Cottrell, James D. Theberge. New York; Washington, DC; London: Praeger, 1974, p. 50-80.

Examines the reserves, production and exports of oil and natural gas from Algeria, the importance of North African oil supplies to Western Europe, and economic development and government policies toward the oil sector.

641 **The African Petroleum Producers' Association: an oil régime with a limited future?**
Peter H. Oppenheimer. *Maghreb Review*, vol. 15, no. 1-2 (1990), p. 48-78.

The APPA was formed by eight African countries, including Algeria, in 1987 for the declared purpose of fostering consultation and cooperation among members in areas of development of hydrocarbon resources. The author examines why it was established, what it aimed to achieve and what it has actually accomplished. He contends that although it has so far been ineffectual, it does address a need and can be made more effective.

642 **Revolution and evolution: the liquified natural gas contracts between the United States and Algeria.**
Pamela Day Pelletreau. PhD thesis, The George Washington University, 1987. 200p. bibliog.

This history of three liquefied natural gas contracts between the United States and Algeria (El Paso Natural Gas Co., Panhandle-Trunkline and Distrigas) illuminates the policy formation process in both countries. The changed global energy market which resulted from the oil embargo of 1973 and the oil price rise of 1979 caused policy responses in the US and Algeria which rendered the contracts uneconomic. The volume also includes a consideration of Algerian natural gas contracts with France, Spain, Belgium and Italy.

643 **The role of the hydrocarbon sector in the Algerian development experience: 1965-1985.**
Mustapha Rechache. PhD thesis, The American University, 1987. 300p. bibliog. (Available from University Microfilms, Ann Arbor, Michigan, order no. 88-02361).

Examines the role of the hydrocarbon sector in the economic development of Algeria between 1965 and 1985. This role is assessed in terms of the sector's contribution to economic growth as well as its overall impact on economic transformation. Rechache uses a national accounting equation and two export growth models to measure and evaluate the contribution to economic growth. The possibility of a negative impact of the fluctuations of oil proceeds on economic growth is also explored. The impact of the diversification of the economy is studied through the use of the concepts of backward, forward, fiscal and consumption linkages.

644 **La politique algérienne des hydrocarbures.** (The Algerian hydrocarbon policy).
Jean-Pierre Séréni. *Maghreb*, no. 45 (1971), p. 31-49.

Séréni discusses the evolution of independent Algeria's hydrocarbon policy between 1962 and 1971 as background to the crisis between France and Algeria which culminated in Algeria's nationalization of French oil companies operating there.

645 **OPEC: twenty-five years of prices and politics.**
Ian Skeet. Cambridge, England; New York: Cambridge University Press, 1988. 248p. bibliog. (Cambridge Energy Studies).

An analysis of oil-pricing policy covering the first twenty-five years of the Organization of Petroleum Exporting Countries (OPEC), with an emphasis on politics, influential individuals and national perspectives. The book is divided into eras, the first being from 1960-73 when oil prices resulted from negotiations between OPEC and the companies, a period when the primacy of national over group interests was institutionalized. The period of OPEC management of prices (1973-78) was similarly flawed by nationalistic policies. The author delineates the micro-structure of high price preference versus low price preference countries, unravelling domestic and international political constraints as well as the structural economic factors. In this context, the actions of states like Algeria, whose position within OPEC can not easily be interpreted as simple reflections of economic self-interest, become comprehensible and even predictable. The cartel era, begining in 1979, illustrates the far greater difficulties facing OPEC than beset the companies during their period of dominance because of the states' dual responsibility for strategic and economic security.

646 **Natural gas in Algeria.**
Keith Sutton. *Geography*, vol. 64, no. 2 (1979), p. 115-19.

Examines Algeria's natural gas potential, the construction of liquefaction plants, and the projects for piping gas directly to Europe.

647 **The prize: the epic quest for oil, money and power.**
Daniel Yergin. New York; London: Pocket Books, 1993. 885p. 9 maps. bibliog.

Includes a short outline of the development of oil exploration in the Algerian Sahara during the period of French colonial rule and the role of the independent Algerian state in OPEC. The work is useful for setting the Algerian oil industry in the context of developments in North Africa and the Middle East.

Algeria: the revolution institutionalized.
See item no. 15.

The Middle East and North Africa.
See item no. 29.

Middle East Economic Digest.
See item no. 30.

Quarterly Economic Review Annual Supplement – Algeria.
See item no. 33.

The United States and North Africa: a cognitive approach to foreign policy.
See item no. 542.

French-Algerian relations, 1980-1990.
See item no. 550.

Algeria's oil economy: liberation or neocolonialism?
See item no. 612.

Oil and regional development: examples from Algeria and Tunisia.
See item no. 619.

The political economy of Maghribi oil: change and development in Algeria and Libya.
See item no. 623.

Algeria's infrastructure. An economic survey of transportation, communication and energy resources.
See item no. 689.

UN Statistical Yearbook.
See item no. 734.

Industry and
Industrialization

648   **Algeria and the politics of energy-based industrialization.**
Philip J. Akre. In: *State and society in Algeria.* Edited by John P.
Entelis, Phillip C. Naylor. Boulder, Colorado: Westview Press, 1992,
p. 73-95.
Argues that the economic and political contours of Algeria's industrial growth from
1970 to 1980 demonstrates the limitations imposed on energy-based development
under conditions of reliance on the international market, represented by US capital.
Akre contends that the partnership with advanced industrial capital did not produce
the outcomes that had been expected, so the era of the 1970s did not usher in the
hoped-for advanced industrial status that had been predicted for the 1980s.

649   **Industrialisation et urbanisation en Algérie.** (Industrialization and
urbanization in Algeria).
J. C. Brulé, G. Mutin. *Maghreb-Machrek*, no. 96 (1982), p. 41-66.
Algeria's industrial strategy since 1970 has played an important role in the rapid urban
growth experienced. Major industrial development projects have brought dramatic
changes to urban peripheries, to the structure of urban employment and to rural-urban
relations. Industrialization has affected mainly the major cities; changes in the
functions of smaller towns are the result of new administrative and socio-cultural
activities rather than of industralization.

650   **Méditerranée occidentale: sécurité et coopération.** (The Western
Mediterranean: security and cooperation).
Edited by Marie-Lucy Dumas. Paris: Fondation pour les Etudes de
Défense Nationale, 1992. 262p. bibliog.
Includes a contribution on industrial cooperation and the transfer of technology in the
Maghreb by Jean-François Daguzan.

651 **Industrial self-management in Algeria.**
Damien Helie. In: *Man, state and society in the contemporary Maghrib*. Edited by I. William Zartman. London: Pall Mall Press, 1973, p. 465-74.

The author examines the problems affecting the industrial self-management sector created in the early years of independence and the attitudes of the workers.

652 **Le complexe sidérurgique d'El-Hadjar: une expérience industrielle en Algérie.** (The iron and steel complex of El-Hadjar: an industrial experiment in Algeria).
Ali El-Kenz. Paris: Editions du Centre National de la Recherche Scientifique (CNRS), 1987. 359p. bibliog. (Collection 'Recherche sur les Sociétés Méditerranéennes').

An important and detailed study about Algeria's first and most important industrial complex at El-Hadjar near the eastern city of Annaba. Through a history of the plant, the author analyses the ideological, politico-institutional and socio-economic factors that have contributed the most to the failure of the Algerian development strategy and examines its profound consequences for the Algerian people and society. He examines the contradictions inherent in the Algerian élite's development ideology and both within and without the complex the new forms of social stratification and segregation that have resulted. The sad story of El-Hadjar is a kind of microcosm for all that has gone wrong with Algerian industrialization. Part of the results of El-Kenz's research on El-Hadjar are available in English in 'Workers' perceptions and practices in Algeria – the case of the El Hadjar iron and steel works and the Rouiba industrial motor car plant' by S. Chikhi and A. El-Kenz, in *Workers in Third World industrialization*, edited by I. Brandell (Basingstoke, England: Macmillan Academic and Professional, 1991, p. 31-48).

653 **Industriels algériens.** (Algerian industrialists).
Jean Peneff. Paris: Editions du CNRS, 1981. 230p.

A valuable study based on a survey of some 220 private industrialists in the Algiers region carried out in 1970-73. It presents a careful analysis of their social origins, economic activities and political opinions.

654 **The use of accounting data in short-run decision-making within Algerian manufacturing public enterprises.**
S. Sefiane. PhD thesis, University of East Anglia, Norwich, England, 1991.

Shows that differences in economic objectives and policies between market economies and the Algerian managed economy appear to have led to different attitudes towards the use of accounting data in pricing, output and product mix decisions. In particular, the dominant philosophy of profit maximization in market economies has resulted in concern for accounting information and increased the importance of accounting as a means of translating economic flows into financial terms. In contrast, in the planned economy of Algeria the key criterion of success is satisfying social needs rather than profit maximization which explains in general the lack of concern given to accounting data in operational decision-making.

655 **Incidences géographiques de l'industrialisation en Algérie.**
(Geographical factors of industrialization in Algeria).
B. Semmoud, A. Prenant. *Cahiers Géographiques de l'Ouest* (Oran),
no. 2-3 (1979), 295p. 42 maps. (Spécial Industrie).
This special issue brings together six separate case-studies, from different parts of
Algeria, of the impact of new factories on urban centres and their surrounding regions
– Arzew, Mostaganem, Saida, Sétif, Berrouaghia and Ghazaouet. They focus on the
effect of the new industries on employment and on migration.

656 **Industrialization and regional development in a centrally-planned
economy – the case of Algeria.**
Keith Sutton. *Tijdschrift voor Economische en Sociale Geografie*,
vol. 67, no. 2 (1976), p. 83-94.
Examines the role of industrialization in the national and regional development of
Algeria during the first decade of independence.

657 **The spatial structure of state-owned industry in the Oran region of
Algeria.**
K. Sutton, B. Tijane. *Tijdschrift voor Economische en Sociale
Geografie*, vol. 76, no. 4 (1985), p. 261-73.
Watt's (1980) large enterprise model is applied here as a framework for studying the
industrial location and spatial behaviour of some ninety-two factories belonging to
seventeen state companies. Despite the difficulties inherent in borrowing from
Western settings, the results are encouraging and suggest the wider applicability of
location theory based on the size of industrial enterprise.

658 **Manufacturing industries in the Oran region of Algeria: their
location, structure and decision-making.**
B. Tijane. PhD thesis, University of Manchester, England, 1983.
A study of the location patterns, structures and changes in the manufacturing industry
of the Oran region since 1966 at the regional, sub-regional and city-district level.
Tijane examines the concepts of different industrial location theories and tests some of
them on industrial locations within the Oran region. The relevance of these concepts
to the Oran region are tested by an empirical analysis based on the author's fieldwork
data.

Contemporary North Africa: issues of development and integration.
See item no. 7.

**The making of contemporary Algeria, 1830-1987: colonial upheavals and
post-independence development.**
See item no. 8.

The Middle East and North Africa.
See item no. 29.

Middle East Economic Digest.
See item no. 30.

Quarterly Economic Review Annual Supplement – Algeria.
See item no. 33.

L'Algérie, volontarisme étatique et aménagement du territoire.
See item no. 60.

L'Algérie ou l'espace retourné.
See item no. 63.

La Mitidja: décolonisation et espace géographique.
See item no. 66.

L'élite dirigeante et la genèse de l'entrepreneur industriel au Maghreb: 'l'exemple algérien'.
See item no. 353.

Planification et développement en Algérie 1962-1980.
See item no. 597.

From central planning to market economy: a study of the political economy of changes in Algerian industrial development.
See item no. 598.

Contradictions in the Algerian development process: the reform of the public sector and the new approach to the private sector in industry.
See item no. 602.

Algeria: the contradictions of rapid industrialisation.
See item no. 606.

Regional disparities and regional development in Algeria.
See item no. 610.

Le capitalisme d'état algérien.
See item no. 614.

Oil and regional development: examples from Algeria and Tunisia.
See item no. 619.

Export promotion of non-hydrocarbon manufactured products from Algeria.
See item no. 624.

The effects of protection in a capital-deficit-oil-exporting country: a case study of Algeria.
See item no. 626.

Effectiveness of industrial democracy in Algeria.
See item no. 720.

UN Statistical Yearbook.
See item no. 734.

Algeria: transformation of a colonial urban system under a planned economy.
See item no. 744.

Urbanisation, reseaux urbains, régionalisation au Maghreb: Fascicule 3, Travaux de la Table Ronde 'Urbanisation au Maghreb'.
See item no. 758.

The transfer and the management of new technology in Algeria.
See item no. 778.

Aspects de l'artisanat en Afrique du Nord.
See item no. 817.

Progress in the human geography of the Maghreb.
See item no. 883.

Agriculture and Agrarian Reform

659 **Rétrospective de la réforme agraire en Algérie.** (Retrospective on agrarian reform in Algeria).
Philippe Adair. *Revue Tiers-Monde*, vol. 24, no. 93 (1983), p. 153-68.
Outlines the major agrarian problems inherited by independent Algeria and tolerated by the Boumediène régime during the 1960's – the sharecropping system, the large landless rural population, subsistence orientation of many producers, inequities of landholdings and export orientation of the modern sector. The author then investigates the effectiveness of the reforms, beginning in 1972, in solving these problems and concludes that none of the goals of the reform have been met.

660 **Peasant or proletarian? Wage labour and peasant economy during industrialization: the Algerian experience.**
Christian Andersson. Göteborg, Sweden: Almqvist & Wiksell International, 1985. 204p. maps.
The study focusses on the interaction of capitalist and traditional peasant economy during the process of industrialization between 1972 and 1982. While following some ten families for ten years the author gets close to Algerian realities and to palpable changes in an agrarian society that was only slightly affected by government-sponsored agrarian reforms, which failed and were abandoned.

661 **'The land to those who work it' Algeria's experiment in workers' management.**
Thomas L. Blair. Garden City, New York: Doubleday, 1969. 275p. 3 maps. bibliog.
Examines the origins, organization and evolution of worker self-management and critically analyses the Algerian experience. It concludes that although rapid socio-economic development did not follow on the heels of self-management, this does not negate the worthiness of the attempt, its potential for socialist change, nor its impact on the national consciousness.

662 **Attentisme et spéculation dans les campagnes algériennes.** (Wait-and-see policy and speculation in the Algerian countryside).
Jean-Claude Brulé. *Maghreb-Machrek*, no. 139 (1993), p. 42-52.

Brulé claims that the Algerian economic revolution has not succeeded in bringing an 'integrated' development project which would have brought about effective reforms in the countryside. The idea of privatization has now run its course, but the hesitation on the part of the authorities to reject collectivism completely and to authorize individual appropriation has resulted in a somewhat vague organization, the collective agricultural farm. Hastily enforced under great social pressure, this reform has opened the door to wide distortion. Today the 'wait-and-see' policy prevails, reflecting latent expectations of real land privatization.

663 **La Mitidja autogérée: enquête sur les exploitations autogérées agricoles d'une région d'Algérie, 1968-1970.** (Worker self-management in the Mitidja plain: enquiry into the agricultural worker self-management units in an Algerian region, 1968-70).
Claudine Chaulet. Algiers: SNED, 1971. 401p. 2 maps. bibliog.

One of the most perceptive case-studies of worker-management in Algerian agriculture, by a leading sociologist. The author seeks to understand the nature of the worker self-management units in the Mitidja plain, south of Algiers, their organization, and the relationship between the members.

664 **Agricultural development experience of Algeria, Morocco, and Tunisia: a comparison of strategies for growth.**
Kevin M. Cleaver. Washington, DC: World Bank, 1982. 60p. bibliog. (World Bank Staff Working Papers, no. 552).

Undertakes a comparison of the agricultural experiences of Algeria, Morocco and Tunisia in order to provide insights into the importance of food and agriculture for development and poverty reduction, and determinants of agricultural growth. The three countries provide special interest because they have very similar agricultural resource endowments, similar cultural and colonial heritages, and similar agricultural potentials, but different policies and agricultural strategies. The report provides recommendations with respect to appropriate government investment and policy strategies in the agricultural sectors of the three countries. It finds that there is considerable agricultural potential in the three countries, but that agricultural development strategy needs reform, particularly with respect to prices, subsidies, land tenure, credit, marketing extension and research.

665 **Problèmes agraires au Maghreb.** (Agrarian problems in the Maghreb).
Bruno Etienne, et al. Paris: Editions du CNRS, 1977. 320p. 5 maps. bibliog. (Centre de Recherches et d'Etudes sur les Sociétés Méditerranéennes).

Seven chapters of this work are devoted to Algeria. They examine the place of agrarian reform in the country's development strategy, investment in the agricultural sector, the programme to build new 'socialist' villages, and the plan to reform the grazing lands of the interior steppelands. In addition, there are three case-studies of the Mitidja, eastern Algeria, and the Kel Ahaggar Tuareg of the Algerian Sahara.

666 **Land, food and rural development in North Africa.**
M. Riad El-Ghonemy. Boulder, Colorado: Westview Press; London:
IT Publications, 1993. 207p. bibliog.

Following a discussion of concepts and regional issues in agriculture, the author
surveys such subjects as the rural economy of Algeria and Tunisia, and food insecurity
in the Nile Valley. The book concludes with a chapter on development challenges
facing North Africa.

667 **Les institutions agricoles algériennes.** (Algeria's agricultural
institutions).
Jean-Pierre Guin. Paris: Centre National de la Recherche
Scientifique, 1974. 182p. (Les Cahiers, no. 2).

A brief description of the evolution of agriculture, its place in the Algerian economy,
and its organization. The second part consists of a systematic bibliography of books
and articles on agriculture and part three includes a collection of all relevant texts
published since independence in the *Journal Officiel de la République Démocratique
et Populaire d'Algérie*, Algeria's official gazette.

668 **Agrarian reform under state capitalism in Algeria.**
Karen Pfeifer. Boulder, Colorado; London: Westview Press, 1985.
258p. maps. bibliog. (Westview Special Studies on the Middle East
and North Africa).

Algeria's dependence on food imports has increased dramatically since 1962 when it
was completely self-sufficient. This study seeks to identify and explain the causes
leading to this condition by critically analysing the government's principal response to
the agricultural dilemma, the three-phase programme of national action known as the
Charter of the Agrarian Revolution initiated in 1971. Based on a detailed micro-
analytical investigation of the manner in which the 'revolution' was implemented in
selected local communities located in the country's five major geo-economic zones, it
concludes that the 'revolution' was nothing more than 'reform' of a bourgeois
capitalist nature. Algerian economic policy-makers did not pursue massive investment
in agriculture and did not promote a profound reorganization of the agrarian sector.
Pfeifer advocates wholesale state intervention, control and mobilization to remedy the
problems of the agricultural sector.

669 **Algeria's agrarian transformation.**
Karen Pfeifer. *MERIP Reports*, no. 99 (September 1981), p. 7-14.

Briefly describes the first and second stages of Algeria's agrarian reform (1971-73 and
1973-76) and points to the differential impact of the reform on Algeria's regions. Two
case-studies (Besbès in the coastal plain of Amata and Thènia in the Mitidja plain
south of Algiers) show how the reform affected two different localities in the rich
coastal plains around the major urban/industrial centres. They clearly illustrate ways
in which the reform maintained and encouraged capitalist agriculture. The article
concludes that capitalism is the main force transforming Algerian agriculture and
paving the way for a new society by setting in place modern class relations.

670   **The development of commercial agriculture in Algeria, 1830-1970.**
Karen Pfeifer.   *Research in Economic History,* no. 10 (1986),
p. 271-308.

An analysis is offered of the evolution of the agrarian sector in Algeria during the era of colonial domination by France and in the immediate post-independence period. This case history reveals some of the structural and institutional foundations in the rural areas which help give rise to 'state capitalism'.

671   **Does food security make a difference? Algeria, Egypt and Turkey in comparative perspective.**
Karen Pfeifer.   In: *The many faces of national security in the Arab world.*   Edited by Bahgat Korany, P. Noble, R. Brynen.
Basingstoke, England: Macmillan, 1993, p. 127-44.

Examines the important issue of food security in Algeria as part of a comparative study which also includes Egypt and Turkey.

672   **Land policy in colonial Algeria: the origins of the rural public domain.**
John Ruedy.   Berkeley, California; Los Angeles: University of California Press, 1967. 115p. bibliog.

This book seeks to discover the origins and trace the early development of the public domain in disposable agricultural lands in Algeria. It examines their juridicial status before 1830, and the methods by which these lands were transformed from their original owners to the French state.

673   **La dépossession des fellahs (1830-1962).** (The dispossession of the peasants, 1830-1962).
Dijlali Sari.   Algiers: Société Nationale d'Edition et de Diffusion, 1978. 2nd ed. 167p. 3 maps. bibliog.

The first part analyses the stages by which the Algerian peasantry were dispossessed from their land after the advent of French colonial rule, and part two looks at the social and economic consequences of the expropriation. This is a valuable background study to the problems affecting the agricultural sector today.

674   **Agrarian reform in Algeria – progess in the face of disappointment, dilution and diversion.**
Keith Sutton.   In: *Rural poverty and agrarian reform.*   Edited by Steve Jones, P. C. Joshi, Miguel Murmis.   New Dehli: Allied Publishers, 1982, p. 356-75.

After the 1960s 'reform' of the autogestion estates, Algeria embarked on a more basic agrarian reform of its private sector during the 1970s. Sutton describes the stages of this reform and provides data on the area involved and the number of beneficiaries, cooperatives, and reform villages which resulted. Several criticisms of the limited results are made, focussing on delays, production shortcomings, and especially on the evidence of evasion by large landowners. Together with successful efforts to avoid expropriation and other means of diluting the measures of reform, the landed classes in Algeria managed to limit the 'Agrarian Revolution' to a shadow of its original plans. More positive was the creation of service cooperatives and the ethos of decentralization left after a decade of activity.

675 Agricultural co-operatives in Algeria.

Keith Sutton. *Yearbook of Agricultural Co-operation 1981* (1982), Plunkett Foundation for Co-operative Studies, Oxford, p. 169-90.

Discusses the different types of cooperatives set up as part of the agrarian reform in the 1970s to regroup beneficiaries of reform land.

676 Agricultural policy in Algeria in the 1980s: progress towards liberalization.

Keith Sutton, Ahmed Aghrout. *Canadian Journal of African Studies*, vol. 26, no. 2 (1992), p. 250-73.

Examines and evaluates the two programmes introduced in the 1980s to restructure the agricultural sector under which the 'self-managed' sector and the agrarian reform units of production were partially privatized.

677 Algeria's vineyards: an Islamic dilemma and a problem of decolonisation.

Keith Sutton. *Journal of Wine Research*, vol. 1, no. 2 (1990), p. 101-20.

Twenty years after independence, Algeria still had nearly half the 1962 area of vineyards, though with markedly lower yields and marketing at lower prices. The colonial legacy has now turned into an economic liability and has been tackled much less vigorously than other decolonization problems. An added dimension is the cultural inappropriateness of viticultural production in an increasingly Islamic country.

678 Algeria's vineyards: a problem of decolonisation.

Keith Sutton. *Méditerranée*, vol. 65, no. 3 (1988), p. 55-66.

Algeria's viticultural industry represents an example of the way that a colonial legacy can turn into a problem of dependency, the solution to which represents an issue of decolonization and adjustment. By late colonial times Algeria's wine exports represented over half of its exports by value. To add economic independence to political independence threatened serious financial and employment losses so any opportunity to avoid the reconversion of the now culturally inappropriate vineyards seemed attractive. Eventually, with the growth of hydrocarbon revenues, the reconversion and reconstitution of Algeria's vineyards proved possible during the 1970s.

679 Agricultural policies and the growing food security crisis.

Will D. Swearingen. In: *State and society in Algeria*. Edited by John P. Entelis, Phillip C. Naylor. Boulder, Colorado: Westview Press, 1992, p. 117-49.

Focusses on the agricultural problems in the Algerian economy. Swearingen points out that in 1992 Algeria had the most precarious food security situation in the region with up to 80 per cent of its food supply imported despite the major emphasis placed on self-sufficiency in food production and extensive agrarian reforms. In order to explain this paradox, he analyses agricultural policies pursued by the government since independence and examines the results of these policies. His explanation centres on the contradictions between official and actual policies, the shortages of funding allocated to the agricultural sector, the relative failure of agrarian reform, the neglect of traditional food production systems, counterproductive pricing policies, peasant resistance, population pressure and environmental constraints.

680　**Algeria's food security crisis.**
Will D. Swearingen. *Middle East Report*, no. 166 (1990), p. 21-25.

This brief article examines why Algeria's food security situation has become so precarious. It points to shortages of funding for agricultural development, peasant resistance, the flawed character of the agrarian reform, neglect of the private agricultural sector, and counterproductive pricing policies.

681　**Terroirs et sociétés au Maghreb et au Moyen Orient.** (Lands and societies in the Maghreb and Middle East).
Lyon: Maison de l'Orient, 1987. 438p. maps. bibliog. (Etudes sur le Monde Arabe, no. 2).

This volume results from a Franco-American seminar held in Lyon in June 1984 under the direction of Byron Cannon. Three of the contributions are on Algeria: 'Invading the village common: the origins of Algeria's modern rural crisis, 1870-1914' by Peter von Sivers; 'Production vivrière et production de marché dans l'agriculture algérienne: les effets de la première guerre mondiale' (Subsistence production and market production in Algerian agriculture: the effects of the First World War) by Gilbert Meynier; and 'Mechanization, mobilization and the market: Algerian agricultural policy in transition' by John P. Entelis. There is also a contribution on 'Les transferts de technologie dans l'agriculture et l'agro-industrie des pays du Maghreb et du Proche Orient' (Technology transfers in agriculture and agro-industry in Maghreb and Middle Eastern countries) by Isabelle Demongeot.

682　**Labor, employment and agricultural development in West Asia and North Africa.**
Edited by Dennis Tully.　Dordrecht, Netherlands; Boston, Massachusetts: Kluwer Academic, 1990. 228p. bibliog.

Includes one contribution on Algeria by Ahmed Bouaita and Claudine Chaulet on 'Agricultural changes in private farms of the Sersou, Algeria'.

The making of contemporary Algeria, 1830-1987: colonial upheavals and post-independence development.
See item no. 8.

Algeria: the revolution institutionalized.
See item no. 15.

Algeria: the challenge of modernity.
See item no. 19.

The Middle East and North Africa.
See item no. 29.

Middle East Economic Digest.
See item no. 30.

Quarterly Economic Review Annual Supplement – Algeria.
See item no. 33.

Polity and society in contemporary North Africa.
See item no. 38.

Le Sahara dans le développement des états maghrébins.
See item no. 57.

L'Algérie, volontarisme étatique et aménagement du territoire.
See item no. 60.

Le Sahara français.
See item no. 61.

L'Algérie ou l'espace retourné.
See item no. 63.

La Mitidja: décolonisation et espace géographique.
See item no. 66.

La politique hydro-agricole de l'Algérie.
See item no. 67.

Oasis du Sahara algérien.
See item no. 69.

Le pays de Ouargla (Sahara algérien): variations et organisation d'un espace rural en milieu désertique.
See item no. 70.

Rural renovation in Algeria.
See item no. 82.

Planification et développement en Algérie 1962-1980.
See item no. 597.

Algeria: the contradictions of rapid industrialisation.
See item no. 606.

Le capitalisme d'état algérien.
See item no. 614.

UN Statistical Yearbook.
See item no. 734.

The United States and Africa: guide to US official documents and government-sponsored publications on Africa: 1785-1975.
See item no. 841.

Progress in the human geography of the Maghreb.
See item no. 883.

Transport and
Communications

683 **Algérie: infrastructure et transport maritime.** (Algeria: maritime
infrastructure and transport).
Maghreb Développement, no. 73 (December 1984), p. 2-12; p. 57-68.
A brief discussion of Algeria's ports and maritime transport system.

684 **Algérie: le transport aérien.** (Algeria: air transport).
Maghreb Développement, no. 70 (September 1984), p. 2-12; p. 57-68.
A brief discussion of Algeria's airports and air communications network.

685 **La compagnie nationale algérienne de navigation.** (The national
Algerian navigation company).
Paul Balta. *Maghreb-Machrek*, no. 83 (1979), p. 52-60.
A study of the development of Algeria's national shipping line created in 1963. It
reveals that Algeria made substantial investment in its national line and examines the
composition of the fleet, the cargoes transported and the company's involvement in
the transportation of liquefied natural gas.

686 **Algérie et route transsaharienne.** (Algeria and the trans-Saharan
road).
Louis Blin. *The Maghreb Review*, vol. 12, no. 3-4 (1987), p. 105-13.
The trans-Saharan road, built by the Algerian army in the 1970s, was named the road
of African unity in 1973 and represented in the official discourse as Algeria's
contribution to African unity. The author describes Algeria's part in this multinational
project, and the project's role in the economy of the Algerian Sahara, especially the
exploitation of the region's mineral wealth, and Algeria's relations with its
neighbours. For a more detailed study of the trans-Saharan road project and Algeria's
relations with its southern neighbours, see Louis Blin, *L'Algérie du Sahara au Sahel:
route transsaharienne, économie petrolière et construction de l'Etat* (Algeria from
Sahara to Sahel: trans-Saharan route, petroleum economy and State construction),
(Paris: L'Harmattan, 1990. 501p. bibliog.).

687 **Railways of North Africa. The railway systems of the Maghreb.**
E. D. Brant. Newton Abbot, England: David & Charles, 1971. 231p.
7 maps. bibliog.

Part one is concerned specifically with Algeria. The main themes covered are the
history of the railway system, the rolling stock, the existing network of railways in
Algeria and travel and touring by train. The work is well-illustrated with maps and
photographs.

688 **Les transports urbains dans l'agglomération d'Alger.** (Urban
transport in Algiers).
Kamel Harouche. Paris: L'Harmattan, 1987. 232p. bibliog.

A detailed examination of the urban transport system of Greater Algiers and the
problems affecting it.

689 **Algeria's infrastructure. An economic survey of transportation,
communication and energy resources.**
J. C. Pawera. New York: Praeger, 1964. 234p. bibliog. (Praeger
Special Studies in International Economics).

Provides a survey of all the major aspects of infrastructure at the time of
independence. The survey of transport includes highways, railways, maritime and air
transport. Radio communications are also considered. Pipelines and energy resources are
discussed with specific chapters on gas, electricity, oil, coal and petroleum products.

690 **Trade routes of Algeria and the Sahara.**
Benjamin E. Thomas. Berkeley, California; Los Angeles: University
of California, 1957. 285p. 36 maps. bibliog. (University of California
Publications in Geography, vol. 8).

Part one covers northern Algeria, examining trade routes in pre-colonial times and the
development of road, rail and air communications during the French occupation. Part
two, on the Sahara, describes traditional forms of transport and the development of
modern transport networks.

691 **Le trafic commercial des ports maghrébins.** (Commercial traffic of
the Maghreb ports).
Maghreb, no. 51 (1972), p. 13-15.

Provides brief notes on the ports of Algeria, Morocco and Tunisia, their import and
export trade, port installations and plans for future development.

The Middle East and North Africa.
See item no. 29.

Middle East Economic Digest.
See item no. 30.

**The United States and Africa: guide to US official documents and
government-sponsored publications on Africa: 1785-1975.**
See item no. 841.

Emigration

692   Nationality and Algerian immigrants in France.
Lahouari Addi.   In: *French and Algerian identities from colonial times to the present: a century of interaction.*   Edited by Alec G. Hargreaves, Michael J. Heffernan.   Lewiston, Idaho; Queenston, Canada; Lampeter, Wales: The Edwin Mellen Press, 1993, p. 217-24.

Examines the question of nationality and the problems which it raises, particularly between different generations. Addi concludes that young men and women of immigrant origin would like to have dual nationality, for this would enable them to enjoy the rights of citizenship in the country where they were born and have decided to live, France, while at the same time avoiding the appearance of an open break with their parents and family roots. However, they cannot settle this issue purely on their own: attitudes on both sides of the Mediterranean have to change so that these youngsters can be accepted in their historical specificity.

693   International migration and dependence.
Stephen Adler.   Farnborough, England: Saxon House, 1977. 235p. bibliog.

An important study of the impact of migrant workers on relationships between France and Algeria, which tests theories of dependency and interdependence as they apply to migratory flows. It examines the history of Algerian emigration to France from 1870 to 1962, the negotiations between France and Algeria on emigration from the Evian Accords to the suspension of emigration in 1971, the status of Algerians in France, and the role of migration, trade and oil in Franco-Algerian relations.

694 **L'émigration maghrébine en Europe: exploitation ou coopération?**
(Maghrebine emigration to Europe: exploitation or cooperation?)
Edited by Rachid Amellal, Malik Kessal with an introduction by
Abdellatif Benachenhou. Algiers: Centre de Recherches en Economie
Appliquée, 1982. 671p.

After an introduction outlining the current crisis affecting Maghrebian migrants in
Europe, this edited volume is divided into three main sections containing articles on
the position of migrants from the Maghreb countries in Europe, state policies towards
the migrants and the perspectives and strategies of the emigrants themselves. Seven
articles are devoted specifically to Algerian migrants, examining the economic crisis
facing them in France and the Algerian government's policy of reinsertion.

695 **Migrant Muslim women in France.**
Sossie Andezian. In: *The new Islamic presence in Western Europe.*
Edited by Tomas Gerholm, Yngve Georg Lithman. London: Mansell,
1988, p. 196-204.

Based on research carried out in the late 1970s and early 1980s in south-east France.
The author examines the part played by North African women in the creation of the
Islamic religious domain in France. The chapter highlights the relative independence
enjoyed by these women in the organization of their religious life both with respect to
institutions and to males. Although considered marginal in terms of the strict canons
of Islam, these practices and representations, which should be linked to a form of
'popular Islam', are nevertheless important in the socializing of children of the second
generation.

696 **Etre Musulman en France.** (To be Muslim in France).
Jocelyne Cesari. Paris: Editions Karthala, IREMAM, 1994. 367p.
bibliog.

Based on a survey carried out among the North African population in Marseilles. The
author, a researcher at the Institut de Recherches et d'Etudes sur le Monde Arabe et
Musulman (IREMAM), points to the extreme diversity of experiences of being
Muslim in France, especially between different generations. She shows how Islam as a
cultural reference point is a factor in the evolving identity of the new generations, who
suffer from exclusion and racism in a country where the republican model of social
and civic integration is in crisis. The weakness of the nation-state and its institutions
seems to mark the end of 'la spécificité française' and the recognition of a
multicultural society.

697 **Berbèrité et émigration Kabyle.** (Berber identity and Kabyle
emigration).
Salem Chaker. *Peuples Méditerranéens* (France), no. 31-32 (1985),
p. 217-25.

Argues that during the past thirty to forty years, Kabyle emigration to France has been
a major factor in strengthening the sense of Berber identity. The first claim to Berber
identity was made by the Fédération de France du Mouvement Nationaliste in 1948-49
which attempted in vain to alter the Arab-Islamic tendencies of Algerian nationalism.
After independence France was used as a base for various activities aimed at

defending and advancing the Berber language and culture among Kabyle immigrants. In the past few years Berber militancy has arisen among the 'second generation'. An English summary is provided on p. 282.

698   **The Gulf war and the Maghrebian community in France.**
Alec G. Hargreaves, Timothy G. Stenhouse.   *Maghreb Review*,
vol. 17, no. 1-2 (1992), p. 42-54.

In France, the Maghrebian community came under intense media scrutiny during the 1990-91 Gulf crisis, with much speculation that it might function as a fifth column against the Allied war effort. The author presents a brief overview of the main images of the Maghrebian community as portrayed by the French press during the Gulf crisis. Data from public opinion polls conducted among the Muslim (mainly Maghrebian) population in France in connection with the war are shown to run counter to much press reporting. The attitudes of élite groups among the Maghrebian population are considered, with a particular emphasis on young political activists.

699   **Hommes et Migrations.** (Men and Migrations).
Paris: 40 rue de la Duée, 1959- . monthly.

Probably the most useful journal on Algerian emigration, and in particular, the Algerian community in France. It contains regular articles on Algerians in France dealing with a wide range of issues – political, social, economic and cultural. See for example *Passions franco-maghrébines* (no. 1183, January 1995), which includes articles on the problem of Algerians seeking refuge in France, Islam and the Islamist threat in France, and the international networks of the Algerian Front Islamique du Salut.

700   **The impact of the 1962 repatriates from Algeria on the French labor-market.**
J. Hunt.   *Industrial and Labor Relations Review*, vol. 45, no. 3 (1992), p. 556-72.

Uses census data to examine the impact on the French labour market of the 900,000 people repatriated from Algeria in 1962. Repatriates settled in regions culturally and climatically similar to Algeria, and represented 1.6 per cent of the total French labour force in 1968. Estimates indicate that the repatriates increased the 1968 unemployment of non-repatriates by at most 0.3 percentage points. Average annual salaries were lower by at most 1.3 per cent in 1967 due to their arrival in France.

701   **The second generation – the children of Muslim immigrants in France.**
Annie Krieger-Krynicki.   In: *The new Islamic presence in Western Europe.*   Edited by Tomas Gerholm, Yngve Georg Lithman.
London; New York: Mansell, 1988, p. 196-205.

A study of the legal and social position of the young *Beurs* – many of whom have a dual nationality which complicates their situation without increasing their opportunities – and the policies of the countries of origin, including Algeria, towards them.

702   **Algerian emigration to France and the Franco-Algerian Accords of 1980.**
Richard I. Lawless, Allan M. Findlay.   *Orient* (Hamburg), vol. 23, no. 3 (September 1982), p. 454-67.
Examines Algeria's incorporation into the French labour market during the colonial period and the negotiations between Algeria and France on emigration during the first decade after Algerian independence. In the early 1970s both the Algerian and French governments sought to terminate all new labour migration from Algeria to France but policies to encourage the return migration of Algerian workers living in France met with little success. In September 1980 the two countries signed a new accord on emigration by which France and Algeria agreed to introduce a range of measures to encourage the voluntary return and to facilitate the reinsertion of Algerian workers and their families into the Algerian economy and society.

703   **Return migration to Algeria: the impact of state intervention.**
Richard Lawless.   In: *Return migration and regional economic problems.*   Edited by R. King.   London: Croom Helm, 1986, p. 213-42.
The closure of the French labour market in 1974 consolidated the third age of emigration from Algeria to France, characterized by family regroupment. A return to Algeria was often delayed and in many cases, perhaps for the majority, it became a retirement movement at the end of the migant's working life. For those who have chosen reinsertion into the productive sector of the Algerian economy, only a small proportion have returned through state-sponsored initiatives. Others have secured employment by applying directly to the state enterprises. There is little evidence that return migration has contributed to the development of those areas outside the major industrial development poles.

704   **Return migration to the Maghreb: people and policies.**
Richard I. Lawless, Allan M. Findlay, Anne M. Findlay.   London: Arab Research Centre, 1982. 47p. (Arab Papers, no. 10).
Compares and contrasts policies on return migration adopted by Algeria and its neighbours, Morocco and Tunisia, in response to the closure of the West European labour markets in the 1970s, and explores the attitudes and responses of the migrants themselves. The study is principally concerned with Algeria.

705   **Le retour des émigrés algériens.** (The return of Algerian emigrants).
Henri Le Masne.   Algiers: Office des Publications Universitaires; Paris: Centre d'Information et d'Etudes sur les Migrations, 1982. 215p. bibliog.
After a brief history of Algerian emigration to France from the colonial period to Algeria's decision in September 1973 to suspend all new emigration, the main part of the text is devoted to the results of the author's survey of some eighty Algerian workers in the Rhône-Alps region in 1972-73, focussing on their attitudes towards a return to Algeria. It also examines the Algerian government's policy of 'reinsertion' and its limitations.

706 **Réflexions sur le non-passage au terrorisme dans l'immigration maghrébine en France.** (Reflections on the lack of terrorism resulting from immigrants from the Maghreb in France).
Rémy Leveau. *Etudes Polémologiques* (France), no. 49 (1989), p. 141-56.

This analysis of the position of North African immigrants in France provides an insight into terrorism; ironically, it is the long-standing strategy of non-violence among these immigrants which provides this insight. Their incorporation into French society reveals a marginalization which, while allowing for a strong identification with the Palestinians in the Occupied Territories, still allows, for example, for French patriotism and a growing sympathy for human rights.

707 **Religion et politique: juifs et musulmans maghrébins en France.** (Religion and politics: Jews and North African Muslims in France).
Rémy Leveau, Dominique Schnapper. *Revue Française de Science Politique* (France), vol. 37, no. 3 (1987), p. 855-85.

The Jewish modes of social integration since the French Revolution cannot be compared summarily with the much more recent ones of the Muslims. However, in both cases a minority group with a strong historical awareness of its cultural and religious identity tends to assert itself in a sort of collective bargaining with the centralized state. The Jews managed to obtain state protection by giving up much of their specificity and by confining the religious element to the private sphere. A comparable evolution is beginning for Muslims, especially those born in France, familiarly known as *beurs*.

708 **Patterns of emigration, 1905-1954: 'Kabyles' and 'Arabs'.**
Neil Macmaster. In: *French and Algerian identities from colonial times to the present: a century of interaction.* Edited by Alec G. Hargreaves, Michael J. Heffernan. Lewiston, Idaho; Queenston, Canada; Lampeter, Wales: The Edwin Mellen Press, 1993, p. 21-38.

Seeks to identify the main factors underlying the emergence and consolidation of zones of high and low labour emigration during the first half of the 20th century. Macmaster highlights the existence of a tradition of internal migration which prepared Kabyles for the emigrant experience. This gave them an advantage over the Arabs, but Kabyle emigration was also encouraged or facilitated by the French in various ways. By the time restrictions were introduced by the colonial authorities, Kabyle emigration had already developed its own internal dynamic, whereas the more weakly organized Arab movement to France was faced with major obstacles that slowed down the formation of a tradition of emigration.

709 **New forms of expression among young people of immigrant stock in France.**
Mohammed Mazouz. *International Social Science Journal* (Great Britain), vol. 37, no. 4 (1985), p. 531-40.

This brief article shows how young French citizens of North African parentage are organizing and participating in sports programmes, engaging in news broadcasting and drama projects, and participating in nationwide demonstrations in an effort to enter the mainstream culture, while still observing their separate heritage.

710 **Aspects of the brain drain in Algeria.**
Fatima-Zohra Oufriha. In: *The Arab brain drain.* Edited by A. B.
Zahlan. London: Ithaca Press (for the United Nations), 1981,
p. 103-13.
The author claims that the brain drain is a problem of recent origin in Algeria although
it has the same consequences as elsewhere. As they lose their high level manpower to
the developed countries – for example there are more Algerian doctors in the Paris
area than in the whole of Algeria – the developing countries are often obliged to seek
'technical co-operation' assistance from the developed countries themselves. In the
case of Algeria this assistance has been massive. The chapter briefly examines the
causes and consequences of the brain drain from Algeria.

711 **Competition for political legitimacy at local and national levels
among young North Africans in France.**
Marie Poinsot. *New Community*, vol. 20, no. 1 (1993), p. 79-92.
Outlines the competition between two major national organizations, SOS Racisme and
France Plus, at a time when they both decided to localize their actions in order to gain
a larger audience and political recognition. Data collected in northern France shows
how local groups reacted after 1988 by building a national federation of grassroots
initiatives. This new trend of mobilization among young North Africans was made
possible thanks to certain changes in the political opportunity structure. This new
structure played a significant role in the outcomes achieved by these groups.

712 **Elites of Maghrebin extraction in France.**
Nadia Rachedi. In: *Muslims in Europe.* Edited by Bernard Lewis,
Dominique Schnapper. London; New York: Pinter Publishers, 1994,
p. 67-78.
Rachedi presents the results of a survey carried out among the Maghrebian élite in
France during the Gulf War. Those interviewed did not claim to represent others of
Maghrebian stock in France or to have a sense of belonging to a community with its
own distinctive culture. They consider themselves to be complete citizens, playing a
full part in communal life. There are in the region of five hundred municipal
councillors of Maghrebian extraction, testifying to fairly recent entry into the political
arena. They show a high degree of professional and social integration. The Gulf crisis
in 1990-91 constituted a test imposed by others, especially the media, of their
membership of French society; as far as they were concerned the war did not give rise
to 'twin loyalties' or call into question their citizenship and involvement in French
society.

713 **Islam in France: religion, ethnic community or social ghetto?**
Olivier Roy. In: *Muslims in Europe.* Edited by Bernard Lewis,
Dominique Schnapper. London; New York: Pinter Publishers, 1994,
p. 54-66.
Points to the fact that *beurs* (North Africans born in France) are perceived as 'Arabs'
or Maghrebians, yet portray virtually no sign of Arab culture or the Muslim religion.
The culture of the urban-zone *beurs* has virtually no Islamic constituent; it is rather a
sub-culture that functions along the lines of popular culture by pirating the dominant
culture.

714   **The *pieds-noirs* in Corsica: the search for identity.**
Peter Savigear.   In: *French and Algerian identities from colonial times to the present: a century of interaction.*   Edited by Alec G. Hargreaves, Michael J. Heffernan.   Lewiston, Idaho; Queenston, Canada; Lampeter, Wales: The Edwin Mellen Press, 1993, p. 240-46.

A discussion of the experience of the *pieds-noirs* (European settlers from Algeria, the majority of whom were repatriated to France during and after the War of Independence) in Corsica since 1962. The author argues that the impact has involved far more than a clash of *rapatriés* and Corsican nationalists. The variety of experience has itself been important and has enabled many to survive the exile. The lesson of their often difficult and special experience has been that integration and identity as a community are not incompatible. They are growing together, aided perhaps by the context of the current strengthening of a sense of a Mediterranean identity. This constitutes one of the few references on the *pieds-noirs* in English.

715   **State intervention and the international labour market: a review of labour emigration policies in the Arab world.**
I. J. Seccombe, R. I. Lawless.   In: *The impact of international migration on developing countries.*   Edited by Reginald Appleyard.   Paris: OECD, 1989, p. 69-89.

Challenges the view that within the Arab world migration for employment occurs virtually unimpeded in a fundamentally *laissez-faire* environment. The range of emigration policies adopted in the Arab labour-supplying countries is revealed, as are the constraints on policy choice and implementation. The authors argue that emigration policies can be successful only when they meet the requirements of, or are backed by, the countries of immigration. This is illustrated by case examples contrasting the successful ban on emigration imposed by Algeria and backed by subsequent action by France and the failure of South Yemen's prohibition on emigration for employment.

716   **The making of family identities among Franco-Algerian couples.**
Jocelyne Streiff-Fenart.   In: *French and Algerian identities from colonial times to the present: a century of interaction.*   Edited by Alec G. Hargreaves, Michael J. Heffernan.   Lewiston, Idaho; Queenston, Canada; Lampeter, Wales: The Edwin Mellen Press, 1993, p. 225-37.

The author examines the role occupied by mixed marriages in Franco-Algerian relations from colonial times to the present day. She points out that Algerian women married to French men have very little chance of making their cultural heritage count within the family home or of transmitting it to their children. Unions between Algerian men and French women are marked even more directly by differential power relations between ethnic groups. In such cases, far from overcoming cultural, religious and political differences between ethnic groups, mixed marriages serve to highlight the effects of those differences, both within the family home and in society at large. This has been seen in the custody disputes over children of estranged Franco-Algerian couples, whose personal conflicts were echoed in cultural and legal disputes between the two states. For a more detailed sociological study of Franco-Algerian mixed marriages see the author's *Les couples franco-maghrébins en France* (Franco-Maghrebian couples in France), (Paris: L'Harmattan, 1989. 155p.).

717 **Migration and development: the case of Algeria.**
Madeleine Trebous. Paris: Organization for Economic Cooperation and Development, Development Centre, 1970. 242p. bibliog.
An important investigation into the evolution and impact of Algerian emigration, which includes a section on the evolution of migration, and the impact of emigration on the Algerian labour market. The problems and characteristics of Algerian migrants in France are also considered. Statistical tables and an introduction to the political agreements are other features of the work.

718 **The *harkis*: a community in the making?**
Catherine Wihtol de Wenden. In: *French and Algerian identities from colonial times to the present: a century of interaction.* Edited by Alec G. Hargreaves, Michael J. Heffernan. Lewiston, Idaho; Queenston, Canada; Lampeter, Wales: The Edwin Mellen Press, 1993, p. 189-201.
One of the few works in English on the *harkis*, Algerian Muslims who supported the French during the War of Independence and who then settled in France rather than remain in an independent Algeria. It points to the diverse origins of the *harkis*, the confusion about the size and distribution of the *harki* population in France and the confused and contradictory policies adopted towards them by the French authorities. While half of the *harki* population has become fully assimilated into French society and requires no special nor distinctive provision, the other half remains in a precarious and marginal state, even though many *harkis* now feel they have found some sense of common identity.

719 **Les immigrés et la politique: cent cinquante ans d'évolution.**
(Immigrants and policy: a hundred and fifty years of development). Catherine Wihtol de Wenden. Paris: Presses de la Fondation Nationale des Sciences Politiques, 1988. 393p. bibliog.
Examines French immigration policies, particularly towards North Africans, the historical factors that account for increased political leverage by immigrants, and their participation in French political life.

Les mémoires de Messali Hadj: aspects du manuscrit original.
See item no. 195.

La 7e wilaya: la guerre du FLN en France, 1954-1962.
See item no. 231.

Le silence du fleuve.
See item no. 259.

Algeria: changes in population distribution 1954-66.
See item no. 266.

Colonialism and after: an Algerian Jewish community.
See item no. 283.

Women of the Mediterranean.
See item no. 351.

French and Algerian identities from colonial times to the present: a century of interaction.
See item no. 535.

French-Algerian relations, 1980-1990.
See item no. 550.

Le Grand Maghreb et l'Europe: enjeux et perspectives.
See item no. 583.

A new trend in Maghrebine culture: the Beurs and their generation.
See item no. 787.

Voices from the North African community in France: immigration and identity in Beur fiction.
See item no. 800.

Nouveaux enjeux culturels au Maghreb.
See item no. 819.

Maghrebians and French television.
See item no. 850.

L'émigration maghrébine de 1962 à 1985: répertoire bibliographique.
See item no. 873.

Labour Relations and Trade Unionism

720 **Effectiveness of industrial democracy in Algeria.**
A. Abada. PhD thesis, Birkbeck College, London, 1990.
Reports on a case-study of the effectiveness of the Algerian Socialist Management of the Units/Enterprises (SMU/E) as a form of representative participation in decision-making or industrial democracy.

721 **Vers un syndicalisme national en Algérie (1946-1956).** (Towards a national trade unionism in Algeria 1946-56).
Charles Robert Ageron. *Revue Histoire Moderne et Contemporaine* (France), no. 36 (July-September 1989), p. 450-63.
A survey of the post-war history of trade unions in Algeria before independence, 1946-56, focussing on the relative influences of French, Tunisian and Moroccan models, the Arab states and the World Trade Union Federation of Communist Obedience and International Confederation of Free Trade Unions. The growth of Algerian trade unions was intimately related to the national independence movement.

722 **Trade unionism.**
Eqbal Ahmad. In: *State and society in independent North Africa.* Edited by Leon Carl Brown. Washington, DC: The Middle East Institute, 1966, p. 146-91.
Examines the origins and development of labour unions in Algeria, Morocco and Tunisia and the problems which they encountered in the early years of independence.

723 **Socialist management of enterprises in Algeria: participation and conflict.**
A. Belghenou. *Relations Industrielles – Industrial Relations,* vol. 47, no. 2 (1992), p. 300-24.
Belghenou attempts to identify the relationship between conflict and participation within the Socialist Management of Enterprises system introduced in Algeria in 1971,

in terms of both its significance and evolution. The article examines the actors within the system to ascertain their objectives and their inter-connections and identifies three areas of conflict: between the two main social actors, the labour movement and the state party; between the elected workers councils and the management; and the fact that those at the level of production did not accept the system and by reference the state party.

724 **The rise and demise of participative management in Algeria.**
M. Branine. *Economic and Industrial Democracy*, vol. 15, no. 4 (1994), p. 595-630.

Evaluates the development and subsequent outcome of the Algerian experience of participative management which was seen as an important determinant in the country's socio-economic development. The outcome was not as expected either by the state, workers or managers. It is argued that the policy's failure was the result of introducing views and ideologies alien to the predominant norms and cultural values.

725 **Les relations de travail en Algérie: le cinquième congrès de l'UGTA.** (Labour relations in Algeria: the fifth congress of the UGTA).
Nicole Grimaud. *Maghreb-Machrek*, no. 80 (1978), p. 57-62.

A study of the trade union movement in Algeria since 1971, examining the issues discussed at the fifth congress of the Union Générale des Travailleurs Algériens held in Algiers in March 1978.

726 **Contribution du syndicalisme au mouvement de libération nationale en Oranie (Ouest Algérien) 1945-56.** (The contribution of trade unionism to the national liberation movement in the Oran region [western Algeria] 1945-56).
Badra Lahouel. *Revue d'Histoire Maghrébine* (Tunisia), vol. 13, no. 43-44 (1986), p. 49-58.

After the Second World War, the number of Algerians in trade unions in Oran province rose dramatically and low pay and unemployment made them more and more militant. The union movement became politicized as workers became aware of colonial exploitation, while French employers tried to divide the movement in order to keep wages down. The impact of unionism was limited by the division of the Algerian working class into several different organizations, but they all came to see that their economic and social goals depended on the end of the colonial régime.

727 **Interest groups and decolonization: American businessmen and organised labour in French North Africa.**
Egya N. Sangmuah. *Maghreb Review*, vol. 13, no. 3-4 (1988), p. 161-74.

Examines the impact of interest groups, particularly the American Federation of Labour and the Congress of Industrial Organizations, on US policy concerning decolonization in French North Africa. Organized labour had more success than business groups because of support from the State Department and CIA. Labour groups also had stronger foreign links through membership of the International Confederation of Free Trade Unions, which gave important support to North African nationalism as a means of aiding workers.

728 **Le mouvement ouvrier maghrébin.** (The Maghrebian labour movement).
     Noureddine Sraieb, et al. Paris: Editions du CNRS, 1985. 327p.

This collection of essays is divided into three parts, dealing with: the history of trade unionism; labour relations and workers' resistance; and trade unions and the state. Several essays are devoted to Algeria and the book forms a useful reference work on labour relations and trade unions in Algeria.

729 **Immigrants and political activists: Algerian nationalists in France, 1945-1954.**
     Benjamin Stora. In: *French and Algerian identities from colonial times to the present: a century of interaction.* Edited by Alec G. Hargreaves, Michael J. Heffernan. Lewiston, Idaho; Queenston, Canada; Lampeter, Wales: The Edwin Mellen Press, 1993, p. 39-75.

Support for the cause of Algerian nationalism had a long tradition among Algerian immigrant workers in France. However, Algerian nationalists in post-war France were faced with a very different situation from that which confronted pre-war activists. The social composition of Algerian immigration had altered and, for political reasons, the Fédération de France was unable to assume the central control in the nationalist organization which the L'Etoile Nord Africaine had played between the wars. By this stage, the Fédération de France was receiving most of its strategic and ideological directives from the Parti du Peuple Algérien and its successor, the Mouvement pour le Triomphe des Libertés Démocratiques.

730 **Doctrine et action syndicales en Algérie.** (Trade union doctrine and action in Algeria).
     François Weiss. Paris: Editions Cujas, 1970. 363p. bibliog.

A study of the origins of the labour movement in colonial Algeria, the creation of the Union Générale des Travailleurs Algériens (UGTA) and the influence of foreign labour movements on it. It describes the organization of the UGTA and analyses the problems resulting from the survival of capitalist economic structures in independent Algeria, and the impact of new socialist structures on the labour movement.

Algeria: the challenge of modernity.
See item no. 19.

State and revolution in Algeria.
See item no. 36.

L'émigration ouvrière italienne dans le Maghreb et les répercussions algériennes après la constitution du comité d'entr'aide des mineurs italiens du groupe de 'Il Minatore' (1907).
See item no. 185.

L'élite dirigeante et la genèse de l'entrepreneur industriel au Maghreb: 'l'exemple algérien'.
See item no. 353.

Algeria: revision of labour legislation.
See item no. 483.

Workers' self-management in Algeria.
See item no. 599.

Le capitalisme d'état algérien.
See item no. 614.

Self-management in Yugoslavia and the developing world.
See item no. 620.

Industrial self-management in Algeria.
See item no. 651.

'The land to those who work it'. Algeria's experiment in workers' management.
See item no. 661.

La Mitidja autogérée: enquête sur les exploitations autogérées agricoles d'une région d'Algérie, 1968-1970.
See item no. 663.

Statistics

731 **Official publications on the Middle East: a selective guide to the statistical sources.**
C. H. Bleaney.   Durham, England: Centre for Middle Eastern and Islamic Studies, 1985. 31p.
A guide to contemporary official statistical data and social and economic documentation available from the nations of the Middle East and North Africa. Bleaney discusses how to use official publications as source materials, and provides lists of international and regional organizations that produce useful materials. In the country-by-country survey, which includes Algeria (p. 9), the history and availability of statistical materials is discussed.

732 **Demographic Yearbook.**
New York: United Nations, 1948- . annual.
Contains up-to-date, official demographic statistics from 220 countries, including Algeria, on size distribution and trends in population, natality, foetal mortality, infant and maternal mortality, general mortality, nuptiality and divorce, and international migration. Data is shown by urban-rural residence in many of the tables.

733 **Statistics – Africa: sources for social, economic and market research.**
Joan Harvey.   Beckenham, England: CBD Research Publication, 1978. 2nd ed. 374p.
This volume lists major Algerian statistical publications (p. 44-52), giving detailed bibliographical information and addresses of useful official bodies.

734 **UN Statistical Yearbook.**
New York: United Nations, 1948- . annual.
Contains up-to-date economic statistics from member countries, including Algeria, showing data on production (agriculture, forestry, fishing, mining and quarrying,

manufacturing, construction), energy, trade (internal and external), on transportation and communications and on total and per capita consumption of agricultural products, fertilizers, etc. Summary statistics are included on the balance of payments, wages and prices, national accounts, finance, budget accounts, and public debt and development assistance. The last section deals with social phenomena, health, housing, education, science and technology and culture.

735   UNESCO Statistical Yearbook.
Paris: UNESCO, 1963- . annual.

Contains up-to-date statistics on education, science and technology, libraries, book production, newspapers, films and cinema, radio broadcasting and television as supplied by over 200 member countries, including Algeria.

736   The Arab world: an international statistical directory.
Rodney Wilson.   Boulder, Colorado: Westview Press, 1984. 15p.
139 tables.

A guide to the most useful statistical sources on the Arab world for social scientists. For each country, sources of statistics on agricultural and industrial production, extractive industry and manufacturing are given, and for the oil producing states, oil production and export data is also included.

The Middle East and North Africa.
See item no. 29.

Middle East Economic Digest.
See item no. 30.

Quarterly Economic Review Annual Supplement – Algeria.
See item no. 33.

Urbanization and Rural Settlement

737 **Habitat, état et société au Maghreb.** (Habitat, state and society in the Maghreb).
Edited by Pierre-Robert Baduel. Paris: Editions du CNRS, 1988. 366p.

A basic reference work on the housing problems affecting Algeria and its neighbours in the Maghreb. The contributions examine housing policies, both rural and urban, at the national and regional levels, and include case-studies of individual cities.

738 **Urban growth and housing policy in Algeria: a case study of a migrant community in the city of Constantine.**
Rabah Boudebaba. Aldershot, England: Avebury, 1992. 316p. bibliog.

Examines the changing political economy of Algeria in order to place the case-study of a single migrant community in the context of the processes of migration and urbanization in which it has been engulfed. There follows an analysis of the city of Constantine and one migrant community as an example of the implications of recent government attempts to meet problems of rural to urban migration and its consequences. The author concludes that there is a vital need for popular democratic participation, especially for the provision of accommodation and services for migrants living on the socio-economic margins of the city.

739 **Urban planning in Algeria – still to achieve a genuine independence.**
Philip Brebner. *The Maghreb Review*, vol. 7, no. 3-4 (1982), p. 82-86.

Brebner examines aspects of the continued reliance of Algeria on French urban planning and highlights some of the repercussions that this has had on the country's post-independence urban development. Planning education is identified as a major contributory factor in maintaining this reliance on France.

740 **Les regroupements de la décolonisation en Algérie.** (The
regroupments of decolonization in Algeria).
Michel Cornaton. Paris: Les Editions Ouvrières, 1967. 295p. 9 maps.
bibliog. (Collection Développement et Civilisations).

A basic study on the massive regroupment of the Algerian rural population by the
French army during the War of Independence, as part of counter-insurgency policy.
The author reveals that half of Algeria's rural population were uprooted from their
homes during the war. He traces the evolution of the policy, describes conditions
within the regroupment centres, and examines the fate of the centres in different parts
of the country after independence.

741 **Algerian housing policies, practices and end product.**
Karim Hadiri. *Third World Planning Review*, vol. 15, no. 3 (1993),
p. 287-305.

A critical discussion of the impact of housing policies and practices in Algeria.

742 **The landscape of colonialism: the impact of French colonial rule on
the Algerian settlement pattern, 1830-1987.**
M. J. Heffernan, K. Sutton. In: *Colonialism and development in the
contemporary world*. Edited by C. Dixon, M. J. Heffernan. London:
Mansell, 1991, p. 121-52.

Examines the impact of French colonial domination on the landscape and settlement
of rural Algeria from the beginning of French rule to the late 1980s, demonstrating
how and why the Algerian rural settlement pattern was progressively modified and
ultimately transformed during the colonial period. Particular atttention is paid to the
creation by French colonial authorities of a network of nucleated rural settlements
which was superimposed on a pre-colonial pattern of dispersed settlement. The
authors analyse how and why the colonial geographies which were created in rural
Algeria have persisted into the post-independence period.

743 **Algeria: decolonization, rapid urbanization, and the functional and
social transformation of a colonial urban system under a planned
economy.**
Richard I. Lawless. *Orient* (Germany), vol. 22, no. 4 (December
1981), p. 557-73.

Lawless discusses how under its centrally planned economy introduced after
independence, the urban network inherited from colonial rule was not abandoned.
Instead rapid urbanization is being reinforced by industrialization.

744 **Algeria: transformation of a colonial urban system under a
planned economy.**
Richard I. Lawless. In: *Development of urban systems in Africa*.
Edited by R. A. Obudho, Salah El-Shakhs. New York: Praeger, 1979,
p. 79-98.

Assesses the effort made since independence to strengthen the urban network inherited
from colonial rule, principally through industrialization.

745 **Tlemcen: continuity and change in an Algerian Islamic town.**
Richard I. Lawless, Gerald H. Blake.   London; New York: Bowker,
1976. 173p. 38 maps. bibliog.
A study of the changing form and functions of Tlemcen, the major pre-colonial urban
centre in western Algeria. It describes the town's location and physical setting, and its
history and development from the Roman period to the end of French control in 1962.
It examines changing land-use patterns over time, the town's traditional craft
industries, its modern status as a regional centre and its place in Algeria's urban
hierarchy.

746 **Algeria.**
Djaffar Lesbet.   In: *Housing policies in the Socialist Third World.*
Edited by K. Mathey.   London. Mansell, 1990, p. 249-73.
A critical discussion of housing policies in Algeria.

747 **La casbah d'Alger entre réhabilitation et réanimation: la casbah
an 2000.** (The Algiers casbah between rehabilitation and recovery:
the casbah year 2000).
Djaffar Lesbet.   *Peuples Méditerranéens*, no. 43 (1988), p. 59-78;
p. 148.
Due to the abandonment of local resources, the lack of control over imported
technology, and especially the absence of clearly defined objectives, the complexity of
everyday life in the Algiers casbah, or pre-colonial city, has eluded the numerous
projects proposed during the past twenty years to save this significant part of a young
capital undergoing renovation. Building up confidence between inhabitants interested
in the future of their neighbourhood and public authorities is necessary to launch a
programme for saving the casbah and to stop demolitions being undertaken for reasons
of 'safety'. An English summary is provided.

748 **Monde arabe, villes, pouvoirs et sociétés.** (Arab world, cities,
power and societies).
Maghreb-Machrek, Special Number (1994), 242p.
This special issue of the journal contains five essays in French on urban issues in
Algeria: 'City dwellers looking to the city: housing in Sétif' by Said Belguidoum
(p. 42-55); 'Islamism in the city' by Smail Hadj Ali (p. 69-74); 'Female territories in
Tlemcen' by Rabia Bekkar (p. 126-41); 'Oran, urbanism without history: destroy to
build' by Fouad Soufi; and 'Effects of the Algerian housing crisis – from makeshift
housing to the state of emergency' by Djaffar Lesbet (p. 212-21).

749 **La médina de Constantine (Algérie): de la ville traditionelle au centre de l'agglomération contemporaine.** (The medina of Constantine [Algeria]: from traditional town to the centre of the contemporary city).
Bernard Pagand. Poitiers, France: Université de Poitiers, Centre Interuniversitaire d'Etudes Méditerranéennes, 1989. 295p. 65 maps. bibliog. (Etudes Méditerrannéennes Fascicule, no. 14).
Examines the changing role of the pre-colonial core or medina of Constantine, Algeria's third largest city. The work also discusses: the current dominance of tertiary activities in the medina; the decay of the urban fabric of the traditional quarters; and studies and projects to restructure and revitalize the area.

750 **Slum clearance and rehousing as a solution to low-income people: the case of Constantine, Algeria.**
T. Sahnoune. PhD thesis, University of Newcastle, England, 1988.
Sahnoune contends that rehabilitation of the historic quarters of the inner cities and upgrading 'bidonvilles' slums will not only improve the residential environment, but also preserve the cultural and social fabric existing therein. Algeria is on the verge of a large-scale enterprise of urban renewal and ought to evolve appropriate methods so that practice will correspond to local and real needs of the citizen.

751 **Algeria.**
Keith Sutton. In: *Urbanization in Africa: a handbook.* Edited by J. D. Tarver. Westport, Connecticut; London: Greenwood Press, 1994, p. 83-104.
Analyses the country's urbanization trends, the sources of population growth, the effect of urbanization on the urban hierarchy, population growth in suburbs and slums, the housing crisis, and policies on urbanization and regional development.

752 **Algeria's socialist villages – a reassessment.**
Keith Sutton. *Journal of Modern African Studies*, no. 22 (1984), p. 223-28.
This article examines the origins and aims of the programme to build a thousand 'Socialist villages', assesses the programme's achievements by 1981, and discusses the limitations of the programme.

753 **The *centres de regroupement*: the French army's final legacy to Algeria's settlement geography.**
Keith Sutton. In: *French and Algerian identities from colonial times to the present: a century of interaction.* Edited by Alec G. Hargreaves, Michael J. Heffernan. Lewiston, Idaho; Queenston, Canada; Lampeter, Wales: The Edwin Mellen Press, 1993, p. 163-88.
The creation of *centres de regroupement* became a definite policy of the French army in Algeria from 1957. This chapter examines the origin and development of the *centres*, the impact of *regroupement* on population change in the period 1954-66, the

survival of the *centres* as permanent rural settlements, and parallels between the *centres de regroupements* and the socialist villages of the 1970s.

754 The growth of Algiers and regional development in Algeria: contradictory themes.

Keith Sutton. *Third World Planning Review*, vol. 10, no. 2 (1988), p. 129-57.

Macrocephalic growth has threatened Algiers since independence, resulting in a range of regional development policies to forestall the threat and a series of urban plans to cope with the continued expansion of the capital city. Continued strong regional disparities attest to the limited impact of the regional development options; hence the urgency for a Greater Algiers growth strategy. The 1975 COMEDOR Plan has been replaced by CNERU's 1983 Plan which contains a major switch from eastwards urban expansion to a south-westwards directional bias.

755 The influence of military policy on Algerian rural settlement.

Keith Sutton. *Geographical Review*, vol. 71, no. 4 (1981), p. 379-94.

The rural settlement system of Algeria had long been characterized by a highly dispersed, poorly structured pattern until a large proportion of the rural population was resettled by the French army during the War of Independence (1954-61). Evidence during the 1960s suggested that many of these temporary settlement centres remained in existence. Data from the 1977 population census permitted a sample of the centres to be traced and an assessment to be made of their role in the rural settlement pattern. The acquisition of service functions by the permanent centres was a significant factor in the restructuring of several rural regions.

756 The socialist villages of Algeria.

Keith Sutton. In: *The Middle Eastern village: changing economic and social relations.* Edited by Richard Lawless. London: Croom Helm, 1987, p. 77-114.

After independence an ambitious 'socialist villages' programme was inaugurated as part of the Agrarian Revolution. This new rural settlement policy aimed to resettle and rehouse in modern dwellings many thousands of rural families still involved in peasant agriculture. The new villages were designed according to urban housing standards and it is argued that urban-based designers and planners have sought to project their own value judgements on the peasantry. Little opportunity for participation or self-help was given to the occupants which could well induce attitudes of dependency with an over-reliance on the central institutions of the state.

757 Vers un Maghreb des villes en l'an 2000. (Towards a Maghreb of cities in the year 2000).

J. F. Troin. *Maghreb-Machrek*, no. 96 (1982), p. 5-18.

Highlights the rapid urbanization of the three Maghreb states, Algeria, Morocco and Tunisia, examines the characteristics of the urbanization process in each country, identifying similarities and differences, and discusses the different urban planning policies adopted in each country.

758 **Urbanisation, reseaux urbains, régionalisation au Maghreb:
Fascicule 3, Travaux de la Table Ronde 'Urbanisation au
Maghreb'.** (Urbanization, urban systems, and regionalization in the
Maghreb: Part 3, Proceedings of the Round Table on 'Urbanization in
the Maghreb').
Poitiers, France: Centre Interuniversitaire d'Etudes Méditerranéennes,
in association with the CNRS and the Conseil Scientifique de
l'Université de Tours, 1978. 289p. 53 maps.

This collection of essays contains a number of important studies on contemporary
aspects of Algerian urbanization, notably the impact of rapid industrialization on the
spatial patterning and economic structure of Algeria's towns and cities, and the new
inter-urban relations created since independence.

**The making of contemporary Algeria, 1830-1987: colonial upheavals and
post-independence development.**
See item no. 8.

Algeria: the challenge of modernity.
See item no. 19.

Le Sahara dans le développement des états maghrébins.
See item no. 57.

L'Algérie, volontarisme étatique et aménagement du territoire.
See item no. 60.

Le Sahara français.
See item no. 61.

L'Algérie ou l'espace retourné.
See item no. 63.

La Mitidja: décolonisation et espace géographique.
See item no. 66.

**Le pays de Ouargla (Sahara algérien): variations et organisation d'un
espace rural en milieu désertique.**
See item no. 70.

Descriptions et iconographie de la ville d'Alger au XVIe siècle.
See item no. 116.

**The impact of Thomas-Robert Bugeaud and the decree of 9 June 1844 on
the development of Constantine, Algeria.**
See item no. 141.

Making Algeria French: colonialism in Bône, 1870-1920.
See item no. 183.

Household census data from Algeria: its content and potentiality.
See item no. 267.

Population changes in Algeria, 1977-1987.
See item no. 268.

Population growth in Algeria, 1966-1977, with some comparisons from Tunisia.
See item no. 269.

Algerian women in development: a case study of the shantytowns in Annaba.
See item no. 338.

Taking up space in Tlemcen. The Islamist occupation of urban Algeria.
See item no. 471.

Industrialisation et urbanisation en Algérie.
See item no. 649.

Incidences géographiques de l'industrialisation en Algérie.
See item no. 655.

La casbah d'Alger.
See item no. 824.

Progress in the human geography of the Maghreb.
See item no. 883.

Nomadism

759 **The state of nomadism in the Sahara.**
R. Capot-Rey. In: *Man, state and society in the contemporary Maghrib.* Edited by I. William Zartman. London: Pall Mall Press, 1973, p. 450-64.
Describes the traditional economy of the Saharan nomads, the political and economic changes which have upset the balance between these pastoral peoples and the desert environment during the 20th century, and current resettlement schemes.

760 **Les Chaanba (leur nomadisme): évolution de la tribu durant l'administration française.** (The Chaanba, their nomadism: evolution of the tribe during the French administration).
A. Cauneille. Paris: Editions du CNRS, 1968. 317p. 16 maps. bibliog.
The author examines the impact of French military occupation of the northern edges of the Algerian Sahara on the Chaanba confederation, analysing the characteristics of their nomadism and the process of sedentarization. This is one of the most perceptive case-studies of the profound changes which have affected Algerian nomads since the late 19th century.

761 **La sémantique au service de l'anthropologie: recherche méthodologique et application à l'étude de la parenté chez les Touaregs de l'Ahaggar.** (Semantics in the service of anthropology: methodogical research and application in the study of kinship among the Tuareg of the Ahaggar).
Hélène Claudot. Paris: Editions du CNRS, 1982. 268p. maps. bibliog.
Focusses on the Kel-Ahaggar Tuareg, pastoral nomads of the Algerian Sahara, based on fieldwork carried out between 1973 and 1977. The basic premise is that the majority of social relations among the Kel-Ahaggar are expressed in terms of kinship. The latter is not only the expression of, and justification for, social rules; it also gives

form to a network of important relations which unite the members of the group – psychological, matrimonial, economic and political.

762 **The nature of nomadism: a comparative study of pastoral migrations in southwestern Asia and northern Africa.**
Douglas L. Johnson. Chicago, Illinois: University of Chicago, 1969. 200p. 20 maps. bibliog. (Department of Geography Research Paper, no. 118).
Chapter three is devoted to pastoral nomadism in northern Africa and includes case-studies of the Arbaa and Saïd Atba and the Chaanba of Algeria.

763 **Changes in political succession, marital strategies and 'noble'/'vassal' relations in precolonial Ahaggar.**
Jeremy Keenan. *Maghreb Review*, vol. 4, no. 4-6 (1979), p. 118-25.
The article discusses three specific issues about pre-colonial Kel Ahaggar society: the question of a transition from patrilineal to matrilineal succession; the marital strategies adopted by the Kel Rela in their rise to and retention of power; and the effects of colonial penetration on 'noble'/'vassal' relations.

764 **A note on the formation of the Kel Ahaggar drum-groups in the 18th century and the meaning of 'Imuhag'.**
Jeremy Keenan. *Maghreb Review*, vol. 3, no. 2 (1979), p. 41-44.
It was not until the middle of the 17th century that the Tuareg of Ahaggar (Kel Ahaggar) emerged as a separate politically autonomous grouping. Their pre-colonial history as a separate independent, political group or confederation covers about two and a half centuries. This article gives a brief historical outline of the emergence and nature of the main political (tribal) groupings that existed during this period, and comments on the division between *Imuhag* (nomadic pastoralists) and *Kel arrem* (sedentary cultivators) that became increasingly significant from the latter part of the 19th century onwards.

765 **The Tuareg: people of the Ahaggar.**
Jeremy H. Keenan. London: Allen Lane, 1977. 385p. map. bibliog.
Examines the people of the vast mountainous area of the Ahaggar in southern Algeria, the nomadic Kel Ahaggar Tuareg, the nature of their society and changes in it that have taken place this century.

766 **Ecology and culture of the pastoral Tuareg with particular reference to the Tuareg of Ahaggar and Ayr.**
Johannes Nicolaisen. Copenhagen: National Museum of Copenhagen, 1963. 548p. map. bibliog.
The result of several years' study of North African pastoralism, this work analyses the development of Tuareg culture with special reference to those groups living in the Ahaggar mountains of southern Algeria and the Ayr mountains of Niger. The study examines their economic activites (stock breeding, hunting, collecting, agriculture and caravan trading), food preparation, crafts, dress and dwellings, and political systems and social organization. It contains nearly 300 black-and-white illustrations.

767 **The nomads of Algeria under French rule: a study of social and economic change.**
Wolfgang Trautmann. *Journal of Historical Geography* (Great Britain), vol. 15, no. 2 (1989), p. 126-38.

The traditional patterns of nomadic life in Algeria were affected by sedentarization which expanded from the northern Tell mountains into the steppelands. The abolition of traditional property rights, European colonization and pastoral crises were the main causes. Social disintegration favoured the concentration of flocks among a few absentee herders and the pauperization of many small-scale pastoralists. Working on French estates became the main incentive for migration.

Enjeux sahariens.
See item no. 6.

Le Sahara dans le développement des états maghrébins.
See item no. 57.

Le Sahara français.
See item no. 61.

Etudes touarègues: bilan des recherches en sciences sociales. Institutions- chercheurs- bibliographie.
See item no. 864.

Education

768 **La politique de l'emploi-formation au Maghreb, 1970-1980.**
(Employment-educational policies in the Maghreb, 1970-1980).
Edited by Chantal Bernard.   Paris: Editions du CNRS, 1982. 472p.

A collection of some twenty articles providing a detailed analysis of the failure of employment-educational policies pursued since independence in Algeria, Morocco and Tunisia, together with a concise and comprehensive critique of their development strategies and their ideological framework. Part one provides an overview of the evolution of the labour force distribution in the region in the 1970s. Part two deals with the inadequacy of the region's educational and vocational training policies and the contradictions between these policies and the economic choices in the agricultural and industrial sectors. Part three discusses the integration into the productive system of two specific categories of manpower, women and the 'non-diplomés-scolarisés'.

769 **Les intellectuels et le pouvoir: Syrie, Egypte, Tunisie, Algérie.**
(Intellectuals and power: Syria, Egypt, Tunisia and Algeria).
T. Al-Bishrie, et al.   Cairo: Centre d'Etudes et de Documentation Economique, Juridique et Sociale, 1985. 221p. (Dossier, no. 3).

This collection of articles considers some of the diverse aspects of the relationship between intellectuals and the state in several Arab countries, including Algeria. It contains several articles on higher education in Algeria and especially on its political implications both during the French colonial period and after independence.

770 **Instituteurs algériens, 1883-1939.** (Algerian school teachers, 1833-1939).
Fanny Colonna.   Paris: Presses de la Fondation Nationale des Sciences Politiques, 1975. 199p. map. bibliog.

A history of those Algerians who were first called 'native adjuncts', then 'native teachers' in colonial Algeria. Colonna examines the role of French education in the colonial domination of Algeria and, more particularly, of the selection and education of an indigenous élite who would help France bridge the gap between herself and her 'native' subjects.

771 **Essai sur l'université et les cadres en Algérie.** (Essay on the university and the cadres in Algeria).
Dominique Glasman, Jean Kremer. Paris: Editions du CNRS, 1978. 258p. (Centre de Recherches et d'Etudes sur les Sociétés Méditerranéennes: Les Cahiers, no. 8).

A perceptive study of the role of higher education in Algerian society since independence. The introductory chapters examine the impact of Algeria's ambitious economic development strategy on 'class' formation, and are followed by a discussion of the social origins of students and their employment after completing their studies. The work concludes that the new cadres being trained for management of modern enterprises lack sound technological training and form a 'technocracy without technology'. This contradiction is seen in terms of the transfer of technology which, in the case of Algeria, means the transfer of equipment without the technological skills to go with it.

772 **L'école algérienne de Ibn Badis à Pavlov.** (The Algerian school from Ibn Badis to Pavlov).
Malika Boudalia Greffou. Algiers: Laphomic, 1989.

The first serious study of the methods employed in the teaching of Arabic in Algerian schools. The author is highly critical of the authoritarian teaching methods employed which are based largely on repetition. However, she does not condemn the Arabization programme itself but calls for more creative teaching methods that will allow Algerian children to discover the richness of the Arabic language. The study first appeared as articles in the Algerian press.

773 **French influence on North African education 1880-1962: an introduction.**
Alf Andrew Heggoy. *Proceedings and Papers of the Georgia Association of Historians*, no. 7 (1986), p. 131-36.

During the 19th century, Algerians, fearing their Muslim youth would be converted to Christianity, generally refused to send their children to French colonial schools. The French settlers in Algeria encouraged a policy of separate education, so as to keep the North Africans in a subordinate position. Attitudes changed after the First World War when Algerians demanded that places be made for their children in colonial schools because these schools offered the best path to better jobs.

774 **Education in post-colonial Algeria: analysis of educational reforms and policies.**
Zohra Kohli. EdD thesis, Boston University, Boston, 1987. 239p. bibliog.

Analyses the educational system in independent Algeria in the light of the colonial French system which preceded it. Kohli examines post-colonial education in order to analyse the factors that influenced the Algerian government to call for a significant educational reform in 1976. This reform and its impact on primary education is investigated to assess the degree to which Algeria had, in fact, produced a system which was not merely an Algerianized colonial system, but a truly Algerian system of education.

775 **Women and the process of educational democratization in the Arab world: the case of Algeria.**
Farida Zouiche.   EdD thesis, Boston University, Boston, 1987. 245p. bibliog.

This study explores whether the Algerian leadership has developed the necessary educational conditions which could assist in the emancipation of Algerian women. The improved access of women to education is seen as the best guarantee for the promotion of their emancipation. Part one examines the major education policies adopted since 1962 and the different strategies utilized to achieve greater democratization of the educational system. Part two contains a content analysis of Algerian elementary readers used in grades 2-5 of the 'Fundamental school' to determine whether the changes in curriculum promoted different role models for Algerian students. The results indicate that the readers tend to reinforce the status quo in that female characters are depicted predominantly in traditional, stereotyped female roles and are also under-represented in all the readers.

The making of contemporary Algeria, 1830-1987: colonial upheavals and post-independence development.
See item no. 8.

North-west Africa: a political and economic survey.
See item no. 21.

Les étudiants algériens de l'université française, 1880-1962.
See item no. 179.

Culture et enseignement en Algérie et au Maghreb.
See item no. 310.

Habous et ministères des habous en Afrique du Nord depuis les indépendances.
See item no. 327.

Human development and adolescent studies in Algeria.
See item no. 352.

The Institut Technologique de la Santé Publique, Constantine, Algeria: preparing health personnel for Algeria.
See item no. 376.

Bâtisseurs et bureaucrates: ingénieurs et société au Maghreb et au Moyen Orient.
See item no. 593.

UNESCO Statistical Yearbook.
See item no. 735.

A needs analysis approach to ESP syllabus design with special reference to English for Science and Technology in the Algerian ESP centres.
See item no. 777.

La politique culturelle de l'Algérie.
See item no. 816.

Affrontements culturels dans l'Algérie coloniale: écoles, médecines, religion, 1830-1880.
See item no. 827.

The United States and Africa: guide to US official documents and government-sponsored publications on Africa: 1785-1975.
See item no. 841.

Arab education, 1956-1978: a bibliography.
See item no. 874.

Science and Technology

776 **Natural science and technology policies in the Arab states: present situation and future outlook.**
Paris: UNESCO, 1976. 214p. (Science Policy Studies and Documents, no. 38).
The section on Algeria (p. 43-55, in French) briefly examines the country's objectives, achievements, and constraints in science and technology policy.

777 **A needs analysis approach to ESP syllabus design with special reference to English for Science and Technology in the Algerian ESP centres.**
A. Remache. PhD thesis, University of Wales, Cardiff, 1993.
Examines the teaching of ESP (English for Scientific Purposes) in the newly established Algerian ESP centres with a view to proposing a new syllabus and teaching materials in English for Science and Technology.

778 **The transfer and the management of new technology in Algeria.**
M. Saad. PhD thesis, Brighton Polytechnic, Brighton, England, 1991.
Examines the process of transfer of AMT (Advanced Management Technology) in two Algerian firms, focussing on a body of technology related to learning, organizational and managerial adaptations.

779 **Science and technology in the development of the Arab states.**
Paris: UNESCO, 1977. 327p. (Science Policy Studies and Documents, no. 41).
The final report of the Conference of Ministers of Arab States, responsible for the application of science and technology to development (Rabat, Morocco, 16-25 August 1976). Sixteen Arab states were represented, including Algeria. It reviews science and technology policies in the Arab states, the present situation, and the prospects of regional cooperation in scientific and technological research.

The relation of French and English as foreign languages in Algeria.
See item no. 303.

Méditerranée occidentale: sécurité et coopération.
See item no. 650.

UNESCO Statistical Yearbook.
See item no. 735.

Essai sur l'université et les cadres en Algérie.
See item no. 771.

Literature

780 **Freedom of expression and the Algerian Arabic novel.**
Farida Abu-Haidar. *Maghreb Review*, vol. 18, no. 1-2 (1993),
p. 70-77.
The first examples of Arabic fiction in Algeria appeared in *Al-Basa'ir* (Insights), the
mouthpiece of the Association of Ulema, founded in 1936. Polemical essays
developed into short narratives which were used to express nationalist sentiments.
Well-known writers of fiction whose works appeared in *Al-Basa'ir* were Mohammed
ibn al-Abid al-Jilali and Reda Houhou. The Arabic short story developed during the
War of Independence, and a number of stories, with a poignant political message,
were published in Tunis, Cairo, Beirut, Damascus and Baghdad. In spite of a few
attempts at novel writing and some long short stories referred to as novels, the Arabic
novel proper did not emerge in Algeria until the early 1970s by which time a national
printing press had been established for the publication of both Arabic and
Francophone works. *Rih al-Janub* (South wind) by Abdelhamid Benhedouga, which
appeared in 1971, is considered to be the first major Algerian Arabic novel. Abu-
Haidar also discusses the work of novelists Tahar Wattar and Rachid Boudjedia.

781 **Veil of shame: the role of women in the contemporary fiction of
North Africa and the Arab world.**
Evelyne Accad. Sherbrooke, Canada: Editions Naaman, 1978. 182p.
bibliog.
A useful reference on the region's literature and on North African women. Accad
compares the sociologically documented condition of women in North Africa and the
Arab East, and the view of women presented by the writers of these regions. A wide
range of novels is examined, including several by Algerian women writers (Djamila
Debèche, Assia Djebar and Zoubeida Bittari) and Algerian male writers (Mouloud
Feraoun, Mohammed Dib, Mouloud Mammeri and Kateb Yacine).

782　The quest for identity: proper names and the narrators in Algerian life-histories.
Christine Achour.　In: *French and Algerian identities from colonial times to the present: a century of interaction*.　Edited by Alec G. Hargreaves, Michael J. Heffernan.　Lewiston, Idaho; Queenston, Canada; Lampeter, Wales: The Edwin Mellen Press, 1993, p. 204-15.

Investigates the system of proper names used in a representative sample of texts, designed to include all the principal sub-genres of the Algerian life history: Mouloud Feraoun's *Le fils du pauvre*, the life-history of a schoolchild during the colonial period; Mohamed Belkacemi's and Alain Gheerbrandt's *Belka*, the life-history of an emigrant worker who, despite not having been to school, has learned to read and write; and Azouz Begag's *Le Gone du Chaâba*, the life-history of a *beur*. The author concludes that in modern societies, the notion of identity involves dynamic processes and a condition of openness rather than a fixed, stable entity.

783　Polémiques autour du premier Grand Prix littéraire de l'Algérie. La situation des lettres algériennes en 1921. (Polemics about the first literary grand prix of Algeria: the state of Algerian literature in 1921). Jeanne Adam.　*Revue de l'Occident Musulman et de la Méditerranée* (France), no. 37 (1984), p. 15-30.

The granting of the first Grand Prix Littéraire de l'Algérie in 1921 led to violent polemics in Algerian literary reviews, underlying which were institutional and ideological conflicts. The Association des Ecrivains Algériens used the occasion to accuse the lawyers and functionaries on the prize jury of corruption and bribery. The association lost its struggle when the decision of the jury was confirmed by the Conseil d'Etat in 1922.

784　Le mouvement intellectuel et littéraire à la fin du XIXe et au debut du XXe siècle. (The Algerian intellectual and literary movement at the end of the 19th and beginning of the 20th centuries). Rachid Bencheneb.　*Revue Française d'Histoire d'Outre-Mer* (France), vol. 70, no. 1-2 (1983), p. 11-24.

Increased urbanization in late 19th-century Algeria gave rise to a new middle class of rural origin who published books and journals and organized discussion groups in an effort to rediscover their Islamic and Arab heritages. Influenced by the approach of reformist Islam, they helped their fellow Algerians to find their national identity in the period between the two World Wars.

785　Anthologie de la littérature algérienne 1950-1987. (Anthology of Algerian literature 1950-1987). Charles Bonn.　Paris: Le Livre de Poche, 1990. 255p.

A selection of annotated texts and commentaries demonstrating the richness, quality and diversity of Algerian literature from the last decade of colonial rule to the present day.

786 **La littérature algérienne de langue française et ses lecteurs.**
(Algerian literature in the French language and its readers).
Charles Bonn.   Sherbrooke, Canada: Editions Naaman, 1974. 251p.
bibliog.
Deals with the factors which motivate the creative imagination of Algerian writers, and the contradictions between free expression and ideology.

787 **A new trend in Maghrebine culture: the *Beurs* and their generation.**
Hedi Bouraoui.   *The Maghreb Review*, vol. 13, no. 3-4 (1988),
p. 218-28.
Describes the position of *beurs* – the second generation born of Maghrebian immigrants – in France, highlighting their double alienation, from French society and also from their own parents. Bouraoui examines the literary and artistic culture of the *beurs* and their impact on French culture.

788 **'Algérie perdue': analyse de titres écrits de français sur l'Algérie,**
publiés apres 1962. ('Lost Algeria': analysis of titles of French
writing on Algeria published since 1962).
Valerie Cabridens.   *Revue de l'Occident Musulman et de la*
Méditerranée (France), no. 37 (1984), p. 175-89.
An analysis of the titles of autobiographies of French Algerians published privately since 1962 show that they work with the semantic fields of 'the person', 'Algeria' and 'drama'. They offer an image of a people in exile, posing as innocent and betrayed victims, clinging to a nostalgic representation of a golden age lost in violence and blood. The present is a purgatory of suffering and incomprehension and the future holds no hope.

789 **Celfan Review.**
Philadelphia: Centre d'Etudes sur la Littérature Francophone de
l'Afrique du Nord (CELFAN), Temple University, 1981- . three issues
per year.
Contains short articles in English and French and provides a valuable source of information on Algerian literature and Algerian writers. Since 1987 CELFAN, under the direction of Eric Sellin, has also published a collection of monographs in either English or French, including for example *An Algerian view of Camus* by Ahmed Taleb-Ibrahimi and *Assia Djebar* by Mildred Mortimer.

790 **Le Grand Prix littéraire de l'Algérie (1921-1961).** (The literary
Grand Prize of Algeria [1921-61]).
Jean Déjeux.   *Revue d'Histoire Littéraire de la France* (France),
vol. 85, no. 1 (1985), p. 60-71.
The Grand Prix littéraire de l'Algérie was established by the Association des Ecrivains Algériens, an organization of French settlers in Algeria who were authors. The article includes an annotated list of laureates awarded the prize.

791 **Mohammed Dib.**
Jean Déjeux. Philadelphia: Celfan Editions, Department of French
and Italian, Temple University, 1987. 60p. bibliog. (Celfan Edition
Monographs).

A brief study in French of Mohammed Dib, one of the most celebrated Algerian
writers of the 20th century. Following brief descriptions of Dib's life and works,
common themes and images in Dib's writings are explored. The monograph benefits
from the author's long association with Dib.

792 **Who remembers the sea.**
Mohammed Dib, translated by Louis Tremaine. Washington, DC:
Three Continents Press, 1985. 134p.

A translation of the French original *Qui se souvient de la mer*. The work provides an
original, and forceful description of the Algerian War of Independence, in both its
external, tangible manifestation as well as the psychological impact it had on the
minds of Algerians. The book is both a journey into the depth of the human soul and a
portrayal of the various reactions to this bewildering event. The fear, the shock and
the feeling of loss which resulted are best described through the experience of the
narrator, as he searches for an understanding of the situation around him.

793 **Images of the Algerian war: French fiction and film, 1954-1962.**
Philip D. Dine. Oxford: Clarendon Press, 1994. bibliog.

An analysis of the images of the Algerian war, communicated in a representative
sample of French fiction and film, produced both during and after the conflict.

794 **Thinking the unthinkable: the generation of meaning in French
literary and cinema images of the Algerian war.**
Philip Dine. *The Maghreb Review*, vol. 19, no. 1-2 (1994), p. 123-32.

Focusses on the substantial 'Franco-French' literature of the Algerian conflict as
opposed to the already extensively documented Algerian French-expression fictions
inspired by the Algerian war of national liberation. Since 1954 the Algerian war
fuelled 'une guerre franco-française de l'écrit et de l'écran' in which generally
partisan commentators have looked to fictional narratives as a privileged means of
fixing and communicating their personal or communal recollections of a peculiarly
traumatic experience. It is this political motivation, Dine argues, which explains the
blurring of generic distinctions, perhaps the most striking feature of the corpus.

795 **Women of Algiers in their apartment.**
Assia Djebar, translated by Marjolijn de Jager, afterword by Clarisse
Zimra. Charlottesville, Virginia: University Press of Virginia, 1992.
211p.

A translation of *Femmes d'Alger dans leur appartement*, a collection of three longer
stories and three short stories about Algerian women's lives, written between 1958
and 1978. There is a theoretical postface and an afterword by Clarisse Zimra. The
stories are located in an almost exclusively female and domestic setting. Djebar
suggest that the first thing a woman learns is to stay in her place. The unknown and
new things heralded here include women forming community, without which they

cannot sing or dance. Clarisse Zimra states that Djebar's 'regressive' feminism has been criticized as uninspiring; however, Djebar's pessimism does not seem in the least out of place, given the precarious situation of contemporary Algerian women. A number of Djebar's other novels have been translated into English: *Fantasia: an Algerian cavalcade* (London: Quartet, 1989. 227p.); *Far from Madina* (London: Quartet, 1994. 279p.); and *A sister for Scheherazade* (London: Quartet, 1988. 159p.).

796 **Un romancier de l'identité perturbée et de l'assimilation impossible: Chukri Khodja.** (A novelist of disturbed identity and impossible assimilation: Chukri Khodja).
Abdelkader Djeghloul. *Revue de l'Occident Musulman et de la Méditerranée* (France), no. 37 (1984), p. 81-96.

Djeghloul discusses how the two novels of Chukri Khodja, *Mamoun, l'ébauche d'un idéal* (Mamoun, sketch of an ideal), (1928) and *El Eudj, captif des Barbaresques* (El Eudj, captive of Barbary), (1929), illustrate the contradictory position of Arab intellectuals in Algeria, educated within the colonial system and assigned the role of reproducing and diffusing colonial values. While approving of modernization and praising a certain idea of France, the texts contain different points of view, underlining the ultimate impossibility of assimilation between Arabs and France. In their hesitations and ambiguities they show the difficulties of Algerian nationalism in laying claim to a national identity and culture.

797 **Prolégomènes à une étude critique de la littérature judéo-maghrébine d'expression française.** (Prolegomena to a critical study of judeo-maghrebine literature in French).
Guy Dugas. *Revue de l'Occident Musulman et de la Méditerranée* (France), no. 37 (1984), p. 195-213.

A preliminary catalogue of literature in French produced by Maghreb Jews between 1896 and 1983 shows original features emerging early from the general justification of colonialism common to all Maghreb literature into the 1930s. Novels portrayed aspects of Jewish life, but after a decline in the number of works between 1936 and 1945, poetry assumed a greater importance as the best way of dealing with the experiences of Nazism and occupation. In the 1950s novels became more personal and autobiographical, while the diaspora after 1960 has continued to produce literature about the Maghreb.

798 **A wife for my son.**
Ali Ghalem, translated by G. Kazolias. London: Zed Press; Chicago: Banner Press, 1984. 211p.

This award-winning novel by the well-known Algerian film-maker tells the story of a very young women forced to marry a man she does not know; her subsequent unhappiness reflects the frustration of women in contemporary Algeria. The book was later made into a film.

799   **Algeria and its history: colonial myths and the forging and deconstructing of identity in *pied-noir* literature.**
Azzedine Haddour.   In: *French and Algerian identities from colonial times to the present: a century of interaction.*   Edited by Alec G. Hargreaves, Michael J. Heffernan.   Lewiston, Idaho; Queenston, Canada; Lampeter, Wales: The Edwin Mellen Press, 1993, p. 78-94.

Examines the two distinct and contrasting conceptions of colonial Algeria in *pied-noir* literature, *Algerianisme* and the so-called *Ecole d'Alger*. The author argues that Camus' work *L'Etranger* is a cultural symbol and reads its essentialist position as symptomatic of colonial malaise. He concludes that Camus' physical alienation from Algeria was the result of the failure to Algerianize colonial politics. The colonist system which blocked the progress of history, disallowing the promulgation of the assimilationist programme advocated by Camus, forced him to leave Algeria and emigrate to France. Camus' withdrawal from the colonial space to become assimilated into the metropolitan literary school replicates this failure, reflecting the malaise of a society and the abortion of a culture.

800   **Voices from the North African community in France: immigration and identity in Beur fiction.**
A. G. Hargreaves.   Oxford; New York: Berg, 1991. 175p. bibliog.

In their daily lives, *beurs* – a popular name in France for the sons and daughters of first generation North African immigrants – have been compelled to migrate constantly between the secular culture of France and the traditions carried with them by their parents from across the Mediterranean. These experiences have been explored by a growing number of *beur* writers in poems, plays and above all prose fiction. This is the first full-length study to be devoted to these writers, the majority of whom are of Algerian descent. The study focusses on the key problematic which has preoccupied *beur* writers, their uncertain sense of identity and *beur* treatment of the theme of identity in their narrative works. The analysis of the formal structures of *beur* fiction also draws on extensive interviews with the authors. The study provides detailed biographical portraits of *beur* authors and places them in their socio-historical context. The basic constituents of the stories recounted by *beur* authors are analysed and compared with the life experiences of the authors. The extent to which narrators and authors appear to position themselves 'within' or 'outside' particular groups is examined together with the interplay between time at the level of narration and time within the flow of the story.

801   **Colonial writers between the wars.**
Alec G. Hargreaves, Peter Fitzgerald.   *Proceedings of the Annual Meeting of the French Colonial Historical Society*, no. 10 (1984), p. 195-208.

The Société des Romanciers et Auteurs Coloniaux Français, based in Paris, attempted to promote the literature of French colonies. This task was made difficult by the rivalries among the various colonial peoples, e.g., between Algerians and Tunisians, by their alienation from metropolitan France, and by the French public's lack of interest in colonial culture.

802   **Location and identity: reflections in three pied-noir novels, 1949-1959.**
Rosemarie Jones.   In: *French and Algerian identities from colonial times to the present: a century of interaction.*   Edited by Alec G. Hargreaves, Michael J. Heffernan.   Lewiston, Idaho; Queenston, Canada; Lampeter, Wales: The Edwin Mellen Press, 1993, p. 95-108.
Discusses three novels by Français d'Algérie (*pied-noirs*) published between the end of the Second World War and the end of the War of Liberation: Jean Pelegri's *Les oliviers de la justice* (The olive trees of justice); Emmanuel Robles' *Federica*; and René-Jean Clot's *Fantômes au soleil* (Ghosts in the sun). Jones analyses the representation of *pied-noir* society offered in these novels and the kind of story told of, and emanating from, that society and suggests certain interpretative possibilities.

803   **Exiles in their native land: Algerian novelists of French expression.**
Donald C. Holsinger.   *Maghreb Review*, vol. 11, no. 2-4 (1986), p. 73-78.
Algerian French-language fiction in the 1950s and 1960s established a respected place for itself in the world literary community. Beginning with ethnographic portraits of Algerian life, it evolved into a literature of combat during the struggle for independence. Since 1962 it has articulated the challenges besetting a newly emergent nation seeking its place in the world. Most significantly, it is an important element in an authentic cultural tradition.

804   **L'allégorie de la féminité: deuil d'une civilisation et mutation d'identité dans *Le fils du pauvre* de M. Feraoun.** (The allegory of womanhood: grieving a civilization and changing identity in *Le fils du pauvre* by M. Feraoun).
Naget Khadda.   *Peuples Méditerranéens*, no. 44-45 (1988), p. 73-88; p. 340.
In M. Feraoun's *Le fils du pauvre* (1950), a woman, though not the central character, serves as the metaphor for the society's social and symbolic changes. This character is constructed not upon idealistic values but as a key element in a code of representation. As an allegory of grief and catastrophy, she is at the height of the extraterritorality experienced by the losers and represents, with humour and discretion, the collision of time and of images. An English summary is provided on p. 340.

805   **Journeys through the French African novel.**
Mildred Mortimer.   London: James Currey; Portsmouth, New Hampshire: Heinemann, 1991. 239p.
This study makes a welcome attempt to find a sort of complementarity between male and female African writers in a literary universe where the norm has been to emphasize cleavages and conflict. It includes a discussion of three Algerian writers: Kateb Yacine, Assia Djebar and Leila Sebbar.

806　**Two lost American plays: ideas of the Muslim Barbary Orient.**
Marwan M. Obeidat.　*The Maghreb Review*, vol. 13, no. 3-4 (1988),
p. 191-98.
Investigates certain ideas from two lost American plays with 'Barbary' themes to
reveal what the Muslim Orient suggested to 19th-century America. One of the plays is
Richard Penn Smith's *The bombardment of Algiers* (1829), an unplayed melodrama
preserved by the Historical Society of Pennsylvania.

807　**Obsession with the white page, the inability to communicate, and
surface aesthetics in the development of contemporary Maghrebian
fiction: the *mal de la page blanche* in Khatibi, Farès and Meddeb.**
Eric Sellin.　*International Journal of Middle East Studies*, no. 20
(1988), p. 165-73.
Writer's block is considered here in the realm of the young and rapidly-developing
Francophone literature of the Maghreb. Sellin suggests that the writer's malaise before
the blank page is a sign of a highly developed authorial relationship with one's
language and materials. The recent increase in the number of testimonials in which
Maghrebian writers bear witness to their sense of impotence when facing the purity of
the white page and reactions symptomatic of that frustration is evident in development
in the literature in question. The article explores the phenomenon in a general way and
then considers the instance of 'white page malaise' in the work of three modern
Maghrebian novelists: Abdelkebir Khatibi from Morocco; Nabile Farès from Algeria;
and Abdelwahab Meddeb from Tunisia.

808　**Desperate spring: lives of Algerian women.**
Fettouma Touati, translated by Ros Schwartz.　London: The Women's
Press, 1987. 156p.
Fettouma Touati's first novel describes the lives of nine women, including: a doctor
who has become educated against all odds and finds tremendous difficulty in attaining
a long-term relationship with an educated man; one who breaks with her background
but whom happiness eludes; one who settles for a traditional life with husband and
children; and other women who suffer pain, cruelty and even death at the hands of
their husbands.

809　**Mémento pour les juifs d'Afrique du Nord.** (Memento for the Jews
of North Africa).
Lucette Valensi.　*Revue de l'Université de Bruxelles* (Belgium),
no. 1-2 (1987), p. 163-68.
Describes the resurgence of collective identity in the biographies and creative writings
of the Jews of North Africa in the 1970s.

810　**The lyrical essays of Albert Camus 'une longue fidélité'.**
Marcia Weiss.　Sherbrooke, Canada: Editions Naaman, 1976. 212p.
bibliog. (English Series, no. 3).
The first full-length study of Camus' lyrical essays. It provides an analysis of three
essay collections – *L'envers et l'endroit*, *Noces* and *L'été* - which are of paramount
importance for a full understanding of Camus' total work.

North-west Africa: a political and economic survey.
See item no. 21.

The French image of Algeria: its origin, its place in colonial ideology, its effects on Algerian acculturation.
See item no. 155.

Albert Camus and the colonial question in Algeria.
See item no. 159.

Colonialism and violence: Camus and Sartre on the Algerian war, 1945-58.
See item no. 220.

The Berbers in Arabic literature.
See item no. 296.

The ambiguous compromise: language, literature, and national identity in Algeria and Morocco.
See item no. 308.

Women and the family in the Middle East: new voices of change.
See item no. 349.

Principales manifestations culturelles en Algérie depuis 1962.
See item no. 815.

Nouveaux enjeux culturels au Maghreb.
See item no. 819.

Bibliographie de la littérature 'algérienne' des français.
See item no. 865.

Bibliographie méthodique et critique de la littérature algérienne d'expression française (1945-1970).
See item no. 866.

Cultural Policy and the Arts

811 **La musique populaire au Sahara algérien.** (Popular music of the Algerian Sahara).
Pierre Augier. In: *Culture et société au Maghreb* (Culture and society in the Maghreb). Paris: Editions du CNRS, 1975, p. 168-69.

Based on extensive research by the Centre de Recherches Anthropologiques, Préhistoriques et Ethnographiques d'Alger, this article examines the different influences – Berber, Arab and African – reflected in the traditional music of the Algerian Sahara, its characteristics, and attempts to classify the different forms according to their function.

812 **Aspects of Algerian cultural policy.**
Sid-Ahmed Baghli. Paris: UNESCO, 1978. 57p. bibliog. (Studies and Documents on Cultural Policies).

Outlines the principles and methods of the state's cultural policy, the evaluation of cultural needs, administrative structures, legislation, the dissemination of culture, training and cultural cooperation.

813 **De la musique avant toute chose: remarques sur le rai.** (Music above all else: remarks on *rai*).
Mohamed Hocine Benkheira. *Peuples Méditerranéens*, no. 35-36 (1986), p. 173-77; p. 344.

Rai is a recent musical creation by Algerian society, specifically by certain urban groups and a sign of a Westernization that is sought after and assumed from inside that society, not imposed from outside. At first it was opposed by centralizing nationalism, whether secular or Islamist; now part of the central as well as the local bureaucracies look upon it with approval. They encourage *rai* as a antidote to the advance of Islamism. An English summary is provided on p. 344.

814   **Naissance du cinéma algérien.** (Birth of Algerian cinema).
Rachid Boudjedra.   Paris: François Maspero, 1971. 101p. bibliog.
Examines the image of Algeria in French cinema before 1954, the War of Independence as portrayed in the French and foreign cinema, and the achievements, difficulties and perspectives of the national cinema in independent Algeria.

815   **Principales manifestations culturelles en Algérie depuis 1962.**
(Principal cultural manifestations in Algeria since 1962).
Jean Déjeux.   In: *Culture et société au Maghreb* (Culture and society in the Maghreb).   Paris: Editions du CNRS, 1975, p. 77-96.
A critical examination of the major developments in the country's cultural life during the first decade of independence, covering the press, literature, cultural festivals, theatre, music festivals, national cinema and fine art.

816   **La politique culturelle de l'Algérie.** (Algeria's cultural policy).
Bruno Etienne, Jean Leca.   In: *Culture et société au Maghreb*
(Culture and society in the Maghreb).   Paris: Editions du CNRS, 1975, p. 45-76.
A comprehensive survey which examines the efforts of the nationalist movements to revive Algerian culture during the colonial period. It also looks at those national organizations responsible for cultural policy in independent Algeria, and discusses various cultural activities – education, cinema, the press and music.

817   **Aspects de l'artisanat en Afrique du Nord.** (Aspects of craft industries in North Africa).
Lucien Golvin.   Paris: Presses Universitaires de France, 1957. 235p. 9 maps. bibliog.
Examines the evolution of craft industries in Algeria, Tunisia and Morocco, describes their situation in the early 1950s and the efforts made to protect and revive them, and indicates the major problems affecting their future. The book is illustrated with black-and-white photographs of some of the main products of the craft industries. It remains a basic reference work on Algeria's traditional crafts, many of which have disappeared since the book was published.

818   **Le legs des Ottomans dans le domaine artistique en Afrique du Nord.** (The Ottoman legacy in the artistic domain in North Africa).
Lucien Golvin.   *Revue de l'Occident Musulman et de la Méditerranée* (France), no. 39 (1985), p. 201-26.
Architecture in Algeria and neighbouring Tunisia during the Ottoman period was little influenced by Turkish models, this influence being seen only in a few religious and funerary buildings. By contrast, artisanal activity in other domains was inspired by Ottoman features. The popularity of the Turkish mode of dress assured its influence on textile crafts, but it may also be seen in tapestry, ceramics and the metal-working crafts.

Cultural Policy and the Arts

819 **Nouveaux enjeux culturels au Maghreb.** (New cultural issues in the Maghreb).
Jean-Robert Henry, et al. Paris: Editions du CNRS, 1986. 449p.
This useful reference work, devoted to Algeria, Morocco and Tunisia, is divided into six parts, containing articles covering: the State and culture; changing linguistic issues; literature; the mass media; a cultural critique of the social sciences; and cultural effects of emigration.

820 **Islamic architecture in North Africa: a photographic survey.**
Derek Hill, with notes and concluding essay by Lucien Golvin, introduction by Robert Hillenbrand. London: Faber & Faber, 1976. 167p. map.
A photographic survey of the architecture and decorative features of the major buildings of North Africa until the 15th century. With its 560 illustrations, this book is a comprehensive source of photographic detail on the Islamic architecture of Algeria, Morocco and Tunisia. There is a short introduction to the historical, cultural and geographical factors which have influenced the North African style in Islamic architecture, together with notes on all the monuments illustrated. A section is devoted to the major monuments of Algeria.

821 **Islamic architecture: North Africa.**
Antony Hutt. London: Scorpion Publications, 1977. 192p. 2 maps. bibliog.
Traces the development of Islamic architecture in North Africa from its simple beginnings in the 8th century to the splendours of the 14th century, and the age of the Barbary corsairs. The work contains colour and black-and-white illustrations and an informative text. Thirty-three of the examples selected are from Algeria and include mosques and palaces in Algiers, Tlemcen and Nedroma.

822 **An uncertain heritage: Berber traditional architecture in the Maghreb.**
A. D. C. Hyland. *The Maghreb Review*, vol. 8, no. 1-2 (1993), p. 109-15.
In the colonial period Berber traditional architecture and historic Berber settlements were singled out for study and some measure of cultural protection, often for political reasons. Since independence, the built heritage of the Berbers has been comparatively neglected. The consequences of this neglect are investigated through a review of historic Berber settlements in the Maghreb and three case-studies, including one on the Aurès region in Algeria.

823 **In a broken dream.**
Chris Kutschera. *The Middle East*, no. 236 (July-August 1994), p. 40-41.
A short article about the Algerian film maker Mohammed Chouikh and his latest film *Yussef*, about a veteran of the war of liberation, waking up after a sleep of almost thirty years to discover the sad realities of how independence has actually worked out. It also gives brief details of Chouikh's life and work and the dangers facing Algerian writers today from Islamist extremists.

824 **La casbah d'Alger.** (The casbah of Algiers).
André Ravereau, preface by Mostefa Lacheraf, photographs by
Manuelle Roche. Paris: Sindbad, 1989. 236p. (La Bibliothèque
Arabe. Hommes et Sociétés).

A description of the architecture of the historic core of Algiers, the casbah, placing it
in its historical context. The work is illustrated with black-and-white and colour
photographs.

825 **Algerian cinema.**
Edited by Hala Salmane, Simon Hartog, David Wilson. London:
British Film Institute, 1976. 58p.

Provides some basic information to introduce British audiences to a national cinema
which is little known outside French-speaking countries. The authors also consider the
experience of Algerian cinema in the context of the history of Algeria, and comment
on the most recent trends in Algerian cinema.

826 **Algerian theatre and protest.**
Youssef Selmane. In: *North Africa – nation, state, and region.*
Edited by George Joffé. London: Routledge, 1993, p. 170-86.

Selmane uses the development of the theatre in post-First World War Algeria to
explore a number of fundamental cultural, as well as political, issues germane to the
country's evolving sense of community. The stage provided a novel forum for
expressing collective grievances against the colonial régime. By eventually employing
colloquial Arabic, Algerian dramatists created a popular theatre which interestingly
enough drew fire after 1932 not only from French administrators but also from
conservative Muslim élites. The history of this indigenous theatre reflects the larger
historical fortunes of Algerian nationalists, the War of Independence and the nation
state. As the war of liberation raged after 1954, an FLN troupe toured the Arab world
as well as the USSR and China to prove that Algeria had its own history and culture
distinct from France. Ironically, in France itself, stage productions decrying French
imperialism, were performed by and for the North African expatriate community.

827 **Affrontements culturels dans l'Algérie coloniale: écoles,
médecines, religion, 1830-1880.** (Cultural confrontations in colonial
Algeria: schools, medicines, religion, 1830-1880).
Yvonne Turin. Paris: François Maspero, 1971. 434p. map. bibliog.

Examines the role of schools and medicine in the 'civilizing mission' of the colonial
power among Algerian Muslims in the early decades of the French occupation. The
author explores the close relationships between the cultural and political policies of
the colonial government, and the influence of the new schools and medicine on the
religious life of the Muslim majority.

828 **Reflections on a Kabyle pot: Algerian women and the decorative
tradition.**
Moira Vincentelli. *Journal of Design History* (Great Britain), vol. 2,
no. 2-3 (1989), p. 123-38.

The shapes, colours, glaze and decoration of the traditional pottery produced in
Kabylia have slowly changed because of outside contact, and distinctions between

villages have been vanishing. Pottery, once restricted to women and made domestically, has been commercialized, and some less traditional work has come to be produced industrially on the potter's wheel by men. In addition, metal, plastic and commercial china are beginning to replace pottery, which now may be primarily for decoration.

Algérie incertaine.
See item no. 2.

Algérie: vers l'état islamique?
See item no. 3.

Annuaire de l'Afrique du Nord.
See item no. 5.

The mosaics of Roman North Africa: studies in iconography and patronage.
See item no. 102.

Les étudiants algériens de l'université française, 1880-1962.
See item no. 179.

The Algerian war on the French stage.
See item no. 218.

Islam: state and society.
See item no. 282.

The reproduction of colonial ideology: the case of the Kabyle Berbers.
See item no. 291.

Berbers in distress.
See item no. 295.

The economics of Berberism: the material basis of the Kabyle question in contemporary Algeria.
See item no. 299.

Towards an understanding of the Kabyle question in contemporary Algeria.
See item no. 300.

The unforeseen development of the Kabyle question in contemporary Algeria.
See item no. 301.

Language, social relations and intellectual production in Algeria.
See item no. 304.

Language and identity.
See item no. 305.

Arabisation et politique linguistique au Maghreb.
See item no. 306.

Arabization and the Kabyle language and cultural issues in Algeria.
See item no. 307.

Culture et enseignement en Algérie et au Maghreb.
See item no. 310.

Amateur theatre in Algeria: choice and use of language.
See item no. 311.

Glasnost **the Algerian way: the role of Berber nationalists in political reform.**
See item no. 440.

Images of the Algerian war: French fiction and film, 1954-1962.
See item no. 793.

Thinking the unthinkable: the generation of meaning in French literary and cinema images of the Algerian war.
See item no. 794.

Libraries and Archives

829 **Problems affecting the development of libraries in Algeria.**
B. Boumarafi, P. Harvard-Williams. *Focus on International and Comparative Librarianship*, no. 14 (1983), p. 15-17.
A brief discussion of the problems facing the development of libraries in Algeria.

830 **The army at Vincennes: archives for the study of North African history in the colonial period.**
James J. Cooke. *Muslim World*, vol. 61, no. 1 (1971), p. 35-38.
A brief introduction to the vast holdings in the colonial section of the French Army historical archives at the Château de Vincennes in Paris and their importance to research on colonial Algeria.

831 **Some useful French depositories for the study of the Algerian revolution.**
Alf Andrew Heggoy. *Muslim World*, vol. 58, no. 4 (1968), p. 345-47.
A brief description of some research facilities located in France where Algerian material covering the period of the War of Independence has been collected and catalogued.

832 **La guerre d'Algérie par les documents. Vol. 1 L'Avertissement: 1943-1946.** (Documents on the Algerian war. Vol. 1 The warning: 1943-1946).
Jean-Charles Jauffret (Dir.), preface by Robert Bassac.   Paris: Service Historique de l'Armée de Terre, 1990. 550p.
The first volume in an ambitious project to publish all the documents concerning the Algerian War of Independence held by the Service Historique de l'Armée de Terre (SHAT). Vol. 1 covers the period from the publication of the *Manifeste du peuple algérien* (Manifesto of the Algerian people) to the proclamation of the amnesty law of 9 March 1946.

833 **Une lettre de l'Emir Abdelkader datée de 1880 aux archives de Sidi bel-Abbes.** (Letter by Emir Abdel Kader of 1880 in the Sidi bel-Abbes archives).
Abdel Kader. *Revue d'Histoire Maghrébine* (Tunisia), vol. 14, no. 45-46 (1987), p. 119-22.

In the archives of the *wilaya* of Sidi bel-Abbes is a letter, probably genuine, written by Emir Abdel Kader to the chief of the forestry service of the Departement of Oran in 1880. The letter requests the annulment of an order evicting some families from their lands on the grounds that the families had undisputed title to the lands, that they were in need, and that they were related to the emir, then living in Damascus. The text of the letter is reproduced in this article.

834 **The French Foreign Office Records on North Africa and the Middle East in Nantes.**
Uri M. Kupferschmidt. *Middle East Studies Association Bulletin*, vol. 23, no. 1 (1989), p. 9-14.

Discusses the records of the French Foreign Office on North Africa, including Algeria, dating from 1585 to 1981, which are held in the Nantes archives.

835 **The central Ottoman archives as a source for Arab history.**
Bernard Lewis. *Revue d'Histoire Maghrébine* (Tunisia), vol. 14, no. 45-46 (1987), p. 75-90.

The Ottoman archives offer a wealth of information for the period of Ottoman rule over Arab lands from 1553 to 1905. Those provinces under direct Ottoman rule are more fully covered than those which where administered by local dynasties, such as Algeria. The records may be divided broadly into diplomatic and statistical information. The latter provide data for social and economic history, the structure of society, and the evolution of institutions and administration, while the former are a major source for 'traditional' history.

836 **Les sources Ottomanes: une source inépuisable pour l'analyse de la société, l'économie et la démographie de l'Algérie moderne.** (Ottoman sources: an inexhaustible source for the analysis of early-modern Algerian society, economy and demography).
Djilali Sari. *Revue d'Histoire Maghrébine* (Tunisia), vol. 12, no. 37-38 (1985), p. 112-20.

Argues that only the systematic utilization of Ottoman administrative material, much of which was dispersed during the French conquest, will allow an accurate evaluation of Algerian history between the 17th century and 1830, and the refutation of ideas put forward to justify colonialism. Fiscal and economic sources, above all relating to the transfer of property, demonstrate the existence of a centralized state, agriculture covering almost all exploitable land, and a population density as high as that of the colonial period. These same sources allow the study of regional differences and the foundations of popular resistance to colonialism.

837 **Guide to federal archives relating to Africa.**
Researched and compiled by Aloha South. Waltham, Massachusetts:
Crossroads Press, 1977. 556p. (African Studies Association – The
Archival and Bibliographic Series).

This guide describes known Africa-related records in the National Archives of the
United States. The records, which include textual material, maps, sound recordings,
motion and still pictures, are located in the National Archives Building, the General
Archives Division in the Washington National Records Center, presidential libraries,
and the regional archives branches that are part of the Federal Archives and Records
Centers. These records document US diplomatic, military, commercial, exploratory,
missionary, philanthropic, educational, scientific and other activities in Africa. The
overall arrangement of the guide is alphabetical by name of agency, with subordinate
organizations listed thereunder in alphabetical order.

838 **Guide to non-Federal archives and manuscripts in the United
States relating to Africa. Volume 1 Alabama-New Mexico, Volume
II New York to Wisconsin.**
Compiled by Aloha South. London; Munich; Paris; New York: Hans
Zell Publisher for the National Archives and Records Administration,
Washington, DC, 1989. 1,259p.

Organized alphabetically by state and within each state by town or city, with each
depository then being treated separately. Africanist holdings are heavily concentrated
in the major depositories of Washington, DC, New York and Pennsylvania. The bulk
of the index appended with Volume II offers a basic listing of all persons,
organizations and institutions. Entries are also made for each country. This constitutes
a companion volume to *Guide to federal archives relating to Africa* (q.v.).

839 **Note sur les 'bulletins d'information' des 'recueils factices' de
la bibliothèque municipale de Bordeaux relatifs au Maghreb
(1664-1690).** (Note on the information bulletins in the 'duplicate
collections' of the Bordeaux Municipal Library relating to the
Maghreb [1664-1690]).
Guy Turbet-Delof. *Revue d'Histoire Maghrébine* (Tunisia), vol. 13,
no. 41-42 (1986), p. 172-74.

Lists, giving publication details and catalogue numbers, sixteen news pamphlets
concerning 17th-century North Africa in the collection of the Bordeaux Municipal
Library, none of which are to be found in the standard bibliographies. Thirteen of
them concern Algiers, and one is on Djidjelli in Algeria. Ten were printed in Paris, the
rest probably in Bordeaux. They are of interest for relations between France and
Algeria in the 17th century.

840 **French colonial Africa – a guide to official sources.**
Gloria D. Westfall. London: Hans Zell Publishers, 1992. 236p.

Each of the five chapters provides an overview explaining the logic behind the French
system of treating official documents. Categories covered include archives, official
and semi-official publications and universities. The final chapter guides the researcher
through the publications of individual colonial governments in Africa and offers the
latest information and bibliography pertinent to each ex-colonial archive.

841   **The United States and Africa: guide to US official documents and government-sponsored publications on Africa, 1785-1975.**
Compiled by Julian W. Witherell.   Washington, DC: Library of Congress, 1978. 949p.

A selection of publications issued by or for the United States government from the late 18th century to September 1975, based on the holdings of the Library of Congress, other federal government collections in Washington, DC, and collections of other American libraries. Entries are grouped into five chronological sections, subdivided by region or country. In the final section, for 1952-75, regional and country listings are further divided by subject. This section, by far the largest in the guide, also includes the widest variety of material. The references on Algeria cover agriculture, assistance programmes, communications and transportation, community development, economic conditions, education, finance, geography and maps, geology and mineral resources, labour, military affairs, politics and government, and the Sahara region.

842   **The African Studies Companion – a resource guide and directory.**
Edited by Hans M. Zell.   London: Hans Zell Publishers, 1989. 175p.

Contains over 600 annotated entries covering major reference tools, bibliographies, journals, libraries and documentation centres, publishers, book dealers and distributors, African and Africanist organizations, African Studies associations, donor agencies and foundations.

843   **Directory of documentation, libraries and archives services in Africa.**
Dominique Zidouemba, revised and enlarged by Eric de Grolier. Paris: UNESCO, 1977. 2nd edition. 311p. (Bibliographies and Reference Works, no. 5).

An attempt to present as complete and accurate a picture as possible of the archives, library and documentary services of forty African countries, including Algeria, as well as a survey of the professional training facilities available for their staff. The work includes national and university libraries, as well as the libraries of other higher education centres, and documentation services of certain administrations and enterprises. For each country there is general information concerning the legal framework of its documentation agencies, the status of their staff, and their cooperation mechanisms both nationally and internationally. This is followed by data on various agencies classified according to their main functions. For the section on Algeria see p. 35-68.

Foreign relations of the United States, 1955-1957. Vol. 18: Africa.
See item no. 531.

British trade with Algeria in the nineteenth century: an ally against France?
See item no. 628.

UNESCO Statistical Yearbook.
See item no. 735.

Mass Media

844   **Algeria: press freedom under the state of emergency.**
Article 19 (International Centre Against Censorship), issue 19 (1992),
27p.
Examines the actions taken by the military-backed régime which came to power in
January 1992 to curtail the press, and to restrict freedom of expression and movement.

845   **Article 19 Bulletin.**
London: International Centre Against Censorship, August/September
1987- . bi-monthly.
The bulletin has carried regular short articles on press censorship in Algeria since the
military coup in January 1992 and has condemned the threats against, and murder of,
journalists by Islamist groups.

846   **The Algerian war of words: broadcasting and revolution, 1954-62.**
Robert J. Bookmiller.   *The Maghreb Review*, vol. 14, no. 3-4 (1989),
p. 198-213.
Presents an analysis of North African radio broadcasts during the War of
Independence. Bookmiller examines the broadcast practices of Egypt, Morocco and
Tunisia, as they relate to the Algerian struggle, progressing chronologically through
the various stages of the broadcast war: broadcasts from Cairo's 'Voice of the Arabs';
FLN programmes transmitted from Egyptian facilities; the entrance of Tunisia and
then Morocco as radio combatants; and the use of radio by the ultra-rightist *colons'*
Organisation Armée Secrète (OAS) near the end of the struggle. He argues that
Algerian independence was partially won by the use of radio, which shaped opinions,
reoriented perceptions and united Algerians in a common struggle.

847 **Broadcasting in the Arab world: a survey of radio and television in the Middle East.**
Douglas A. Boyd. Philadelphia: Temple University Press, 1982. 306p. bibliog. map.

Most of the book consists of a country-by-country description of radio and television systems, practices and history. The historical role of broadcasting, particularly that of radio, is examined within the separate country studies.

848 **Le pouvoir, la presse et les intellectuels en Algérie.** (Power, the press and intellectuals in Algeria).
Brahim Brahimi. Paris: L'Harmattan, 1990. 390p.

A history of the Algerian press from 1962 to 1988 and an analysis of the complex relations which determine its ideological, political and cultural environment. The author identifies three periods in the development of the press: 1962-65, when the editors of newspapers were intellectuals of the FLN who enjoyed a certain autonomy; 1965-85, a period when the intellectuals were replaced by civil servants who were docile instruments of the state bureaucracy; and the period after 1985 when the press enjoyed greater freedom and several new papers appeared.

849 **La communication inégale: l'accès aux média dans les campagnes algériennes.** (Unequal communication: access to the media in the Algerian countryside).
François Chevaldonné. Paris: Editions du CNRS, 1981. 222p. bibliog.

A sociological study of the role and effects of mass communications in post-colonial Algeria. The author points to some glaring problems with the media's ability to spread information to the different socio-economic classes. The educated and affluent élite which controls the content and dissemination of mass media to the whole of Algerian society often fails to reach classes outside it. Many rural Algerians are illiterate and too poor to own a radio or television. Those who do have access may not understand the Standard Arabic used in all forms of the media, only dialectical Arabic or Berber. In addition, the content of films or entertainment is shaped by a class of Algerians with close ties to Western culture and is often foreign to the mass of uneducated Algerians. The special problems of reaching rural Algerian women who seem virtually disenfranchised by mass communications are also explored.

850 **Maghrebians and French television.**
Alec G. Hargreaves. *Maghreb Review*, vol. 18, no. 1-2 (1993), p. 97-108.

Maghrebians have yet to establish a position in French television commensurate with their position as the largest ethnic minority in France. They are seen in only a limited range of programmes, which often associate them with negative images in the eyes of the viewing public. With the aid of recent research into prime-time programming, the author illustrates the fragmentary and frequently unflattering images of Maghrebians purveyed by French television, considers the limited but growing role of Maghrebians as programme makers, and examines the position of Maghrebians as consumers of television programmes.

851 **The state centralization and control of the broadcasting media in Algeria from 1962 to 1982: application and shortcomings.**
Ahmed Kaci. PhD thesis, University of Illinois at Urbana-Champaign, 1988. 876p. bibliog. (Available on microfilm from University Microfilms).

A case-study of the post-independence Algerian broadcasting media from a cultural-critical perspective. Kaci argues that Radiodiffusion Télévision Algérienne developed five main characteristics: a failure of the élites to re-think broadcasting in the post-independence era; a broadcasting monopoly which privileged the dissemination of official political discourse; a toleration of financial, personnel and production mismanagement in exchange for political allegiance; the control of the broadcasting profession; and a paternalist conception of the audiences.

852 **The Middle East and North Africa on film: an annotated filmography.**
Marsha Hamilton McClintock. New York; London: Garland Publishing Inc., 1982. 542p. (Garland Reference Library of the Humanities).

A comprehensive listing of films and videotapes produced between 1903 and 1980, which groups films by subject matter or by countries. In addition to the annotations, the film information given includes: production or release date; running time; technical information; producer; director; distributor; and locations where films are found. All films and tapes are indexed by titles and alternate titles, and a separate index lists the addresses of producers and distributors. The introduction discusses some of the restrictions of the medium and the availability of major collections of film and tape resources.

853 **Professionalism in broadcasting: case-studies of Algeria and Senegal.**
Rita Cruise O'Brien. Brighton, England: Institute of Development Studies, University of Sussex, 1976. 50p. (Discussion Paper, no. 10).

Examines the influence of professonal modes and organizational structures transferred from industrialized to developing countries in the field of broadcasting in Algeria and Senegal. The effects of socialization through training and the perpetuation of standards and norms are traced. Problems of recruitment and local working methods are considered in relation to metropolitan influences. The crucial influence of the state on broadcasting in developing countries is also examined, as are the constraints which imported characteristics have had on the broadcasting systems in that they impair support for national development and cultural policies.

854 **The African press.**
M. Ochs. Cairo: American University in Cairo Press, 1986. 138p.

A discussion of the press of Arabic- and French-speaking Africa, including Algeria, appears on p. 91-108.

855 **Radical radio: an emancipatory cultural practice.**
Marc Raboy. *Border/Lines* (Canada), no. 1 (1984), p. 28-31.
A 1983 World Conference on Community Radio, held in Montreal and representing 500 groups, promoted community radio as a means to oppose domination by commercial and government interests in Europe, North America, and countries such as Algeria, Cuba and El Salvador.

856 **The Arab press: news media and political process in the Arab world.**
William A. Rugh. Syracuse, New York: Syracuse University Press, 1987. rev. ed. 205p.
Analyses the news media as institutions to see what forms they have taken in the independent Arab states, how self-governing Arab societies have chosen to control them, and how they relate to the political processes in the Arab world. The work includes useful references to the Algerian mass media – newspapers, television and radio.

857 **Secret decree: new attack on the media in Algeria.**
Article 19 (International Centre Against Censorship), issue 38 (10 November 1994), 19p.
Discusses a recent, secret Inter-Ministerial Decree which prohibits the media from publishing information about political violence and security-related issues from any source other than the government, which has already been used to ban temporarily two newspapers.

Between two fires.
See item no. 9.

Algeria: the challenge of modernity.
See item no. 19.

The violent decade.
See item no. 156.

A study in radio propaganda broadcasts in French from North and West African radio stations, 8 November 1942-14 December 1942.
See item no. 171.

Le Monde and the Algerian war during the Fourth Republic.
See item no. 236.

Partiality and biases: the coverage of the Algerian Liberation War (1954-1962) by Al-Ahram and *Le Monde*.
See item no. 239.

La réaction de la presse et de l'opinion publique américaines à la politique du gouvernement Eisenhower envers la Révolution Algérienne.
See item no. 252.

Algeria: assassination in the name of religion.
See item no. 384.

Algeria's infrastructure. An economic survey of transportation, communication and energy resources.
See item no. 689.

The Gulf war and the Maghrebian community in France.
See item no. 698.

UNESCO Statistical Yearbook.
See item no. 735.

Principales manifestations culturelles en Algérie depuis 1962.
See item no. 815.

La politique culturelle de l'Algérie.
See item no. 816.

Nouveaux enjeux culturels au Maghreb.
See item no. 819.

Bibliographies

858 Le Maghreb: repères bibliographiques, chronologie, documents.
(The Maghreb: bibliographical references, chronology, documents).
Amine Ait-Chaalal. *Les Cahiers du Monde Arabe*, no. 104 (1993),
Centre d'Etudes et de Recherches sur le Monde Arabe Contemporaine,
Université Catholique de Louvain, 131p.
Contains references on the recent history, politics and economy of Algeria, some with
short annotations.

859 Le tourisme au Maghreb: repères bibliographiques. (Tourism in the
Maghreb: bibliographical references).
René Baretje. In: *Annuaire de l'Afrique du Nord*. Paris: Edition du
CNRS, 1980, p. 939-63.
The section on Algeria (p. 939-42) includes references to official publications as well
as to books and articles.

**860 Index Islamicus 1665-1905: a bibliography of articles on Islamic
subjects in periodicals and other collective publications.**
W. H. Behn. Millersville, Pennsylvania: Adiyok, 1989. 899p.
Lists articles from a wide range of periodicals, arranged by country and subject.

861 A current North African bibliography.
Mohamed Ben-Madani. *Maghreb Review*, no. 4 (1979), p. 152-55.
A selective listing of new books, periodicals and newspaper material dealing with the
Maghreb countries. It covers books in all languages and surveys the leading English-
language periodicals and newspapers.

862 **Bibliographie des publications de G. Turbet-Delof relatives au Maghreb.** (Bibliography of the publications by G. Turbet-Delof relating to the Magheb).
Revue d'Histoire Maghrébine (Tunisia), vol. 11, no. 33-34 (1984), p. 191-94.

Turbet-Delof founded the Centre for Maghreb, African and Antilles Studies in 1969. The aim of his studies was not the Maghreb *per se*, but the ideas that the French developed concerning it in the three hundred years that preceded the conquest of Algeria. The items in the bibliography cover: Africa as portrayed in French literature in the 16th and 17th centuries; the French press and Africa in the 17th century; and the Moors and the Huguenots.

863 **Bibliographie raisonnée sur l'émir Abdelkader.** (Descriptive bibliography on the emir Abdelkader).
Oran: Office des Publications Universitaires, 1985. 166p. (Centre de Recherche et d'Information Documentaire en Sciences Sociales et Humaines, Série 'Histoire').

A collection of works on Abdel Kader published since 1840 in German, English, French, Italian, Polish and Russian.

864 **Etudes touarègues: bilan des recherches en sciences sociales. Institutions- chercheurs- bibliographie.** (Tuareg studies: schedule of research in the social sciences. Institutions- researchers- bibliography).
Under the direction of Salem Chaker. Aix-en-Provence, France: Edisud and IREMAM-LAPMO, 1988. 192p. (Travaux et Documents de l'IREMAM, no. 5).

A bibliography of works on the Tuareg language, culture and society published between 1977 and 1987 is found on p. 92-192. There is a section devoted to research on the Tuareg in Algeria on p. 40-43.

865 **Bibliographie de la littérature 'algérienne' des français.** (Bibliography of French 'Algerian' literature).
J. Déjeux. Paris: Centre National de la Recherche Scientifique, 1978. 116p.

A bibliography of 'Algerian' literature written by French authors born in Algeria or inspired by Algeria before and after independence. It includes both original works and critiques of them.

866 **Bibliographie méthodique et critique de la littérature algérienne d'expression française (1945-1970).** (Systematic and critical bibliography of Algerian literature written in French [1945-70]).
Jean Déjeux. *Revue de l'Occident Musulman et de la Méditerranée* (France), no. 10 (2ème semestre, 1971), p. 111-307.

This annotated bibliography lists 1,398 novels, stories, poems and plays by Algerian writers written in French. It constitutes a basic source of references on Algerian literature.

867   **Books on the Algerian revolution in English: translations and Anglo-American contributions.**
Alf Andrew Heggoy.   *African Historical Studies*, vol. 3, no. 1 (1970), p. 163-68.

A review of work by Anglo-American authors on the final phase of French rule in Algeria. It concludes that many books related to the Algerian revolution are available in English either in translation or through original research, but that more specific studies of the war and its effects on Algerian society are needed.

868   **Russian works on the Maghreb.**
Jacob M. Landau.   *Middle Eastern Studies*, vol. 23, no. 1 (1987), p. 116-19.

A review article of Soviet titles on the Maghreb, including Algeria.

869   **American and Canadian doctoral dissertations and Master's theses on Africa 1974-1987.**
Compiled by Joseph J. Lauer, Gregory V. Larkin, Alfred Kagan.
Atlanta, Georgia: Crossroads Press (for The African Studies Association), 1989. 396p.

Designed to continue the earlier *American and Canadian doctoral disssertations and Master's theses on Africa 1886-1974,* compiled by Michael Sims and Alfred Kagan (Waltham, Massachusetts: African Studies Association, 1976). Entries are arranged primarily by country, with works on the continent as a whole or a region of it listed separately at the front, and within this framework into broad disciplines with further subdivisions by year of submission. There are three indexes by author, academic institution and subject.

870   **Algerian bibliography: English language publications, 1830-1973.**
Richard I. Lawless.   London; New York: Bowker, 1976. 117p.

Includes some 1,490 references to books and articles in English on Algeria published between 1830 (the year of the French conquest) and 1973. References have been abstracted from over 300 journals. There are twelve major sections (some subdivided) on: general reference works; geography/geology; travel/exploration guides; history; politics; economics; anthropology; language; religion; and the Sahara. The first section attempts to list all the key bibliographies available on Algeria.

871   **Nota de lecturas (El Magreb Arabe y Marruecos).** (Reading notes: the Arab Maghreb and Morocco).
Victor Morales Lezcano.   *Revista de Estudios Internacionales* (Spain), vol. 6, no. 4 (1985), p. 965-70.

Reviews books and articles on North Africa published mainly in Spanish and French between 1983 and 1985.

872 **Bibliographie algérienne – répertoire des sources documentaires relatives à l'Algérie.** (Algerian bibliography – catalogue of documentary sources on Algeria).
Michel Maynadies. Algiers: Office des Publications Universitaires, 1989. 338p.

This reference work, prepared by a long-serving archivist at the library of Algiers University, is divided into two parts, general and specialized documentary sources. Subjects covered include geography, anthropology, sociology, demography, medicine, history, law, economy, politics and culture.

873 **L'émigration maghrébine de 1962 à 1985: répertoire bibliographique.** (Maghrebian emigration from 1962 to 1985: bibliographical list).
Simone Nassé, Marie-José Bianquis, Mireille Meyer, Mireille Tièche. Aix-en-Provence, France: CNRS, Université d'Aix-Marseille, Institut de Recherches et d'Etudes sur le Monde Arabe et Musulman, 1986. 253p. (Travaux et Documents de l'IREMAM, no. 1).

Includes over 2,000 references organized under the following categories: religion and culture; political and social life; legal matters; work and employment; education and training; and health and social security. Within these categories references are further subdivided according to whether they refer to Maghrebians as a whole, Algerians, Tunisians or Moroccans. A geographical index is provided.

874 **Arab education, 1956-1978: a bibliography.**
Veronica S. Pandelidis. Bronx, New York; London: Mansell Publishing, 1982. 570p.

An annotated bibliography of works in European languages and Arabic dealing with Arab education. The bibliography is organized according to country and there is an author-title subject index.

875 **Index Islamicus 1906-1955: a catalogue of articles on Islamic subjects in periodicals and other collective publications.**
Compiled by J. D. Pearson. Cambridge, England: Heffer, 1958. 807p. Supplements published for 1956-60 (Cambridge, England: Heffer, 1962), 284p.; 1961-65 (Cambridge, England: Heffer, 1967), 308p.; 1966-70 (London: Mansell, 1972), 358p.; 1971-75 (London: Mansell, 1977), 400p.; 1976-80 Part 1 Articles (London: Mansell, 1983), 539p.; 1976-80 Part 2 Monographs (Compiled by J. D. Pearson, W. Behn. London: Mansell, 1983), 348p.

Lists articles on many subjects including history, politics, economy, society, culture and religion, from a very wide range of periodicals published mainly in European languages, together with books and monographs. Entries are arranged by country and subject. This is a basic bibliographical reference work for Algeria, especially for periodical articles in English and French.

876 **The Quarterly Index Islamicus – current books and articles on Islam and the Muslim world.**
Compiled by J. D. Pearson, continued by G. J. Roper, C. H. Bleaney at the Islamic Bibliography Unit, Cambridge University Library, England. London: Mansell, January 1977-92. London: Bowker-Saur, 1992- . quarterly.

This basic bibliographical reference work lists articles from a wide range of journals and also books and monographs, covering education, religion, law, philosophy, art and architecture, music and drama, geography and ecology, anthropology and sociology, archaeology, history, economics, politics, Arabic language and literature. In addition to subject listings, there are also listings by country. See in particular the sections on the Maghreb and Algeria and also the section on Muslim minorities which includes references on Algerian communities in Europe. A name index, including authors and all other persons occuring in entries, is also provided.

877 **A bibliography of Algeria from the expedition of Charles V in 1541 to 1887.**
Sir R. Lambert Playfair. *Royal Geographical Society Supplementary Papers* (London), pt. 2 (1888), p. 127-430.

An essential bibliography for early works in European languages, with some annotations, and subject and author indexes. It has been reprinted in one volume, together with *Supplement to the bibliography of Algeria from earliest times to 1895* (London: Murray, 1898; reprinted, Farnborough, England: Gregg International, 1971. 271p.).

878 **Guide to theses and dissertations: an international bibliography of bibliographies.**
Michael M. Reynolds. Phoenix, Arizona: Oryx Press, 1985. rev. and enlarged. 263p.

Provides access to almost 3,000 bibliographies of dissertations, theses and research in progress published as books, journal articles, or pamphlets. It is arranged in nineteen broad subject sections. One section covers national lists of dissertations from Algeria to Yugoslavia. Each entry has complete bibliographical information and a lengthy annotation. There are three indexes by institution, by author and journal, and by subject.

879 **Essai de bibliographie sélective et annotée sur l'Islam maghrébin contemporain: Maroc, Algérie, Tunisie, Libye (1830-1978).**
(Selective and annotated bibliographic essay on contemporary Maghrebian Islam: Morocco, Algeria, Tunisia, Libya [1830-1978]).
Pessah Shinar. Paris: Editions du CNRS, 1983. 530p.

This annotated bibliography, containing over 2,000 works in Arabic, French, English, German, Italian and Spanish, includes sections on Maghrebian Islam in its entirety and on Algerian Islam.

880 **United States foreign policy and the Middle East/North Africa: a bibliography of twentieth century research.**
Sanford R. Silverburg, Bernard Reich. New York; London: Garland Publishing, 1990. 407p. (Garland Reference Library of Social Science, no. 570).

Contains 3,676 bibliographical entries, arranged alphabetically and by subject. The work includes material published to the end of 1988.

881 **Theses on Islam, the Middle East and North-West Africa 1880-1978 accepted by universities in the United Kingdom and Ireland.**
P. Sluglett. London: Mansell, 1983. 147p.

This work includes a listing of theses on Algeria. For a listing of theses on Algeria accepted for higher degrees by Universities in Great Britain and Ireland since 1978 see *Index to theses* – with abstracts accepted for higher degrees by the Universities of Great Britain and Ireland and the Council for National Academic Awards (London: ASLIB, quarterly).

882 **Soils of Algeria.**
Farnham Royal, England: Commonwealth Agricultural Bureaux, 1977. 8p. (Annotated Bibliography, No. SG 1877).

Contains 100 annotated references on soil biology, fertility and management, and ecology, together with an author index.

883 **Progress in the human geography of the Maghreb.**
K. Sutton, R. I. Lawless. *Progess in Human Geography* (1986), p. 60-105.

A review of the literature on the human geography of the Maghreb (Algeria, Morocco, Tunisia and Libya) published from the late 1970s under the following headings: environmental, historical and political background; population geography, agriculture and rural settlement; economic development, industrialization and tourism; urban, social and transport issues; and regional development planning and regional geography.

884 **Periodicals from Africa: a bibliography and union list of periodicals published in Africa.**
Compiled by Carole Travis, Miriam Alman. Boston, Massachusetts: G. K. Hall, 1977. 619p. (Standing Conference on Library Materials on Africa).

Includes a list of over 700 periodicals published in Algeria from the early French colonial period to the present on a wide range of topics. Titles are arranged in alphabetical order in the country sections and an alphabetical index is included.

885 **Petit supplément bibliographique pour servir à l'histoire du Maghreb.** (Short bibliographical supplement to the history of the Maghreb).
Guy Turbet-Delof. *Revue d'Histoire Maghrébine* (Tunisia), vol. 15, no. 49-50 (1988), p. 128-30.

Provides additions and corrections to Turbet-Delof's *Bibliographie critique du Maghreb dans la littérature française, 1532-1715* (1976), consisting mainly of travellers' accounts of Algeria, Morocco and Tunisia plus Raymond Gleize's 1914 life of Jean Le Vacher, apostolic vicar and French consul in Algiers and Tunis during the period 1619-83.

886 **French and English bibliography of the Arab world 1988-1992.**
Compiled by Vincent Van Gulck. Louvain-la-Neuve, Belgium: Catholic University of Louvain, Centre d'Etudes et de Recherches sur le Monde Arabe Contemporain, 1993. 87p. (Les Cahiers du Monde Arabe, no. 101-02).

Algeria is covered on p. 22-27. The references, mainly books, cover a wide range of topics – recent history, politics, economy and society. Almost all the items included are in French.

Algeria-Britain Academic Network Newsletter.
See item no. 1.

Annuaire de l'Afrique du Nord.
See item no. 5.

La guerre d'Algérie: la fin des secrets et le secret d'une guerre doublement nationale.
See item no. 226.

Les institutions agricoles algériennes.
See item no. 667.

Statistics – Africa: sources for social, economic and market research.
See item no. 733.

The African Studies Companion – a resource guide and directory.
See item no. 842.

Indexes

There follow three separate indexes: authors (personal and corporate); titles; and subjects. Title entries are italicized and refer either to the main titles, or to other works cited in the annotations. The numbers refer to bibliographical entry rather than page numbers. Individual index entries are arranged in alphabetical sequence.

Index of Authors

Rouvillois-Brigol, M. 69-70
Roy, Jayanta, 616
Roy, Jules 251
Roy, Olivier 713
Ruedy, J. 34, 98, 252, 287, 318, 400, 408, 421, 431, 455, 463, 478, 672
Rugh, W. A. 856
Rummel, L. 617

S

Saad, M. 778
Saadallah, B. 333
Sahnoune, T. 750
Saivetz, C. R. 558
Salacuse, J. W. 500, 503
Salem, N. 424
Salmane, H. 825
Sangmuah, E. N. 727
Sanson, H. 373
Santa, S. 81
Santucci, J.-C. 544
Sari, D. 264, 629, 673, 836
Savage, E. 630
Savigear, P. 714
Sayad, A. 373
Sayigh, Y. A. 618
Sbih, M. 510
Schalk, D. L. 253-54
Schemm, P. 464-65
Shlaim, A. 589
Schliephake, K. 619, 637
Schnapper, D. 707, 712-13
Schofield, R. N. 58
Schurmann, H. M. E. 71
Schwartz, R. 808
Seccombe, I. J. 715
Seers, D. 586, 588
Sefiane, S. 654
Seddon, D. 559
Seibel, H. D. 620
Sellin, E. 789, 807
Selmane, Y. 826
Semmari, F. A. al- 334
Semmoud, B. 655
Sengupta, J. 616
Séréni, J.-P. 644
Servan-Schreiber, J.-J. 255
Shaaban, B. 366
Shaikh, F. 466

Shakhs, S. El- 744
Sharabi, H. 467
Sharman, M. 45
Shinar, P. 879
Siagh, Z. 311
Silverberg, S. R. 880
Silvers, R. 214
Singh, K. 560
Sivers, P. von 191-92, 335, 387, 511, 681
Skeet, I. 645
Sluglett, P. 881
Slyomovics, S. 367
Smith, G. M. 322
Smith, R. P. 806
Smith, Tony 193
Smyth, D. 194
Sorum, P. C. 256
Soufi, F. 748
South, A. 837-38
Spencer, C. 35
Spencer, W. 123
Spiro, D. E. 401
Sraieb, N. 728
Stenhouse, T. G. 698
Stevens, Jon 48
Stevens, Valerie 48
Stewart, C. C. 95
Stewart, J. 138
Stewart, P. 82
Stillman, N. A. 302
Stohr, W. B. 621
Stokes, R. G. 363
Stokke, B. R. 631
Stone, R. A. 612
Stookey, R. W. 20
Stora, B. 195-96, 257, 729
Streiff-Fenart, J. 351, 716
Sturgill, C. C. 284
Sullivan, A. T. 197
Sullivan, D. J. 604
Sutton, K. 1, 72-73, 84, 266-69, 468-69, 567, 610, 621, 646, 656-57, 674-78, 742, 751-56, 883
Swearingen, W. D. 679-80
Swift, J. 49
Sykes, C. 439

T

Tabory, E. 312

Tabory, M. 312
Taha, A. D. 112
Tahi, M. S. 470
Talbott, J. 258
Taleb-Ibrahimi, A. 789
Tarver, J. D. 751
Tayib, S. D. Z. el- 198, 336
Taylor, D. R. F. 621
Taylor, M. 199
Temime, E. 270
Temimi, A. 124
Tessler, M. 472
Theberge, J. D. 640
Thomas, B. E. 690
Thomson, A. 125-26
Thrift, N. 610
Tidy, M. 244
Tièche, M. 873
Tijane, B. 657-58
Tillion, G. 368
Tlemcani, R. 36, 369, 622
Touati, F. 808
Touati, H. 127
Tourneau, R. Le 95, 111
Tozy, M. 473
Trautmann, W. 767
Travis, C. 884
Trebous, M. 717
Trench, R. 51
Tristan, A. 259
Troin, J.-F. 74, 757
Trout, F. E. 561
Tully, D. 682
Turbet-Delof, G. 128, 839, 885
Turin, Y. 827

U

United States Board on Geographic Names 55
Utas, B. 370

V

Vaes, B. 52
Vaitsas, C. 586
Valensi, L. 129, 809
Vallet, J. 69
Vallin, J. 271

Index of Titles

292

Index of Subjects

Boudjedia, Rachid 780
Boumediène, President
  Houari
  Algerian élite 479, 481
  and the Islamist
    movement 459
  economic strategy
    597-98, 601
  nature of political
    leadership 451
  policies 447
  régime 433, 449, 458
Boundaries 58
Boundary disputes
  with Morocco 68, 519,
    561
Bourgeat, François 218
Bourgeoisie
  industrial 353
Boutouizerat brothers see
  History
Brain drain
  from Algeria 710
Britain
  attitude to French
    conquest of Algeria
    186
  role in North Africa 176
British
  colony in Algiers 188
  trade with Algeria in
    19th century 628
Broadcasting 846-47
  professionalism 853
  state control 851, 853
  see also Mass Media;
    Radio; Television
Bu Akkaz see History
Bugeaud, Thomas Robert
  see History
Bureaux Arabes see
  History
Bureaucracy 453

C

Camus, Albert see History
Centres de regroupement
  740, 753
Chaanba
  impact of French military
    occupation 760, 762

Chapelle, Fernand Bonnier
  de la see History
Chouikh, Mohammed 823
Christianity
  conversion to 314
  effect of Muslim
    invasion 105
  movements of dissent
    104
Cinema 814, 825
  images of Algeria in
    French 814
  images of the War of
    Independence 793-94,
    814
  national 814-16
Class relations 36
Clientalism 347
Clot, René-Jean 802
Colonial period see History
Colons see Settlers
Conseil National de la
  Révolution Algérienne
  see History: War of
  Independence
Constantine 141, 143, 413
  department of 178
  Institut Technologique de
    la Santé Publique 376
  Islamist movement 461
  medina 749
  migrant community 738
Constantinois
  anti-Jewish violence 276
  notable families 192
Constitution   497
  of 1963 485-86, 495
  of 1976 493, 495
  of 1989 495
Crémieux decree see
  History
Cuba
  foreign policy towards
    Algeria 530
Culural
  festivals 815
  life 815
  policy 812, 816
Culture 5, 23, 815
  Beur 787
  effects of emigration on
    Algerian 819
  state and 819

D

Darlan, Admiral see
  History
Debèche, Djamila 781
Decentralization policies
  610
Deforestation 83
De Gaulle, Charles see
  History
Dib, Mohammed 781,
  791-92
Dissertations
  bibliography of 869, 878,
    881
Djebar, Assia 781, 789, 795
Donatist Church 104
Durif, Eugène 218
Dutch Republic
  relations with Ottoman
    province of Algiers
    117
Duveyrier, Henri see
  History

E

Eberhardt, Isabelle see
  History
Economic
  adjustment policies 616
  development 8, 14-16,
    19, 24-25, 35-36,
    597, 609, 611, 618
    political consequences
      622-23
    regional disparities
      610, 614, 621
    rent-financed 601
    role of hydrocarbon
      sector 643
    social consequences
      614, 652
  external relations 615
  issues 3
  liberalization 2, 613
  money supply and
    inflation 595-96
  planning 597-98
  policies 8, 13, 38,
    596-97
  problems 606, 608, 652

301

303

Maghrebian
  community in France
    images on French
      television 850
    and the Gulf crisis
      (1990-91) 698
  élites in France 712
Majjawi, Abd al-Qadir al-
  see History
Mammeri, Mouloud, 781
Marseilles 190
  North African population
    696
Marriages (mixed)
  and Franco-Algerian
    relations 716
Mass media 819
  access of Algeria's rural
    population 849
  censorship 857
  political process 856
  see also Press; Radio;
    Television
Mécili, Ali-André 382
Merchant friars see History
Mers el-Kebir 238
Messali Hadj see History
Middle classes 373
Military
  coup (1992) 408, 419,
    438
  forces 395-96
  régime 398
  role in the succession to
    Boumediène 480
  see also Army
Minorities 273-302
  human rights 427
  see also Aurès
    Mountains; Berbers;
    Jews; Mzab; Kabylia;
    Kabyles; Tuareg
Mitidja
  agricultural economy 66,
    665
  worker self-management
    units 663
Modernity
  challenge of 19
Modernization
  contradictions of 17
Moorish cafe
  social functions 345

Morali, Rabbi Isaac see
  History
Morocco
  frontier disputes with
    Algeria 68, 519, 561,
    564
  reactions to French
    occupation of Algeria
    168
  relations with Algeria 13,
    517, 519, 523-25, 536
Mosques
  Hanafite mosques of
    Algiers 330
Mostaganem
  Jews 277
Mouvement de la Nahda
  Islamique (MNI) 434,
  460
Mouvement de la Société
  Islamique (HAMAS)
  434, 460
Mouvement pour le
  Triomphe des Libertés
  Démocratiques 729
Mozaics
  Roman 102
Muqrani, Muhammad al-
  Hajj al- see History
Music 816
  festivals 815
  popular 811
  rai 813
Muslim
  civil and political rights
    147
  court system in colonial
    Algeria 488
  intellectual life 143
  judicial system in
    colonial Algeria 491-92
  law 142, 417
    courts during colonial
      period 492
    magistrates in late 19th
      century 490, 492
    students during
      pre-independence
      period 179
Mzab 373
  economic system 288
  French occupation 287,
    289

inhabitants 274
opposition to French rule
  292
political systems 294
traditional institutions
  293
travel guide 47

N

Nantes
  French Foreign Office
    archives 834
Nasser, Abdel
  and the Algerian
    revolution see History
National Charter 388, 498
Nationalism
  contribution of ulemas
    333-34
  effects of Anglo-
    American presence
    169
Nationalist movements
  and the Front Populaire
    174
  see also Front de
    Libération Nationale
    (FLN)
Nedroma
  architecture 821
Nemenchas
  French administration
    505-06
Nomadism 6, 57, 60, 759,
  762
  Chaanba 760, 762
  impact of French rule
    767
  Tuareg 761, 763-66
North Africa
  British role 176
  Catholic Church 189
  France's 'Mission
    civilisatrice' 167
  Jews 273, 285-86, 302
  modern history 18
  Muslim invasion 105,
    112
  intraregional conflicts 7
  under Roman rule
    99-100, 103-04

Z

Map of Algeria

This map shows the more important towns and other features.

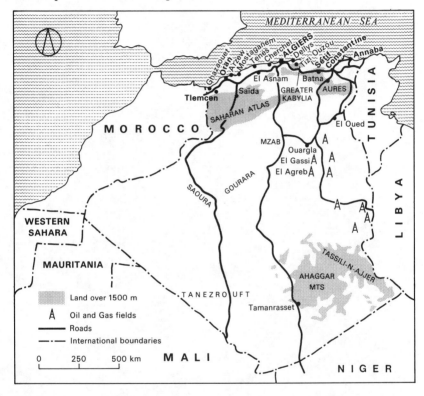

ALSO FROM CLIO PRESS

INTERNATIONAL ORGANIZATIONS SERIES

Each volume in the International Organizations Series is either devoted to one specific organization, or to a number of different organizations operating in a particular region, or engaged in a specific field of activity. The scope of the series is wide-ranging and includes intergovernmental organizations, international non-governmental organizations, and national bodies dealing with international issues. The series is aimed mainly at the English-speaker and each volume provides a selective, annotated, critical bibliography of the organization, or organizations, concerned. The bibliographies cover books, articles, pamphlets, directories, databases and theses and, wherever possible, attention is focused on material about the organizations rather than on the organizations' own publications. Notwithstanding this, the most important official publications, and guides to those publications, will be included. The views expressed in individual volumes, however, are not necessarily those of the publishers.

VOLUMES IN THE SERIES

1 *European Communities*, John Paxton
2 *Arab Regional Organizations*, Frank A. Clements
3 *Comecon: The Rise and Fall of an International Socialist Organization*, Jenny Brine
4 *International Monetary Fund*, Anne C. M. Salda
5 *The Commonwealth*, Patricia M. Larby and Harry Hannam
6 *The French Secret Services*, Martyn Cornick and Peter Morris
7 *Organization of African Unity*, Gordon Harris
8 *North Atlantic Treaty Organization*, Phil Williams
9 *World Bank*, Anne C. M. Salda
10 *United Nations System*, Joseph P. Baratta
11 *Organization of American States*, David Sheinin

TITLES IN PREPARATION

British Secret Services, Philip H. J. Davies

Israeli Secret Services, Frank A. Clements